Context, Individual Differences and Pragmatic Competence

CW01496569

MIX
Paper from
responsible sources
FSC® C014540
www.fsc.org

SECOND LANGUAGE ACQUISITION
Series Editor: Professor David Singleton, *Trinity College, Dublin, Ireland*

This series brings together titles dealing with a variety of aspects of language acquisition and processing in situations where a language or languages other than the native language is involved. Second language is thus interpreted in its broadest possible sense. The volumes included in the series all offer in their different ways, on the one hand, exposition and discussion of empirical findings and, on the other, some degree of theoretical reflection. In this latter connection, no particular theoretical stance is privileged in the series; nor is any relevant perspective – sociolinguistic, psycholinguistic, neurolinguistic, etc. – deemed out of place. The intended readership of the series includes final-year undergraduates working on second language acquisition projects, postgraduate students involved in second language acquisition research, and researchers and teachers in general whose interests include a second language acquisition component.

Full details of all the books in this series and of all our other publications can be found on http://www.multilingual-matters.com, or by writing to Multilingual Matters, St Nicholas House, 31–34 High Street, Bristol BS1 2AW, UK.

SECOND LANGUAGE ACQUISITION
Series Editor: David Singleton, *Trinity College, Dublin, Ireland*

Context, Individual Differences and Pragmatic Competence

Naoko Taguchi

MULTILINGUAL MATTERS
Bristol • Buffalo • Toronto

Library of Congress Cataloging in Publication Data
Taguchi, Naoko
Context, Individual Differences and Pragmatic Competence/Naoko Taguchi.
Second Language Acquisition: 62
Includes bibliographical references and index.
1. English language—Study and teaching—Japan. 2. Pragmatics. 3. Communicative competence. I. Title.
PE1068.J3T23 2012
428.0071'052–dc23 2011048968

British Library Cataloguing in Publication Data
A catalogue entry for this book is available from the British Library.

ISBN-13: 978-1-84769-609-0 (hbk)
ISBN-13: 978-1-84769-608-3 (pbk)

Multilingual Matters
UK: St Nicholas House, 31–34 High Street, Bristol BS1 2AW, UK.
USA: UTP, 2250 Military Road, Tonawanda, NY 14150, USA.
Canada: UTP, 5201 Dufferin Street, North York, Ontario M3H 5T8, Canada.

The policy of Multilingual Matters/Channel View Publications is to use papers that are natural, renewable and recyclable products, made from wood grown in sustainable forests. In the manufacturing process of our books, and to further support our policy, preference is given to printers that have FSC and PEFC Chain of Custody certification. The FSC and/or PEFC logos will appear on those books where full certification has been granted to the printer concerned.

Typeset by Techset Composition Ltd., Salisbury, UK.
Printed and bound in Great Britain by Short Run Press Ltd.

Contents

Preface

Second language acquisition researchers often ask: How do people develop competence in a second language (L2)? What internal and external factors affect the development? What variations are observed in the process and outcome of the development? This book addresses such questions as they are found in the domain of interlanguage pragmatics. It presents a longitudinal study of pragmatic development among Japanese learners of English in Japan. The study was guided by two questions: (1) What pattern and rate of development can we observe across different pragmatic functions and attributes? and (2) What types of learning resources and experiences are available in the context and how do they shape developmental trajectories of individuals?

Participants were 48 Japanese students studying English in a bilingual university in Japan. They completed two pragmatic measures: a pragmatic listening test assessing their ability to comprehend conversational implicatures and a pragmatic speaking test assessing their ability to produce speech acts. These measures were given three times over one academic year in order to capture changes in their pragmatic competence. In addition to the quantitative data, this study used qualitative analyses by sampling a subset of the participants for case studies. Eight participants were interviewed for the nature of their social contacts, domains of contacts and activity types to examine the relationship between pragmatic gains and types of sociocultural experiences. Interview data were supplemented with class observations, journal entries and field notes. Through the process of synthesizing the extensive body of triangulated data, an interesting portrayal emerged about the opportunities for pragmatic practice, learners' stance in accessing the opportunities and context-specific factors that promoted or constrained the access.

Throughout this project, I have been fortunate to have the assistance and support of many people. First and foremost, I would like to thank students and teachers at Akita International University who participated in this study with serious commitment. Thanks also go to faculty and staff members in the institution for their tremendous support throughout the study. I would particularly like to thank Al Lehner and Kirby Record for giving me permission to conduct this study and arranging my research stay, and for Hongyon Wei who gave me crucial technological support for my data collection.

I am grateful to a large number of colleagues, former teachers, students and friends for their support and inspiration during this project. I cannot possibly list everyone, but I would specifically like to thank Kiriko Mashima, Mizuho Suzuki, Shuai Li, Yun Zhao and Pooja Reddy, graduate students at Akita International University and Carnegie Mellon University, for their tireless help with data analysis. I also extend my thanks to Ben Weaver, Lindsay Mcgaan and Sylvia Rebholz, graduate students in the English Department at Carnegie Mellon, for their time in editing the chapters. I also wish to thank Howard Seltman in the Statistics Department at Carnegie Mellon for his generous assistance with data analysis. I am also indebted to Marc Siskin in the Modern Languages Department for his assistance with the instrument development. Thanks also goes to Bruce Cornrich for his help with creating the index for this book. I would also like to thank Mary McGroarty, my mentor and advisor at Northern Arizona University, for her invaluable research training when I was a PhD student in the Applied Linguistics program. I am grateful for the *Language Learning* Small Research Grant and the Berkman Faculty Development Grant for supporting this research. The research was also supported by the sabbatical year arrangement made by the Modern Languages Department at Carnegie Mellon, and I would like to thank Susan Polansky, the chair of the department, for providing me time to concentrate on this project. I feel privileged to be associated with these many people and organizations whose efforts directly led to the publication of this book.

Naoko Taguchi
Pittsburgh, PA
December 1, 2011

1 Context, Individual Differences and Pragmatic Development: An Introduction

Introduction

Interlanguage pragmatics (ILP), analogous to interlanguage grammar or interlanguage lexicon, is a branch of study in second language acquisition (SLA) that focuses on second language learners' knowledge, use and development in performance of sociocultural functions in context. The original definition of ILP can be traced back to Kasper and Dahl, who stated that '*interlanguage pragmatics* will be defined in a narrow sense, referring to non-native speakers' (NNSs') comprehension and production of speech acts, and how their L2-related speech act knowledge is acquired' (Kasper & Dahl, 1991: 216).

Two decades after this definition debuted in the field, we have accumulated a large, diverse body of international literature that has collectively expanded the scope of ILP research beyond 'comprehension and production of speech acts' and beyond an examination of pragmatic 'knowledge'. 'Ability to perform language functions' and 'knowledge of socially appropriate language use' are now defining characteristics of pragmatic competence in the theoretical models of communicative competence (Bachman & Palmer, 1996, 2010; Canale & Swain, 1980; Hymes, 1972). These features have been operationalized in a variety of ways as measurable constructs, and specific tasks and analytical methods have since been identified to elicit and examine these constructs. Target pragmatic features investigated to date are wide ranging, including: speech acts, conversational implicature, formal vs. informal speech styles, honorifics and politeness terms, terms of address, rituals of small talk and other discourse genres, routines and formulaic expressions and conversation management devices (e.g. reactive tokens, discourse markers and turn-taking). Learners' knowledge of

1

these pragmatic features as well as their processing efficiency in using this knowledge in real time have been examined through a variety of methods, ranging from ethnographic studies that involve observation of naturalistic interaction to descriptive–experimental studies that use construct-eliciting instruments.

Numerous ILP studies introduced over the last few decades – whether descriptive, quasi-experimental, qualitative or quantitative – have centered on developmental issues of pragmatic competence. Such studies have addressed a range of questions about pragmatic development among individuals who have learned an additional language through various venues, such as formal schooling, sojourns or in naturalistic settings. These studies have posed many questions: Do learners register meaningful gains in pragmatic competence, outside of grammatical, lexical and phonological competence? Do they demonstrate an even pace in development across pragmatic functions, or do some functions develop more quickly than others? Does pragmatic competence develop naturally with 'time', or does its development require instructional intervention, feedback and modeling? Do L1–L2 similarities and differences in forms, conventions and cultural norms lead to positive or negative L1 transfer, consequently affecting the rate and patterns of development? Is pragmatic growth constrained by learners' grammatical knowledge and general proficiency? Does exposure to target language input and learners' amount of contact with native speakers facilitate pragmatic development, or do formal classroom settings afford ample sociocultural opportunities that lead to increased pragmatic abilities?

Accumulated research findings have, either individually or collectively, provided answers to these empirical questions. Particularly relevant to this monograph is a line of longitudinal studies, which, by definition, involve observation of the same participant(s) over an extended period of time. Ortega and Iberri-Shea (2005) proposed four criteria by which to evaluate longitudinal investigation: (1) the length of the study, (2) the presence of multiwave data collection, (3) a conceptual focus on capturing change by design and (4) a focus on establishing antecedent–consequent relationships by tracking a phenomenon in its naturalistic context. By 2010, about two dozen ILP studies conformed to these criteria. These studies have brought to light relevant insights into learners' pathways in evolving pragmatic abilities, helping to establish causal relationships between change and time (see Chapter 2 for a review of these studies).

Development of pragmatic competence is best observed longitudinally for several reasons. First, pragmatic development is a long-term process because it requires abilities to manage a complex interplay of language, language users and context of interaction. This complexity is reflected in the distinction between the concept of pragmalinguistics and sociopragmatics. Pragmalinguistics refers to the linguistic resources available for performing language functions, while sociopragmatics refers to a language user's assessment of the context in which those linguistic resources are implemented (Leech, 1983; Thomas, 1983). Pragmatic development entails acquisition of both these knowledge bases and efficient control of each of them in spontaneous communication. Learners need to have a range of linguistic resources, as well as the ability to evaluate layers of contextual information, select the most appropriate resources and use them efficiently. For instance, when a speaker wants to refuse someone's invitation, they need to know what syntactic forms and lexis to use. They also need to know whether such a refusal is acceptable in this particular situation in the target culture, and if it is acceptable, they need to know what language to use to express refusal to whom under what circumstances. This combination of linguistic ability and sociocultural sensitivity that is involved in pragmatic competence takes time to acquire.

The distinction between pragmalinguistics and sociopragmatics also indicates that pragmatic competence may not develop hand in hand with grammatical ability. Instead, these two abilities may follow separate trajectories toward their full development. In fact, previous literature showed that while a threshold level of grammatical ability (or general proficiency) is needed for a learner to encode pragmatic functions, a high level of grammatical competence does not always guarantee a corresponding high level of pragmatic competence (Bardovi-Harlig, 1999, 2000). Empirical evidence has shown that L2 learners sometimes fail to approximate native-like pragmalinguistic forms even at a rather advanced stage of L2 learning or after an extended period of residence in a target language community. For example, in a study conducted by Bardovi-Harlig and Hartford (1993) that examined the speech acts of suggestions and rejections performed by international graduate students at a US university, naturalistic data of advising sessions between the students and professors revealed little learners' progress in applying the target pragmalinguistic forms. The students gained in their ability to initiate suggestions about the courses they wanted to take and offer credible reasons when rejecting their advisors' suggestions about courses. However, they continued to use direct linguistic forms of rejections and did not employ any mitigating expressions. These findings support the assertion that grammatical competence is not sufficient for pragmatic performance. Even advanced learners who live in the target language context sometimes may fail to express pragmatic sentiments, due to their lack of understanding of L2 norms and linguistic conventions of social interaction.

Another complex aspect of pragmatic competence is its sociocultural nature. Sociocultural functions such as those found in academic advising sessions are not easy to perform because learners need to know the conventions of the advising session – the goal of the session and roles of the advisor and advisee, in addition to the linguistic forms associated with the session. Some pragmatic functions are universal but linguistic and nonlinguistic means to practice those functions, as well as norms and conventions behind the practice, exhibit considerable variation across cultures. These observations are evident in an extensive body of literature in the field of contrastive pragmatics and cross-cultural communication (e.g. Blum-Kulka *et al.*, 1989; Boxer, 2002; Gudykunst & Kim, 2004). These studies revealed great variations across languages in their realizations of pragmatic acts, which are often intertwined with norms and values in a given culture. As linguistic behaviors and social conventions of speaking are not easily observable, learners often experience difficulty in noticing how people project appropriate levels of politeness or how they communicate meaning indirectly to avoid confrontation. Furthermore, learners may transfer their L1 sociocultural norms to L2 practice and end up with what Thomas (1983) calls 'pragmatic failure' or a failure to convey the intended meaning, which occurs when two languages operate under different conventions.

A classic example of pragmatic failure is found in a documentary about interethnic communication called 'Crosstalk'. This video was made in the late 1970s by a sociolinguist, John Gumpurz, and some of his colleagues at the University of California-Berkley to illustrate instances of cross-cultural miscommunication between Indians and British people in England (Gumperz *et al.*, 1979). The video shows that cross-cultural miscommunication occurs at three levels: differing cultural assumptions, differing ways of structuring talk and differing ways of speaking (e.g. how to emphasize a point or use various tones of voice). For instance, in the video, an Indian applicant failed miserably at a job interview because he was not aware of certain interview conventions in British culture. Following south Asian conventions of being less direct and less presumptuous, he did not provide straightforward answers to the interviewers' questions and failed to initiate bringing up relevant topics. As the video demonstrates, consequences of these cross-cultural miscommunications can be serious, leading to cultural stereotyping and prejudice.

Taken together, these observations found in ILP research suggest that complete pragmatic competence is an aspect of L2 abilities that take some time to acquire. Pragmatic development involves mastery of linguistic and nonlinguistic knowledge and the sociocultural norms underlying them, together with efficient control of both these knowledge types when encoding and decoding language functions in social contact. Given these complexities, pragmatic development is best described from longitudinal lenses, which, by tracking learners over time, can provide fuller insights into L2 learners' pathways toward evolving pragmatic abilities.

Contributions of this Book

This book reports a longitudinal investigation conducted in 2008 about pragmatic development among 48 Japanese students of English in an

English-medium university in Japan. Over the course of one academic year, this research traced students' progress in two aspects of pragmatic competence: pragmatic comprehension – the ability to comprehend speakers' implied meaning, and pragmatic production – the ability to produce speech acts appropriately. This study aimed at revealing patterns of pragmatic development, and individual and contextual factors that affect this development. Two research questions guided the study: (1) What patterns and rate of pragmatic development can we observe across different pragmatic functions and attributes?; and (2) What types of learning resources and experiences are available in various contexts and how do these factors shape developmental trajectories of individual learners?

The 48 participants in this study completed two pragmatic measures: a pragmatic listening test that assessed their ability to comprehend conversational implicatures and a pragmatic speaking test that assessed their ability to produce two speech acts: 'requests' and 'opinions (disagreements)'. These measures were administered three times over one academic year to capture changes in pragmatic competence. In addition, qualitative data were collected by sampling a subset of the participants through case studies. The focal informants were interviewed with regard to the nature and domains of their social contacts in order to examine the relationship between pragmatic gains and available sociocultural experiences for various individuals. Interview data were supplemented with class observations, journal entries and field notes.

This study has several merits. First, it reveals patterns of pragmatic development that have not been examined extensively in a longitudinal design. Second, the study extends beyond the usual measures of accuracy and appropriateness of pragmatic language use, by analyzing learners' processing speed in performance of pragmatic functions. Finally, this study explains, not just describes, pragmatic development, by examining factors that may be related to this development. These three lines of investigation combine to contribute to the accumulated knowledge regarding what features define pragmatic competence and what factors influence it, as well as contributing to a more robust understanding of the theoretical models of L2 proficiency. Below I will explain distinctly the features of this study, which uniquely situate it within the literature of SLA and ILP.

Contribution to Greater Understanding of the Development of Pragmatic Competence

The last few decades have seen rapid development in studies on L2 pragmatic competence. This trend corresponds to growing recognition among researchers and teachers that proficient use of a language involves mastery of functional usage of the language within a social context. Hymes' (1972) notion of communicative competence has had a significant impact in shaping this recognition and has enhanced our interest in investigating L2 communicative competence. Pragmatic competence – the ability to convey and interpret meaning appropriately in a social situation – has occupied a distinct place in the theoretical models of communicative competence and attracted much interest in modern SLA research (Bachman & Palmer, 1996, 2010; Canale & Swain, 1980; Hymes, 1972).

Following these trends, over two dozen books on L2 pragmatics have been published since the 1990s. Some of these are research monographs that documented pragmatic performance of particular individuals and groups (Barron, 2003; Gass & Houck, 1999; Kinginger, 2008; Ohta, 2001; Schauer, 2009; Trosborg, 1995). Others are edited volumes with specific themes, including: cross-cultural pragmatics (Blum-Kulka et al., 1989; Gass & Neu, 1996; Kasper & Blum-Kulka, 1993; Spencer-Oatey, 2005), pragmatic development (Kasper & Rose, 2002), pragmatic teaching (Bardovi-Harlig & Mahan-Taylor, 2003; Ishihara & Cohen, 2010; LoCastro, 2003; Martínez Flor et al., 2003; Rose & Kasper, 2001; Sóler & Martinez-Flór, 2008), pragmatic assessment (Hudson et al., 1995; Röver, 2005; Yamashita, 1996), and pragmatics in institutional context (Bardovi-Harlig & Hartford, 2005). A few volumes have focused on pragmatics in L2 other than English (Kasper, 1992a, 1995; Márquez-Reiter & Placencia, 2004; Taguchi, 2009a). Among these books, those by Barron, Gass and Houck, Kinginger, Ohta and Schauer are the only research monographs available in the field, from which only Ohta, Barron, Kinginger and Schauer are longitudinal studies.

Ohta (2001) investigated the development of acknowledgement and alignment expressions by American learners of Japanese in a formal classroom setting. She documented developmental patterns of these two expressions, along with classroom experiences that influenced the development. Barron (2003), on the other hand, examined the development of German address forms over a 14-month study-abroad. Data elicited through discourse completion test (DCT) at seven-month intervals revealed only modest progress on learners' ability to distinguish between formal and informal address forms. Kinginger's (2008) study, another longitudinal study in study-abroad, examined the development of the knowledge of sociolinguistic variation (e.g. address forms, colloquial expressions) in L2 French in a semester-length residence in France. Pre- and post-test comparisons revealed a significant gain and considerable individual differences. Qualitative data revealed the qualities of learners' experiences, and the specifics of context and its impact on development.

This study aims to contribute to the rather limited body of longitudinal studies in ILP. Specifically, this research addresses pragmatic development in terms of both comprehension and production skills, which has rarely been explored in the literature. Longitudinal development of pragmatic competence has predominantly been studied in terms of production skills, such as production of speech acts (Barron, 2002; Schauer, 2009), reactive expressions

(Ohta, 2001) and production and perception of formal and informal expressions (Kinginger, 2008). Very few studies have examined pragmatic comprehension in a longitudinal design, and studies that have examined both comprehension and production together are even scarcer. As a result, research has not provided a comprehensive picture of the nature of pragmatic competence, namely what learners can do as producers and interpreters of pragmatic meaning. In addition, questions related to the development of pragmatic competence, for example, whether comprehension and production abilities are related to each other, or whether comprehension precedes production, still remain unanswered. To help fill these gaps in the literature, this study examines the development of pragmatic competence from two perspectives: comprehension and production of pragmatic intentions. The study documents L2 learners' ability to accurately comprehend speaker intention, ability to appropriately produce communicative intention and the degree to which these two abilities are related to each other in their stage of L2 development (see Chapter 3 for the descriptions of pragmatic comprehension and production measures).

Contribution to Greater Understanding of the Theoretical L2 Proficiency Model

This monograph uses an original theoretical framework that combines a psycholinguistic and pragmatic approach in analysis, with a goal to contribute to our understanding of what is involved in becoming a proficient L2 user. Traditionally, the acquisition of language knowledge (e.g. grammar and lexis) has been considered the end state of SLA. However, researchers have recently paid more attention to the processing dimension of language acquisition by examining how learners access and process linguistic information in real time. Language acquisition is now typically considered to have two complementary aspects: accurate demonstration of language knowledge and efficient processing of this knowledge. Analyses of linguistic knowledge and processing capacity are considered to offer alternative means for examining L2 use, and consequently provide complementary descriptions of L2 proficiency.

This partnership between competence and processing is apparent by the growing body of L2 research measuring fluency. Segalowitz (2007: 181) defines fluency as the 'aspects of productive and receptive language ability characterized by fluidity (smoothness) of performance'. The concept of processing differs from knowledge but subsumes knowledge. Language knowledge involves a variety of components, including: an underlying representation of linguistic systems (e.g. syntax, lexis), functional knowledge (form–meaning associations), knowledge of discourse (coherence and cohesion) and knowledge of pragmatic conventions (e.g. notion of politeness and rules of interaction). Fluency is thus a reflection of processing capacities in implementing these various knowledge bases. It is affected by cognitive and affective factors, and mediated by external factors relevant to task demands, settings and interactional requirements (Bialystok, 1990a; Hymes, 1972; Segalowitz, 2003; Segalowitz & Hulstjin, 2005; Skehan, 1996; Widdowson, 1989).

The body of research measuring fluency has been rapidly expanding over the last decade as a result of technology development and its application to L2 research. Digitalization of sound systems has promoted efficiency in oral fluency analysis, allowing researchers to analyze speech rate and pause length relatively easily. Computer-delivered tasks have enabled researchers to record reaction times with a large group of participants at one time. These changes have expanded our options of interlanguage analysis: rather than relying on language knowledge inferred from performance accuracy, these advances allow us to directly measure processing capacities that characterize speedy implementation of knowledge.

Empirical findings published to date have enhanced our understanding of the construct and development of fluency, as well as factors that affect fluency. For instance, although fluency is often used as a cover term for global language proficiency (Lennon, 1990) and is reflected in the standardized assessments (ACTFL, 1999; Council of Europe, 2001), empirical evidence suggests that oral fluency does not develop in parallel with other aspects of L2 ability (e.g. accuracy, complexity and lexical density) (Norris, 2006). Speedy processing of aural input does not perfectly coincide with proficiency in the course of L2 development (Taguchi, 2007a). These findings indicate that performance fluency forms distinct characteristics on its own, apart from general proficiency and accuracy.

Concerning the development of fluency, corroborating the theory of skill acquisition and automatization (Anderson, 1990; Anderson *et al.*, 2004), previous research has shown that acquisition of grammatical rules follows a learning curve, moving from the stage that involves conscious and slow application of rules to the stage where rules are retrieved quickly at minimal error rate (DeKeyser, 1997). Extensive practice and time-on-task are claimed to facilitate development of speedy, skilled performance (DeKeyser, 2007; Ellis, 2003; Gatbonton & Segalowitz, 2005), and a few studies have empirically tested the impact of practice in reading fluency development (Fukkink *et al.*, 2005), word and phrase recognition fluency (Akamatsu, 2006) and oral fluency (Taguchi, 2007b, 2008a; Taguchi & Iwasaki, 2008).

Another line of research has revealed a number of factors that affect fluency. Cognitive factors such as lexical access, sentence processing and working memory are found to have a correlation with fluency in spoken and written skills (e.g. O'Brian *et al.*, 2006; Segalowitz & Freed, 2004). A personality factor, extraversion, is found to be related to oral fluency (see Dewaele & Furnham, 1999, for review). Task-specific factors such as availability of planning time are found to affect fluency, aside from accuracy and complexity of spoken production (e.g. Skehan, 2001). Learning context also plays a significant role in fluency development, as learners in a study-abroad context showed greater gains in oral fluency (Segalowitz & Freed, 2004) and processing speed of indirect meaning (Taguchi, 2008b), compared with their counterparts who were learning in a domestic, formal instructional context.

To sum up, fluency is represented widely in the recent SLA literature and has been measured in both oral and written skills, in various constructs and tasks (e.g. word recognition, grammar, pragmatics, formulaic processing), using various measurement standards (e.g. word per minute, pause length, reaction times). Fluency is a distinct feature of L2 proficiency and exhibits characteristic patterns of development. It can be promoted through specific forms of practice and instruction, and is influenced by learner-specific factors (cognitive and affective), as well as by external factors related to task characteristics and learning context.

Increasing interest in fluency is also evident in ILP research. Although empirical effort in measuring pragmatic fluency is relatively recent, the knowledge-processing dichotomy in pragmatics is hardly new and dates back to the 1980s in Faerch and Kasper's (1984) original model of pragmatic competence. These authors conceptualized pragmatic knowledge in terms of both declarative and procedural components. Declarative knowledge consists of resources necessary for pragmatic performance, including linguistic knowledge, sociocultural knowledge, knowledge of speech acts and knowledge of discourse. Procedural knowledge refers to knowledge that 'selects and combines parts of declarative knowledge for the purpose of reaching specific communicative goals, observing constraints imposed by language processing in real time' (Faerch & Kasper, 1984: 215), and it subsumes processes of context analysis and goal formation, verbal planning and monitoring. Acquisition of pragmatic competence entails development of both declarative and procedural knowledge. Echoing Kasper (2001), pragmatic development refers to acquisition of pragmatic knowledge and to gaining automatic control in processing this knowledge in real time.

While the majority of the previous ILP research has focused on the development of declarative knowledge, a growing body of recent research has examined fluency or processing aspect of pragmatic performance. Many of these studies examined fluency in pragmatic comprehension – specifically how accurately and rapidly learners can draw inferences of conversational implicatures (Taguchi, 2005, 2007a, 2008b, 2008c, 2008d). Findings generally confirmed that accuracy and fluency form distinct dimensions and do not develop in parallel in pragmatic comprehension. There are two studies that measured fluency using production tasks. House (1996) examined the effect of explicit and implicit teaching in developing learners' control of routines, discourse strategies and speech acts. Results showed that the explicit group used more gambits and discourse strategies, but instruction did not improve the learners' use of routines, which is considered an aspect of discourse-level fluency. More recently, Taguchi (2007b) examined the effects of proficiency and task type on fluent speech act production. In this study, Japanese students of English produced speech acts of requests and refusals in a role-playing task. Students' productions were analyzed for appropriateness (rated on a six-point scale), planning time (amount of time taken to prepare for each role play) and rate of speech (number of words spoken per minute). It was found that proficiency has a significant impact on appropriateness and speech rate, but not on planning time.

Following this emerging interest, the present study explores the relationship between knowledge and processing in pragmatic competence. Pragmatic knowledge is measured based on learners' accurate and appropriate comprehension and production of speech intentions, while processing capacity is measured as fluency in comprehension and production. By analyzing the two aspects together longitudinally, this research reveals whether the two attributes, the acquisition of pragmatic knowledge and the achievement of fluent processing of this knowledge, develop in parallel and whether these features jointly characterize the course of pragmatic development (see Chapter 3 for the methodology that guided this investigation).

Contribution to Greater Understanding of the Factors Affecting Pragmatic Development

Among those building theories in SLA, there is a burgeoning interest in the dynamicity and complexity of the language development process in a social context. Dynamic Systems Theory (DST) (de Bot, 2008), chaos/complexity theory (Larsen-Freeman & Cameron, 2008) and the emergentist approach (Ellis & Larsen-Freeman, 2006) provide key support toward this new epistemological trend. Common among this body of research are the following views toward language development (see Chapter 2 for a more detailed description of these theoretical paradigms):

(1) Language development is a nonlinear, nonstatic process shaped by socially coregulated interactions of multiple influences.
(2) Language development is inseparable from context: language emerges from agents (individuals) and their interactions with the environment.
(3) Language development entails intra- and intervariability. Variability data provide idiosyncratic details of individual learners' developmental trajectories that are otherwise masked out in the analysis of group-level means.

This trend in recent approaches to this topic suggests that the SLA field is in transition, moving away from the traditional reductionist approach which explores a simple cause–effect relationship isolated from context, and moving toward a more ecologically oriented approach which includes context as part of the systems under investigation and considers reciprocal relationships among multiple variables over time.

In line with this epistemological trend, this study adopts a dynamic, complex system paradigm in pragmatic development analysis in an attempt to enhance our understanding of ways that both individual and contextual factors affect pragmatic development. The study adopts a mixed-method approach, combining quantitative and qualitative methods, and uses a variety of research instruments and analytical methods to seek explanations for observed developmental trajectories. This study provides an in-depth account of context and explores the quality of sociocultural experiences that affect pragmatic gains. From the pool of 48 participants, a subset of 12 participants were recruited as informants for the qualitative analyses and were interviewed several times during the course of the study. The entire data set consists of 50 interviews with students and teachers, 60 class observations and about 1150 journal entries produced by a subset of students. Through the process of synthesizing this extensive body of triangulated data, an interesting portrayal emerged regarding the opportunities for pragmatic practice, learners' stances in accessing these opportunities and context-specific factors that constrained such access. Using data from 12 participants, this monograph reports eight idiosyncratic case histories that exemplify the intricate interaction among individuals, context and changes in pragmatic competence.

To sum, this study pursues a multimodal, multidimensional investigation of pragmatic development. It examines both knowledge and processing dimension of pragmatic performance, and uses a variety of research instruments and methods, both quantitative and qualitative, to describe changes in pragmatic competence and explain the changes. A situated analysis of multiple data sets generates meaningful interpretations of individual variations in pragmatic development, and learner-specific and contextual factors that shape developmental trajectories.

Context of the Study

English as an International Language in Japan

This study was conducted at Akita International University, a small liberal arts college located in Akita City with a population of 300,000. The college is unique in that it is one of the few English-medium universities currently existing in Japan. Responding to the emphasis on globalization and English as an international language, many Asian countries have emphasized development of functional English abilities in young adults in order for them to gain mobility across the international community (Block

& Cameron, 2002). Japan is no exception in this trend. In 2003, the Japanese Ministry of Education, Culture, Sports, Science and Technology (MEXT) announced an 'Action Plan' aimed at producing Japanese citizens who can function effectively in English in international settings (Ministry, 2003). The five-year plan titled the 'Action Plan to Cultivate Japanese People with English Abilities' emphasized the teaching of English as a means of practical communication tools (Tanabe, 2004). The budget of 11 hundred million yen (approximately $10 million) approved under the plan was designated to attain various goals in seven main areas: (1) improving English classes; (2) improving English teaching methods; (3) motivating students' learning through study-abroad programs and meaning-oriented language use; (4) improving entrance examination systems; (5) supporting English education in elementary schools; (6) improving Japanese language abilities; and (7) promoting research on English education.

The 'English as an international language' slogan endorsed by the central government is closely tied with the discourse of *kokusaika* or internationalization seen elsewhere in present-day Japan. Internationalization refers to increased local diversity resulting from contact among people of various cultural and linguistic backgrounds, as well as from exchange of information and commodities among countries. The goal is achieved by gaining knowledge about other cultures, acquiring foreign language skills, situating one's own expertise within the global community and obtaining opportunities to experience other cultures. The impact of this goal of internationalization is particularly prominent in educational systems. To give a few examples, in 1987, the government launched the JET (Japan Exchange and Teaching) program to promote cultural exchange between Japan and English-speaking countries. The purpose of the program is to invite university graduates from overseas who can participate in English teaching throughout Japan. The number of the JET teachers has grown immensely since its launch, from below 1000 in 1987, to the current number of close to 50,000 participants from over 50 countries. The majority of these teachers come from the United States and England.

Another notable trend is an increasing number of international students in Japanese universities as a result of a number of organized efforts. One example of these efforts is the 'International Student 100,000 Plan' (*ryugakusei 10 man-nin keikaku*) initiated in the 1980s by several committees commissioned by the central government, which had a goal of bringing the number of international students in Japan up to 100,000 by early 21st century. In 2004, the Japanese Student-Services Organization, in support of similar goals, began promoting short-term international education programs, resulting in nationwide establishment of a number of such programs in national universities.

These milestone events in recent Japan recapitulate the government-promoted emphasis on English education. Kubota (2002) summarizes four premises in the typical approach to foreign language education in Japan, stemming from this internationalization movement: (1) 'foreign language' is 'English'; (2) the model for 'English' should be either standard North American or British varieties; (3) learning English leads to international understanding; and (4) national identity is fostered through learning English. In her paper, Kubota criticizes that learning English, particularly with an emphasis on the Inner Circle such as the United States or England, does not promote intercultural understanding. Rather, it may lead to a skewed view of world diversity and limit opportunities for cross-cultural understanding to just Anglophone countries and Japan. The linguistic imperialism of English in Japan has also been criticized in other publications that challenge the widespread view of English as a beneficial language (e.g. Kubota, 2002; Kubota & McKay, 2009; Pennycook, 1994; Phillipson, 1992). While we share a concern that the elevated status of English goes against the current global society where increased ethnic and linguistic diversity is a reality, the symbolic power attached to English still remains great, and the mastery of functional English ability is a top priority in the national educational policy in Japan.

Emphasis on English prevails in all levels of education in Japan. In elementary schools, English conversation activities have been part of standard curriculum since 2002, and English officially became a required subject for the fifth and sixth graders in 2011. In junior and senior high schools, English has been part of the curriculum since the postwar period and gained the status of a mandatory foreign language in 2002. The teaching of communicative English has been reinforced through several revisions of national curriculum guidelines, or the so-called 'Course of Study' (*gakushu shido yoryo*). One landmark event in terms of educational policy was the 1989 revision of the Course of Study, which showed a drastic departure from an emphasis on grammar instruction to a functional, communication-oriented teaching approach. At the high-school level, for the first time in the history, the government introduced Oral Communication courses into the curriculum. The general objectives of these courses were: (1) to improve students' ability to comprehend English in everyday situations and to express their ideas in English; and (2) to cultivate students' positive attitudes in attempting communication. This 1989 curriculum was further revised in 1999 to promote a more integrated approach to the development of spoken English abilities. This curriculum has been effective since 2002.

Higher-Education Reform and English-Medium Curriculums

At the university level, emphasis on English is evident in the growing trend among public and private universities to establish an English-medium curriculum. Some universities have an entire campus operating in bilingual mode, English and Japanese, like the target institution in this study. English-medium universities refer to institutions in which all college-level courses in basic and advanced education areas, as well as language courses, are taught in English to improve students' academic English proficiency. The goal of this type of university is to broaden students' general and specialized knowledge, and to promote professional expertise in English so that they can take leadership in the international arena. In such a university, English is viewed as a tool of academic study, not as a subject itself. Attaining English skills are expected to be a by-product of the process of gaining content knowledge in academic subjects.

The growing trend toward the English-only curriculums in universities is closely intertwined with the higher-education reform that has been progressing rapidly since the 1990s. In 1996, the 18-member University Deliberation Council (*daigaku shingikai*) published a report titled the 'Future of Higher Education' in which the pressing need for reform was emphasized as a means to ensure that Japan would gain the capacity to compete internationally in the next century. This university reform was also meant to cope with the pressing societal problem of the decline of 18-year-old Japanese citizens in the population and corresponding low Japanese university enrollments. After the second peak of baby boomers in 1992, the college population shrunk by approximately half. In 2008, 50% of private universities faced a situation where optimal university capacity exceeded the number of applicants, while the percentage was only 10% 10 years ago. Under these circumstances, survival has become an immediate concern among many universities, and the reform that promotes universities with unique characteristics has become a pressing need.[1]

The council's report urged the government to improve the quality of college education and research, strengthen decision-making systems in each university and add more flexibility to course sequences and curriculum. In addition, the report strongly emphasized the need for external evaluations, which would be used to determine the amount of subsidies provided by the central government. The report also proposed an increase of graduate programs aimed at sharpening the professional skills of those already in the work force.

These council recommendations informed the 'Toyama Plan' announced in 2002 by the Minister of MEXT, Atsuko Toyama (Ministry, 2002). The plan was announced as part of the 'National Restructuring Plan' (*kozo kaikaku*) launched under the Koizumi cabinet, which served as official guidelines for university reform. A number of drastic measures were announced, including restructuring and merging of national universities, privatization of national universities (*daigaku hojinka*), implementation of external evaluation systems and budget allocation favoring the top 30 colleges in Japan. Responding to the Toyama Plan, all national universities became independent administrative corporations in 2004 (*daigaku hojinka*). With this change, universities gained autonomous decision-making over a range of curricular and administrative issues, but in exchange they were required to submit a six-year plan to the central government and be evaluated according to the achievement of their goals. The Toyama Plan was further strengthened in 2007 through the most recent report issued by the Education Revitalization Council. This second report added several new areas to reform plans: introduction of a college exit exam, expansion of fall semester admission to attract foreign students, reform of college entrance exams and expansion of English classes.

The establishment of English-medium curriculum is one representative example of this nationwide education reform movement. Due to relaxation of the government's regulations in curricula planning, combined with the urgent need for survival in this era of declining college population, many universities have faced the need to define their individual character and promote a unique learning environment to remain competitive in the current higher-education market. English-medium curriculum has formed part of strategic plans in some universities to attract applicants and endure top-down evaluation. English-medium curriculum is considered timely and strategic because it is a place where the key elements of internationalization – acquisition of English as a common international language and situating one's own expertise within the global society – are clearly intertwined. Whether or not such curriculum could actually produce the intended outcome is yet to be seen. The next section describes Akita International University, an English-medium university opened in 2004, which is the research site in the present study.

Research Site

Akita International University is one of the three English-medium universities that currently exist in Japan.[2] It is a small liberal arts college with a student population of 820. In the era of higher-education reform, it is the first *daigaku hojin* opened in Japan. Having gained flexibility in administration and curriculum structures, the university is committed to implement some of the human resource strategies promoted through national agendas (Ministry, 2002). Following the government's initiative in globalization and internationalization, the aim of the university is to produce well-educated individuals who are fully competent in English, at the same time equipped with rich knowledge of the world and global visions. Hence, the school was established as an arena where key elements in a global society (acquisition English ability and general/specialized knowledge) are clearly intertwined. The goal of the school is to broaden students' general and specialized knowledge and build professional expertise in English so that they can take leadership in the international arena. In the university brochure the president writes:

> Our goal is very simple. We produce future leaders who will effectively conduct business and lead international organizations of the 21st century. In achieving this goal, we reform Japanese higher education and

create a university that can compete and communicate with prestigious counterparts around the world.

The university offers several unique features which parallel those of the prototypical immersion program described by Swain and Johnson (1997): an L2 serves as a medium of instruction, the curriculum parallels the local L1 curriculum, the program aims for additive bilingualism, students have proficiency levels similar to one another and the classroom culture is that of the local L1 community. To illustrate these characteristics, first, all courses – both language and content courses – are offered in English. The school currently has about 70 faculty members, of which close to 50% are foreign nationals. Japanese instructors are fully bilingual, and many of them have received a degree overseas. Another unique characteristic of the school is its multicultural environment. As of 2011, the school has 118 partner institutions from over 34 countries and regions. International students spend a semester or a year on campus studying Japanese language and related courses. The international student population, which occupies about 10–15% of the student population, is highly multi-cultural/multilingual. The majority of these students come from English-speaking countries such as the United States, Britain and Canada, and a fair number of students represent European countries, China, Taiwan and South Korea.[3] Because all first-year Japanese students are required to live in a dormitory, they have frequent contact with international students on a daily basis. The Japanese and international students share routines such as dining in the cafeteria, studying in the library and participating in club activities. Another unique feature of this institution is that, after students declare their major (Global Business or Global Studies), most of them go one-year study-abroad typically during their junior year. They return to the main campus in their senior year and transfer their credits required for graduation. Integrating study-abroad into the degree requirement has many incentives. For one, it serves as a source of integrative and instrumental motivation for the students and adds practical value and utility to their English study. It also closely corresponds to the institution's mission – to produce Japanese citizens who can function in the global community.[4]

The university has six academic programs: Global Business, Global Studies, Basic Education, English for Academic Purposes (EAP), Japanese Studies and Japanese Language. All new students are placed into one of three levels in the EAP program. The levels are divided according to proficiency: students with a TOEFL score below 460 are placed in Level 1, students with a score between 460 and 480 in Level 2 and those with a score of higher than 480 are placed in Level 3. The main objective of the EAP program is to develop students' academic English abilities and prepare them for more advanced content-area courses. After students exit the EAP, they proceed to the Basic Education program and then move on to upper-level courses in their major – Global Business or Global Studies.

The participants in this study were all first-year students in the EAP program. The program has three levels, and students are promoted to the next level after they meet the course requirements and achieve the required proficiency measured by TOEFL. The class size in the EAP program is relatively small, 15–18 students per class. There are 13 full-time EAP instructors, including 11 native English speakers and two Japanese instructors who speak English fluently. All instructors have a Master's or PhD degree in TESOL or Applied Linguistics from a university in the United States, Canada or Britain.

The next section provides descriptions of EAP classes. These descriptions are based on my on-site observation and participation in the target institution. During the period of this study in 2008, I was a visiting scholar at the university and collected all the data by myself. I went to school two days a week and spent my entire day on campus visiting classes, interviewing students and teachers and taking field notes. I also commuted with the EAP instructors on the same train and had frequent informal conversations about their classes, teaching and students (see Chapter 3 for the descriptions of the researcher).

English for academic purposes (EAP) program

The goal of the EAP program is to prepare students for typical academic work in English such as writing academic papers, reading academic texts and participating in discussion. Students have four main classes: reading (4–6 hours per week; 50 minutes per class period), writing (4 hours per week), speaking (3 hours per week) and listening (3 hours per week). In addition to these four skill courses, students have self-learning hours where they polish their listening skill using a variety of audio-visual materials (e.g. movies, news clips, TV dramas). They also have a TOEFL preparation class three times per week.

The aim of the EAP reading class is to develop reading strategies, reading comprehension ability, reading fluency and knowledge of academic vocabulary. Students are expected not only to recall and describe what they have read but also to identify the main points of readings. They are also expected to provide an in-depth explanation of their own opinions about the readings. In class, students practice a variety of reading skills (e.g. skimming, scanning, previewing, guessing meaning from context), expand their vocabulary, develop reading fluency via timed reading activities and engage in extensive reading. The main textbook used in the course is the *Reading Power* series published by Pearson Education (2004). The book has four parts. Part 1 introduces students to the concept of reading for pleasure and provides guidelines on how to choose a book to read, how to keep a record of reading and how to talk about reading with peers and teachers. Part 2 engages students with a variety of comprehension exercises, for instance, previewing a text and making predictions about its content, scanning, making inferences about information in the readings, building vocabulary, understanding main ideas, understanding paragraph structures and summarizing. Part 3 is aimed at developing students' critical thinking skills based on reading and Part 4 provides timed reading exercises. Each part contains from about five to 20 exercises based on a variety of reading materials, including newspaper articles, advertisements, TV schedules, conversations, classified ads, book reviews and short passages.

In the classes I observed, teachers followed the textbook closely but there were variations across EAP levels. For example, in a more advanced class, emphasis was placed on academic vocabulary and collocations, but in a lower-level class, students were reading more of the short stories and narratives. Inferential skill was of great interest to me because of its relevance to the target pragmatic construct in this study – comprehension of implied meaning. Although the modality was different (i.e. reading vs. listening), the underlying construct is considered applicable to both skills. In all the classes I observed, inferential skill was practiced with a variety of reading materials. For instance, textbook exercises posed questions such as: What does the writer mean by the title? What can you tell about the main character's past? and What is the relationship between the speakers? There were about 50 inferential questions in the textbook.

The first semester writing course covers grammar units (e.g. parts of speech, tense and subordination), whereas students in the second semester focus on paragraph development and essay writing. The purpose of the writing course is to provide students with opportunities to engage in a variety of English language writing and thinking activities to help them master basic, sentence-level English grammatical structures and forms, while increasing their writing fluency to paragraph- and essay-writing level so that students develop fluency in informal writing and improve grammatical accuracy in formal writing assignments. Throughout the course, students are trained to pay attention to the content of their writing and also to conventions of writing (e.g. grammar and word usage). Students are also encouraged to think about how to write sentences and paragraphs that are logical and easily understood by their readers. They write a variety of texts, for instance, presenting facts, feelings and opinions, responding to a text, or synthesizing and summarizing various texts.

Through my class observations and textbook analyses, I paid attention to specific grammatical structures relevant to the target speech acts assessed in this study. In order to produce the target speech acts (i.e. requests and opinions), students need to have basic control of grammar including relevant parts of speech, verb tense, question formation and conjunctions. Moreover, they need to know some grammatical forms specific to the target speech acts, for instance, modals (e.g. 'could', 'may' and 'would'), and bi-clausal sentence structures (e.g. 'I think that' + clause, 'I wonder if' + clause), as well as conditional sentence structures (e.g. 'If' + clause, 'I wish' + clause). These structures were covered in their writing classes at all levels, although these forms were introduced as isolated grammatical points and not practiced together within the frame of speech acts.

The EAP listening class focuses on bottom-up listening activities where students listen to short academic lectures and write down what they hear (i.e. dictation). Hence, global, top-down forms of listening, such as pragmatic listening which involves making inferences about speakers' intentions, are completely absent in class. The class is conducted in a computer lab with each session structured according to exactly the same format containing the following three parts: (1) vocabulary previews in preparation for listening to a scripted segment; (2) repeated listening to audio files and writing down what they hear verbatim; (3) checking and scoring the manuscript for accuracy. Each audio file contains a three to four minute mini-lecture recorded by EAP instructors. The topic of each lecture varies, ranging from cultural customs and celebrations, to famous places, to historical events. Students also have a quiz each week in class, which takes the format of dictation based on the listening materials covered in the previous week.

The speaking class focuses on informal communication skills in a variety of formats, including small talk between peers, interviews, discussions and formal presentations. Through these activities, students are encouraged to express their feelings, opinions and ideas. The topics are kept informal, concentrated on daily, personal experiences such as family, vacations, media, weekend plans and university life. Pair and group activities are arranged in a way such that students speak as much English as possible across a variety of situations. The core textbook is the *New English Upgrade* series published by Macmillan Ltd (2008). The textbook has 12 thematic units, each containing six main sections: dialogue listening, introduction of key expressions, pattern practice with key expressions, oral dialogue practice, extended conversation practice, activities related to each topic and various key expressions and vocabulary practice. There is no formal assessment, but on a regular basis, the class instructors evaluate students' speaking in class using a rubric, whereby informal feedback is provided periodically. In the speaking classes I observed (a total of 26 sessions), the amount of time that the students spent speaking in pairs or group ranged from 5 to 45 minutes, with an average of 28 minutes. They also frequently volunteered answers and asked questions to the teachers.

At the time of my study, there were two instructors who were teaching different speaking class sections. There was great variation between these two instructors in terms of their teaching style, instructional materials and classroom arrangements. One instructor followed the textbook very closely, exercise-by-exercise, and took a fluency-oriented approach with his students by having them speak in pairs for a large chunk of class time. He circulated among the pairs and facilitated conversation, but rarely interrupted students' conversations or corrected their mistakes. There were no homework or tests in this class outside of occasional vocabulary assignments taken directly from the textbook. Students were quizzed on vocabulary every other week. There was no additional assignment in class.

The other instructor, on the other hand, used the textbook very minimally, once a week at most. Instead, he prepared a variety of original materials and activities. Once he brought a series of YouTube video clips to class and had students narrate them. Another time he had students prepare an email message presenting their own life problems and afterwards had them give advice to each other. While the activities were communicative, the teacher's instruction method was form-focused. The instructor circulated among students and constantly gave corrective feedback on their grammar and lexical mistakes. Students were usually seated in a group of four or five, not in pairs, so their actual speaking time was rather small. The instructor preferred structured communication activities with explicit directions, rather than fluency-based, extended conversation tasks.

In this instructor's class, all 18 students had a weekly speaking journal assignment in which they were required to converse with an English-speaker outside of class and write a reflection about their experiences. Each student wrote three to five entries per week, approximately half a page per entry, and turned their journal in every Friday for credit (see Chapter 3 for more information about the speaking journal assignments). Sample journal entries are given in the next section). Students were also regularly evaluated for their listening, speaking and vocabulary in class. In addition to the informal in-class assessment like that provided by the other instructor, this instructor arranged a one-to-one interview session with each student outside of class five times during the semester. Each session lasted for about 10 to 15 minutes and involved informal, small talk. Students recorded the interview and transcribed it at home. In a follow-up session, they analyzed their speech by identifying mistakes and weaknesses.

I surveyed the textbook for target speech acts and found one exercise on requesting a favor and expressing an opinion. In a short dialog between classmates, several expressions indicating requests for permission and help surfaced: 'Can I' + verb, 'Do you mind if' + clause, 'Is it OK if' + clause, and 'I was wondering if' + clause. These key expressions were followed by a pattern drill and short conversation practice. However, there was no sociolinguistic information provided by the instructor or textbook about these forms – when and under what circumstances to use one form over another and what situational features constrain their use. This was also true in the case of the speech act of expressing opinions. Contextual variables such as interlocutor relationship, power difference and topic of conversation were usually fixed, and the textbook did not engage students in practicing this speech act in a variety of sociocultural settings.

In summary, the analyses of course materials and class observations revealed that students had plenty of opportunities for general speaking and listening practice in class. Each session was only taught in English and students received skill-focused practice based on textbook exercises. Regarding target pragmatic knowledge and abilities, it appears that these skills were addressed indirectly. Inferential listening was practiced mainly through reading exercises focused on making inferences in written texts, but not through auditory input because the EAP listening class was a dictation class. Speech acts of requests and opinions appeared in the speaking textbook, but students only learned linguistic forms without sociocultural information about appropriateness or politeness of those forms. Target linguistic forms were also covered in the writing class, but they were presented as isolated grammar points, and social functions involved in these forms were not introduced. The next section presents descriptions of students' target language use outside the class.

Opportunities to use English outside class

A close look into students' experiences revealed a unique immersion context in the institution, in which students have access to target input on daily basis outside of class. To support this, throughout the period of this study, I administered a 10-item survey called the Language Contact Profile (LCP) adapted from Freed *et al.* (2004) in order to document the students' reported amounts of outside class contact with the target language across a variety of activities (e.g. time spent on interacting with fluent English speakers, time spent on homework, time spent browsing the internet) (see Appendix A for a copy of this survey). Students recorded an estimation of total time per week for each activity. The survey was given six times over the academic year at about five- to six-week intervals. In the first week, the amount of language contact was small, but in the remaining weeks, students reported a relatively stable amount, at an average of 30.23 hours per week (SD = 14.7). Table 1.1

TABLE 1.1 Descriptive statistics of the amount of English contact per week reported in LCP

	Time of administration	Mean	SD	Min.	Max.
LCP 1	April	27.01	14.29	4.00	59.00
LCP 2	June	35.16	26.48	3.00	107.00
LCP 3	July	35.51	25.96	6.00	109.50
LCP 4	September	34.49	20.16	6.50	90.00
LCP 5	November	37.33	25.18	0.00	123.00
LCP 6	December	39.64	23.48	10.50	131.50

Note: Japanese academic year begins in April. Mean refers to the sum of all the weekly English contact hours reported on LCP.

displays descriptive statistics of contact time in each time period (see Appendix B for descriptive statistics by activity type).

In addition to the LCP, I analyzed speaking journal entries provided by 18 students in which they kept records of their communication experiences on campus. A total of 1150 entries accumulated over two semesters revealed a range of language contact each student had on campus. About 60% of the time, the students recorded experiences related to vocabulary and grammar, for example, asking international students how to use certain words or trying out a new word with someone. About 20% of the time, participants recorded topics they discussed with international students, for example, about their hometown, family and friends, part-time job, traveling, study habits, Japanese language and culture and future goals. About 10% of the time, students recorded speech acts they produced or observed, including greetings, thanking, complements, requests, suggestions and persuasion. In a post hoc survey I administered to the 18 students, 16 reported that they talked to international students for this assignment and two reported that they talked to teachers. They typically spent 30 minutes to one hour per week to complete the journal entry. Below are example entries from three students in their first semester:

Student #33 (female)

When I talked with an international student, I was glad to talk with him but I was tired a little bit, so I said 'I'm tired,' and he said 'I'm sorry.' At the time, I misunderstood. I thought he apologized me. So I said 'It's not your fault.' He said 'I know. It's not my fault.' I didn't understand why he said 'I'm sorry.' So I asked him that. He told me that he showed his sympathy to me. The word 'I'm sorry' is very easy words, but I thought the meanings depend on situation. It is hard to judge which one is right meaning.

Student #25 (female)

When I was studying in the library, an international student came. I told him I had a test the next day. He said 'That's too bad.' But I said 'It's a piece of cake!' He said 'Wow! Do your best.' But actually I made a bluff to him. In fact, it's never a piece of cake. Actually, I got a terrible score the next day. It's a very interesting word because there's no connect between 'a piece of cake' and that's mean 'It's easy.' I wonder why a 'piece of cake'. Why it is not 'a piece of bread' or 'a piece of pie' or 'a piece of something'. By the way, there is a Japanese phrase which means the same as 'a piece of cake'. We say 'It's before a breakfast.' Maybe it means 'it's very easy so I can do it before I eat breakfast.'

Student #24 (female)

Today Masako, Kayoko and I visited Ms Naomi and we talked a lot. I asked her how to improve speaking skill. When I have a problem, I ask various people the same question to solve my problem. This time, my problem is how to improve my speaking skill. So I asked her. It was second time to ask her because I couldn't be convinced last time. At first, she talked about 'dream'. If our mind changes from Japanese to English, we dream in English. I have never dreamed in English. Even if foreigners appear in my dream, they speak Japanese. It's very strange. So my mind hasn't changed. Second, she told me that we don't have to prepare Japanese when we talk English. But I always do that. It takes a long time to start speaking English. I prepare Japanese sentence at first in my mind. Next, I put Japanese to English. I try to translate very correctly, so I can't find words which I want to say. Thanks to her advice, I could know what I should do next. So I was very happy today. I'll do that in tomorrow's reading class.

In summary, these descriptions, both inside and outside of the class, indicate that the target institution offers abundant opportunities to use English for authentic purposes, both academic and interpersonal. Students use English to digest class materials, comprehend lectures, express themselves in essays and exchange opinions. English also serves as a medium for entertainment: They watch movies in English and browse the internet in English, and converse with international students in English. In all of these venues, English is used to perform real-life functions – to perform academic tasks as well as mundane everyday tasks.

Given these characteristics, the research site offers a particularly interesting context to examine pragmatic development because it presents an optimal environment for both academic and social language use. To gain the ability to politely communicate intentions or comprehend one's indirect intentions, students need refined linguistic skills. However, the social nature of pragmatic competence also implies that opportunities to engage in social interactions are indispensable for pragmatic growth. As the target institution is likely to afford such opportunities, it is worth examining the emerging patterns of pragmatic competence within this unique immersion context, by studying the interaction between this context and students' characteristics that are considered to affect their pragmatic development.

Organization of the Book

The remaining part of this book has five chapters encompassing four major sections: literature review, research questions and methodology, research findings and conclusion.

Chapter 2: Longitudinal Studies in Interlanguage Pragmatics

This chapter reviews previous longitudinal studies in ILP. Exhaustive bibliographic searches of refereed journals, books and book chapters and conference monographs yielded a body of 23 unique longitudinal studies published throughout 2010. This chapter compares findings across the studies and explores the patterns and inconsistencies that emerge among them. These studies are evaluated in terms of what they contribute to the accumulated knowledge of SLA. Because SLA research focuses primarily on developmental patterns, variation among learners and factors (individual, social and cognitive) that influence development, these issues are used as benchmarks to synthesize the findings of these studies. These criteria are meant to strengthen connections between ILP and SLA at large, and to profile ILP as specific area of inquiry in SLA research. Based on the review of these 23 studies, this chapter presents critical areas in developmental ILP that merit future attention.

Chapter 3: Theoretical Framework, Purpose and Methodology of the Study

Chapter 3 first presents the theoretical framework that guides the present study, and then introduces research questions: (1) What patterns and rate of pragmatic development can we observe across different pragmatic functions and attributes? and (2) What types of resources and experiences are available in the learning context and how do these factors shape developmental trajectories of individual learners? The chapter then describes the methodology of the study over five sections: (1) descriptions of the participants; (2) descriptions of the researcher; (3) descriptions of the measures used in this study (i.e. pragmatic listening and speaking tests and qualitative data sources); and (4) data collection procedures.

Chapter 4: Patterns and Rate of Pragmatic Development

This chapter presents results of the first research question regarding the patterns and rate of pragmatic development. The chapter presents descriptive statistics of six data sets collected from the pragmatic measures over three time points:

Pragmatic listening test
(1) Accuracy scores
(2) Response times

Pragmatic speaking test
(3) Appropriateness scores
(4) Grammaticality scores

(5) Planning time
(6) Speech rate

Finally, this chapter presents results of statistical analyses to demonstrate which aspects of pragmatic competence showed significant gains over time and which aspects did not. Statistical analyses are accompanied with graphic illustrations of changing means over time. In addition, qualitative data from interviews, class observations and students' journals are discussed in detail to account for the patterns of pragmatic changes found in this study.

Chapter 5: Individual Differences in Pragmatic Development

This chapter presents results of the second research question related to the individual variation in pragmatic development. This chapter presents qualitative analyses of the developmental patterns observed among the eight informants recruited from the whole participant group. First, the chapter provides background information of the focal participants and a rationale for choosing these participants. The chapter then provides descriptions of the qualitative data collection methods employed in the study (i.e. interviews, class observations and journals). Finally, the chapter presents case histories of the eight informants to reveal a complex interplay among individuals, context and change in pragmatic development. The eight cases demonstrate idiosyncratic developmental trajectories, and variations are explained based on different types of learning opportunities and resources available to individuals.

Chapter 6: Summary and Conclusion

The last chapter presents summary and interpretations of the findings, as well as implications that the study generates about the construct of pragmatic competence and SLA process. The chapter concludes with limitations of the study and directions for future research.

Notes

(1) As of 2009, Japan has 773 four-year universities and colleges, consisting of 86 national universities, 92 public universities and 595 private universities. As a result of the declining birthrate, universities are now competing to attract students.
(2) Other two English-medium universities are Ritsumeikan Asia Pacific University in Beppu City and Miyazaki International University in Miyazaki City.
(3) Located in the town of Yuwa with a population of 8000, Akita International University promotes open campus environment and offers students a number of extra-curricular activities and community outreach programs with an aim of improving their understanding of local culture and people. For example, international students are invited to participate in the 'Home Visit Program' arranged by a local organization. They are introduced to volunteer host families and visit their home during weekends and holidays. Other community activities include: rice harvesting

with local community members, assistant English teaching in local elementary schools and international cooking parties.

(4) Akita International University has been successful in attracting prospective students. For the academic year 2010, 1562 students applied for the quota of 150. In addition, graduates of the university have attained competitive employment. In the year 2009, despite the depressing economy, students received a job offer from large corporations, including Mitsubishi Material, Meiji Holdings, Honda and Sumitomo Trading, which media praises as a model of successful new universities in Japan.

2 Longitudinal Studies in Interlanguage Pragmatics[1]

After Kasper and Dahl's (1991) definition of *interlanguage pragmatics* (see Chapter 1), the field of pragmatics has accomplished a major leap in terms of the quantity and quality of empirical studies of L2 pragmatic competence. An enriched body of research has shed light on critical issues related to pragmatic development, learning and teaching. While Kasper and Dahl's definition instantiates that acquisitional research is a desideratum in ILP, longitudinal investigation into pragmatic competence is still underrepresented. Existing research has predominantly focused on pragmatic use, not development. Relative paucity of developmental ILP research was originally noted by Kasper (1992b) and later emphasized by Kasper and Schmidt, who observed:

> Unlike other areas of second language study, which are primarily concerned with acquisitional patterns of interlanguage knowledge over time, the great majority of studies in ILP has not been developmental. Rather, focus is given to the ways NNS' pragmalinguistic and sociopragmatic knowledge differs from that of native speakers (NSs) and among learners with different linguistic and cultural backgrounds. To date, ILP has thus been primarily a study of second language use rather than second language acquisition. (Kasper & Schmidt, 1996: 150)

Their call for developmental research has generated much discussion over a range of seminal publications that aim to enrich the acquisitional body of ILP research (Bardovi-Harlig, 1999, 2000; Kasper & Rose, 1999, 2002). A handful of longitudinal studies that exist in the field today echo this important voice. This chapter examines the findings of existing longitudinal studies for oft-cited topics of SLA research: developmental patterns, variation among learners and factors that affect development. Based on the analysis, this chapter highlights critical areas in developmental ILP that merit future attention.

On Issues of Pragmatic Development: A Review of Longitudinal ILP Studies

This section reviews about two dozen longitudinal studies found in the field of interlanguage pragmatics. Exhaustive bibliographic searches were conducted to identify all longitudinal ILP studies published throughout 2010 when this book was written. All the refereed journals, books, book chapters and conference monographs were searched through the databases of ERIC, LLBA, World Cat and Web of Science. Eligibility of the studies for analysis was determined based on these criteria:

(1) The study observed the development of the same participant(s) over a period of time.
(2) The study examined the development of specific pragmatic features.
(3) The study chronologically documented development, change and gains by analyzing learner data collected systematically over time (e.g. pre- and post-test results, linguistic analysis).
(4) The study did not involve instructional intervention or other types of training.
(5) The study observed participants of secondary or postsecondary school age.

Several studies based on the same sample and data were counted only once as a unique study. A total of 23 unique ILP longitudinal studies were found for this review: four studies on comprehension of pragmatic meaning, five studies on perception and recognition of pragmatic features and 14 studies on the production of pragmatic functions. The studies are discussed according to these three categories.

Development in the Comprehension of Pragmatic Meaning

Pragmatic comprehension involves an inferential process of understanding speakers' intentions in utterances. Meaning is conveyed at two levels: utterance meaning, or literal sense of words uttered; and force, or speaker's intention behind the words (Thomas, 1995). Pragmatic comprehension entails understanding meaning at both levels. It requires decoding linguistic and contextual cues and using them to make inferences of speakers' intentions behind the cues. This is a difficult task for L2 learners because they have to recognize the mismatch between the literal utterance and the intended meaning, and reprocess the literal information to infer implied message. The greater the mismatch is, the greater the processing effort becomes.

The mechanisms of inferencing were first explained by Grice in 1975. Grice explained that when people communicate, they conform to Cooperative Principles, a set of assumptions that guide human communication. According to the principles, when the speaker says something, the listener assumes that the linguistic message is relevant to the discourse and draws the most plausible interpretation based on the context. Grice said that conversation is built upon a set of 'conversation maxims', or rules of communication shared by the speaker and listener. One of the conversation maxims, the maxim of relevance, for example, helps people to interpret implicature, such as in B's response:

A: I'm out of eggs.
B: There is a grocery store around the corner.

The listener, assuming that the speaker is following the maxim of relevance and has made an appropriate comment to A, draws the conclusion that the grocery store has eggs. As illustrated here, understanding a message is a process of working out what the speaker means based on the linguistic knowledge, context and the assumption of relevance. Implied meaning is understood based on the assumption that the speaker operates under cooperative norms, as well as the listener's ability to supply contextual information to make inferences from seemingly unrelated utterances. Implied meaning is understood from what is said, and the assumption that the relevance maxim is maintained (Levinson, 1983).

Building on Grice's theory, Relevance Theory by Sperber and Wilson (1995) further explicated the mechanisms operating under utterance interpretation. The theory claims that the central aspect of communication is the recognition of speaker intentions guided by ordinary cognitive inferential processes. Communication is achieved by decoding linguistic stimuli, as well as by interpreting contextual cues and using them as evidence toward the correct inferencing of speaker intentions. In Relevance Theory, context is not limited to external factors such as physical environment or the preceding discourse. A set of all the assumptions that the hearer has about the world, including 'expectations about future, scientific hypotheses or religious beliefs, anecdotal memories, general cultural assumptions, beliefs about the mental state of the speaker' (Sperber & Wilson, 1995: 15) contribute to meaning interpretation. These expectations and assumptions are termed as 'cognitive environment', the set of all the facts that the hearer is aware of or is capable of becoming aware of in the environment of an utterance. The concept of cognitive environment is also closely related to processing effort. According to the theory, when people interpret a message, many different assumptions from diverse sources come to mind. Among the assumptions, they select the interpretation that has the greatest contextual effects (i.e. most relevant in the context) for the smallest processing effort. Processing effort is determined by utterance complexity, size of context and accessibility of the context. See an example below:

A: Has George left for the basketball game?
B: It's after ten.

Based on the assumption that Speaker B provided information relevant to the question, Speaker A can only understand B's reply (i.e. whether George is still home or not) if he or she has ability to comprehend B's reply and has sufficient contextual knowledge such as George's routine, basketball practice, and the time of the day. If Speaker A does not have those contextual assumptions, comprehension of B's utterance becomes either impossible or requires considerable effort.

These mechanisms of inferencing have been exploited in the ILP research. As decades of studies in cognitive psychology documented that the ability to interpret implied meaning is part of people's social cognition and is acquired along with their normal development of communicative competence (e.g. Bezuidenhout & Sroda, 1998; Shatz, 1977), the premise that has guided L2 studies is that the relevance processing is directly transferable from L1 to L2 acquisition process. Despite this premise, pragmatic comprehension has been the most underrepresented domain of ILP research (Kasper & Rose, 2002), and a handful of longitudinal studies available to date confirm this observation. Among the 23 studies located for the present review, only four deal with comprehension of pragmatic meaning or conversational implicatures. English was the target language in all of them, and the studies were by two authors. These facts indicate that longitudinal investigation into pragmatic comprehension has not come so far in scope over the last few decades. Table 2.1 summarizes the characteristics of the four studies.

Bouton (1992) investigated ESL learners' comprehension of conversational implicatures. ESL learners of mixed L1s took a written multiple-choice test that composed of 33 short written dialogues that included different types of implicatures. See simplified example items:

Relevance implicature
David: Mandy just broke our date for the play. Now I've got two tickets for Saturday and no one to go with.
Mark: Have you met my sister? She's coming down to see me this weekend.
(a)   Mark can't remember if David has met his sister.
(b)   There is nothing Mark can do to help David.
(c)   Mark suggests that David take Mark's sister to the play.

Pope implicature (saying 'Is the Pope Catholic?' to mean that something is obvious)
A: Are you sure you can take care of yourself this weekend?
B: Can a duck swim, mother?
(a)   She is doing homework about ducks and is asking her mother for help with one of the questions.
(b)   She is asking her mother if she can go with her for the weekend.

TABLE 2.1 Longitudinal studies of comprehension of pragmatic meaning

	Target language	Target pragmatic features	Measures	Participants	Context	Study length
Bouton (1992)	English	Implicatures	Written multiple-choice test	30 learners of mixed L1s	SL	4.5 years
Bouton (1994)	English	Implicatures	Written multiple-choice test	375 learners of mixed L1s	SL	17 months
Taguchi (2007a)	English	Indirect opinions and refusals	Listening test with yes–no questions	92 learners of L1 Japanese	FL	2 months
Taguchi (2008c)	English	Indirect opinions and refusals	Listening test with yes–no questions	44 learners of L1 Japanese	SL	4 months

Notes: SL: second language context; FL: foreign language context

(c) She is trying to change the subject. She is a little nervous about being left alone and doesn't want to talk about it.
(d) She is telling her mother hat she will be able to take care of herself okay.

Irony
    Bill and Peter have been good friends since they were children. They roomed together in college and travelled Europe together after graduation. Now friend have told Bill that they saw Peter dancing with Bill's wife while Bill was away. Bill said, 'Frank knows how to be a good friend.' What does Bill mean?

(a) Peter is not acting the way a good friend should.
(b) Peter and Bill's wife are becoming really good friends while Peter is away.
(c) Peter is a good friend, so Bill can trust him.
(d) Nothing should be allowed to interfere with Bill and Peter's friendship.

Indirect criticism
A: What did you think of Mark's term paper?
B: It was well-typed.
(a) He liked the paper; he thought it was good.
(b) He thought it was certainly well typed.
(c) He thought it was a good paper; he did like the form, though not the content.
(d) He didn't like it.

    Bouton found that the L2 learners became native-like in their comprehension of relevance-based implicatures after four-and-a-half years, but some formulaic implicatures (e.g. sequence implicatures, Pope question implicatures) remained difficult to comprehend. His second study in 1994 analyzed learners' comprehension at a 17-month interval. Unlike the learners in his first study, these learners did not achieve native-like comprehension, and they still struggled with four types of implicatures after 17 months. The challenging implicatures were indirect criticism, Pope questions, sequence implicatures and irony.
    Longitudinal studies by Taguchi (2007a, 2008c), on the other hand, examined the comprehension of indirect refusals and indirect opinions among Japanese EFL and ESL learners. Indirect refusals were considered conventional because they followed a common, predictable discourse pattern (giving a reason for refusal). In contrast, indirect opinions were considered less conventional and idiosyncratic in nature because meaning was not attached to specific linguistic expressions or predictable patterns, and linguistic options regarding how to express the opinion are wide open (e.g.

endless qualifications of liking or disliking). These two item types (24 items each) were incorporated into a computerized listening test that had a series of short dialogues followed by a yes–no question. See example items below:

Indirect refusal
Ben: Hey, what are we doing for dinner tonight?
Barbara: Um … I don't know.
Ben: How about if we go out to eat tonight. How about Chinese food?
Barbara: That sounds good, but don't you think we should finish the food from yesterday before we spend more money? We still have the chicken and rice.
Question: Does Barbara want Chinese food?

Indirect opinion
Ben: I can't believe I fell asleep in the middle of the movie last night. Did you watch it till the end?
Barbara: Yeah, I did.
Ben: How was it? Did you like it?
Barbara: Well, I was glad when it was over.
Question: Did Barbara like the movie?

Development of pragmatic comprehension was analyzed for two attributes: accuracy of comprehension (scores) and response times (average time taken to answer items correctly). These two attributes were measured in order to illustrate different patterns of development that correspond to different processing loads encoded in the target implicatures. According to Relevance Theory, the degree of indirectness is closely related to the amount of processing effort, which is affected by a number of linguistic and nonlinguistic features, such as features of conventions, cultural and linguistic knowledge and frequency of the utterances. Different degree of processing effort manifests in differences in accuracy and speed of comprehension (i.e. response times) across implicature types. Comprehension is predicted to be faster when the preceding proposition is immediately accessible. But when the proposition is not salient, listeners need to construct some sort of bridging structure, resulting in longer response times. Conventionality enhances comprehension speed because, due to the rouitinalized associative connections in long-term memory, conventional utterances do not require extensive analytical procedures.

Supporting this assumption, both of Taguchi's studies revealed that, regardless of learning context, indirect refusals were easier and faster to comprehend, and showed larger gain size than indirect opinions. In her 2007 study, the learners made significant gains in both accuracy and comprehension speed over a period of seven weeks, but the degree of gain was much larger for accuracy than it was for response time when effect sizes were compared. The pattern was reversed in her 2008b study of ESL learners; they showed much more profound development in comprehension speed with a sizable effect size, but with only marginal improvement in accuracy over a five-week period.

Together, the four longitudinal studies revealed a developmental order in the comprehension of implicatures, which is intertwined with the difficulty order of implicatures. When meaning is based on shared conventions, it is easier to comprehend for L2 learners, not only because it poses fewer processing demands, but also because it allows for successful transfer of pragmatic knowledge from L1. This was the case in Bouton's studies in which learners' comprehension of relevance implicatures became native-like over time because, as their general comprehension ability in the target L2 matured, learners became able to use their L1-based inferential skills to seek relevance in the information. Taguchi's studies also lend support to these generalizations. Comprehension of indirect refusals preceded that of indirect opinions because the means to encode refusals (i.e. giving a reason for refusal) were conventional and shared between L1 and L2. However, when the convention is culture specific, or not shared between L1 and L2, meaning becomes difficult for L2 learners to recognize, as shown in Bouton's studies in which Pope implicatures remained difficult for learners even after four years.

The ability to comprehend less conventional implicatures does not seem to develop as quickly due to the extensive inferential bridge that learners need to arrive at correct interpretations. This was the case in Taguchi's studies where comprehension of indirect opinions showed slower development than that of indirect refusals. Since there were no constant symbolic representations, comprehension of indirect opinions demands more word-by-word bottom-up processing that involves analysis of syntactic and lexical information and contextual cues. Using these analyses, learners have to first understand the literal meaning of the opinion expressions, and then work deductively toward the implied speakers' intentions. Due to the multiple levels of processing, along with more drastic deviation from the Gricean maxims, the degree of inferencing that learners have to make becomes extensive, resulting in more absolute difficulty and slower-paced improvement in comprehension over time.

Regarding the developmental patterns of accuracy and comprehension speed of implied meaning, both aspects are found to develop naturally over time without instruction or training, but they showed different pace of development, and the differences were explained in the context of learning. ESL learners showed more profound gain in comprehension speed than accuracy over time, while the pattern was reversed for EFL learners who made little gain in comprehension speed over time. These findings imply two things: (1) In the course of L2 development, speed and accuracy may not develop in parallel; and (2) Different environments may support different aspects of pragmatic comprehension ability. The processing of pragmatic meaning involves coordinated action of a number of factors, including linguistic, cognitive and sociocultural processes, which must be automatized to achieve speedy comprehension. These underlying components might take a longer time to be automatized in the EFL context due to the limited amount of exposure to input and processing practice available in the environment. The small gain in comprehension speed found among the EFL learners may be due to the fact that they lacked sufficient opportunities for associative practices to develop performance speed. In a foreign language environment, EFL learners had limited incidental exposure to L2; as a result, mapping practices between form and meaning did not occur frequently. Greater gains in comprehension speed shown by ESL learners, on the other hand, could be due to the abundant incidental processing practice available in the environment.

In summary, meanings that are more conventionalized, regular and thus require fewer linguistic and cognitive resources are more easily processed, as long as learners can take advantage of the conventionality. In contrast, meanings that are more context dependent and less common or highly culture specific are more difficult to comprehend. Learners' comprehension progresses from the stage where meaning has strong signals, to the stage where message does not involve any obvious signals and thus requires a series of inferential stages to arrive at the intended meaning.

Development in the Recognition and Perception of Pragmatic Features

Shifting from the studies of pragmatic comprehension, this section discusses longitudinal studies in the area of meta-pragmatic awareness and recognition of appropriate pragmalinguistic forms. Comprehension of implied meaning and recognition of pragmatic forms are similar in that both deal with the receptive aspect of learners' pragmatic abilities. However, they differ in that the former deals with inferential skills and recognition of speakers' intentions, while the latter deals with recognition of pragmalinguistic forms and their contextual requirements. When comprehending nonliteral meaning, learners require knowledge that encompasses a wide range of properties, including: linguistic knowledge, knowledge of Gricean maxims of conversation (i.e. assumption of relevance), conventions of language use and sociocultural norms of interaction. In order to comprehend indirect utterances, learners need to know the vocabulary and grammar of the utterances, as well as the cultural conventions and rules of language use that accompany the utterances. Successful pragmatic comprehension depends on learners' ability to draw on these knowledge bases and integrate them to infer speakers' intentions encoded in the utterances.

Recognition of appropriate pragmatic forms, on the other hand, draws on similar knowledge bases of linguistic forms and their conventions but requires learners to use the knowledge to detect correct form-context mappings. In this regard, studies of recognition of pragmalinguistic forms more directly observe the central concern of the study of pragmatics – language use in social context. One of the assumptions in pragmatics is that production and perception of language are affected by social variables, such as settings, social status of the interlocutors and topics of conversation. Under this assumption, ILP research has mainly examined learners' knowledge of proper linguistic forms to convey the intentions or semantic strategies used to project politeness in particular social encounters. A typical task used to elicit such knowledge is multiple-choice questionnaires. These questions specify the situational context and provide several response alternatives to choose from. As a variation, some studies have used a scaled-response questionnaire in which learners evaluated the degree of appropriateness of the target expression on a Likert scale. See the example below from Jianda's study on pragmatic knowledge of apology expressions in L2 English:

Situation: You are a student. You are now rushing to the classroom as you are going to be late for the class. When you turn a corner, you accidentally bump into a student whom you do not know and the books he is carrying fall onto the ground. You stop, pick the books up, and apologize.

A: Oops, sorry, my fault. I'm in such a hurry. Here, let me help pick these up for you.
B: I'm sorry, I will be late if I'm not in a hurry. I'll pay attention to this when I turn corner next time.
C: Oh, I'm very sorry. I'm going to be late for my class, and if I'm late, I won't be allowed to enter the classroom. But I like this course very much. So, sorry again! (Jianda, 2007: 415)

These multiple-choice items measure learners' understanding of situational characteristics (e.g. participants' power difference and social distance) and their knowledge of preferred linguistic options in the situation. Advantage of these tasks is that the constructs under study are well defined. Researchers can build in the exact context variables in the stimulus situations and preselect the pragmatic expressions to test learners' knowledge, allowing a direct examination of learners' knowledge of specific form–context mappings.

Another advantage of recognition tasks is that, in contrast to performance-based tasks, they could reduce the influence of learners' subjectivity and identity that could mask pragmatic knowledge that the learners actually possess.

When performing a sociocultural function on the spot, learners may intentionally choose to opt out for particular pragmatic expressions simply because these expressions do not appeal to them. Subjectivity and identity become an issue here because of the nature of pragmatics that involves language use affected by considerations of language users, social context and norms of interaction. When facing pragmatic tasks in another language, learners bring in their own perceptions of the world based on their educational, professional and generational backgrounds. Some learners may want to conform to the pragmatic norms and forms of the given culture, but others may avoid using the forms, signaling a desire to maintain their identity (e.g. Davis, 2007; Ishihara & Tarone, 2009). While the issues of subjectivity and identity are critical in making sense of learners' pragmatic abilities, if researchers are purely interested in the range of pragmatic knowledge that learners have – whether they do or do not implement it – recognition tasks that directly tap learners' awareness of pragmatic forms and norms could be an appropriate option.

Kinginger and Blattner (2008) engagingly discuss this point in their longitudinal investigation of awareness of French colloquial expressions. They used a receptive task in which learners were presented with a series of social situations illustrating different parameters that influence the choice of address forms. The authors claim that choice of variable sociolinguistic features such as formal vs. informal forms or second-person pronouns of address is indexical, meaning that the choice of particular form over another may index the speaker's identity – how he/she wants to be perceived in the particular interaction (e.g. wanting to sound friendly or reserved). Hence, it is not clear whether learners' use of a particular form reflects their pragmatic knowledge or their desire to project their identity in certain ways. The authors wrote:

> [The] use of variable sociolinguitic features is inherently ambiguous; we cannot tell the extent to which a certain form has been employed or avoided due to first or second order indexicality, or a combination of both. The double indexicality of sociolinguistic variables means that learners need to assess not only how these forms relate to contexts of use, but also the extent to which they want these forms in the communicative repertoire in the first place. ... When we add to this the finding that second language learners tend toward hesitance to claim identities as second language speakers empowered to use informal variants (Belz and Kinginger, 2002, 2004; Dewaele, 2004), it becomes clear that performance data alone cannot reveal what learners know about sociolinguistic variation. (Kinginger & Blattner, 2008: 228)

Observing these strengths of recognition tasks, several longitudinal studies in ILP investigated learners' development of meta-pragmatic awareness of appropriate linguistic expressions in specific social settings. Table 2.2 displays a summary of features of those studies.

TABLE 2.2 Longitudinal studies of recognition of pragmatic features

	Target language	Target pragmatic features	Measures	Participants	Context	Study length
Kinginger and Blattner (2008)	French	Colloquial expressions	Awareness survey & interview	17 American learners	SL	3 months
Kinginger and Farrell (2004)	French	Address forms	Awareness survey & interview	23 American learners	SL	3 months
Matsumura (2001)	English	Advice-giving expressions	Multiple-choice survey	102 Japanese in Japan and 97 in Canada	SL and FL	8 months
Matsumura (2007)	English	Advice-giving expressions	Multiple-choice survey	15 Japanese learners	FL	12 months
Schauer (2006, 2009)	English	Apologies, refusals, requests & suggestions	Pragmatic and grammatical error detection test	17 Germans in England and 16 in Germany	SL and FL	9 months

Matsumura (2001) examined changes in learners' recognition of appropriate advice-giving expressions over time. Japanese learners of English read 12 advice-giving scenarios in English and Japanese, and selected the most appropriate advice-giving expression out of four options: direct advice (with the use of 'should'), hedged advice, indirect comments with no advice and opting out. See the example item below:

Situation 1. You and the instructor P.D. are in a restaurant. The instructor says something about ordering a hamburger. You ordered a hamburger in this restaurant before and, in your opinion, it was really greasy. What do you think would be appropriate to say in this situation?

A: You shouldn't order the hamburger. I had it here before, and it was really greasy.

B: Maybe it's not a good idea to order a hamburger. I had one here before, and it was really greasy.

C: I had it here before, and it was really greasy.

D: Nothing. (Matsumura, 2001: 767)

In the example above, Option A is direct advice, Option B is hedged advice, Option C is indirect comments and Option D is opting out.

Learners in Canada and Japan took the questionnaire four times during one-year of study. Initially, both groups preferred using indirect and hedged forms of advice in the situation of high-status interlocutors (i.e. instructors), and the tendency, which was congruent with that of native speakers, remained the same throughout the year. Matsumura attributed the results to L1 socialization. Because Japanese students are status-sensitive and tend to use indirect expressions with individuals of higher status, the learners referenced their L1 sociocultural norms when speaking in their L2 English. When advising interlocutors of equal or lower-status (e.g. friends), or in situations where their advice was legitimate, the study-abroad group outperformed the at-home group by choosing more direct advice forms. The fact that they showed this tendency even in their early stages of their stay tells us that the study-abroad group appeared to have had more opportunities to understand how native speakers perceive social status.

The perception of social status and its effect on the choice of advice-giving expressions also became apparent in Matsumura's (2007) study that examined the aftereffects of study-abroad in pragmatic changes. After returning from Canada, 15 Japanese students completed the same multiple-choice test three times: one month, six months and one year after their return to Japan. The results showed that students retained their ability in lower- and equal-status situations but diverged in higher-status situations. After the six-month point of reentry, the students increasingly preferred not to give advice to their instructors. Follow-up interviews revealed that the students' perceptions of casual relationships between professors and students in Canada were altered after they returned to Japan because hierarchical relationships between professors and students are assumed in Japanese universities. Due to their increasing reanalysis of social status in Japan triggered by L1-based sociopragmatic norms, the students gradually rerealized that expressing opinions directly to higher-status persons is not a social norm in Japan. As a result, they began to opt out in giving advice in such situations. However, the students maintained their pragmatic knowledge in lower- and equal-status situations because they maintained contact with their Canadian friends via emails and other measures.

These findings indicate that learners' understanding of sociopragmatic norms affect patterns of pragmatic changes. As shown in Matsumura's studies, learners' choice of particular advice-giving expression was strongly influenced by their perception of social status and evaluation of appropriate behavior. Pragmatic development could take place at an early stage of study-abroad if learners have ample opportunities to observe the native speaker norms of sociopragmatic patterns. However, pragmatic development may be obstructed in a home country environment, especially when sociocultural conventions differ between L1 and L2 culture.

Schauer's (2006, 2009) study also examined the changes in the awareness of pragmatic appropriateness in a study-abroad context. Using Bardovi-Harlig and Dörnyei's (1998) instrument, she examined learners' progress in the detection of pragmatic as well as grammatical errors and the perceived severity of those errors. German learners of ESL and EFL watched a series of video interactions, and then judged the appropriateness of the interlocutors' speech act expressions. The target speech acts were apologies, refusals, requests and suggestions. Eight items contained pragmatic errors, eight had grammatical errors, and the remaining four were control items. Below is an example item:

Teacher: Anna, it's your turn to give your talk.
Anna: I can't do it today, but I will do it next week.
 Was the last part appropriate/correct?
  Yes   No
 If there was a problem how bad do you think it was?
  Not bad at all   ___: ___: ___: ___: ___: ___: Very bad
 (Schauer, 2006: 286)

Results showed that, compared with the EFL learners, the ESL learners recognized a larger number of pragmatic errors than grammatical errors, even after staying in England for just one month. Their pragmatic awareness continued to improve during their nine-month stay in the target country, almost nearing the level of native speakers. ESL learners also improved when making judgments about the severity of pragmatic errors, even exceeding the native speaker levels, as indicated by the post-tests. Like Matsumura's study, Schauer's study showed that pragmatic development could occur even after a short period of residence abroad. Living in a target language context, learners probably make gains more easily in the pragmatic awareness because they can directly analyze pragmatic features as found in native speaker models.

Although Matsumura and Schauer's studies revealed learners' development in pragmatic recognitions, other study-abroad studies revealed variation among individual learners in the pace of development (Kinginger, 2008; Kinginger & Blattner, 2008; Kinginger & Farrell, 2004). Kinginger and Blattner's study, cited above, examined gains in the awareness of French colloquial expressions among 17 American students over a semester abroad. While most students progressed with interpretations of colloquial phrases, their pre- and post-test scores showed a considerable individual variation, and the variation was explained by the intensity and range of the learners' experiences. The learner who gained the most frequently engaged in conversations with host family on a variety of topics at dinner table, whereas the learner who gained the least ate dinner in front of the TV and had little contact with the target community.

Kinginger's book-length research monograph (2008) provides a more in-depth account of the interplay among context, learners and development of sociopragmatic awareness. From the 17 participants in Kinginger and Blattener's study, Kinginger explored case histories of six participants in detail. She collected data from interviews, bi-weekly journals and calendar diaries in which the participants recorded their language use at hourly intervals. Qualitative data revealed how learners negotiated their access to opportunities and established their membership in the community despite the challenges and constraints imposed on them. For example, one learner, Louis, was placed in a host family who preferred a quiet environment and did not talk much at home. To compensate for the absence of interaction with his host family, he actively developed a social network in French by talking with his American friends in French and participating in volunteer activities. Quite opposite was the case of Liza. She was a highly skilled and motivated student. She was fortunate in her home stay placement and developed a close relationship with her host mother. However, she ended up spending a substantial amount of time speaking in English because her family and friends visited her in France for an extended period of time. She also spent much time traveling and reinforcing links to home via email and chat.

These stories revealed the types of learning resources available in host communities and learners' various stances toward them. Learners may be confronted with many challenges to language learning during their time abroad. Although initially they might construct the study-abroad experience as an opportunity for learning, they might get discouraged from unexpected home stay arrangement or close connections they maintain with their home country peers. In those circumstances, it is the learners' agency and investment that help reshape the context and learning opportunities available in it.

Taken together, the studies on the awareness of pragmatic features summarized above shed light on the patterns of pragmatic development, individual variations and the factors affecting both. Pragmatic learning does kick off at the very early stages of study-abroad, facilitated by the opportunities to observe target sociopragmatic norms. However, the gains may be lost after learners return to their home country, due to the influence of L1-based sociopragmatic norms. There is considerable variation in the pace of development among learners because of the differential amount and intensity of sociolinguistic contact, as well as the range of social experiences.

Development in the Production of Pragmatic Functions

Different from pragmatic comprehension or recognition, the production of pragmatic functions involves the knowledge of pragmalinguistics and sociopragmatics in unison with the processing capacity to articulate the knowledge in online production. While pragmatic comprehension and recognition form a process of attending to linguistic stimuli and understanding meaning attached to them, production is a process of attending to linguistic stimuli and conveying meaning with the stimuli. Pragmatic production requires a greater processing load than comprehension or recognition. In pragmatic comprehension, it is possible for learners to infer overall meaning of input without precise linguistic analysis of it by relying on paralinguistic and contextual cues, but production of pragmatic meaning requires precise linguistic processing. Likewise, complete linguistic processing may not be necessary in the recognition of appropriate pragmatic expressions because the learners' job is to compare linguistic alternatives and to select pragmatically appropriate option over the other. But when producing pragmatic expressions, learners' lexis and morphosyntax must be exact and accurate so that the meaning encoded in the forms is understood correctly. Incorrect linguistic knowledge, as seen in wrong word order or word choice, may obscure meaning or lead to misunderstanding.

The precise linguistic processing required for pragmatic production implies that the patterns of development in pragmatic production are, in part, constrained by learners' grammar. Although advanced grammatical competence does not automatically lead to skilled pragmatic performance, learners need to have basic linguistic resources to encode pragmatic functions. For instance, they need to know that lexis such as 'possibly' and 'a bit/a little' could effectively mitigate potential face-threat acts in complaints or refusals. Bi-clausal structures like 'I am wondering if' + clause and 'Would it be possible for you to' + verb could soften the request intention as opposed to more direct structures such as 'Please' + verb or 'I want you to' + verb. Learners' knowledge of these linguistic forms becomes more directly observable in production-based tasks that require them to actually use the forms.

This interdependence between pragmatics and grammatical development has been recapitulated over several seminal publications (Bardovi-Harlig, 1999, 2000; Kasper & Rose, 2002), although very few studies to date have actually documented staged development of pragmatic competence in accordance to grammatical maturity. Some exceptions are found in studies of children's pragmatic development (Achiba, 2002; R. Ellis, 1992). These studies documented learners' evolving pragmatic competence, corresponding to the increasing level of syntactic complexity. R. Ellis analyzed request-making expressions of two ESL children and revealed three-stage developmental sequence. In the first stage, children conveyed request intentions drawing on contextual resources. In the second stage, they mostly relied on formulaic language use. In the third stage, they started unpacking formulas for productive use, and at the same time, they began to exhibit conventional indirect forms. This three-staged sequence was later expanded to five by Kasper and Rose (2002) with addition of two stages: pragmatic expansion and fine-tuning. See the summary below (Kasper & Rose, 2002: 140):

Stage	Characteristics	Examples
(1) Pre-basic	Highly context dependent No syntax, no relational goals	'Me no blue,' Sir
(2) Formulaic	Reliance on unanalyzed formulas and imperatives	'Let's play the game.' 'Let's each breakfast.' 'Don't look.'
(3) Unpacking	Formulas incorporated into productive language use, shift to conventional indirectness	'Can you pass the pencil please?' 'Can you do another one for me?'
(4) Pragmatic expansion	Addition of new forms to pragma- linguistic repertoire, increased use of mitigation, more complex syntax	'Can I see it so I can copy it?'
(5) Fine- tuning	Fine-tuning of requestive force to participants, goals and contexts	'Is there any more white?'

What has not been revealed in the previous ILP studies are the detailed developmental trajectories beyond Stage 3. At Stage 4, learners are gradually exiting from simple, conventional request forms with modals such as 'could', 'may' and 'would' and moving toward more complex, bi-clausal structures (e.g. 'I am wondering if' + clause, 'Do you think you can' + verb, and 'Is there any way that you could' + verb). Having those forms in their repertoire, at Stage 5, learners begin to form a firm understanding of appropriate form–context mappings – which form to use to make a request to whom in what situation. The bi-clausal request forms merit attention in illuminating developmental sequences of a request speech act because previous research showed that those forms were difficult to acquire. For instance, Takahashi (1996) used a transferability judgement scale and tested whether or not Japanese college students of EFL perceive certain request strategies in L1 Japanese transferable to L2 English. She found that, regardless of proficiency levels, learners overall projected false form–function mappings between L1 and L2; they did not perceive syntactically complex English forms, especially bi-clausal structures, as functionally equivalent to Japanese polite request utterances.

The bi-clausal request forms were also found to be mostly absent in learners' production. Taguchi (2006) investigated the appropriateness of speech acts of requests produced by 59 Japanese EFL students in a bilingual college. Learners' requests were analyzed quantitatively by having native speakers rate their appropriateness on a six-point scale, as well as qualitatively by analyzing the types of linguistic forms used to produce the requests. Results revealed a significant proficiency influence on overall appropriateness ratings, but only a marginal difference in the types of linguistic expressions used between the two proficiency groups. Particularly noteworthy was an almost complete absence of bi-clausal structures in learners' requests. While all 20 native speakers used requests embedded in clause structures (e.g. 'I'm wondering if' + verb) when making a formal request (e.g. asking a professor for an extension of assignment), this linguistic form was used only 7% of the time in the higher-proficiency L2 group and never appeared in the lower-proficiency group. The following excerpts illustrate expressions used in a high-imposition request situation (i.e. asking a professor to reschedule a test). The native speaker participant used the bi-clausal structure ('Is there any chance I can' + verb), while the form was absent in the L2 learners' production.

Native Speaker (NS) sample
NS: I, look, I have a big favor to ask you. I know our exam is this week
          on Friday, but my friend is getting married that day. Is there any
          chance, like, maybe I can take it earlier or later or some other time?

Higher proficiency L2 learner sample
('L' refers to 'learner' and 'I' refers to 'interlocutor'):

L: Ah, so I'm here to ah, can you do me a favor? Because I
heard there is gonna be test next Friday, but I do need to go to
my friend's wedding. ((gap))

I: OK, ah, yeah, ah ((pause)) what kind of favor do you want me to do?

L: Ah, I hope I can do, I can shift the test date.

Lower proficiency L2 learner sample

L: Test, test?

I: Test.

L: Test.
((gap))

I: Ok, ah, so what do you want to do?

L: I want, I want to, I want to go to marriage ceremony, maybe.

I: OK↑ What do you want to do about your test.

L: Ah ((pause)).other day.

I: Another day?

L: Another day.

These findings suggest that the bi-clausal request forms are largely unfamiliar to L2 learners. As shown in the excerpts above, both L2 groups relied heavily on hinting expressions. In total, about 36% of hinting expressions appeared in the higher L2 group and 50% in the lower L2 group. As hints were not conventional form of requests, they required more inferencing on the part of the interlocutor, often resulting in more extended negotiations and clarifications. Investigation into the emergence of more complex request forms in learners' requests, as well as reasons behind the late-emerging nature of the forms, will provide more insights into the acquisitional trajectories of this particular speech act.

While fine-tuned analyses of conjoined development of pragmatics and grammar have not been seriously attested in the previous research, past longitudinal studies have illustrated the mediating role of grammatical knowledge in pragmatic development. Table 2.3 lists those 14 studies in the area of pragmatic production. Among the 14, seven studied speech acts, two studied address forms and the remaining five studies examined discourse features.

One notable finding common in these studies is the learners' initial tendency to adhere to simple, one-to-one correspondence between form and function, which was followed by the gradual expansion of the pragmalinguistic repertoire to encode functions. Salsbury and Bardovi-Harlig (2001) examined the development of the speech act of disagreements by three ESL learners in a US university over a period of 10–12 months. Naturalistic conversation data between the learners and native speakers were collected monthly. Types and tokens of modal expressions that appeared in conversation (e.g. 'can', 'might', 'want to', 'think', 'possible', 'maybe') were recorded and analyzed for how they functioned to frame disagreements.

TABLE 2.3 Longitudinal studies of production of pragmatic functions

	Target language	Target pragmatic features	Measures/data	Participants	Context	Study length
Barron (2006)	German	Refusal and offer	DCT	33 Irish learners	SL	14 months
Barron (2003)	German	Address forms	DCT	33 Irish learners	SL	14 months
Belz and Kinginger (2003)	German	Address forms	CMC	11 American learners	FL	2 months
Bardovi-Harlig and Hartford (1993)	English	Suggestion & rejection	Recordings of conversation	10 graduate students of mixed L1s	SL	7–14 weeks
Code and Anderson (2001)	English	Request	DCT	35 learners of	SL	10 months
DuFon (2000)	Indonesian	Negative responses	Naturalistic conversation	6 learners	SL	4 months
Hassall (2006)	Indonesian	Leave-taking	Diary	1 Australian learner (author)	SL	3 months
Ishida (2009)	Japanese	Sentence-final particle *ne*	Naturalistic conversation	1 American learner	SL	9 months
Iwasaki (2010)	Japanese	Speech style	Oral Proficiency Interview	5 American learners	SL	1 academic year
Ohta (2001)	Japanese	Acknowledgment & alignment	Recordings of class periods	2 American learners	FL	9 months
Salsbury and Bardovi-Harlig (2001)	English	Disagreement	Naturalistic conversation	3 US college students of mixed L1s	SL	10–12 months
Sawyer (1992)	Japanese	Sentence-final particle *ne*	Interview	11 learners of mixed L1s	FL	9 months
Schauer (2004)	English	Request	Multimedia DCT	12 German learners	SL	9 months
Warga and Scholmberger (2007)	French	Apology	DCT	7 Australian learners	SL	10 months

The data showed that a learner with a high type/token ratio of modals efficiently used a variety of modal forms as qualifying expressions, while a learner with a low type/token ratio either used strong forms of disagreement or recycled the same modal expressions throughout the conversation. The first excerpt below is from a learner with a high type/token ratio of modals. Here, the learner, MD, disagrees with the native speaker interlocutor (Int 1) about the use of the term 'test anxiety'. MD mitigates his disagreement with the hedge 'quite', 'a little' and other modal expressions such as 'I think' and 'can':

Int 1:   ... it's called test anxiety.
MD: I don't have quite like this, but I have a little, but not quite like this, always in, I think, in, every exam, we, don't, the most thing, the most important thing for me is time, like I'm not someone who can work like very fast, yeah ...
(Salsbury & Bardovi-Harlig, 2001: 139)

In stark contrast, the excerpt below from the learner, MR, with a low type/high token of modals uses the hedge 'maybe' throughout to mitigate the disagreement, and her linguistic resources are exhausted:

MR: I, I, maybe I had, many, taboo, taboo, because, ok, I grow in the family, religion, I think you, you like the life, depends, maybe your mother, ah education you, only don't do this and this, maybe your mother say, oh, you free, is different ...
(Salsbury & Bardovi-Harlig, 2001: 144)

As illustrated in these excerpts, with expressions of disagreements, grammatically weak learners seemed to be constrained by the range of modal expressions they have at their disposal.

The slow development in the acquisition of grammatical forms and their pragmatic functions was also found in Bardovi-Harlig and Hartford's (1993) study, which analyzed the development of speech acts of suggestions and rejections by 10 international graduate students at an American university. Data were naturalistic advising sessions recorded twice over a period of 7–14 weeks. While learners acquired sociopragmatic rules of advising rather quickly, they were slow to acquire the target pragmalinguistic forms. Over time, learners became able to initiate course nominations and offer credible reasons when rejecting advisors' suggestions about courses. Learners struggled more with appropriate forms of rejection; indeed, they continually used various forms of aggravators and ignored mitigating devices. The excerpts below illustrate this point. Here the advisor suggests that the student takes Linguistics 560. The student responds with a series of questions. Repeated questions is the student's strategy to reject the professor's suggestion on taking L560 or to avoid commitment, but it is nontarget-like and clearly ineffective because the advisor never withdraws his/her suggestion despite the long exchange.

(A = faculty advisor, S = graduate student)

A: Then, you'll have to do L560.
S: Which one is that one? Oh.
A: It's American culture.
S: That one's required?
A: Yes it is. It's right ... there.
S: It's American Culture. What time is it? 4:20. [mumbles as looks at schedule] (softly) L560. This was ... I was thinking if I could take your class Mondays and Wednesdays. 15 credits. It'd be crazy, too many credits.
[20 turns later]
S: So you know about 560, who teaches?
A: Mr Smith.
S: Mr Smith, is the one who is next to Professor Brown?
A: No, no, Mr Smith is not here. He's in Malaysia, so he'll be back next semester.
         (Bardovi-Harlig & Hartford, 1993: 47).

This instance illustrates the learner's lack of sociopragmatic knowledge related to advising sessions – the learner was not able to assess when it is appropriate and effective to use repeated questions. However, at later advising sessions, the learner demonstrated increasing awareness of appropriate sociopragmatic behaviors. The excerpt below is from an advising session that took place around the end of the semester.

NNS, Korean [second session]

A: Have you ever taken Second Language Acquisition? Is this something that interests you?
S: Yes, but I wan to, uh, receive transfer for that course.
A: Oh, I see.
S: Applied, uh, Linguistics.
A: Well what is, but I'm not sure what ...
S: Appli-, applied, uh ...
A: Applied Linguistics. But is Applied linguistics Second
S: Yes
A: Language Acquisition? Oh, is that, that's what they call it?
S: Yes, yes
A: Um ... I see, okay.
         (Bardovi-Harlig & Hartford, 1993: 296–297)

Over time, the learner made improvement in the content and manner of his rejections. He provided a credible reason for rejecting the course nominated by the advisor, saying that he had taken an equivalent course. He communicated his intention directly in his first turn, without resorting to nontarget-like strategies such as repeated questions as found in the previous excerpt. While the gain of sociopragmatic knowledge is clear, what remained the same in the learner's manner of rejection is the pragmalinguistics aspect. When conveying his wish, the student used the direct form, 'I want to receive a transfer for that', without any mitigating devices. Compare this with a native-speaker excerpt from the same corpus:

S: Perhaps, I should also mention that I have an interest in sociolinguistics and would like, if I can, to structure things in such a way that I might do as much sociolinguistics as I can.
(Bardovi-Harlig & Hartford, 1993: 284)

This excerpt forms a sharp contrast with the learner's speech act. It contains hedging devices and modal expressions such as 'perhaps', 'maybe', 'if I can', and 'would like' to soften the intent. The utterance appears less direct with the use of embedded clauses, which are absent in the L2 learner's data. These data illustrate that, in advising sessions, learners came to expect certain settings, rituals and strategies to use, which lead to the increased knowledge of sociopragmatics over time. However, learners did not fully master the pragmalinguistics of the target speech acts because, as the authors suggested, they lacked explicit advisor corrections and had few opportunities to observe native-speaker models of rejections in advising sessions.

The slow acquisition of pragmalinguistic forms, as compared with that of strategies, also appeared in Warga and Scholmberger (2007) and Schauer (2004). Schauer examined the development of requests among 12 German ESL learners, focusing on the use of internal and external modifications. A computerized DCT was administered three times over a nine-month study abroad period. The frequency of external modifiers was similar to that of native speakers from the onset of the study. A few modifiers that were initially under-employed (small talk, flattering, showing consideration) approached the native-level after the four-month stay. In contrast, several internal modifiers involving lexical and syntactic downgraders remained underdeveloped. Consultation devices (e.g. *Would you mind*), imposition minimizers (e.g. *a bit*) and tag questions were used 25–50% less frequently than native speakers, and the degree of progress was negligible. In addition, divergence from native-speaker norms was found in the increased use of appreciation expressions (e.g. *It'd be nice*) and conditional clauses (*I'd like to ask if you could do this*). As shown in the findings, rituals and manners of requesting, for example, establishing a positive atmosphere through a small talk or showing consideration for the requestee's situation, were learned over time, but morphosyntax devices showed slow development.

Longitudinal studies by Hassall (2006) and DuFon (2000) more clearly illustrated the slow but gradual expansion of the form–function associations in learners' system. Using the diary method, Hassall recorded his own acquisition of leave-taking expressions in Indonesian during a three-month travel. The 272-page diary documented that the author exclusively used *permisi* when taking leave, which was too formal for certain occasions. After the mid-point, another expression, *dulu*, entered his repertoire through observation of others' leave-takings, experiences of misuse and correction, and noticing the form in the media. The author did not use *dulu* initially because it literally meant *formally*, and he took it for another social question. The author's pragmatic development is shown in his gradual understanding of the contextual requirements of these two leave-taking forms – which form to use when. The following excerpt from the author's diary illustrates a learning episode:

> As I was trudging home on the final stretch after a long hot walk, I was called over to chat by two women in the yard of a house nearby. We chatted amiably enough, but I suddenly got the impression that I'd overstayed my welcome – one of them seemed to be casting around rather awkwardly for further questions to ask me. So I rather hastily took my leave, with a dulu statement: *Puland dulu ya* 'I'm going home for now, okay' (literally, 'Go-home for-now, yes'). I said it a bit tensely and unsmilingly and it felt a bit abrupt as I said it. As I then turned to go, one of them said softly, in English, 'Excuse me'. I turned around in puzzlement. She then repeated it in Indonesian: *Permisi*, and laughed. So her 'excuse me' had been a gentle correction; a supplying of what I'd omitted to say. (Diary entry, *Padang Week* 2, 9/1/02) (Hassall, 2006: 39)

In reflection of this occasion, the author wrote that the native speaker's implicit correction helped him to learn that the expression *dulu* could be impolite. Two weeks later, in another occasion of a casual chat with an acquaintance, the author recalled this earlier instance and successfully used *permisi* when he took leave.

Similar to Hassall's study, DuFon's study was on L2 Indonesian abroad, but about the acquisition of negative responses to experiential questions. Indonesian language has two forms of negative response to a question asking about one's experience: *tidak* (meaning *no*) and *balum* (meaning *not yet*). DuFon recorded naturalistic interactions between six learners of Indonesian and native speakers over a period of four months. Comparisons of three transcripts at two-month intervals revealed that *tidak* was initially dominant in learners' system because it corresponded L1 English form; however, by the end of the four-month sojourn, they became able to use *belum* occasionally when responding to experiential questions, although the response was not automatic. The events that triggered the learning included native speakers' corrective feedback and modeling of appropriate responses.

Similar conclusions are drawn from Ohta's (2001) study on the expressions of acknowledgement and alignment in L2 Japanese. Acknowledgment is a feedback signal used to show attentiveness in conversation (e.g. *so desu ka* meaning 'oh really'), while alignment is an emphatic feedback signal that carries the sentence final particle *ne* (e.g. *ii desu ne*, meaning 'That's great, isn't it?'). These response forms were also studied earlier by Sawyer (1992) in the acquisition of sentence-final particle *ne*. The 11 learners in his study were slow in their acquisition of this particle, except for the case of formulaic expressions, suggesting the relative difficulty in mastering this pragmatic target.

In Ohta's study, five naturalistic recordings of classroom interactions were collected over one academic year. The focal participants, Candace and Rob, showed a similar, six-staged development of the target expressions: (1) no use of acknowledgement and alignment; (2) use of repetition and laughter for acknowledgement; (3) use *of aa so desu ka* and minimal response (e.g. *hai*, meaning 'yes') for acknowledgement; (4) use of *aa so desu ka* with facility and emergence of alignment expression; (5) spontaneous use of a limited range of alignment expressions; and (6) appropriate use of a range of acknowledgment expressions, as well as greater lexical variety in alignment expressions.

This six-staged development found in Ohta's study is in line with the five-staged developmental sequence of a request speech act in the previous literature (Ellis, 1992; Kasper & Rose, 2002). L2 learners start out with expressing meaning in a highly context-dependent manner, relying on extra-linguistic resources such as laughter or conversation strategies (i.e. repetition). Then, they shift to the formulaic use of the target expressions in restricted discourse contexts. More advanced stages involve expansion of the target pragmalinguistic repertoire, together with creative and productive use of the target forms. In Ohta's study, the emergence of the acknowledgement expression preceded that of the alignment expression. This developmental order was probably constrained by the different grammatical requirements between the two expressions. The acknowledgement expression, *soo desu ka*, is a fixed, formulaic sequence, while the alignment expression is a syntactic frame that requires grammatical manipulations: learners have to attach the particle *ne* to verbs, adjective or nouns, which require different conjugations. Here again, grammar seems to mediate the developmental patterns of pragmalinguistic forms. While the sequence of development exhibited little individual difference among learners, the difference was found in the pace of development: One learner showed stable, frequent use of the alignment earlier than the other learner because her partner consistently used listener responses with frequency and variety.

While Ohta's study examined the development of *ne* in a formal classroom setting, Ishida (2009) analyzed the use of *ne* by one American learner of Japanese (Fred, pseudonym) in a naturalistic setting during his nine-month study abroad. The data consisted of eight 30-minute video-recorded informal conversations collected during Fred's stay in Japan. While *ne* never appeared in his conversation initially, it appeared 13 times at the end of the nine-month period. A large portion of the particle was found in the formulaic expression of acknowledgment (i.e. *so desu ne*), but it emerged only mid-way through his study-abroad, confirming Ohta's finding that the formulaic use of *ne* does not appear at the beginning. After the mid-point, Fred continuously expanded his repertoire of *so desu ne* over a variety of functions, including: signaling confirmation and agreement, acknowledging the interlocutor's comments and information, displaying understanding, showing alignment and seeking agreement. His developmental path was similar to that of Ohta's participants in that the acknowledgment use emerged before alignment. What was notable in his developmental path was his use of *ne* in a wider range of sequential organizations: he gradually shifted from using the particle in turns that do not require adjustment toward the previous interlocutor's turn, to using it as an immediate response to the previous turn. Hence, Fred's use of *ne* was an indicator of his evolving interactional competence and contribution to the collaborative achievement of talk-in-interaction.

Iwasaki (2010), on the other hand, examined the change in the use of the polite and plain speech styles among five American male students of Japanese during their study-abroad in Japan for one academic year. In Japanese, forms of finite verbs and copulas index social meaning. There are at least two types of finite verb–copula combinations: polite and plain forms. The choice between these two forms needs to be made with consideration of various social, situational and attitudinal factors, and style shifts occur routinely even in a conversation with fixed interlocutor roles and situations. Iwasaki compared the participants' frequency and use of the polite/plain forms in the OPI (oral proficiency interview) recordings between pre- and post-study-abroad. She found that two of the learners overused the plain forms upon their return to the United States, diverging from the target norm. However, all participants gained some competence in making moment-by-moment of style choices in response to an ongoing interaction. For instance, they became able to switch to the plain form when expressing self-directed thoughts and emotions, as well as when providing a summary statement.

Belz and Kinginger's (2003) study also examined learners' style shift between formal and informal register and illustrated their gradual expansion of form–function repertoire. However, different from Iwasaki's study, they demonstrated the facilitative role of explicit feedback and modeling on the expansion. Using CMC (computer-mediated communication), the authors examined the acquisition of German address forms by 11 American college students over a two-month period. The authors documented learners' growing tendency to replace the formal *V*-form with the informal *T*-form of solidarity when addressing peers in their age group. Although some learners started using the *T*-form after encountering it in the speech of peers, the majority of learners improved only after they had received peer feedback on their inappropriate use of the *V*-form. The peer feedback took the form of explicit correction:

> When you write in German, I understand you very well, Tom. However, there are a few little things that you could improve. When you write to me, you can say 'DU' to me. So better: 'Ich mochte eine Frage an Dich [you–T] stellen'. You only say 'SIE' or 'Ihnen' when you speak in a polite way to people like your lecturer, or people who are not your mate. (Belz & Kinginger, 2003: 624)

Before receiving this type of feedback, most learners did not pick up the *T*-form in their German peers' emails, suggesting the strong effect of explicit feedback in the development of this pragmatic target. Two types of development were identified: abrupt development in which learners stopped using the *V*-form after receiving peer assistance, and gradual development in which the *V*- and *T*-forms occurred together before complete acquisition. There was also one case of nondevelopment, a case of heritage speaker. This learner, Irene, who was born and grew up in a German-speaking family, was highly communicative in German. Her peers corrected her use of the *V*-form several times, but she never conformed to the correction. Instead, she continued to use the *T*-form throughout the semester. The authors attributed these findings to her heritage background. Because German was an integral part of her everyday life, peer assistance probably did not serve as a critical moment of noticing and learning for Irene. These findings suggest that feedback facilitates development, and that individual variation exists in the course of development.

The rate of development of address forms revealed in Belz and Kinginger's study is striking when compared with Barron's (2003) study of the same German address forms. Thirty-three Irish learners of L2 German were studied over a 14-month study-abroad period. DCT data collected at seven-month intervals revealed only modest progress of learners' use of the *T*- and *V*-forms. Learners switched between the two forms in all DCT situations, although the case of switching decreased by 7% by the end of the study. The findings further support the importance of attention in pragmatic development. In study-abroad contexts where learners are presumably exposed to target language input and patterns of interaction, without opportunities for corrective feedback and explicit explanation, acquisition of pragmalinguistic forms is a slow process.

In summary, previous studies of pragmatic production showed that early stage of pragmatic development is often characterized by learners' limited range of pragmalinguistic resources. Once particular form–function–context mapping is established, it takes some time for another form to enter the repertoire to encode the same function. Some critical events such as native speaker modeling, corrective feedback, observation and self-reflection seem necessary to trigger the entry of a new mapping into the interlanguage systems.

Summary of the Study Findings

Longitudinal studies surveyed in this chapter revealed 'changes' in the pace and pattern of pragmatic development. Concerning the comprehension of implicature, patterns of development can be inferred from the intensity of contextual cues available in the input. It seems that learners progress from the stage where meaning is marked via strong contextual signals (e.g. universal or shared conventionality between L1 and L2, frequency and saliency of input, and predicted discourse moves) to the stage where meaning does not involve those signals and thus requires a series of inferential stages to comprehend (Bouton, 1992, 1994; Taguchi, 2007a, 2008c).

In the area of pragmatic recognition, exposure to the target sociopragmatic norms seems to be one of the factors that help enhance learners' development of meta-pragmatic awareness. Form–function–context mappings can be registered even during the early stages of study-abroad if there are opportunities to observe native-speaker patterns of interaction (Matsumura, 2001, 2007; Schauer, 2006). However, this newly acquired pragmatic knowledge may gradually disappear from learners' systems after their reentry to the home country, this time, being shaped by their L1 sociopragmatic norms. Although the experience in the host environment strongly influences the awareness that learners gain, individual variation exists in the pace and size of the gains due to differential quality and quantity of contextual experience.

In the area of pragmatic production, however, it appears that form–function–context mappings are not internalized in a linear manner, even among advanced-level learners living in a target language context. Learners usually begin with a limited range of pragmalinguistic forms, often symbolized by the overgeneralization of a few forms over a range of functions or the use of formulaic language. They gradually expand their pragmalinguistic repertoire by adopting a new form–function mapping into their systems. This process is slow, unless learners are exposed to explicit feedback, or modeling. The complete replacement of one pragmatic form with another also takes time, as shown by the coexistence of forms and learners' tendency to switch between them. Previous studies examined the development of form–function mappings in two different directions: expansion of forms linked to single function (e.g. Barron, 2003, 2006; Hassall, 2006; Salsbury & Bardovi-Harlig, 2001; Schauer, 2004; Warga & Scholmberger, 2007) and expansion of functions linked to single form (Ishida, 2009; Iwasaki, 2010; Ohta, 2001).

In sharp contrast with the slow acquisition of pragmalinguistic forms, learners' strategies to perform the target illocutionary act seem to show a solid progress. Studies by Bardovi-Harlig and Hartford (1993), Warga and Schölmberger (2007) and Schauer (2004) showed that, over time, learners gained competence in coping strategies in the target pragmatic act. In academic advising sessions, they learned to provide credible reasons to reject their advisors' suggestions on courses to take. When apologizing, learners understood not to justify their misconduct and learned to offer repair for the damage they had caused. They also began to soften their requests by establishing a friendly atmosphere with small-talk and expressions of consideration. These findings imply that the knowledge of the logistics specific to a pragmatic event develop naturally over time. However, precise syntax and lexis needed to encode pragmatic intentions did not develop as quickly. Limited progress in the acquisition of pragmalinguistic forms as compared with that of tactics and rituals of pragmatic acts, as well as the slow expansion of learners' pragmalinguistic repertoires, all support the potentiality of the unbalanced development of grammar and pragmatics among adult L2 learners. Koike observes:

> Simply because learners do not employ L2 pragmatic forms corresponding to those of the L1, even when they have studied a number of possibilities to express the speech act, does not signify that those forms are not present in their competence. Rather ... since the grammatical competence cannot develop as quickly as the already present pragmaticconcepts require, the pragmatic concepts are expressed in ways conforming to the level of grammatical complexity acquired. (Koike, 1989: 286)

If pragmatic competence does not develop in conjunction with grammatical ability, what factors could facilitate the acquisition of pragmalinguistic forms? Several possibilities are drawn from the previous longitudinal studies. One potential factor for pragmalinguistic gain is the learning context. Although living in the target language environment is no panacea for pragmatic development, the target community has potential to offer unique sociocultural experiences that foster the acquisition of pragmalinguistic forms. Qualitative analyses by DuFon (2000), Hassall (2006), Kinginger and Farrell (2004) and Kinginger and Blattner (2008) revealed a range of social encounters and activities that could foster the acquisition of new form–function–context associations. Another promising factor for pragmatic gain relates to the features of context, particularly input and peer feedback. Ohta's (2001) study conducted in a formal instructional context proves that pragmatic competence could develop in a domestic environment, as long as learners are exposed to the target pragmatic input and have opportunities to practice the target language. In Belz and Kinginger's (2003) CMC study, cases of abrupt development after peer assistance indicate the even stronger effect of feedback on learners' progress. Saliency of the target form–function mappings, promoted through input frequency and direct attention to forms, could facilitate the pace and grain size of pragmatic development.

Taken together, these longitudinal findings lend support to the two theoretical positions proposed in Kasper and Blum-Kulka's seminal book *Interlanguage Pragmatics* (1993): Bialystok's two-dimensional model and Schmidt's Noticing Hypothesis. The two-dimensional model (Bialystok, 1993) emphasizes the differences between children's and adult L2 learners' acquisition process of pragmatic competence. Bialystok claimed that, unlike children whose pragmatic and linguistic competences develop simultaneously, adult learners are already fully competent in L1 pragmatics. They possess a rich foundation of universal pragmatic knowledge and strategies. They already have implicit knowledge of politeness (Brown & Levinson, 1983; Leech, 1983), sociolinguistic variability (Hymes, 1972), rituals of conversation such as turn-taking and repair (Drew & Heritage, 1992; Goffman, 1976), specific pragmatic acts such as greetings, leave takings and invitations (Austin, 1962; Ochs, 1996; Searle, 1976), inferencing heuristics and presuppositions (Grice, 1975; Holtgraves, 2008), and routine formulae in recurrent communicative situations (Kecskes, 2003; Pawley & Syder, 1983; Schmitt, 2004). Acquisition of this knowledge is a part of the socialization process in which children become enculturated into society and acquire specific manners of communication that reflect the beliefs and values of the culture (Schieffelin & Ochs, 1986). According to Bialystok, after having gone through this process once in their L1 acquisition, a challenge for adult L2 learners is to acquire processing control over preexisting pragmatic representations in L2. They must relearn the form–function relations appropriate to the L2, which requires them to learn new pragmalinguistic forms, along with the social contexts in which they occur. This theoretical claim is supported by slow-developing pragmalinguistics compared with the knowledge of sociopragmatics found in the previous literature. Adult learners could pick up what is expected in the given L2 situation relatively quickly. They come to learn about the setting, rituals, and strategies to cope with the pragmatic act. However, the learning of actual morphosyntax involved in the act takes place slowly, unless supported by explicit correction, feedback and modeling.

The facilitative role of feedback and correction found in the literature, in turn, lends support to Schmidt's (1993, 1995) Noticing Hypothesis, which is a psycholinguistically oriented theory that situates consciousness and attention in its central claim. According to the hypothesis, input becomes intake and leads to acquisition only if it is noticed by learners. Attention to linguistic forms, functional meanings and relevant contextual features are necessary conditions for pragmatic input to become intake. Schmidt claimed that global alertness to target input is not sufficient, and attention has to be allocated to specific learning objects.

Schmidt (1995) further distinguished noticing from understanding. Noticing refers to a conscious registration of an event, while understanding refers to the recognition of rules or patterns in the event. Hence, understanding involves 'deeper level(s) of abstraction related to (semantic, syntactic or communicative) meaning and system learning' (Schmidt, 1995: 29). The longitudinal studies reviewed here exemplify a range of communicative encounters that promoted the noticing of form–function–context mappings and subsequent understanding of them. In Belz and Kinginger's (2003) telecollaboration study, learners of German saw the informal *T*-forms elsewhere in their peers' emails, but they actually started using them only after their peers pointed out and explained their misuse of formal *V*-forms. Similar cases were found in DuFon's (2000) study in which native speakers' corrective feedback and modeling facilitated acquisition of the contextually appropriate use of the form *belum* ('not yet') in Indonesian. In Hassall's (2006) diary study, the author expanded his pragmalinguistic resources of leave-taking expressions after noticing new forms in the media and having been corrected on his misuse. These findings reiterate the critical role that consciousness, attention, noticing and understanding play in naturalistic development of pragmatic competence.

Future of Longitudinal Investigation in ILP

This chapter reviewed about two dozens longitudinal studies available in the field of ILP. From these studies, a meaningful portrayal of how learners gradually attain pragmatic competence within various contexts has emerged. Based on the review, I will present issues critical to future investigation of pragmatic development.

Study Duration

In longitudinal design, optimal length of observation is an important methodological concern, yet little consensus exists in response to the important question: how long is long enough. According to Ortega and Iberri-Shea (2005), most longitudinal studies in SLA span from a few months to six years. The authors attributed this diversity to the nature of SLA research that involves both developmental scaling (from emergence to mastery of linguistic targets) and convenient scaling based on institutional time (one semester, one year and duration of study abroad program). Researchers often consider key events and turning points in a social or institutional context when deciding on the appropriate length of observation. Longitudinal ILP studies reviewed here largely confirm this observation. A wide range of study lengths were found, ranging from two months to four years. The majority of them used convenient scaling due to curriculum constraint and were conducted within a time frame of one semester or one academic year.

All of these studies revealed pragmatic gains of some sort, indicating that the timescales used in the studies were appropriate in illuminating development to some extent. However, because there has been little discussion about the optimal length of study, the standard of longitudinal ILP practice could be raised by theorizing sensible metric for time. Such effort is important because comprehension, recognition and the production of pragmatic functions examined in this chapter present very different interpretations of the pattern and pace of pragmatic progress, owing to different construct orientations, modalities and task demands. Studies on pragmatic comprehension and recognition revealed meaningful gains size even after two or three months of study, while target-like pragmalinguistic forms rarely appeared in production studies after the same time period. These findings suggest an intimate relationship among pragmatic construct, time and change. Hence, the metric for time in a longitudinal study should be articulated more clearly at the design stage based on informed predictions and hypotheses. To do this, we need more longitudinal findings over a variety of pragmatic features, target languages and instructional arrangements. Those studies will help us determine the optimal time period needed to detect meaningful gains. Once an average time span is established, researchers can examine individual variations in the pace and outcome of development, with an aim to reveal learner-specific and contextual factors that affect the variations.

Frequency of Data Points and Data Collection Methods

Another important feature of longitudinal research is the frequency of data collection. Without collecting data systematically over time using comparable tasks, inferences about changes toward full pragmatic competence are hard to make. While some key ethnographic studies have provided qualitative data that is rich enough to suggest a causal relationship between individuals, context and gained pragmatic knowledge (e.g. Schmidt, 1983; Siegal, 1996), the picture of 'changes' in those studies is rather blurry because they did not collect data systematically at equal intervals. Given the rich, in-depth naturalistic data collected on context and learner agency, future ethnographic studies will gain strength if they incorporate waves of systematic data collection to capture learners' changing pragmatic abilities.

Similar to the study duration, there is little consensus regarding the optimal number of data points and their spacing in the current longitudinal practice (Ortega & Iberri-Shea, 2005). Confirming this observation, pragmatic development was mapped with as few as two data points (pre- and post-test), and as many as eight in CMC studies. Intervals of those data points spread from weekly observation to seven-month intervals. Of the 23 studies, 17 studies had only two or three data points. The small number of data points in the majority of ILP studies can be attributed to their use of an elicitation instrument, such as DCT, multiple-choice questionnaires and tests. As using the same instrument multiple times at short intervals poses the risk of practice effects and diminished interest, researchers tend to keep low frequency of data collection to control for this potential design flaw.

Popularity of the use of data elicitation method, as opposed to naturalistic observation, comes from the reality that pragmatic features do not occur frequently enough in naturalistic interaction to form a reliable data set. This is especially true when situational variables (e.g. interlocutors' power relationships, distance) become part of the investigation. For example, McGroarty and Taguchi's (2005) analysis of a corpus of student–professor conversations found only a few instances of high-imposition request (e.g. asking a professor for a letter of recommendation) in a 50,000-word corpus. In a larger-scale corpus study, Garcia (2004) examined speech acts in three types of conversations occurring in United States university settings: professor–student conversations, service encounter conversations, and study group discussions. Each corpus was similar in length, consisting of about 14,000–16,000 words. Through a line-by-line analysis of the conversation, she identified speech acts and categorized them by situations and speakers (i.e. students, professors and service providers), and analyzed them for lexico-syntactic features. The results revealed a strong association between situations and speech act types. While student-initiated requests were most frequent in service encounter situations, occurring 80 times in the corpus, it was found only about 20 times in the office hour and study session corpora. These findings suggest that, in naturalistic discourse, not all speech acts are equally represented across different conversational situations; as a result, compiling a sizable sample of speech acts from authentic data is difficult. It is even more daunting in the case of L2 speech act samples because there are not many L2 corpora that represent a variety of situations.

One possible avenue for recurring speech samples is to go beyond typical speech acts and target pragmatic features that occur more frequently. Discourse markers, response forms (e.g. acknowledgement expressions), address terms and routine encounters such as greetings and leave-takings are more likely to occur in naturalistic interactions, and are therefore easier to record over time, as shown in the longitudinal studies in this chapter (e.g. Belz & Kinginger, 2003; Ohta, 2001; Sawyer, 1992). Another possibility is to look into institutional discourse that consists of highly constrained social interactions. Some literature (Bardovi-Harlig, 2010; Bardovi-Harlig & Hartford, 2005) argues that institutional talk is replicable due to its recurrent and consequential nature. It takes place with many speakers even during a short period of time. What is more, contextual features such as setting, participant roles and relations and goals of interaction are relatively fixed, which make the data points comparable across time and place. Drew and Heritage summarize characteristics of institutional talk as follows:

(1) Institutional interaction involves an orientation by at least one of the participants to some core goal, task or identity (or set of them

conventionally associated with the institution in question. In short, institutional talk is normally informed by goal orientations of a relatively restricted conventional form.
(2) Institutional interaction may often involve special and particular constraints on what one or both of the participants will treat as allowable contributions to the business at hand.
(3) Institutional talk may be associated with inferential frameworks and procedures that are particular to specific institutional contexts. (Drew & Heritage, 1992: 22)

Bardovi-Harlig (2010) claims that these characteristics – goal orientation, constraints and frameworks, make institutional discourse suitable for ILP research because the data are comparable over multiple interactions, following similar frames, expectations and participant roles and relationships. Bardovi-Harlig and Hartford's (1993) study of academic advising sessions is the only longitudinal study found in the ILP literature that deals with institutional discourse, suggesting much potential for future research in this area.

Grammar–Pragmatics Intersect

Developmental characteristics observed in pragmalinguistics forms call for future examinations of pragmatic development with the in-depth study of specific, related grammatical subsystems. This proposal builds on previous recommendations from the analysis of the relationship between grammar and pragmatics (e.g. Bardovi-Harlig, 1999, 2000; Kasper, 2001), a model of which can be found in Salsbury and Bardovi-Harlig's (2001) study. Independent analyses of learners' knowledge and the development of grammatical forms that are necessary for pragmatic performance (e.g. modal expressions in disagreements, syntactic mitigators in requests) could reveal how the knowledge of the forms mediates the pace and pattern of development in pragmatic functions that necessitate the forms. Since very few longitudinal studies have actually examined the presence or absence of the target pragmalinguistic forms in learners' systems, a separate analysis of grammar and pragmatics would help illuminate the sequential stages of development, as well as the linguistic factors and learners' proficiency that affect development.

Beyond Speech Acts: Expanding the Construct of Pragmatic Competence

As Kasper and Rose (2002) noted, studies of the development of speech acts are the most represented in the ILP literature. Supporting this,

Bardovi-Harlig's (2010) recent research synthesis showed that, out of 152 ILP studies found in seven major journals and edited volumes of pragmatic topics, 99 studies (65%) either named 'speech acts' or a specific speech act in the research questions, or operationalized pragmatic competence in a speech act framework. This trend applies also to the longitudinal practices as evidenced by the fact that 10 of the 23 studies examined this pragmatic target.

The popularity of speech acts evidently reflects disciplinary histories. Some of the early influential pragmatic theories – Austin's (1962) Speech Act Theory, Searle's (1976) taxonomy of speech acts and direct vs. indirect speech acts, politeness theories (Brown & Levinson, 1983; Leech, 1983), and Grice's (1975) conversation maxims – all make an explicit reference to speech acts. The concepts and terminologies from these theories have provided a platform for organizing units of analysis in ILP research. In addition, speech acts present clear connections among linguistic forms, functions and social context. There are certain syntactic forms and strategies that co-occur with speech acts, and those forms align with situational characteristics (i.e. power relationship and social distance between the interlocutors, degree of imposition) that are assumed to determine the degree of politeness and indirectness of the forms. For these reasons, speech acts have served as a convenient unit for the examination of form–function–context mappings in ILP research. However, this trend has given an impression that pragmatics barely ever means more than speech acts, while in broader areas of linguistics it encompasses a wider range of issues. In order to gain a more balanced understanding of pragmatic competence and the field of ILP, below I will discuss several areas beyond speech acts to be explored in the future research.

Speech Acts in Interaction

Recently, there has been an increasing interest in the field to move beyond the traditional speech act theory and examination of speech acts in isolation from situated interaction. Corresponding to Kasper's (2006) approach of discursive pragmatics, an increasing number of recent studies have applied conversational analysis (CA) to study action, meaning, and context in speech acts. CA utilizes the *emic* approach to analyze talk-in-interaction to reveal how participants co-construct an action sequentially turn-by-turn, and design their turns to jointly accomplish the activity at hand. Together with the CA approach, an emerging body of studies in interactional linguistics and discoursal–functional linguistics have analyzed ongoing social activities and sequential contexts where specific linguistic forms are used, along with nonverbal and paralinguistic features that co-occur with the forms (e.g. Mori, 2006). These studies have revealed how a particular linguistic form emerges from the 'moment-by-moment unfolding of talk-in-interaction and in conjunction with other types of multimodal semiotic resources available for interactional participants' (Mori, 2009: 344). Although these studies have mainly analyzed L1 speakers, the approach could be applied to L2 pragmatics research, providing alternative methods to examining L2 pragmatic competence.

The recent poststructuralist movement also responds to some of the criticisms toward speech act theory discussed in the literature for quite some time. As noted by Verschueren (1999), Mey (2003), Cutting (2008) and other scholars of pragmatics, a limitation of speech act theory is that it assumes one-to-one correspondence between utterance and force. It disregards the interactive, dynamic nature of conversation in which a speech function is jointly constructed between the speaker and hearer, and negotiated over a number of sequences and turns. The excerpt below from Cutting illustrates this point:

> **BM:** You do you do Language Planning don't you?
> **DM:** Yeah, I've stopped doing that though. I did stop doing that last week. SLA?
> **BM:** I'm not doing that.
> **DM:** Ah. We haven't got many things in common then.
> **BM:** Wow. We've parted ways.
> **DM:** That's right. That's right. Yes.
> →**BM:** We'll have to go out sometime.
> **DM:** Yeah.
> **BM:** Before we forget each other's faces. (Cutting, 2008: 22)

In this excerpt, the speech act of 'invitation' is identified at BM's fourth turn, 'We'll have to go out sometime.' However, this is not a pre-planned action nor occurs in isolation out of context. It arises in the course of the flow of conversation through participants' mutual understandings of the topic and reactions to each other's contribution to the on-going discourse. BM's invitation to catch up emerges from the shared knowledge that the two participants who, perhaps, started in the same graduate program and are now rarely see either other. Without this background established over the preceding turns, BM might not have extended the invitation. Traditional speech act theory does not account for this interactive, dynamic nature of speech acts that emerges from the interplay of social context, action and linguistics resources.

This limitation is also reflected in the mainstream practice of ILP research. Common data collection methods in speech act studies such as DCT and questionnaires neglect sequential and discourse factors that influence speech acts. In fact, Bardovi-Harlig's (2010) research synthesis found that only 60% of the studies (78 out of 129) used two-way communication data (e.g. synchronous and asynchronous telecollaboration and roleplay) to examine production of pragmatic functions. The rest of the studies used written instruments or monologue tasks to examine features of spoken production. Bardovi-Harlig argues:

> In order to meet the explicitly stated goals of studying use, interaction, and effect of speakers' contributions on other speakers, samples of authentic and consequential language use should be collected whenever possible. Given the focus of pragmatics research, this should be the default design for studies of production. Authentic and consequential data best reveal language use and where two-way communication occurs, interaction and effect on participants as well. (Bardovi-Harlig, 2010: 242)

Future longitudinal studies should follow this important call and explore alternative methods to analyze L2 learners' language use in situated interaction. As naturalistic data are not easily controllable or predictable, it is difficult to use it to compare learners' language use at different times. However, the use of institutional discourse, as described in the previous section, could provide an optimal ground to analyze recurrent pragmatic acts in naturalistic settings. In such a genre, we can examine speech acts in dynamic social structure embedded within situated concrete activities.

When analyzing speech acts in naturalistic interactions, we need to adopt different types of analytical frameworks and approaches (Mori, 2009). Traditionally, speech acts have been analyzed at linguistics levels – directness of syntactic forms, appropriate use of lexical devices and semantic strategies. Learners' pragmatic development has been inferred from how closely their forms approximate native speakers' forms. However, when we use interactive data, we can apply performance-based analysis that involves examination of wide-ranging features of interactional competence, not limited to linguistic elements. Fluency and promptness, discourse competence, conversation management skills, ability to accomplish mutual understanding, and ability to recover from communicative breakdowns are some of the interactional features that could be analyzed to make sense of learners' ability to accomplish a speech act. These features can be traced over time through recurring speech events with the same participant(s), and their ability to participate in discourse successfully could serve as an indicator of pragmatic development. Recent conceptualization and discussion of interactional competence should be certainly helpful in identifying a range of resources that learners draw on in pragmatic-act-in-interaction (e.g. Hellerman, 2008; Walter, 2007; Young, 2002; Young & He, 1998). In addition, as Mori (2009) argues, analyses of language use can be combined with the analysis of learners' identity and agency behind their linguistic choices, and pragmatic development can be conceptualized as a process of language socialization (Schieffelin & Ochs, 1986) or the learning of community of practices (Lave & Wenger, 1991), extending beyond the mere mastery of target pragmatic features (Mori, 2009). To date, there have been very few such longitudinal studies, and thus this awaits future research.

Pragmatic competence as a multifacet construct

Another gap in the existing literature is that very few studies to date have included a longitudinal analysis of multiple pragmatic targets. Most studies have pursued a separate analysis of one or two speech acts, implicature types or discourse features, and almost no studies have tracked down the development of different pragmatic subcompetencies simultaneously. As the three strands of longitudinal research discussed in this chapter (comprehension, recognition and production of pragmatic features) revealed very different pictures of the pattern and pace of development, a combined analysis of different pragmatic targets in a longitudinal design will provide us more complete understanding of learners' pragmatic competence and development. Developmental trajectories might differ depending on the nature of pragmatic constructs, modality, task type and processing mechanisms involved. So far, almost no studies have examined the longitudinal development of pragmatic comprehension and production combined. As a result, research has not revealed what L2 learners can do as producers and interpreters of pragmatic meaning and how their subcompetencies develop. Furthermore, questions related to the developmental aspect of L2 pragmatic competence, for example, whether comprehension and production are related to each other, or whether ability to comprehend meaning communicated indirectly develop in parallel with the ability to convey meaning appropriately, still remain unanswered.

In a cross-sectional design, however, there is a study that examined multiple aspects of pragmatic competence. Using a web-based assessment battery, Röver (2005) compared ESL and EFL learners on three pragmatic subconstructs: comprehension of implicatures, comprehension of routines and production of speech acts. The implicature section tested learners' comprehension of two types of implicatures: conventional, formulaic implicatures and idiosyncratic, nonconventional implicatures. The routine items tested recognition of situational routines that were tied to specific situations and functional routines that were not situation bound. The speech act section had 12 items that elicited requests, refusals and apologies. He found a significant effect of residence abroad on the comprehension of routines but no effect of context on the comprehension of implicatures and production of speech acts, although there was a significant L2 proficiency effect on both. These findings suggest that the structure of pragmatic objects, along with proficiency and residence experience in the host country, interact with each other and jointly affect one's ability to perform pragmatic functions. This implication may well apply to developmental investigation. Learners of different proficiency levels and experience with residence abroad may exhibit different levels of mastery across pragmatic functions.

Pragmatic development from knowledge and processing perspectives

To further expand the construct of pragmatic competence, future longitudinal research should attend to the development of processing aspect of pragmatic competence. Although the studies reviewed in this chapter have provided a relatively well-formed analysis of the patterns of development in pragmalinguistic and sociopragmatic knowledge, what is lacking in the literature are the studies that examined the development of fluency in using those knowledge bases in pragmatic production, comprehension, and recognition tasks. As Kasper (2001) argues, pragmatic competence entails the acquisition of pragmatic knowledge and gaining automatic control in processing it in real time. Following this claim, several studies have examined the longitudinal development of processing speed when comprehending conversational implicatures (Taguchi, 2007a, 2008b, 2008c). These studies showed that comprehension speed, measured by response times, develops naturally overtime, along with the accuracy of comprehension, but learning context has significant effect on the pace of development. Learners in an EFL context showed more profound development in accuracy than comprehension speed, but the pattern was reversed for the ESL learners. Since there is no succeeding study in the production of pragmatic functions, future research that investigates gains in fluent pragmatic production, combined with gains in pragmatic knowledge, will add to the literature.

The conjoined analysis of accuracy and processing speed in pragmatic competence situates ILP research in a wider field comprised of SLA, cognitive psychology and psycholinguistics. Corresponding to the growing interface between linguistics and psychology, there is a burgeoning interest in the field to investigate the processing dimensions of language-related performance by examining how learners access and process linguistic information in real time (DeKeyser, 2007; Dörnyei, 2009). This trend is, in part, represented through the application of several well-known models of skill acquisition in SLA research. For instance, ACT-R (Adaptive Control of Thought-Rational) proposed by John Anderson and his colleagues (Anderson et al., 2004), which was grown out of Anderson's earlier ACT theory (Anderson, 1990; Anderson & Lebiere, 1998), distinguishes between declarative and procedural memory, emphasizing that skill acquisition involves a transition from the stage of declarative knowledge to the stage of procedural knowledge. Declarative knowledge refers to the knowledge of 'what', which is conscious and analyzable. Procedural knowledge refers to the knowledge of 'how' and involves the state in which one's knowledge is executed in actual behaviors. Skill acquisition is a process in which declarative knowledge becomes proceduralized via an associative stage where rules are practiced repeatedly in a consistent manner. The end point of acquisition is characterized as a stage where rules are executed unconsciously and automatically. Fluency, or speed, is a metric of the extent to which declarative knowledge is proceduralized, while accuracy is a general measure of declarative knowledge (Segalowitz, 2001, 2003).

These theoretical claims suggest the importance of a conjoined analysis of accuracy and processing speed (fluency) in the development of pragmatic competence. Pragmatic acquisition has two complementary aspects: accurate demonstration of pragmatic knowledge and efficient processing of that knowledge. Accurate demonstration of pragmatic competence is considered as a general measure of underlying knowledge bases that are either newly learned in L2 or transferred from L1. Speed or fluency involved in the demonstration of pragmatic knowledge, on the other hand, is a property of general skill execution. It is an indication that the knowledge bases have been proceduralized through extensive practice and use, and that learners have acquired efficient and speedy control over the knowledge. Developmental analyses of accuracy and speed combined will enrich our longitudinal investigation because they will help reveal whether or not these two dimensions demonstrate parallel developmental pattern in pragmatic competence.

Dynamic Systems Theory, Chaos/Complexity Theory and the Emergentism Approach to Longitudinal ILP Research

SLA theory builders have recently focused on the dynamicity and complexity of L2 acquisition process in a social context, and this new perspective could also inform longitudinal investigations of pragmatic competence. Dynamic Systems Theory (DST) (de Bot et al., 2007; de Bot, 2008), chaos/complexity theory (Larsen-Freeman & Cameron, 2008) and the emergentism approach (N. Ellis & Larsen-Freeman, 2006; MacWhinney, 2006) are the major proponents of this epistemological trend that argues that language develops through interactions between context and individuals, and variability is central in development. With this approach, context is essential to acquisition, and the interdependence of variables – both at individual and contextual level – forms the explanation of development. While these three paradigms have different focuses and emphases, they all share a view that language development is a nonlinear, nonstatic process, and language emerges from socially coregulated interactions of multiple influences. Some of the key characteristics of these paradigms are summarized below, largely drawn from Larsen-Freeman and Cameron's book (2008), *Complex Systems and Applied Linguistics*.

(1) Dynamicity

DST, complexity theory and emergentism take a socially grounded approach. Cognitive, social and environmental factors continuously interact, resulting in coregulated emergence of language behaviors and changes in the behaviors over time. Language is co-constructed and emerges via interactions between agents (individuals) and their interactions with environments.

(2)   Nonlinearity

Language development is a nonlinear process in which elements and agents interact, and coregulate the course of development. In a nonlinear process, 'the elements or agents are not independent, and relations or interactions between elements are not fixed but may themselves change' (Larsen-Freeman & Cameron, 2008: 31). L2 development is a nonlinear, fluid and transient process that displays an unevenly paced progress over time. Different rates of change are found for different aspects of language abilities, and a change in one aspect does not directly cause a change in other aspects. The growth curve is nonlinear, involving backslidings, jumps and stagnations (Larsen-Freeman & Cameron, 2008).

(3)   Variability

Language development entails a great deal of intra- and inter-variability. Different from traditional quantitative studies that consider variability as 'noise' which should be controlled or eliminated, DST and complexity theory consider variability as a valuable source of information that illuminates the underlying developmental process. Variability data provide idiosyncratic details of individual learners' developmental trajectories that are otherwise hidden in the analysis of group means.

(4)   Coadaptation and interconnectedness of variables

Developmental trajectories are shaped by the interconnectedness of the components of a system in producing the whole. Coadaptation refers to a change in a system that is motivated by change in another system connected to it. It is the 'interaction of two or more complex system, each changing in response to the other' (Larsen-Freeman & Cameron, 2008: 67). There is no single explanation for changes or simple cause–effect relationships: Multiple, interconnected factors underlie a complex event or outcome (de Bot, 2008; N. Ellis & Larsen-Freeman, 2006). Larsen-Freeman and Cameron use the term 'collective variables' to explain this aspect. Collective variables are 'actions and responses that index the cooperativity of a multidimensional system' (Thelen & Smith, 1994: 99). Variables collectively explain the changes, but not in isolation.

(5)   Attractors in state space and control parameters

An attractor is a 'preferred region of a system's state space into which the system tends to move' (Larsen-Freeman & Cameron, 2008: 50–53). Transitions to an attractor's state space are influenced by 'control parameters'. Using Larsen-Freeman and Cameron's example to illustrate this, in L2 learning, motivation could be a control parameter that helps the learning system move forward to more advanced stages of learning, avoiding attractors such as preference of going to a party rather than doing homework.

(6) Self-organization

The term 'self-organization' is used to explain a phase shift from one attractor into a new attractor in its state space. Once systems reach a critical stage, they reorganize themselves and transform themselves into a new pattern of behavior (de Bot, 2008). According to Larsen-Freeman and Cameron, self-organization leads to new phenomena called 'emergence' (2008: 59). Emergence is the appearance of new properties of systems at a higher level of organization than the elements or agents that produced the new properties. Language development is characterized as a continuous process of self-organization and emergence in which simple elements and agents produce complex language behaviors. Systems that undergo a phase shift display behavior that has been described as 'self-organized criticality' (Bak, 1997), which is also referred to as the 'tipping point' (Gladwell, 2000) – the point where the sudden change occurs. According to de Bot (2008), example phenomena in L2 acquisition include 'breakthrough' or sudden jumps in proficiency, or the 'threshold hypotheses' (i.e. the point at which the system is re-organized in a way that knowledge becomes stable).

(7) Sensitivity to onset conditions

Language development is sensitive to the initial condition. Relatively small differences in initial conditions may result in larger differences in growth trajectories across individuals in the same participant sample. The initial condition itself is also in an ongoing state of change.

These concepts and guiding principles also collaborate with the recent shift in the views of individual difference (ID) factors from stable and monolithic learner attributes free from contextual influence, to dynamically changing and evolving characteristics contingent upon context. In traditional SLA research, common individual characteristics such as motivation, language aptitude, personality, anxiety and learning style have been treated as fixed variables, and linear relationships between the variables and learning outcomes have been sought. However, in light of the growing recognition of the process-oriented and situated nature of IDs, variations in learners' performance and achievement are now seen stemming from individual characteristics mediated through context and time (e.g. Dörnyei, 2000, 2005; Ushioda, 2009). IDs are no longer viewed as isolated factors independent from each other: they form a complex constellation of factors that interact with each other and the environment at multiple levels.

These key terms associated with the reconceptualization of ID factors – dynamicity, variability, multi-component and context-dependence – situate ID research well within the paradigm of DST, complexity theory and emergentism. The explicit connection between the two research fields has been made recently by Dörnyei (2009) who claims that learners' contribution to the learning process can be best understood from a Dynamic Systems Theory perspective. One area of connection is found in the understanding of the function of attractors and attractor states. According to Dörnyei, certain ID variables may act as potentially powerful attractors. Factors such as motivation, affect and interest, and cognition systems such as working memory, attention and abstract thinking could serve as a force that gravitates the language system to a stable pattern. The stability of the system depends on the power of the attractors as well as the number of regions where the attractors concentrate (i.e. attractor basin). Optimal combination of ID factors, rather than factors in isolation, is considered to have great predictive power because they form a broader attractor basin. Idiosyncratic developmental trajectories are explained by the ongoing interrelations between learner characteristics and environment, which contribute to the complex system of learning.

Another example for the intersect between ID research and the complexity theory paradigm is the 'L2 motivation self system', which illustrates the interaction between motivation and environment (Dörnyei, 2005, 2009). According to Dörnyei, learning is organized along with three components: ideal L2 self, ought-to L2 self and L2 learning experience. The ideal L2 self refers to what one wishes to become as a L2 speaker. It is a strong motivating force because of the desire to close the gap between the actual and ideal selves. The ought-to L2 self involves a set of attributes that one believes he/she should possess to accomplish learning goals. L2 learning experience concerns motivation related to the immediate learning environment and experience, and includes a variety contextual elements, such as influence of the teacher and curriculum, experience of success and peer group. Dörnyei claimed that these three components function as attractor basins, providing learners with persistence in behavior and guiding them toward the higher stage of the learning process.

Taken together, the field of SLA is in a transition period, doing away from the traditional reductionist approach that pursues a simple cause–effect explanation in isolation from context, to a more ecologically oriented approach that includes context as part of the systems under investigation and considers reciprocal relationships among variables over time. As Larsen-Freeman and Cameron argue, the focus in this growing epistemology is not on learner or language but on learning process where a learner assembles his/her linguistic resources while interacting with a changing context. Larsen-Freeman and Cameron (2008: 158) observe:

> Learning is not the taking in of linguistic forms by learners, but the constant adaptation and enactment of language-using patterns in the service of meaning-making in response to the affordances that emerge in a dynamic communicative situation. Thus, this view assumes that

language development is not about learning and manipulating abstract symbols, but is enacted in real-life experiences.

While these paradigms offer a useful conceptual framework and vocabulary for studying language development under complex systems, most longitudinal studies in SLA are still placed within a traditional framework that presupposes a simple, linear development of systems with single factor explanations. In the recent volume of longitudinal studies and advanced L2 capacities, Ortega and Byrnes (2008: 286) note:

> Diverse disclaimers notwithstanding, the bulk of existing research has, at least implicitly, suggested the existence of simple linearities and simple causalities, expressing these in terms of single features seen as decontextualized 'variables' that change along a single time line – one development leading to or 'causing' another. As Ortega and Iberri-Shea (2005) note, such thinking continues to prevail when longitudinal change is recast through the lens of repeated cross-sectional comparisons or when it emphasizes the discovery of continuities that, by and large, privilege notions of developmental stability over time. In this picture, the importance of two key characteristics of language learning, the phenomenon to be investigated, has been underestimated: variability and non-linearity.

This observation also applies to the longitudinal ILP research. In the current database, only a few ILP studies conform to some of the methodological principles of dynamic, complexity systems research. Those studies are Ohta (2001), Barron (2003) and Kinginger (2008). As discussed in the previous section, Ohta investigated the development of acknowledgement and alignment expressions by learners of Japanese in a formal classroom. She identified developmental patterns of the expressions and revealed specific classroom experiences that promoted the gains. Barron, on the other hand, examined the development of German address forms over a 14-month study-abroad. Data elicited through DCT at 7-month intervals revealed only modest progress of learners' ability to produce the pragmatic targets, which was closely related to individual experiences. Kinginger's study, another longitudinal investigation in study-abroad, examined the development of the knowledge of sociolinguistic variation (e.g. address forms, colloquial expressions) in L2 French in a semester-length residence in France. Pre- and post-test comparisons revealed significant gains and considerable individual differences. Qualitative data revealed the qualities of learners' experiences, and the specifics of context and its impact on development.

These three studies are all book-length longitudinal studies that used mixed methods approaches – the combination of qualitative and quantitative methods. They collected data about both the individual and the context, and provided multilevel analyses of pragmatic development. They closely documented the interactions between individuals and the environment, focusing on how they shape the developmental paths and how the paths converge or diverge across individuals. Rich, qualitative data triangulated from multiple sources shed light on the complexity and dynamicity of pragmatic development in which multiple factors – learners' subjectivity; stance; affect; resources, such as proficiency, input and feedback; and interaction in the target language – were indeed interconnected and jointly influenced the developmental trajectories as they changed.

These studies suggest that longitudinal research in pragmatic development should benefit from this emerging theoretical perspective that focuses on the dynamicity and complexity of L2 development because, similar to other aspects of linguistics, the multiple factors that influence pragmatic gains are inherent to contexts and individuals. The coadaptation between context and individuals might manifest even more strongly in pragmatics, given the complex nature of the construct. Many aspects of pragmatic competence are inseparable not only from cognitive considerations but also from sociocultural practices and individuals' orientations toward them. To become able to communicate intentions appropriately in a situation or to comprehend meaning that is not explicitly stated, one needs a refined knowledge of linguistic systems and target language skills to mobilize the knowledge in real-time interaction. To this end, pragmatic abilities are built on threshold-level proficiency and cognitive capacities. However, the social nature of pragmatic competence also implies that exposure to the target pragmatic input, combined with opportunities to engage in social interaction and practice pragmatic functions, are indispensable to pragmatic growth.

In addition, pragmatics is not separable from personal considerations. Politeness, appropriateness and formality in learners' pragmatic performance reflect not only their linguistic abilities but also their personalities and styles. Learners have their own preferences and beliefs about how formal or polite they want to sound in certain situation. Their previous experiences with family, friends and professionals inevitably influence the manner in which they project politeness and the criteria they use to judge the appropriateness of language behaviors. Some may want to conform to the pragmatic norms and forms of the given culture, but others elect not to use the forms, perhaps signaling a desire to maintain their identity. Empirical evidence supporting this comes from Ishihara and Tarone's (2009) study. They reported cases in which learners of Japanese resisted pragmatic use of higher-level honorifics or gendered language, and their decisions were guided by their subjectivity, identity and stance.

To summarize, the cognitive, social and personal nature of pragmatic competence is the very reason that the dynamic and complexity systems approach is a potentially useful framework to adopt in a longitudinal investigation of pragmatic development. It could reveal coadaptation of linked subsystems and help unveil connected growth of the subsystems. A future challenge in this perspective is the construction of a concrete research design that facilitates a dynamic analysis of context and individuals. Ethnographic studies will certainly fall under such an endeavor if they can accumulate data points systematically. Quantitative–descriptive studies should expand their data sources to include qualitative data, allowing researchers to find meanings behind developmental phenomena. Measures such as observations, interviews and diaries are valuable in documenting learners' access to pragmatic input at the individual levels. Detailed reports of the nature of social contacts, the domains of those contacts and activity types could clarify the extent to which different types of sociocultural experiences affect pragmatic development.

The present longitudinal study is an effort to adopt the dynamic, complexity theory perspective in the examination of pragmatic development. It presents a group-level analysis of pragmatic change among 48 Japanese college students studying English in an English-medium university in Japan. Variations in developmental trajectories across different pragmatic subconstructs are presented, and the meanings behind the variations are explored through a situated, individual-level analysis of learners' characteristics and investment in the learning environment. The next chapter presents guiding theoretical framework, research questions and methodologies used in this investigation.

Note

(1) This chapter is an expanded version of Taguchi (2010).

3 Theoretical Framework, Research Questions and Methodology of the Study

Chapter 2 presented a review of longitudinal studies in ILP. About two dozen studies published to date have generated important discussion about changes within the L2 pragmatic system and influence on that system. This study aims to contribute to the body of longitudinal research in ILP. Building on the synthetic review of previous studies, several critical areas to explore in the future longitudinal research are identified. This study attends some of those areas. First, the study views pragmatic competence as a multifaceted construct and aims to reveal patterns and rate of change across different pragmatic functions and attributes. By collecting data systematically via cyclical elicitation using comparable tasks, the study aims to establish developmental scaling among subconstructs of pragmatic competence. This study also extends beyond the usual measures of accuracy and appropriateness of pragmatic language use by analyzing learners' processing speed when performing pragmatic functions. Hence, developmental pathways are projected for changes in learners' pragmatic knowledge, as well as in their efficiency in controlling the knowledge base. Finally, this study explains, not only describes, pragmatic development by examining individual and contextual factors that may affect the development. In-depth analyses of individuals, context and interaction between them are carried out by synthesizing an extensive body of triangulated data. To this end, this study takes an ecological approach to longitudinal investigation. It adopts the dynamic, complex systems' views of language development that context is part of the system, variability is central to its development, and language abilities emerge from co-regulated interactions of multiple influences in an environment. Next section presents the theoretical framework of communicative competence that guided this study.

Theoretical Framework of Communicative Competence

The guiding theoretical framework for this study is illustrated below based on the synthesis of existing models of communicative competence (Bachman & Palmer, 1996, 2010; Bialystok, 1990b; Canale & Swain, 1980; Hymes, 1972). The framework includes *knowledge* and *processing* as two major components of performance, supporting Hymes that language performance is based on language knowledge, but cognitive and noncognitive factors that underlie processing also affect performance. Below I will describe each component in the model and explain how this study addresses each component in the investigation of pragmatic development (Figure 3.1).

Communicative Competence

Based on Hymes (1972), communicative competence is defined as underlying potential or capabilities to perform language-related functions in communicative situations. Communicative competence consists of two underlying subcompetencies: language knowledge and the processing dimension of language performance. These two subcompetencies function interactively and simultaneously for performance.

Performance

Performance is the actual instances of language use in real time (Hymes, 1972). It consists of any observable language-related behavior elicited through a task involving learners in interacting with the target language. Performance

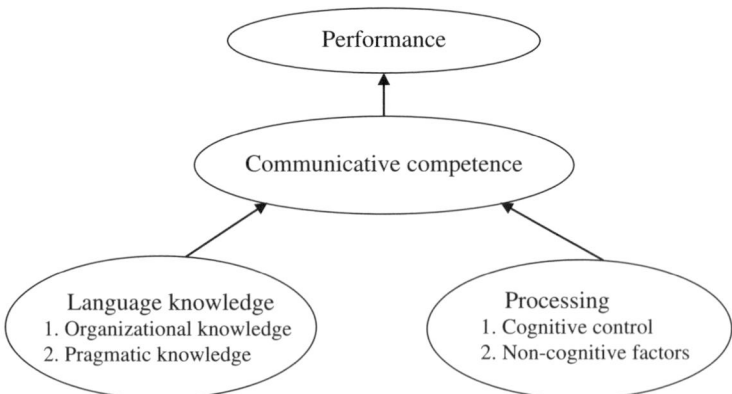

Figure 3.1 The guiding theoretical framework

is considered as the manifestation of communicative competence and its underlying constructs. However, performance is not necessary a direct reflection of the competence. Various factors contributing to performance (e.g. memory, situational constraints, task demands) are considered to affect the realization of competence possibilities. Imperfections of performance are the reflections of these performance-specific factors affecting underlying competence.

Language Knowledge

Language knowledge is a set of language factors that potentially affect language-related performance. Conceptualization of language knowledge follows Bachman and Palmer (1996, 2010). Language knowledge refers to an underlying domain of information available for use in producing and interpreting discourse in language use. Language knowledge has two types: organizational knowledge and pragmatic knowledge. Organizational knowledge deals with formal aspects of language, specifically the grammatical aspects (e.g. syntax, lexis, phonology) and the textual aspects (e.g. cohesion and rhetorical structure). Pragmatic knowledge, on the other hand, deals with language use in relation to language users and language use settings. There are two types of pragmatic knowledge: functional knowledge, which enables us to interpret relationships between utterances and communicative goals of language users (e.g. knowledge of how to perform instrumental functions such as requests and suggestions), and sociolinguistic knowledge, which enables us to interpret or create utterances that are appropriate to specific language use settings (e.g. knowledge of genres and register).

Bachman and Palmer's concept of pragmatic knowledge is related to the concepts of pragmalinguistics (linguistic resources available in contexts) and sociopragmatics (assessment of contextual information) introduced earlier by Leech (1983) and Thomas (1983), and later applied to L2 pragmatics by Kasper (1992b). Functional knowledge determines the range of linguistic resources available to perform language functions, while sociolinguistic knowledge enables us to select the most appropriate resource in a given context. As Leech (1983) argues, pragmalinguistics is applied to the study of the more linguistic end of pragmatics, while sociopragmatics is applied more toward the socio-cultural end.

When defining pragmatics, the term 'context' is a recurring theme. Context is crucial in our understanding of pragmatic knowledge because the ability to interpret and produce speech intentions is realized only through our understanding of context. Pragmatic knowledge entails the ability to assess contextual information and to choose appropriate linguistic means to perform functions according to context. Wrong assessment of context or limited use of contextual cues inevitably leads to inadequate representation of pragmatic knowledge. Thus, the central feature of L2 pragmatic knowledge is learners' understanding of contextual information – external factors surrounding the language use setting, as well as their ability to access experiences, memory and background knowledge (Duranti & Goodwin, 1992; Sperber & Wilson, 1995; Verschueren, 1999).

Processing

Processing, the other component of communicative competence, synthesizes three concepts from previous models: Hymes's (1972) 'ability for use', Bialystok's (1990b) control of processing and Bachman and Palmer's (1996, 2010) strategic competence. It involves higher-order executive abilities that promote efficient integration of subcomponents and knowledge bases, and maximize the effectiveness of performance. The processing component subsumes two subcomponents: cognitive control and noncognitive factors.

Cognitive control, corresponding to Bialystok's notion of control of processing, is an overarching term for all the functions used when we access and process information (e.g. memory and attention). Cognitive control is an obligatory process that enables us to focus attention on relevant parts of information, without being distracted by irrelevant or misleading cues, and enables us to select and coordinate information in real time. Performance of any complex skill (e.g. listening, speaking) involves the coordinated action of a number of component processes, both at a lower level (e.g. word recognition) and at a higher level (e.g. making inferences, summarizing). When underlying components are automatized, the performance is carried out rapidly and fluently in a stable manner (Segalowitz, 2003, 2007).

The other subcomponent is noncognitive factors. It subsumes the individual factors that have been adapted from Bachman and Palmer's framework. Personal characteristics (e.g. age, gender, personality and nationality), background/topical knowledge and affective state are part of the noncognitive factors. Similar to cognitive control, individual factors are considered as underlying nonlanguage factors that have potential for affecting performance.

Following this theoretical framework, this study measures two subcomponents of pragmatic performance: *knowledge* as pragmatic knowledge of comprehending and producing speech intentions, and *processing* as ability to demonstrate the knowledge efficiently in real-time tasks. Inferences about pragmatic knowledge are drawn from the analysis of accuracy of pragmatic comprehension and appropriateness of pragmatic production. Inferences about processing are drawn from the analysis of fluency in comprehension and production. Changes across these different aspects of pragmatic competence are traced over one academic year, in relation to participants' target language contact and sociocultural experiences gleaned from qualitative data.

Research Questions

This study is guided by research questions in two broad areas: general patterns of pragmatic development and individual differences in development.

(1) *General patterns of pragmatic development: What patterns and rate of development can we observe across different pragmatic functions and attributes?*
Do L2 learners show even-paced development across pragmatic functions or do some functions develop more quickly than others? For instance, do learners' ability to comprehend implied meaning precede their ability to produce meaning appropriately? Is there comparable development over time in fluency, accuracy and appropriateness of pragmatic comprehension and production? Do the knowledge and processing aspects of pragmatic competence unfold in parallel development, or does one lag behind the other?

(2) *Individual differences in pragmatic development: What types of learning resources and experiences are available in context and how do these factors shape developmental trajectories of individual learners?*
What are the sources of individual variation observed in pragmatic change? Do the nature and domains of social contact explain variations in pragmatic change among individual learners? Do learners have equal access to opportunities for pragmatic practice? Do learners' subjectivity, stance and context-deriving factors promote or constrain their access to opportunity, consequently affecting individual trajectories of pragmatic development?

To address these questions, a variety of instruments and data collection methods are arranged. A unique feature of this study is that it uses mixed method approach by interrelating quantitative and qualitative data and triangulating multiple data sources. Mixed methods approach has several strengths. For example, multilevel analysis promotes deeper understanding of a phenomenon at hand by converging numeric trends from quantitative data and contextualized details from qualitative data (Dörnyei, 2007). This convergence of findings and data triangulation are considered to improve the validity of research because they help us examine hypotheses from multiple angles. Each data source highlights the reality in a different yet complementary manner. Specifics of the methodology in this study are described in the following section that encompasses three parts: participants and the researcher, the constructs and instruments used in this study and procedures for data collection.

Methodology

Participants

Participants were 48 Japanese students of English as a foreign language (EFL) at Akita International University, an English-medium university located in Akita prefecture in Japan (see Chapter 1 for the descriptions of the institution). The participants (hereafter EFL learners) were all first-semester students enrolled in the intensive English for Academic Purposes (EAP) program (see Chapter 1 for the description of the EAP program).[1] There were 16 males and 32 females, ranging in age from 18 to 21 with an average age of 18.33 (SD = 0.66). They averaged 6.1 years of formal English education in Japan, indicating that almost all of them just graduated from high school. About 80% of the students reported that Japanese was the medium of instruction in their high-school English classes, and about 19% said that the classes were taught both in English and in Japanese. One student reported that the classes were taught only in English. Three students had experienced living in an English-speaking country for longer than one month. Their entry TOEFL score was 459.35 (SD = 17.76) in average, ranging from 413 and 497. Their TOEFL score at the end of the academic year was 524.32 in average (SD = 24.02; range: 467–563). From the group of the 48 participants, a subset of 12 participants was recruited as target informants for qualitative analysis (see Chapter 5 for the descriptions of the informants and how they were selected). Of the 12 participants, this book reports eight cases in Chapter 6. In addition to the EFL learners, 25 native speakers of English (14 males and 11 females) participated in the study and provided the baseline data. They were undergraduate students in the United States in a comparable age range with the Japanese participants.

The Researcher

I was born and grew up in Akita City where the target institution was located. I graduated from a local college and taught in a high school located in the city. After several years of teaching, I moved to the United States for my doctorate study. After I completed my PhD in Applied Linguistics at Northern Arizona University, I was hired as a full-time faculty in the target institution and taught there during the year 2004, the year when the school opened. Prior to the opening of the school, I served as a member of the university foundation committee in the prefectural office, and helped to develop the EAP curriculum and academic policies. My responsibilities in the institution during the first year involved teaching in the EAP program and General Education division. I taught academic listening courses and Speech Communication courses to Japanese students in an intensive format, all in English. I was also involved in academic advising and extracurricular activities. In 2005, I left the institution and relocated to the United States for my job at Carnegie Mellon University.

During the eight-month period of the present study in 2008, I was a visiting scholar at the target institution. I stayed in the institution for the entire study period and collected data. I was given an office in the main building where EAP instructors' offices were located. I went to school two days a week from April through December except when the school was in recess during August. I spent my entire day on campus visiting classes, interviewing students and teachers and taking field notes. I introduced myself to the students as a visiting researcher from a US university. My interaction with the students was limited to class visits and interviews, but there were a few instances when the students dropped in my office for a chat. I spoke English with them when I went to observe classes, but in all other occasions, I talked to them in Japanese. The students called me 'Taguchi *sensei*', meaning 'Teacher Taguchi', which is a common address term in Japanese schools. This indicates that they regarded me as a teacher, not as a near-peer advisor or a total stranger. They used *keigo* (honorifics) with me, which is also a common way of talking to someone older. My relationship with the EAP instructors, on the other hand, was on a first-name basis. We commuted on the same train and talked frequently for an extended time about classes, teaching and students. I also developed a rapport with several instructors through after-school shopping and dining.

Target Pragmatic Constructs and Instrumentation

Pragmatic comprehension[2]

This study investigated the longitudinal development of pragmatic comprehension – the ability to comprehend speakers' implied intentions accurately and in a speedy manner. Implied meaning is defined as meaning 'that goes beyond what is given by the language form itself or what is literally said' (Verschueren, 1999: 25). According to Thomas (1995), meaning has two levels: utterance meaning, or assigning sense to words uttered; and force, or speaker's intention behind the words. Pragmatic comprehension entails understanding meaning at both levels. This study focused on intentions that were not explicitly stated and thus were only implied.

This study investigated the development of learners' ability to comprehend conventional and nonconventional implicatures. Conventional implicatures are considered to convey meaning that is relatively fixed and invariable across contexts. Many idioms, formulaic expressions, situational routines and metaphors exhibit this quality. For instance, the expression 'How can I help you?' represents a speech act of offer that takes place within the frame of shopping. When one is familiar with sociocultural rules and conventions of the frame (i.e. shopping), the expression is understood as formulaic, and comprehension becomes automatic. Another example of conventional implicatures is a refusal routine of giving an excuse to refuse someone's invitation or request (e.g. saying 'I'm busy' when refusing someone's invitation to a party). These implicatures convey indirect meanings through fixed linguistic forms or predictable discourse patterns.

Nonconventional implicatures, on the other hand, represent indirect meanings that vary according to context, for example:

A: How was your presentation?
B: It's over, so it's OK.

In this example, an open set of expressions is possible as B's reply. Thus, compared with the more conventional implicatures, expressions used for the nonconventional implicatures are more idiosyncratic and less stable across language users and contexts. As a result, they require more extensive inferential processing to derive meaning because the listener needs to process a greater number of contextual cues.

This study adopted these two implicature types to measure learners' pragmatic comprehension over time. Comprehension of conventional implicatures was operationalized as ability to interpret indirect refusals and routines, while nonconventional ones referred to the ability to infer meaning of indirect opinions and comments. These two implicature types were sought for in corpora of naturalistic conversations. Two corpora of face-to-face conversations of American English were selected for the present study, representing two registers: family/friends interactions and service encounter interactions. Family/friends interactions were taken from the Santa Barbara Corpus of Spoken American English (SBC) (DuBois *et al.*, 2000), and the service encounter interactions were taken from the TOEFL 2000 Spoken and Written Academic Language Corpus (T2K-SWALC) (see Biber *et al.*, 2002, for descriptions). The SBC was used to locate all implicature types, while service encounter interaction in the T2K-SWALC was analyzed to find routines.

The SBC included a large body of recordings of naturally occurring spoken interaction from all over the United States, representing a wide variety of people of diverse regional origins, ages, occupations, genders and ethnic and social backgrounds. The corpus mainly consists of face-to-face informal conversations, but it also includes other forms of spoken texts, such as classroom lectures, sermons, story-telling, town hall meetings and tour-guide spiels. The corpus has 60 wave-format speech files, representing about 200,000 words in transcription. Forty-six of those 60 files were available in my institution and were surveyed. Of the 46 files analyzed, 20 files involved face-to-face casual conversations among family members, friends and colleagues. Files were excluded if they were: monologues (e.g. lectures sermons, scripted tours, public story telling), telephone conversations, large group discussions, bilingual conversations and those that involved technical topics that are not easily accessible to EFL learners (e.g. medical conversation and business talk).

The T2K-SWAL is a collection of audio-taped recordings and transcriptions of office hour and study group conversations, service encounter interactions and lectures that took place in a US university setting. This study used a subcorpus of various service encounter conversations on campus (11 files; a total of approximately 56,000 words). It was selected because routines are typically associated with specific situations or functions (e.g. Kecskes, 2003; Wray, 2000). Relatively fixed and recurrent service encounter situations were considered to yield a sizable collection of routine expressions.

I read the transcriptions of the corpora line-by-line, and the target implicatures were identified and hand-coded based on the criteria below:

(1) Conventional implicatures:
  (a) Indirect refusals: refusal responses to invitations, requests, and suggestions with a reason (e.g. saying 'I'm busy' when refusing someone's request for help).
  (b) Routines: fixed or semi-fixed expressions that commonly occur under certain situational conditions and functions. (e.g. 'It comes to $2' in a service encounter exchange and 'That's so sweet of you' in thanking someone.)
(2) Nonconventional implicatures: nonliteral comments or opinions that do not involve conventional linguistic features or language-use patterns. (e.g. indicating a negative opinion of a restaurant dinner by saying 'The food was late.')

The implicatures were adapted from the corpora if the conversational context was judged accessible to the beginner EFL learners who this study targeted. Dialogs that required culture-specific knowledge to understand meaning (e.g. politics, religion and medical practices) or that involved educationally inappropriate content (e.g. drugs and sex) were excluded. The excerpts that contained technical language and slang were also excluded. This initial process yielded a total of 26 situations involving conventional implicatures (14 indirect refusals and 12 unique routines) and 24 situations involving nonconventional implicatures. Rather than taking directly from the corpus, when necessary, dialogs and implicatures were modified and adapted to better serve the level of the target learner group and goals of the research.

Several factors were considered when writing dialogs. Length of the dialog and number of speaker turns had to be similar across items in order to maintain consistency. Because authentic conversation involved a long stretch of discourse that sometimes runs over 20 speakers' turns per topic, the conversation was shortened significantly to reduce the effect of short-term memory. Proper nouns or vocabulary items that were considered unfamiliar to the target EFL learners were replaced with familiar equivalents (e.g. 'mud pie' changed to 'apple pie'). The dialogs were written as a conversation between a male and female speaker so that the test takers can easily distinguish the voice. Another characteristic of naturalistic conversation that had to be adjusted was frequent use of pronouns, stemming from the great degree of shared context among speakers. Because in the testing situation learners are 'overhearing' the conversations, not participating in them, excessive pronouns pose unfair demand on comprehension. To avoid the problem, pronouns were replaced with their referents or supplied contextual information to make the pronoun referent explicit. Other characteristics of spoken discourse, such as ellipsis, incomplete sentences, overlaps, interruptions and disfluency (e.g. repetitions, pauses and false starts), were also reduced to make the test dialogs comparable to each other. These modifications, of course, beg the question of the degree of authenticity of the test items. While these modifications were necessary for the EFL group in this study, the balance between authenticity and practicality remains an issue for further research.

The following example shows how a naturalistic dialog was adapted and modified to a listening test dialog. The excerpt below is from the SBC file #035, a conversation among a mother (Patty), daughter (Stephanie) and sister (Gail). Patty suggests that Stephanie should look into Adrian College (line 5). In line 9, Stephanie turns down the suggestion by saying that the college does not have many majors, and she wants to go to a school with a variety of majors.

(1) **Patty:**	How about this school called Adrian College in Michigan,
(2) **Stephanie:**	Yeah,
(3) **Patty:**	It's real
(4) **Stephanie:**	it's in Adrian Michigan.
(5) **Patty:**	not very far from uh Ann Arbor.
	... They sent you a lotta information.
	... Sounds like a neat school.
(6) **Stephanie:**	But,
	.. they don't ha = ve a lot of
(7) **Patty:**	It's a smaller school.
(8) **Gail:**	.. I had a really good book that I should give you.
(9) **Stephanie:**	They don't have that many4] majors Mom.
	... I wanna go to a school that has a .. large variety of majors, and so if I change,
	I have something to look at.

While maintaining the gist of the target refusal utterance (line 9 above), several modifications were made to the rest of the conversation to create a plausible test item (see below). First, the mother–daughter conversation was changed to a mother–son conversation to distinguish gender in voice. Second, the sister's interruption (line 8 above) was eliminated. Third, the first utterance by the mother was changed to provide a sense of beginning.

The son's response was inserted in line 2 to clarify the situation and topic of the conversation.

(1) **Mother:**   Hey Steve, you're still on the internet. What are you doing?
(2) **Son:**   I'm checking out some colleges to see which one I should apply to.
(3) **Mother:**   How about this school called Adrian college in Michigan. They sent us a lot of information. It sounds like a neat school.
(4) **Son:**   They don't have many majors.

A set of 26 dialogs of conventional implicatures and 24 dialogs of nonconventional implicatures were prepared, and a native English speaker checked the plausibility of the dialogs. Although the intended meaning of the conventional implicatures was relatively straightforward, concerning the nonconventional implicatures, it was questionable whether the same intended interpretations arise across people due to their variable nature. Hence, a pilot study was conducted to confirm the reliability of the interpretations. An open-ended survey containing the 24 dialogs was prepared. In each dialog, the target indirect utterance was underlined. Participants were instructed to supply the interpretation for the underlined nonliteral utterance. See the sample pilot items below:

Sample pilot item #1

A: Thank you for this birthday present, Mike. It's a really pretty sweater.
B: You're welcome, Nancy. If it's too big, your mother can take it.
A: Or I can get some shirts underneath it. Let me try it on.
B: Is it too big?
A: I still got room for another ten pounds.

Sample pilot item #2

A: Hey Nancy, happy birthday. I want you to open this gift. It's from me.
B: Oh, thank you, Mike. This is a pretty package. When did you have a chance to wrap this?
A: At school.
B: Look at this. A Mickey Mouse watch. That's just what I always wanted.

The survey was administered to 10 native English speakers enrolled in an American university, and follow-up individual interviews were conducted to gain insights about their interpretations. For the majority of the items, they showed relatively uniformed interpretation. For example, in the first sample item above, all native speakers wrote that the sweater is too big for Speaker

A. However, some items showed a mixed interpretation. In the second sample item above, five respondents interpreted the target utterance as positive (i.e. Speaker B likes the gift), while four people wrote the opposite (i.e. Speaker B is not thrilled with the gift), and one person indicated both. Follow-up interviews revealed that this utterance could be taken as sarcasm and hence could imply negative opinion about the gift. Based on the results of the pilot study, three items that showed inconsistent interpretations were eliminated, resulting in a pool of 21 nonconventional implicatures. Certain items were selected from the pool to make the test length appropriate for the target EFL group.

The first version of the listening test (hereafter, pragmatic listening test or PLT) had a total of 42 items: two practice items, eight filler items and 32 experimental items. The filler items tested literal comprehension and were developed from the corpora. The experimental items had two types: 16 conventional implicatures and 16 nonconventional implicatures. Each item had a brief dialog followed by multiple-choice questions with four answer options (see Table 3.1 for sample items). The test asked participants to listen to the dialog and select the correct statement based on the content of the conversation. In the experimental dialogs, the correct answer was the speaker's implied intention. Conversations were counterbalanced over four interlocutor relationships: college friends, housemates, coworkers and family members.

The lengths of the conversations were kept relatively similar to control their impacts on short-term memory. Each conversation had between 47 and 52 words, with an average of 49 words (SD = 1.55), involving four to six speaker turns (about 25 seconds in length). In addition, since the time taken to answer multiple-choice questions was part of the investigation, the number of words used in question and option sentences had to be equal to make those response times more comparable. Therefore, the number of words in the option sentences was kept approximately the same across items, either 26 or 27 words (SD = 0.50). Furthermore, to reduce the extraneous effect coming from the learners' different vocabulary knowledge, all vocabulary in conversations and option sentences was drawn from the JACET List of 8000 Basic Words (JACET, 2003). The JACET list is based on the British National Corpus (BNC) and JACET original corpus of high-school English textbooks in Japan. The developers of the JACET list compared a list of words appearing more than 10 times in each corpus and determined the frequency order of 8000 words that were common in the two corpora. Since the top 3000 words are determined to be high-school level, they were used to write the conversations and option sentences. These vocabulary items were considered attainable by the EFL learners in this study because they were all high-school graduates and passed the college entrance exam to enter the university.

Finally, options in the multiple-choice questions were written in a consistent manner. The multiple-choice questions in the test had four answer

TABLE 3.1 Sample PLT items

Conventional implicatures

Refusal

Mother	Hey Steve, you're still on the internet. What are you doing?
Steve	I'm checking out some colleges to see which one I should apply to.
Mother	How about this school called St. Joes college in Indiana. They sent us a lot of information. It sounds like a neat school.
Steve	They don't have many majors.
	(1) Steve wants to apply for St. Joes college.
	(2) Steve knows about many majors.
	(3) Steve lived in Indiana before.
	(4) Steve is not interested in St. Joes college. (CORRECT)

Routine

Salesclerk:	Hi how can I help you?
Customer:	Ah, could I get a small regular coffee, with milk? And a slice of apple pie.
Salesclerk:	For here or to go?
Customer:	To go please.
Salesclerk:	Here's a large cup, we don't have small because we ran out of the small ones.
Customer:	OK, thank you.
	(1) The man ordered cake.
	(2) The man is taking the coffee out. (CORRECT)
	(3) The man is having coffee in the shop.
	(4) The man ordered a large cup.

Nonconventional implicatures

Nancy:	Hey Mike, you're home. Aren't you supposed to be at work?
Mike:	Hey Nancy. I quit that job yesterday. I just didn't wanna work in the factory any longer.
Nancy:	What? Really? Do your parents know about this?
Mike:	When they come back from their trip, they'll be pretty shocked.
	(1) Mike's parents think he's still working. (CORRECT)
	(2) Mike's parents know that he quit his job.
	(3) Mike's parents just came back from their trip.
	(4) Mike's parents work in a factory.

option statements, one correct statement and three distractor statements. The following principles were used to write distracter options:

Principle 1: The option contains a meaning opposite to the implied meaning.
Principle 2: The option contains words related to the last part of the conversation.
Principle 3: The option is related to the overall conversation.

The PLT was computerized using the software 'Revolution' (Runtime Revolution Ltd., 1997) and the test was piloted with 25 native English speakers and 12 ESL students in a US university. There were four items that were revised because the native speakers achieved lower than a 90% accuracy rate (two nonconventional implicatures, one routine, and one distracter item). The revised items were then checked with the same native speakers. After administering the test to the EFL learners, internal consistency reliability was assessed. Cronbach's alpha was 0.92 for the full test. It was 0.85 for conventional implicatures (0.76 for indirect refusals and 0.72 for routines) and 0.84 for nonconventional implicatures. Table 3.1 displays sample items (see Appendix C for the complete instrument). A parallel version of the test was prepared to minimize the practice effect coming from repeated administration. Different filler items were used, male and female speakers' roles were reversed and slight modifications were made to proper nouns, prices and object names. Besides those minor changes, the conversations and answer options were kept exactly the same in the two versions of the test.

In summary, this study operationalized pragmatic comprehension as L2 learners' correct identification of the PLT items, and the speed with which they chose an answer. Accuracy scores had an interval scale between 0 and 32 across three item types: conventional implicatures of two types (indirect refusals, scale of 0–8, and routines, scale of 0–8) and nonconventional implicatures (scale of 0–16). Comprehension speed, also interval data, was operationalized as response times and was calculated by averaging the number of seconds taken to answer items correctly. Gains in accurate, speedy comprehension were analyzed using repeated-measures ANOVA by comparing accuracy scores and response times across the three test sessions.

Pragmatic production [3]

In addition to pragmatic comprehension, this study examined the development of pragmatic production – the ability to convey intentions appropriately and fluently in speech acts. This ability requires learners to evaluate situational information, and to select and use appropriate linguistic resources to convey illocutionary force while coping with the processing demand. The concept of appropriateness entails knowledge of pragmalinguistics and sociopragmatics. Learners need to know both the linguistic forms and socio-cultural rules of appropriate speech acts in the given situation.

A computerized pragmatic speaking test (PST) was developed to exam-ine this ability. The test took the format of an oral discourse completion task (DCT) in which participants read situational descriptions and pro-duced speech acts. Two types of speech acts were tested: requests (a direc-tive speech act; $k = 4$) and opinions (an expressive speech act; k = 4). These two were selected after consulting Garcia's (2004) corpus-based study on naturalistic conversations in university settings. Using the T2K-SWALC (see previous section for descriptions), Garcia analyzed conversations across three registers: conversations between a professor and student, conversa-tions among study group members and service encounter conversations. She documented representative speech acts in each register along with the linguistic characteristics of them. Analyses of professor–student conversa-tions and study group conversations were relevant to this study because these two registers exhibit different levels of formality. The findings revealed that speech acts of directives (request) and expressives (opinions) are common in both registers. From the examples in the corpus data, four request and four opinion situations were adapted for this study. The requests and opinions taken from the study group conversations were dis-tinctively different from those of the office hour conversations. They occurred between interlocutors of equal power relationship and the size of imposition was small (e.g. asking a friend for a pen). The teacher–student conversations generated speech acts between interlocutors of a different power relationship, and the degree of imposition was large (e.g. asking a professor for an extension on an assignment). Hence, the speech acts from study group conversations were called low-imposition speech acts, while those from office hour conversations were called high-imposition speech acts.

To confirm the distinction between low- and high-imposition situations, a pilot study was conducted. This involved developing a survey that asked participants to indicate the degree of perceived ease/difficulty in performing the target speech act on a Likert scale of 1 (easy) to 5 (difficult). The survey also asked the participants to indicate the degree of commonality of each speech act on a scale from 1 (very rare) to 5 (very common). The survey was given to 20 native speakers of English in a US university. The low-impo-sition situations received a mean difficulty rating of 1.6 (SD = 0.8) for requests and 2.2 (SD = 0.9) for opinions. High-imposition situations received a mean difficulty rating of 3.1 (SD = 1.1) for request and 3.8 (SD = 0.9) for opinion speech acts. Paired-sample t-test revealed a significant difference between the two situation types, $t = 6.76$ ($p = 0.00$) for requests, and $t = 6.26$ ($p = 0.00$) for opinions, indicating that high-imposition speech acts were perceived to be more difficult to perform socially than low-imposition speech acts. Regarding the perceived level of commonality, low-imposition requests received a commonality rating of 4.1 (SD = 1.2), while low-imposition opinions received a rating of 3.3 (SD = 0.9). High-imposition situations received a commonality rating of 2.7 (SD = 1.0) for request and 3.6 (SD = 0.9) for opinions. All situations were around or above the rating of 3.0 on the 5-point scale, indicating that they were perceived not rare and thus acceptable. Table 3.2 displays simplified scenarios used in the PST. Appendix D contains the complete scenario.

TABLE 3.2 Simplified PST situations

(1) Low-imposition speech acts
(a) Requests
You have a free writing task in class, but you forgot to bring a pen. You need a pen to write the essay. You want to borrow a pen from your friend, Ken. What do you say to Ken?
You and your close friend John are talking about your group presentation for class. John said something about English class to you, but you didn't understand. What do you say to John?
(b) Opinions
You are shopping for clothes with your close friend, Jeff. Jeff tried on a brown jacket. You don't think he looks good in brown. He says, 'What do you think?' What do you say to Jeff?
Your close friend, Cindy, asked you to check her paper. The paper is well-written, but you think the introduction is too long. What do you say to Cindy?
(2) High-imposition speech acts
(a) Requests
You have a small test in Professor Smith's class, but you realized that you have your cousin's wedding on the same day. You want to take the test at some other time. What do you say to Professor Smith?
Paper for Professor's Land's class is due tomorrow. You caught a cold, and you've written only two pages so far. You want to ask for two extra days. What do you say to Professor Land?
(b) Opinions
You got a mid-semester grade of C from Professor William's class, but you don't think it's fair. You missed three classes and didn't speak up, but you turned in homework and got 80% on the test. You go to his office to explain. What do you say?
You like Professor Young's French culture class, but she mostly talks about French history and doesn't address recent things. She says, 'What do you think about the class?' What do you say to Professor Young?

The length of the situational description was controlled across items. The number of words used in each description ranged from 55 to 57 with a mean of 55.55 (SD = 0.60). The vocabulary used to write the descriptions came from the JACET list of basic words. The grammatical structures used to write sentences were kept at a basic level. In addition to the two target speech acts, four routine situations were included as filler items. The final version of the PST had a total of 14 items: four low-imposition speech acts, four high-imposition speech acts, four filler items and two practice items. In order to avoid practice effect coming from administering the same test multiple times, two parallel versions of the test were prepared by making slight changes in the situational scenarios. The PST was computerized using the Revolution software. The items were presented in written form on the screen. The PST was piloted with 25 native speakers of English and 12 ESL students in the United States prior to the main study.

Participants' speech acts were evaluated on three aspects: appropriateness, grammaticality and fluency. Appropriateness was defined as the ability to perform speech acts at the proper level of politeness, directness and formality in the given situations. It was assessed using a five-point rating scale ranging from 1 (very poor) to 5 (excellent). Grammaticality was also evaluated based on a five-point rating scale ranging from 1 (very poor) to 5 (excellent). For both appropriateness and grammaticality, the sum of the ratings of the four low-imposition and four high-imposition speech acts were used for analysis. Tables 3.3 and 3.4 display the rating scales. Appendices E and F present complete rating scales with examples.

Four native speakers of English evaluated the samples (see Taguchi, 2011a for the descriptions of the raters). They were asked to listen to the speech acts, along with the transcripts, and to indicate the rating based on the rating

TABLE 3.3 Appropriateness rating scale

5 Excellent
Almost perfectly appropriate and effective in the level of directness, politeness and formality.
4 Good
Not perfect but adequately appropriate in the level of directness, politeness and formality. Expressions are a little off from target-like, but pretty good.
3 Fair
Somewhat appropriate in the level of directness, politeness and formality. Expressions are more direct or indirect than the situation requires.
2 Poor
Clearly inappropriate. Expressions sound almost rude or too demanding.
1 Very poor
Not sure if the target speech act is performed.

TABLE 3.4 Grammaticality rating scale

5 Excellent
Almost perfect. There are almost no grammatical and lexical errors.
4 Good
There are one or two minor grammatical and lexical errors, which are hardly noticeable.
3 Fair
There are a few major grammar and lexical errors, but they do not interfere with understanding.
2 Poor
There are many major grammatical and lexical errors that cause misunderstanding.
1 Very poor
Expression incomprehensible due to fragmental nature or excessive grammatical mistakes.

descriptions. Interrater reliability was $r = 0.92$. About 2% of the samples had two points off in rating. They were discussed in the follow-up meetings to reach a consensus. For the cases with one point off, the average score between the two raters was assigned as the final score.

Two temporal measures were used to assess fluency: pretask planning time and speech rate. These two measures were applied because they were used in previous ILP research (Taguchi, 2007c) and produced reliable contrast in measuring processing aspect of pragmatic production. Planning time was operationalized as the time taken to prepare for each speech act. Speech rate refers to fluidity or 'smoothness' of language use (Freed, 2000) and has served as a common measure of oral fluency (see Riggenbach, 2000, for summary). In this study, speech rate was measured as the number of words spoken per minute, excluding false starts and repetitions. Although restricting the fluency analysis to speech rate and not incorporating other measures (e.g. pause length) is a limitation of the study, previous research showed that speech rate positively correlated with other measures of fluency (Segalowitz & Freed, 2004).

In conjunction with the PST, I administered a grammar test to measure learners' receptive knowledge of typical linguistic forms used in the target speech acts. The forms were sampled from native speakers' baseline data and included these syntactic and lexical items:

Hedging and amplifiers:
    a bit, a little, really, maybe, probably, just, completely, absolutely,
        I think, I'm not sure, I feel, I know

Modal auxiliaries:
> can, could, may, might, must, should, will, would

Syntactic structures:
> I wish + clause, if + clause, I wonder if + clause, is there any chance/way to + verb, would it be possible + verb

The test had a total of 28 items: 20 items asking the participants to choose Japanese translations for the target English word/phrase and eight items asking them to rearrange words to construct a sentence. The test was given in the first data collection session (see Appendix G for the copy of the grammar test). On average the learners scored 95.5% on the test, indicating that they had almost complete receptive knowledge of these linguistic forms at the onset of the study. They knew the meaning and use of these linguistic items, although their understanding of pragmatic functions of these forms was uncertain.

Introspective verbal interviews

In addition to the pragmatic measures, qualitative data were collected to examine learners' cognitive processes while completing the measures. After the last data collection session, I conducted introspective verbal interviews in Japanese with individual learners, that is, asking them to report their thought processes upon completing the tasks. Twelve students (six males and six females) who served as focal participants for the qualitative analysis participated in the follow-up interview in my office. They completed nine items from the PLT with me, one by one. The nine items involved three indirect refusals, three routines and three nonconventional implicatures. The participants listened to each dialog and chose the answer from the multiple-choice options. After they chose the answer, I asked them to report their thoughts upon their choice. I facilitated the interview by asking questions such as: 'Why did you choose the answer?' and 'What were you thinking when you chose the answer?'

The same participants also completed five PST items with me, one-by-one. The PST items involved two low-imposition and three high-imposition speech act items. They read the situational scenarios and produced target speech acts accordingly. After they produced the speech acts, I asked questions such as: 'What did you focus most when preparing for the speech act?,' 'Did you express all you wanted to say?' and 'Were you aware of the situational differences between the items?' As I was interested in the students' knowledge of a range of pragmalinguistic forms related to the target speech acts, I asked them if they knew other expressions that could convey the same intentions than the ones they used. For example, if they said, 'May I submit the paper next week?,' in the speech act of asking a professor for an extension, I asked them to say all other alternative expressions they knew to perform the same speech function. The interview sessions, each lasting about 30–40 minutes, were recorded and later transcribed. A total of 168 verbal reports (nine PLT and five PST items per learner; 12 learners in total) were analyzed for particular strategies used to complete the task items. Data from these introspective verbal interviews were used to identify the source of difficulty involved in the pragmatic tasks and strategies that the participants used to cope with the tasks.

Additional Measures and Data Sources

In addition to the pragmatic measures, this study collected data from additional sources: language contact profile, institutional TOEFL and qualitative data.

Language contact profile (LCP)

In order to document the learners' language history and language use in the context of their learning, a survey instrument, a modified version of the Language Contact Profile (Freed et al., 2004), was administered in their L1 (Japanese) six times at about 1.5 month intervals. The purpose of the questionnaire was to document the amount of outside-class contact with the target language. The questions in the survey asked learners to indicate how many days per week and how many hours per day they spent using four language skills in English (i.e. speaking, reading, writing and listening) and interacting with native or fluent speakers of English. The product of these two numbers (i.e. the number of days per week and hours per day) provided an estimate of total time per week in English. Appendix A provides an English translation of the survey. Appendix B presents descriptive statistics of the LCP results.

The ITP TOEFL

In order to examine the learners' development of pragmatic comprehension and production in relation to their general language ability, the institutional TOEFL (ITP TOEFL) was used to determine general L2 proficiency. Educational Testing Services (ETS) provides the opportunity to administer the TOEFL locally to students at their home institutions throughout the world, through a program called the Institutional Testing Program (ITP). Because the ITP uses previous versions of the TOEFL test, the format, content and scoring of the ITP TOEFL are identical to the actual TOEFL (ETS, 2003). The ITP TOEFL was given three times to the Japanese participants at about same timing with the pragmatic measures.

Qualitative data

In addition to the quantitative data, this study collected qualitative data in order to gather information about the types of social experiences available on campus and to explain the individual variation in pragmatic development stemming from individual and contextual factors. Qualitative data involved five sources: student interviews, teacher interviews, class observations, journals and field notes. These data sources are meant to reveal the nature of participants' social contacts, domains of contacts and activity types and shed light on the relationship between pragmatic gains and types of sociocultural experiences available for individuals. In addition to the five major data sources, I also analyzed textbooks used in the EAP program in order to examine the extent of pragmatic instruction in classrooms.

The main data source in this study was student interviews. The interviews were conducted in my office in Japanese for about 40 minutes to one hour. The interviews were semi-structured to include certain preselected themes but allowed flexibility in incorporating themes nominated by the informants. First interview was focused on the informants' educational background and experiences. I asked questions about their high-school English classes (e.g. the number of class hours, medium of instruction, teaching style, typical classroom activities), amount of contact with native English speakers in high school, goals of their English study, the degree of adjustment difficulties in the new university environment (both academically and socially) and the degree of satisfaction they felt about their university life. I also asked questions about their class participation, amount of time they spend using English, amount of time contact with ESL teachers, club activities and the degree of social network (e.g. the number of English-speaking friends they have). Because the target pragmatic tasks involved listening and speaking skills, I asked questions about the amount and type of listening and speaking activities that they were engaged outside the class.

Many of these questions were followed up in the second interview, but the topic was extended to more detailed accounts of their communication opportunities: with whom they speak English most in what situations on which topics. Because the pragmatic speaking task measured their sociocultural sensitivity and pragmalinguistic style shift between formal and informal situations (i.e. talking to a friend vs. talking to a professor), I asked questions about the frequency, types, and nature of their contact with friends and teachers. I also tried to gain insight into their metapragmatic awareness: I solicited their opinions about the similarities and differences between Japanese and English communication styles, formality and politeness practices, by using examples from Japanese language that explicitly marks sociolinguistic variation in speech style (e.g. honorifics, polite vs. plain forms).

The last interview was conducted a few days after the last testing session. I revisited the questions from the first interview to gain information about changes over the semester. I also asked specific questions about the pragmatic listening and speaking tasks: how they thought they did, what aspects of the tests were easy or difficult, and whether or not they had experienced similar conversations or situations in their daily lives. In addition, I conducted introspective verbal interviews using a portion of the pragmatic tasks (i.e. PLT and PST). The informants completed nine PLT items and five PST items with me, one-by-one, and verbalized their thoughts while completing the tasks (see previous section for descriptions).

In addition to the students' interviews, I visited EAP classes regularly to gather information about the eight target informants in class. I observed 60 classes over two semesters: 13 reading, 13 writing, 31 speaking and three listening classes (see Chapter 1 for descriptions of the EAP classes). Each EAP section was observed from 18 to 22 times, over a total of 12 instructors. I visited the speaking class most often because it was the target skill area in the pragmatic task. Although listening was another target skill area, I visited the listening class only three times because it was a dictation class (see Chapter 1 for description of the listening class).

I did not tape record the classes because it would make the students feel uneasy. Instead, I took detailed notes of them. I recoded all the class activities, both teacher- and student-initiated, and jotted down the names of the students who volunteered answers. Since the target speech acts were requests and opinions, I wrote down the linguistic forms used by the students when they produced these two speech acts in class. I did the same for the teachers. I also recorded the length of time spent speaking in pairs or group in English. Class exercises and activities that involved the target speech acts were pre-identified through course schedule and textbook analyses. Those sessions were either observed or later interviewed with the teachers to learn how they covered the materials. I also recorded the instances of jokes and sarcasms produced by the teachers because they were expressed in nonliteral forms and thus were relevant to the target construct of pragmatic comprehension – comprehension of implied meaning.

While student interviews and class observations formed two major sources of qualitative data, other forms of data were also collected to supplement the present analysis. I interviewed 11 EAP instructors for two to eight times each (a total of 26 interviews conducted in English; each lasting from 30 minutes to one hour). I asked them about typical class activities and assignment, strong and weak students in class, frequency and types of interaction with individual students in and outside of class, and their perceptions of students' attitudes and manner, both verbal and nonverbal. Their observations and impressions about the target eight informants were explored in detail.

A subset of 18 participants retained a journal as part of the assignment for their speaking class, and so I obtained permission to use it as data. The purpose of the journal was to provide students with opportunities to speak English outside of the class. The students were instructed to have a small talk with international students or teachers in English. They recorded their experiences in three to five, half-page entries every week over a period of two semesters, totalling over 60 entries, and the instructor graded each entry. I analyzed the focal informants' entries carefully, by comparing the range and nature of their English use experiences on and off campus. These four forms of qualitative data: student interviews, teacher interviews, class observation notes and journal entries, along with field notes and emails I exchanged with EAP instructors, were triangulated when analyzing case histories of the focal eight participants.

I recorded all the student and teacher interviews in a digital voice recorder and transcribed them. The data were analyzed using the strategy of analytic induction. I examined the interview data for impressions and trends by noting salient, recurring comments and grouping the comments for similarity. Because the goal of this study was to capture the patterns of pragmatic development over different pragmatic functions and attributes, and then to match them up with individuals' socio-pragmatic experiences in the target context, I paid special attention to the participants' narratives that touched upon their sociocultural practices and social interaction. I highlighted these features of data that directly indicate changes in pragmatic development and evidence of pragmatic learning.

Data Collection Procedures

The PLT and PST were administered individually to the participants three times over the academic year: Time 1 (April), Time 2 (July) and Time 3 (December). Each testing session was scheduled outside of the participants' regular class hours. The tests were given using Windows machines in a computer lab on campus. After sitting in front of the computer, the participants started with the PST. They put on headphones with an attached microphone and read directions in English with Japanese translations. They were told to read each situational scenario and respond as if they were in a real situation performing the role. After a sound check and two practice items, they proceeded to the 12 test items. Each item started with a situational scenario on the computer screen. They were allowed to take as much time as they needed to read the scenario and prepare for the speech act. When they were ready, they clicked on the 'continue' button. Once they clicked the button, the scenario disappeared and the message 'start speaking' appeared on the screen. After they finished the item, they clicked on the 'continue' button to move on to the next item. The computer recorded their speech and planning time. The planning time was recorded from the moment the scenario appeared on the screen until the moment the students clicked on the 'continue' button to begin speaking.

After the PST, the participants proceeded to the PLT. They read English and Japanese instructions, practiced two listening items and then proceeded to the 40 test items. Each item followed the same format: immediately following a dialog, a multiple-choice question with four answer options in

English appeared on the screen. Participants were told to read each answer option and choose the correct statement based on the content of the dialog by pressing the corresponding key from '1' to '4'. Once they chose the answer, the computer automatically took them to the next item. After completing half of the items, the participants were allowed to take a short break before moving on to the last half. Response time was measured between the moment when the question appeared on the screen and the moment when the participants pressed the number key. The computer recorded all responses and their latencies. After completing the PST and PLT, the LCP was administered. The entire testing session took about one hour. The ITP-TOEFL was administered on a separate day as part of the EAP curriculum. In addition to the quantitative data, I collected qualitative data from interviews with students and teachers, class observations, students' journals, textbook analyses and field notes. Figure 3.2 provides an overview of the data collection process.

The next two chapters present the findings of the study. Chapter 4 presents quantitative analyses in response to the first research question: What patterns and rate of development can we observe across different pragmatic functions and attributes? Chapter 5 provides qualitative analyses and

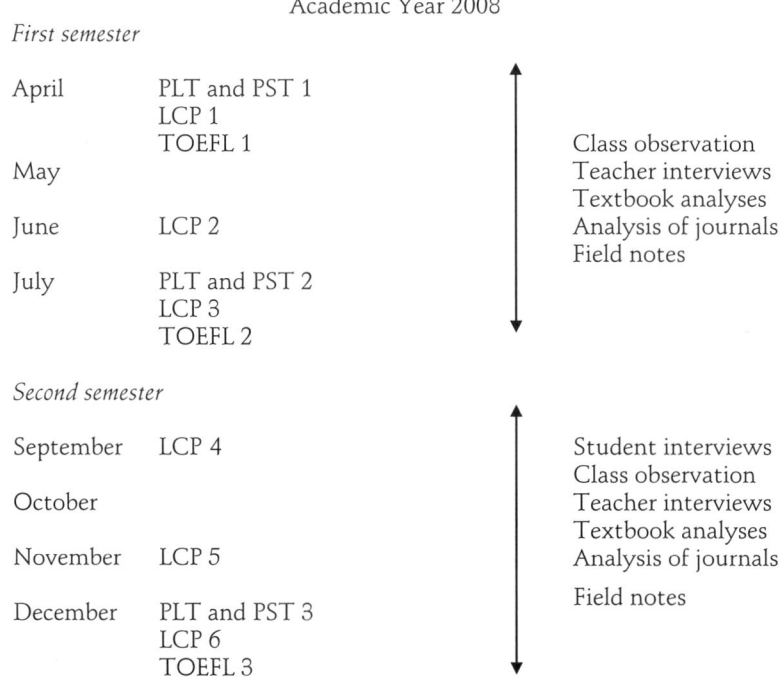

Figure 3.2 Data collection timeline

presents eight case histories in response to the second research question: What types of learning resources and experiences are available in context and how do these factors shape developmental trajectories of individual learners? Quantitative and qualitative findings are synthesized and interpreted in Chapter 6, the conclusion chapter, and implications of the findings for pragmatic competence and second language acquisition process are discussed.

Note

(1) The participants were recruited from the first two levels in the EAP program (three levels in total) because students in these two levels are relatively homogenous in terms of general proficiency and prior experience in English study. I visited each class and solicited volunteer participations. Out of the pool of 54 students, 48 agreed to participate.
(2) Partial descriptions of the test development process appeared in Taguchi (2009).
(3) Partial descriptions of the test development process appeared in Taguchi (2011b).

4 Patterns and Rate of Pragmatic Development

The purpose of this study was to investigate the longitudinal development of pragmatic competence among 48 Japanese EFL learners in an English-medium university in Japan. Two aspects of pragmatic competence – pragmatic comprehension and production – were traced. The study focused on two main areas of investigation: (1) the general patterns and rate of pragmatic development and (2) individual variations in this development. (See Chapter 3 for research questions and methodology.) This chapter presents the findings from the first area of inquiry, which responds to the question: What patterns and rate of pragmatic development can we observe across different pragmatic functions and attributes? To address this question, this study administered two measures: a pragmatic listening test (PLT) and pragmatic speaking test (PST). The PLT assessed learners' ability to comprehend conventional and nonconventional implicatures, while the PST assessed their ability to produce speech acts of requests and opinions in low- and high-imposition situations. The measures were given three times in the course of two semesters to capture change in pragmatic abilities.

I will present the analyses of quantitative data collected from these pragmatic measures. Qualitative data from interviews, class observations, journals and introspective verbal protocols are also discussed in the interpretation sections to provide explanations for the patterns of change gleaned from the data. For the statistical analyses of pragmatic comprehension, the alpha level was adjusted to 0.017 using the Bonferroni correction because it involved three statistical comparisons (indirect refusals, routines and nonconventional implicatures). For pragmatic production, the alpha level was adjusted to 0.025 because it involved two comparisons (high- and low-imposition speech acts).

Findings for Pragmatic Comprehension

Effect of Item Type on Pragmatic Comprehension

Tables 4.1 and 4.2 display the descriptive statistics of accuracy scores and response times for the three test sessions. Not surprisingly, the native speakers' comprehension was almost completely accurate and much faster than the EFL learners, and their response times were relatively uniform across implicature types.

Unlike native speakers, EFL learners' comprehension differed across item types. They displayed lower accuracy scores and slower response times when comprehending nonconventional implicatures than conventional implicatures. (See Appendix C for the copy of the implicature items.) Indeed, the difference was statistically significant for accuracy scores at all time points: $t = -3.13$ ($p = 0.000$, $\eta2 = 0.17$) at Time 1, $t = -5.59$ ($p = 0.000$, $\eta2 = 0.41$) at Time 2 and $t = -14.37$ ($p = 0.000$, $\eta2 = 0.81$) at Time 3. Comparisons of effect size ($\eta2$) indicate that the score difference between these two item types became greater over time. Differences in response times also exhibited similar patterns. A significant difference was detected at all time points: $t = 4.38$ ($p = 0.000$, $\eta2 = 0.29$) at Time 1, $t = 5.57$ ($p = 0.000$, $\eta2 = 0.40$) at Time 2 and

TABLE 4.1 Descriptive statistics, PLT accuracy scores

	Mean	SD	Min.	Max.
EFL learners ($n = 48$)				
Time 1				
Conventional imp ($k = 16$)	8.35	2.84	3.00	14.00
Refusals ($k = 8$)	4.31	1.74	0.00	7.00
Routines ($k = 8$)	4.04	1.75	0.00	8.00
Nonconventional imp ($k = 16$)	6.98	2.31	2.00	12.00
Time 2				
Conventional imp ($k = 16$)	8.97	2.76	4.00	15.00
Refusals ($k = 8$)	5.13	1.59	2.00	8.00
Routines ($k = 8$)	3.85	1.60	1.00	8.00
Nonconventional imp ($k = 16$)	6.77	2.27	3.00	12.00
Time 3				
Conventional imp ($k = 16$)	2.04	2.27	7.00	16.00
Refusals ($k = 8$)	6.32	1.16	4.00	8.00
Routines ($k = 8$)	5.72	1.41	3.00	8.00
Nonconventional imp ($k = 16$)	7.98	1.96	3.00	12.00
Native speakers ($n = 25$)				
Conventional imp ($k = 16$)	15.29	0.75	14.00	16.00
Refusals ($k = 8$)	7.88	0.34	7.00	8.00
Routines ($k = 8$)	7.42	0.72	6.00	8.00
Nonconventional imp ($k = 16$)	14.67	0.96	12.00	16.00

Notes: k = the number of items. One point was assigned per correct answer. Imp = implicatures

$t = 2.67$ ($p = 0.000$, $\eta2 = 0.13$) at Time 3, but this time, the gap narrowed toward the end of the study period.

Of the two conventional implicature types, indirect refusals were generally easier and took less time to comprehend than routines for the EFL learners. Although the data from Time 1 revealed no significant difference in accuracy scores between refusals and routines ($t= 0.93$, $p = 0.36$), a significant difference was found in Time 2 ($t = 5.52$, $p = 0.000$, $\eta2 = 0.63$), and again in Time 3 ($t = 3.28$, $p = 0.000$, $\eta2 = 0.21$). The same patterns were found in the response time data. There was no significant difference at Time 1 ($t = 2.33$, $p = 0.024$), but significant differences were detected at Time 2 ($t = 2.51$, $p = 0.015$, $\eta2 = 0.12$) and again at Time 3 ($t = -4.36$, $p = 0.000$, $\eta2 = 0.29$). The order of difficulty of the PLT item types is summarized in Table 4.3. Initially, the two subcategories of conventional

TABLE 4.2 Descriptive statistics, PLT response times

	Mean	SD	Min.	Max.
EFL learners ($n = 48$)				
Time 1				
Conventional imp ($k = 16$)	14.32	5.11	6.39	31.17
Refusals ($k = 8$)	13.39	4.81	7.18	26.37
Routines ($k = 8$)	14.86	6.02	4.46	35.96
Nonconventional imp ($k = 16$)	16.98	5.96	9.35	43.77
Time 2				
Conventional imp ($k = 16$)	12.12	2.46	6.74	17.79
Refusals ($k = 8$)	11.63	3.22	5.89	23.16
Routines ($k = 8$)	13.05	3.26	5.67	22.04
Nonconventional imp ($k = 16$)	15.60	5.10	7.87	33.56
Time 3				
Conventional imp ($k = 16$)	12.54	2.75	7.30	20.36
Refusals ($k = 8$)	11.37	3.44	6.23	23.63
Routines ($k = 8$)	13.78	3.00	6.33	22.90
Nonconventional imp ($k = 16$)	13.80	3.61	6.43	21.84
Native speakers ($n = 25$)				
Conventional imp ($k = 16$)	7.61	1.32	5.14	10.14
Refusals ($k = 8$)	6.67	1.46	4.40	10.48
Routines ($k = 8$)	8.63	2.00	4.09	12.28
Nonconventional imp ($k = 16$)	8.33	2.40	5.15	16.32

Notes: k = the number of items. The time refers to the average number of seconds taken to answer each item correctly. Imp = implicatures

TABLE 4.3 Summary of order of difficulty in pragmatic comprehension

Accuracy

Conventional implicatures > Nonconventional implicatures	
Conventional implicatures	
Time 1	refusals = routines
Time 2 and 3	refusals > routines

Note. A > B: Accuracy score of A is greater than that of B.

A = B: Accuracy score of A is equal with that of B.

Response times

Conventional implicatures < Nonconventional implicatures	
Conventional implicatures	
Time 1	refusals = routines
Time 2 & 3	refusals < routines

Note. A < B: Response time of A is shorter than that of B.

Notes: Because the analysis required three statistical comparisons (indirect refusals, routines and nonconventional implicatures), alpha level was adjusted to 0.017 using the Bonferroni correction. The results are based on the adjusted alpha level.

implicatures (i.e. indirect refusals and routines) were at the same level of difficulty and they were both easier and faster to comprehend for the students than nonconventional implicatures. As time progressed, indirect refusals became easier and faster to comprehend than routines. Nonconventional implicatures remained the most difficult of all throughout the period.

Patterns and Rate of Development in Pragmatic Comprehension

Figures 4.1 and 4.2 display changes in comprehension accuracy scores over time.

Repeated-measures ANOVA were applied to compare accuracy scores and response times across the three time points. There was a significant gain in accuracy scores for both item types: $F = 53.38$ ($p = 0.000$, $\eta 2 = 0.70$) for conventional implicatures, and $F = 7.00$ ($p = 0.000$, $\eta 2 = 0.24$) for nonconventional implicatures. Significant gain was also detected for each subcategory of the conventional implicatures: $F = 32.92$ ($p = 0.000$, $\eta 2 = 0.59$) for indirect refusals, and $F = 35.51$ ($p = 0.000$, $\eta 2 = 0.61$) for routines. Hence, learners made significant progress in comprehending speakers' implied intentions over time, regardless the degree of conventionality involved in the items. However, when effect sizes were compared, the increase was almost three times larger for the conventional implicatures than for the nonconventional implicatures.

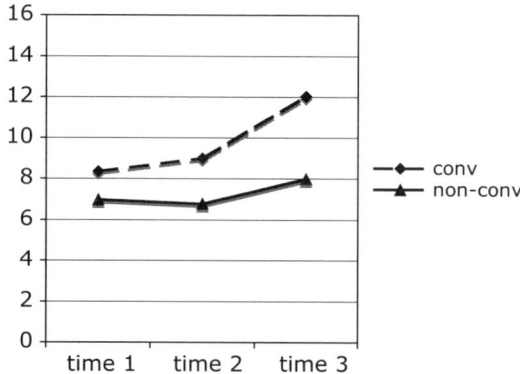

Figure 4.1 Changes in PLT accuracy scores, conventional and nonconventional implicatures

Post hoc analyses were conducted to find the differences in accuracy scores between Time 1–2 and Time 2–3. See Table 4.4 for the summary.

Significant gains in accuracy were identified during the second half of the study period (Time 2–3). Such gains were not identified in the first half (Time 1–2), with the exception of comprehension of indirect refusals, which showed an incremental, even-paced score increase over time. In the initial period, learners demonstrated little gain in their comprehension of nonconventional implicatures and routines, but they showed gain in the later period. The degree of gain was strong, particularly for routines, marking an increase of two points in average. These findings suggest that the effect of time did not kick in immediately for routines and nonconventional implicatures. Learners needed longer than three months to register measurable gains in these two areas. In contrast, their development of the comprehension of refusals began immediately, and the pace paralleled that of the learners' listening proficiency measured by TOEFL. Learners improved their TOEFL

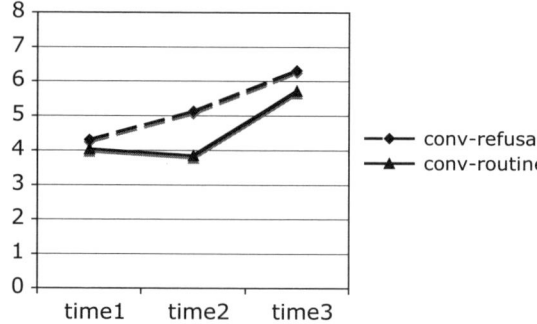

Figure 4.2 Changes in PLT accuracy scores, indirect refusals and routines

TABLE 4.4 Post hoc analyses of PLT accuracy scores between time points

| | Differences | |
	Time 1–2	Time 2–3
Conventional implicatures	*n.s.*	$t = -9.06*$
Indirect refusals	$t = -3.50*$	$t = -6.00*$
Routines	*n.s.*	$t = -7.80*$
Nonconventional implicatures	*n.s.*	$t = -3.58*$

Note: $*p < 0.017$. The results are based on the paired-sample *t*-test.

listening scores at every time junctures, mean = 44.60 (SD = 3.13) at Time 1, mean = 50.23 (SD = 2.97) at Time 2 and mean = 52.21 (SD = 2.87) at Time 3, and the score differences were all statistically significant. Hence, it seemed that, as general listening skill improved, so did learners' ability to comprehend indirect refusals. There was indeed a significant correlation between TOEFL scores and accuracy scores of indirect refusal items, $r = 0.53$ ($p = 0.000$), while such a correlation was absent between TOEFL and nonconventional implicatures ($r = 0.12, p = 0.43$).

Changes in response times are displayed in Figures 4.3 and 4.4. A significant decrease in response times was found for the nonconventional implicatures, $F = 9.04$ ($p = 0.000, \eta2 = 0.29$), and post hoc analyses detected the change only in the second time period (Time 2–3), $t = 2.59$ ($p = 0.000$): There was no decrease of response times in the first time period (Time 1–2) ($t = 1.83, p = 0.07$). Conventional implicatures also showed the significant decrease in response times, but the decrease occurred at Time 1–2 ($t = 2.81, p = 0.007$), not at Time 2–3 ($t = 0.89, p = 0.38$).

The significant drop in response times for conventional implicatures at Time 1–2 was largely due to the decrease in the response times for indirect

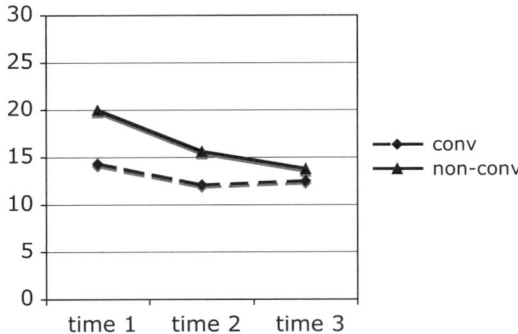

Figure 4.3 Changes in PLT response times, conventional and nonconventional implicatures

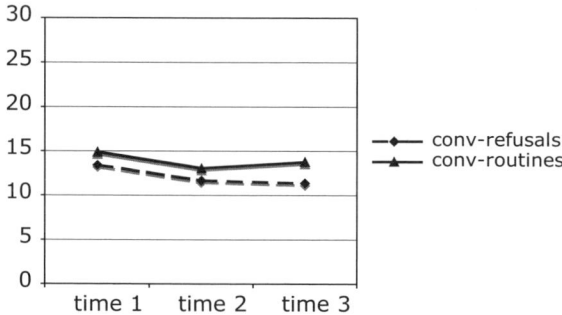

Figure 4.4 Changes in PLT response times, indirect refusals and routines

TABLE 4.5 Post hoc analyses of PLT response times between time points

	Differences	
	Time 1–2	Time 2–3
Conventional implicatures	$t = 2.81*$	n.s.
Indirect refusals	$t = 2.39*$	n.s.
Routines	n.s.	n.s.
Nonconventional implicatures	n.s.	$t = 2.59*$

Notes: *$p < 0.017$. The results are based on the paired-sample t-test.

refusal items. The nonconventional implicatures noted an opposite pattern: response times remained the same in the initial period, but dropped later at Time 2–3. Hence, for this item type, both accuracy and comprehension speed were found to develop later, showing progress at later time period rather than initially.

Table 4.5 shows post hoc analyses of differences in response times for each time period.

Summary and Interpretations of the Findings for Pragmatic Comprehension

This study revealed an interaction between implicature type, comprehension difficulty and the development of pragmatic comprehension. Conventional and nonconventional implicatures were clearly ordered by difficulty level, with conventional implicatures being easier and faster to comprehend than their nonconventional counterparts. In particular, comprehension of indirect refusals was the easiest and fastest to process for the learners: they showed a profound development over a relatively short period of three months, and continued to develop throughout the rest of the study period. The conventionality encoded in this item type probably assisted learners' comprehension and further facilitated their development. The learners were able to draw on their knowledge of convention of normative patterns of refusal, that is, giving a reason for refusal, in order to correctly identify the speaker's refusal intention. As this discourse pattern was shared between L1 Japanese and L2 English, they were able to transfer their L1-based convention to L2 comprehension and made further progress as their general listening ability improved over time.

These patterns found in this study are also supported by the pragmatic theories of utterance comprehension and inferencing. According to Relevance Theory (Sperber & Wilson, 1995), communication is achieved by decoding linguistic stimuli, as well as by interpreting contextual cues and using them as evidence toward the correct inferencing of speaker intentions. This process draws on the relation between context and processing effort. Humans process information as productively as possible. When people interpret a message, many different assumptions from diverse sources come to mind. Among the assumptions, they select the most relevant interpretation that has the greatest contextual effects for the smallest processing effort. Processing effort is determined in three dimensions: utterance complexity, size of context and accessibility of the context.

Conventionality is one of the factors that could reduce processing effort. When implicatures convey conventional meaning, that is, when speaker intentions are linguistically coded or embedded within predictable, fixed patterns of discourse, the listener may not attend to many contextual cues such as background knowledge, mutual understanding or flow of discourse, consequently reducing the processing effort. Some indirect speech acts are a more conventionalized form of implicatures because of certain syntactic forms or language use patterns that are available for them. For instance, the linguistic form 'Could you' + verb is often used when one is making a request (Blum-Kulka et al., 1989). When refusing someone's invitation, it is customary that one provides a reason for not accepting the invitation (Beebe et al., 1990; Nelson et al., 2002). Morgan (1978) called indirect speech acts 'short-circuited implicatures', meaning they are types of implicature that do not require extensive inferencing: listeners understand the intended meaning based on the conventions of language and language use, and they do not have to process a large number of contextual cues. Indirect refusals are one type of the 'short-circuited implicatures' in which the speakers' intentions are more easily inferred from the normative pattern of conversational exchange or from what is expected in the 'next turn' – giving an excuse when refusing.

Facilitated by this universal convention, EFL learners in this study were able to comprehend indirect refusals faster and better overall, compared with the other item types. An increase in accuracy and a decrease in response times of this item type were detected in the first three-month period. While the gain in accuracy was maintained in the second period, response times stayed the same in Time 2–3, suggesting that the developmental scaling for the accurate comprehension of this item type is different from that of the speedy processing of these items. Larger time intervals might be necessary to capture the development of the fluency aspect of comprehension than the accuracy, at least for indirect refusals.

Compared with the strong gain found in indirect refusal items, gains with routines, the other type of conventional items, were less impressive. There was no significant gain in accuracy scores or response times in the first time period. Significant gains in accuracy were found only in the second period, but response times remained the same throughout the period. The findings indicate that the nature of conventionality encoded in the refusals and routines is different, and the difference manifested as distinct developmental patterns of pragmatic comprehension. Compared with refusals, routines have stronger associations with specific situations or communicative functions. For instance, the phrase 'For here or to go?' occurs in a service encounter situation of buying food, and the meaning is fixed across similar situations. The phrase 'Here you go' is uttered when giving something to someone, and the form–function correspondence remains the same across situations. Conventionality encoded in routines can be explained by the concept of 'frames' or schemata (van Dijk, 1977). Frames constitute the hierarchical organizing principle that relates purposes of utterances to contextual states. For instance, the expression 'How can I help you?' symbolizes a function of offering help that takes place within the frame of shopping. As a highly conventionalized situation, shopping calls for this linguistic expression, and comprehension of the expression depends on whether one is familiar with sociocultural rules and conventions of this frame. When there is a great degree of familiarity, the expression is understood as formulaic. Consequently, comprehension of illocution becomes easier and takes less time. This fixedness and invariant nature of the routines typically assists our comprehension because they are processed as a chunk rather than a series of isolated words. Meaning is thus immediately retrievable from long-term memory, as long as people are aware of the forms and their contextual requirements.

Despite these comprehension advantages involved in routines, the EFL learners studied here showed little development in accuracy or response times in the first three-month period. Significant gain was found at the second period, but only for the accuracy. Several reasons can account for the slow-developing nature of the routine items. First, the EFL learners studied here were not so familiar with the target routine expressions. Due to the highly situation-dependent, culture-specific nature of the routines, they were probably not able to pick them up naturally in a foreign language environment that is limited in the situations where routines occur. As the frames that organize the target routines were not abundant in the learners' surroundings, it took a longer time for them to learn and accumulate the routine expressions. Without the knowledge of higher-order frames, learners had to use both top-down and bottom-up processing in which they analyzed syntax and lexical information as well as contextual information to comprehend meaning, consequently slowing down the overall comprehension speed.

Another reason for the late-developing nature of the routines is due to the format of the instrument used in this study. This study used multiple-choice questions to measure learners' comprehension ability. The task required learners to listen to a conversation in which the target routine expression was embedded, and to choose the option that was correct according to the content of the conversation. The correct answer was a paraphrasing of the routine expression. See the example below.

Son: Hey Mom, this is the birthday gift I want you to open.
Mother: Oh, is this from you Steve? This is a pretty package. When did
              you have a chance to wrap this?
Son: Last night. At home.
Mother: Look at this. A pair of gloves. <u>That's so sweet of you.</u>

(1) Mother thanked Steve for the gloves. (CORRECT)
(2) Mother didn't like the gloves much.
(3) Mother likes sweets.
(4) Mother wrapped the gift at home.

In this gift-giving/receiving situation, the target routine is the last utterance by the mother, 'That's so sweet of you.' This is a type of functional routine that is tied with one, invariant function (Röver, 2005), in this case, the function of 'thanking' or 'expressing appreciation.' In order to be able to identify the correct statement (Option 1), learners have to pay attention to the specifics of the conversation – settings, topic of conversation and flow of the discourse – including the meaning of the target routine, and match them up with the four answer options one by one, comparing and contrasting them, then select the one that is correct according to the content of dialog. This is a demanding task because if learners miss the target routine, or if they hear it incorrectly, they will not be able to identify the correct option. All information packaged in the dialogs other than the target routine is potentially distracting. Hence, the correct identification of routines in this study requires a precise understanding of the target expression and the ability to focus on the expression by ruling out irrelevant cues. Because of this demand at multiple levels, the comprehension of routines in the format measured in this study took longer time than the comprehension of indirect refusals.

This interpretation is supported by the results of a retrospective verbal interview conducted with a subset of 12 participants. One notable tendency gleaned from the interview data is that the participants were much more verbose about their decision making when comprehending routines than indirect refusals. Learners verbalized very few strategies when comprehending refusals.

For example, in item 37, a woman refused a man's invitation to the movies by saying, 'I don't feel that great.' All participants responded only that the woman does not want to go to the movie because she is sick. They did not utilize many strategies for understanding the illocutionary intent of refusals, probably because they were embedded in conventional, easily recognizable contexts.

In sharp contrast, routine items evoked a number of inferential strategies. In the example item above (the gift-giving conversation), I found that learners were paying attention to a variety of contextual cues before arriving at the correct interpretation of the target routine (Option 1). Here is the sample excerpt of verbal protocol:

Learner #28 (EAP Level 2, female)

I think the answer is Option 1 (Mother thanked Steve for the gloves) because she sounded pleased at the end. She said 'sweet.' Also, other options don't apply. The mother didn't say that she didn't like gloves (Option 2). Steve did the wrapping, not the mother (Option 4).

I asked this participant whether she knows the exact meaning of the target routine, 'That's so sweet of you.' She said no, and she was not able to translate it into Japanese, but she indicated that the word 'sweet' has a positive connotation. This example shows that the comprehension process of routine items, given in the format of the PLT used here, was strategic – learners relied on their memories, retrieving details of the conversation and measuring them up with each answer option so they could eliminate those that did not fit with what they heard and understood. Arriving at the correct option was a process of purging irrelevant information. The precise understanding of the target routine could even be absent: learners could still identify the correct option by attending a range of linguistic and contextual cues encoded in the conversation, not restricted to the target routine. For this particular item, out of the 12 interview participants, seven chose the correct option, yet none of them relied solely on the target expression when making a decision. In fact, only three mentioned the target routine, among other cues. As shown in the excerpt below, multiple contextual cues, including linguistic information, common sense knowledge and the target routine expression, were equally accessible and salient to the student:

Learner #40 (EAP Level 2, female)

The answer is Option 1. The son gave a present to his mother. Option 2 is out because mothers usually don't feel bad about receiving a gift from their son. Also, she didn't say that. Option 3 is out because she didn't say 'sweets.' And the son did the wrapping, not mother (Option 4). At the end, she said 'sweet of you.' It means, 'You did a nice thing.'

Due to the greater number of cues to be processed, the amount of 'work' involved in the comprehension of routines was greater than that of indirect refusals in which the cue of normative response (i.e. giving a reason for refusal) was so salient that the learners did not have to focus on other pieces of information. These observations also explain the nonsignificant development of comprehension speed found in routines. Learners showed gains in accuracy, but response times remained the same for the entire period.

In summary, this study revealed distinct patterns of development between routines and indirect refusals due to the different nature of conventionality involved. When meaning is based on shared conventions, it is easier and faster to comprehend. This is not only because it poses fewer processing demands, but also because it allows the successful transfer of pragmatic knowledge from L1, as shown in the comprehension of indirect refusals. Learners' comprehension of refusals improved greatly over time because, as they became accustomed to the target language input and their listening proficiency improved, they became more efficient in using their L1-based inferential skills in listening to understand the relevance of the indirect refusals. However, when the convention is culture specific, or not shared between L1 and L2, as in the routine expressions, meaning becomes difficult to recognize for the learners. This was shown in this study when the learners' comprehension of routines did not show any gains during the first semester. The linguistic conventions encoded in the routines were not salient enough to improve their comprehension speed, as seen in the marginal decrease in response times in both the first and second time periods.

Similar to routines, nonconventional implicatures were also found to be both difficult to comprehend and late-developing for the learners: there was no gain in accuracy and comprehension speed in the first time period but only a marginal gain in the second period. The nonconventional implicatures in this study involved utterances used to express opinions or provide information in a nonliteral manner. Different from conventional implicatures, they were context dependent and did not involve fixed linguistic forms of routines or customized discourse patterns of refusals. They were idiosyncratic and required learners to make inferences from the overall context of a conversation, beyond understanding the target indirect utterance. Findings of this study suggest that the ability to comprehend nonconventional implicatures does not develop as quickly as conventional ones due to the extensive inferential bridge that learners have to use to arrive at correct interpretations. Without constant symbolic representations, the comprehension of nonconventional implicatures relies more on word-by-word bottom-up processing, such as the analysis of syntactic and lexical information, or that of a number of contextual cues. Using these analyses, learners must understand the literal meaning of the expressions first, and then work deductively toward the speakers' implied intentions. Multiple levels of processing add to the greater degree of inferencing that learners must go through, thereby increasing difficulty and slowing down their processing speed.

These observations are supported by the comparison of the comprehension speed between nonconventional implicatures and routines. Although the accuracy rate was the same, the comprehension speed was faster for the routines than for the nonconventional implicatures. The findings suggest that, although the linguistic conventions encoded in the routines were unfamiliar and difficult to access for the EFL learners, once they understood the conventions, they were able to derive meaning quickly by taking advantage of the linguistic conventions. Nonconventional implicatures, on the other hand, did not have such an advantage on comprehension speed.

A more extensive inferencing involved in the comprehension of nonconventional implicatures was also evident in the learners' introspective verbal interviews. The learners reported using a variety of strategies during the task of inferencing. Interviews revealed the types of contextual and cognitive cues that were most immediately accessible to them when determining the relevance of implicit input. One common strategy in the comprehension of nonconventional implicatures was the use of para-linguistic cues. Out of 36 verbal protocols (three nonconventional implicature items × 12 participants), 18 included a mention of the speaker's tone of voice and intonation. There was no mention of these cues in the comprehension of conventional implicatures. See the example excerpt below:

Mary: Hi Kevin.
Kevin: Mary you're late today.
Mary: Yeah, I got on a train, and then realized I left my bag at home. Did I miss something?
Kevin: No, ah, we were just talking about getting a new coffee maker for the office.
          Don't you want a new one with timer?
Mary: I'm happy with ours.

(1) Mary is interested in a new coffee maker.
(2) Mary is happy today.
(3) Mary left her bag in the bus.
(4) Mary doesn't care for a new coffee maker. (CORRECT)

Learner #46 (EAP Level 2, female)

The answer is Option 4. At the end the woman said 'happy' or something, but ... Her tone of voice indicates that she is not so willing. And I think I also heard 'well'. I imagined that she is fine with the one they have.

This learner was not able to articulate the target utterance (the last utterance in the dialogue), but she noticed the sign of hesitation in the speaker's voice and related it to a negative meaning. Hence, she was able to correctly infer the answer through the speaker's intonation.

Although late-developing, successful comprehension of nonconventional implicatures did eventually take place for the learners, indicating that such competence does develop naturally as learners are exposed to input and as they gain competence in general listening ability. As the EFL learners in this study did not receive any classroom instructions targeted at their inferential skills in listening (see Chapter 1 for descriptions of EAP listening class), the small but significant gain they made in this area at Time 2–3 could be attributed to their ability to transfer their L1-based inferential skills to L2 comprehension of implied meaning as their listening proficiency developed over time. Another potential factor for development is the transfer of training. Being a different modality, the inferential strategies that they practiced in their EAP reading class – for instance, making inferences about the writer's point and guessing vocabulary meaning in context – might have assisted their comprehension of nonconventional implicatures. While these skills are different from the pragmatic inferencing that involves deductive processing based on Gricean maxims and contextual cues, they are similar in that they involve the processing of nonstraightforward meaning, and thus are transferable to pragmatic listening.

Another factor that might have contributed to the gain is classroom input that involves nonliteral comprehension. Class observation notes revealed a number of jokes and sarcastic comments presented in a classroom. See example below from an EAP writing class (November, 2008):

(1) **Teacher:** 'Cafeteria food in this university is _____.' What do you put in the blank to make it a startling statement?

(2) **Students:** [silence]

(3) **Teacher:** I think everybody is worried about saying a bad thing about cafeteria food. I don't think anyone here is working at cafeteria.

(4) **Students:** [laugh]

(5) **Teacher:** Haruko, what do you think?

(6) **Haruko:** Cafeteria food is my lifeline to survive this busy school life.

(7) **Teacher:** Wow, this is startling because someone has a good opinion about the cafeteria food.

(8) **Students:** [laugh]

(9) **Teacher:** To make it more startling, you can say, 'Cafeteria food is the most delicious food I have ever had.'

(10) **Students:** [laugh]

In this interaction, the teacher was being sarcastic about the cafeteria food. He was soliciting students' comments about the food to complete the sentence in a way that was startling (line 1). The students' laughter in line 4 indicates that they were aware of the teacher's negative opinion of the cafeteria food as well as his intention in soliciting the discussion about it. In contrast to the teacher's intention, Haruko, in line 6, made a positive comment about the cafeteria food. In response, the teacher once again used sarcasm and told to the class that it was indeed startling to hear something positive about the cafeteria food. The teacher was sarcastic yet again in line 9. The students' laughter in line 8 and again in line 10 indicates that they understood the teacher's use of sarcasm and its nonliteral meaning.

The following examples of classroom jokes illustrate similar instances because they require contextual information in order to understand their meaning. In the first excerpt below, the teacher's comment on Shoko and Yosuke had an underlying meaning that their missing class together was probably not a coincidence because they were boyfriend and girlfriend. Students picked up the implied meaning and laughed at his joke in line 2.

(1) **Teacher:**   I just noticed that both Shoko and Yosuke are absent. I'm not quick on the uptake.
(2) **Students:** [laugh]

Below is another example of joking. Following a silent response to the question, the teacher jokes in line 3 that she can hear snow falling outside. The students laughed at the joke in line 4 because they knew what it meant: nobody was responding to the question.

(1) **Teacher:**   What are the three major rhetorical modes?
(2) **Students:** [silence]
(3) **Teacher:**   I can almost hear the snow.
(4) **Students:** [laugh]
(5) **Teacher:**   You guys are quiet.

These observations of classroom discourse and student–teacher interactions revealed that opportunities to comprehend indirect meaning were abundant in class, taking a form of jokes, sarcasm and nonliteral communication that assumed a shared context and background knowledge between teachers and students. The students were able to pick up the underlying meanings as shown in their reactions (e.g. laughter). Hence, it is possible that the accumulation of experiences with nonliteral communication in naturalistic classroom input has contributed to the slow, but significant, development of comprehension of nonconventional implicatures, despite the absence of direct, focused instruction and practice of them in the classroom.

In summary, pragmatic comprehension involves a simultaneous calculation of three layers of meaning: the linguistic meaning based on the structure of language, the conventional meaning based on the norms of how language is typically used and the intended meaning based on the context of the discourse. The perceived comprehension difficulty is based on the degree of the processing effort required in each of these three layers. Some of this effort is monotonic, due to the strong signal present in the input, but some of this effort is nonmonotonic and requires the combination of inference processes. The strength of signals is determined in part by the level of conventionality. This study found that the conventional pattern of interaction in indirect refusals had a relative edge over the linguistic conventions of routines, as shown in the learners' immediate gains in the former but not in the latter. The absence of conventionality slows down the development even more, as found in the slow progress of comprehending nonconventional implicatures. While the lack of conventionality might have slowed down the development of this item type, qualitative data revealed frequent instances of nonliteral communication in classroom discourse, which might have contributed to the small, slow and yet significant gain in the comprehension of nonconventional implicatures in the later period.

Findings for Pragmatic Production

Effect of Situation Type on Pragmatic Production[1]

Tables 4.6 through 4.9 display descriptive statistics of four aspects of speech act production (requests and opinions combined) analyzed in this study: appropriateness scores, grammaticality scores, planning time and speech rate. There was a large discrepancy between low- and high-imposition speech acts in all three measures at all time points. (See Appendix D for the situations.) Low-imposition speech acts were easier and faster to produce and took less

TABLE 4.6 Descriptive statistics, PST appropriateness scores

	Mean	SD	Min.	Max.
Low-imposition speech acts				
Time 1	3.88	1.02	1.25	5.00
Time 2	4.08	0.46	2.38	4.75
Time 3	4.73	0.31	3.50	5.00
High-imposition speech acts				
Time 1	2.63	0.64	1.00	4.00
Time 2	2.71	0.50	1.75	4.25
Time 3	3.13	0.48	2.13	4.25

Notes. Low- and high-imposition situations included speech acts of requests and opinions combined. Appropriateness was assessed on a five-point scale ranging from 1 to 5. See Appendix F for the copy of the rating scale.

TABLE 4.7 Descriptive statistics, PST grammaticality scores

	Mean	SD	Min.	Max.
Low-imposition speech acts				
Time 1	3.77	0.64	2.50	5.00
Time 2	4.04	0.42	3.25	5.00
Time 3	4.26	0.45	3.50	5.00
High-imposition speech acts				
Time 1	3.46	0.44	2.50	5.00
Time 2	3.79	0.43	3.00	4.75
Time 3	3.86	0.42	3.00	4.88

Notes: Grammaticality was assessed on a five-point scale ranging from 1 to 5. See Appendix E for the copy of the rating scale.

time to prepare than high-imposition speech acts. As this tendency was similar in native speaker data, it seemed that these two situation types were distinctively different in terms of their cognitive and psychological demands.

Indeed, the paired-sample *t*-test revealed that the situational differences were statistically significant for all variables at all time points. Hence, results confirmed that low-imposition speech acts were easier to produce, both pragmatically and grammatically, and took less time to plan and articulate than high-imposition speech acts. These tendencies remained the same for the entire study period. Although the gap between the two situation types was largest for the appropriateness score, it was smallest for the grammaticality score, suggesting the relatively small impact of situation type on accuracy of speech act production.

TABLE 4.8 Descriptive statistics, PST planning time

	Mean	SD	Min.	Max.
Low-imposition speech acts				
Time 1	48.13	14.80	22.63	90.31
Time 2	43.13	11.40	21.93	97.22
Time 3	33.32	9.79	16.32	68.62
NS	20.10	7.36	8.09	36.68
High-imposition speech acts				
Time 1	63.04	20.72	27.27	124.28
Time 2	53.43	14.96	17.50	107.29
Time 3	41.87	13.26	17.27	86.60
NS	28.09	13.89	8.70	62.26

Notes. Planning time = average number of seconds taken to prepare for each speech act. NS = native speakers (*n* = 24).[3]

TABLE 4.9 Descriptive statistics, PST speech rate

	Mean	SD	Min.	Max.
Low-imposition speech acts				
Time 1	84.03	23.36	44.89	139.96
Time 2	92.45	19.94	56.10	153.35
Time 3	90.23	22.37	48.65	157.64
NS	167.92	31.30	117.62	236.55
High-imposition speech acts				
Time 1	72.86	18.66	36.62	117.34
Time 2	78.17	19.95	37.73	143.92
Time 3	83.40	17.99	52.41	140.85
NS	158.96	24.10	119.15	206.32

Notes. Speech rate refers to the average number of words spoken per minute.
NS = native speakers ($n = 24$)

When subcategories of each speech act type were compared, high-imposition requests and opinions showed no significant difference on any of the measures at any time point, except for the appropriateness score at Time 3 ($t = 4.10$, $p = 0.001$). Hence, in the high-imposition situations, requests and opinions were in general at equal levels of difficulty and took about the same amount of time to plan and to produce. However, the significant difference in the appropriateness scores detected at the end suggests that learners' progress was faster for requests than opinions, but this tendency was found only in the appropriateness.

Comparisons between low-imposition requests and opinions, on the other hand, revealed somewhat different patterns. These two situation speech acts did not differ on appropriateness score or planning time, and this tendency remained consistent over time. Significant difference was found with grammaticality and speech rate in favor of requests, at all time points. Relative ease of low-imposition requests than opinions in these two aspects is probably due to the formulaic nature of the low-imposition requests used in this study. When asking a friend for a pen, we typically use conventional expressions such as 'Can I borrow a pen?' or 'Do you have a pen I can borrow?' Similarly, when we miss what someone has said, it is common to use a routine formula such as 'Say it again?' or 'Pardon?' Due to the relative fixedness of these routine expressions, learners were probably able to retrieve them as a chunk from long-term memory, without going through grammatical analysis. For the same reason, once retrieved as an unanalyzed unit, the expressions were articulated fluently without attending to individual words and phrases. In contrast, low-imposition opinions are much more idiosyncratic, consisting of multiple linguistic expressions and semantic moves. For instance, when expressing a negative opinion about someone's clothes, we could use a myriad of strategies: we could preface the negative comment with a minor compliment (e.g. 'It's all right, but ...'), or we might make a suggestion for alternatives (e.g. 'How about another color?'). This less restricted nature of opinion expressions probably led to slower speech rates and lower grammaticality, because learners had to construct novel utterances from scratch, rather than retrieving them from memory.

However, whether retrieved from memory or constructed from rule, planning time (the amount of time spent reading situational scenarios and preparing for speech acts) was the same between requests and opinions. This is probably because situational factors were the same between the two speech acts, both involving a conversation on a mundane topic between people of equal status. The length and linguistic difficulty of the descriptions were also the same. As a result, the actual amount of time required for reading and understanding the scenarios, as well as for searching for appropriate expressions to match the situations, did not differ between requests and opinions. See Table 4.10 for a summary of the order of difficulty among situation types and speech act types found in this study.

Patterns and Rate of Development in Pragmatic Production

Figures 4.5 through 4.8 display changes in appropriateness scores, grammaticality scores, planning time and speech rate in pragmatic production. The changes are plotted separately for low- and high-imposition speech acts.

Over time, there was a gain in all aspects of pragmatic production. Repeated-measures ANOVA revealed a significant gain in appropriateness scores for the low-imposition speech acts: $F = 73.83$ ($p = 0.000$, $\eta2 = 0.77$), and the difference was significant at all time contrasts: $t = -3.42$ ($p = 0.001$) between Time 1 and 2, and $t = -10.46$ ($p = 0.000$) between Time 2 and 3. High-imposition speech acts also showed significant gains, $F = 16.56$, $p = 0.000$ ($\eta2 = 0.42$), but the gain was detected only in the second period, between Time 2 and 3 ($t = -4.84$, $p = 0.000$). There was no gain from Time 1 to 2 ($t = -0.26$, $p = 0.78$). Hence, appropriate production of high-imposition speech acts was found to be slow-developing. In contrast, low-imposition speech acts showed a steady, even-paced gain over time increments, and the development kicked in immediately in the first time period.

As for the grammaticality of speech acts, there was a significant gain over time for the low-imposition speech acts: $F = 9.21$ ($p = 0.000$, $\eta2 = 0.29$), and the gains were detected at all time contrasts: $t = -2.34$ ($p = 0.024$) between Time 1 and 2, and $t = -2.87$ ($p = 0.006$) between Time 2 and 3. The grammaticality score of high-imposition speech acts also showed a significant overall gain, $F = 11.42$, $p = 0.000$ ($\eta2 = 0.34$), but the gain was detected for Time 1–2 ($t = -3.74$, $p = 0.000$) and not for Time 2–3 ($t = -67$, $p = 0.52$). Hence, similar to appropriateness, the grammaticality of speech acts showed a steady, incremental development across three

TABLE 4.10 Summary of order of difficulty in pragmatic production

Appropriateness

Low-imposition speech acts > High-imposition speech acts

Low-imposition speech acts:

| Time 1, 2 and 3 | requests = opinions |

High-imposition speech acts:

| Time 1 and 2 | requests = opinions |
| Time 3 | requests > opinions |

Notes. A > B: Appropriateness score of A is greater than that of B.

A = B: Appropriateness score of A is equal to that of B.

Grammaticality

Low-imposition speech acts > High-imposition speech acts

Low-imposition speech acts:

| Time 1, 2 and 3 | requests > opinions |

High-imposition speech acts:

| Time 1, 2 and 3 | requests = opinions |

Notes. A > B: Grammar score of A is greater than that of B.

A = B: Grammar score of A is equal to that of B.

Planning time

Low-imposition speech acts < High-imposition speech acts

Low-imposition speech acts:

| Time 1, 2 and 3 | requests = opinions |

High-imposition speech acts:

| Time 1, 2 and 3 | requests = opinions |

Notes. A < B: Planning time of A is shorter than that of B.

A = B: Planning time of A is equal to that of B.

Speech rate

Low-imposition speech acts > High-imposition speech acts

Low-imposition speech acts:

| Time 1, 2 and 3 | requests > opinions |

High-imposition speech acts:

| Time 1, 2 and 3 | requests = opinions |

Notes. A > B: Speech rate of A is faster than that of B.

A = B: Speech rate of A is equal to that of B.

Notes. Because the analysis required two statistical comparisons (low- and high-imposition speech acts), alpha level was adjusted to 0.025 using the Bonferroni correction. The results are based on the adjusted alpha level

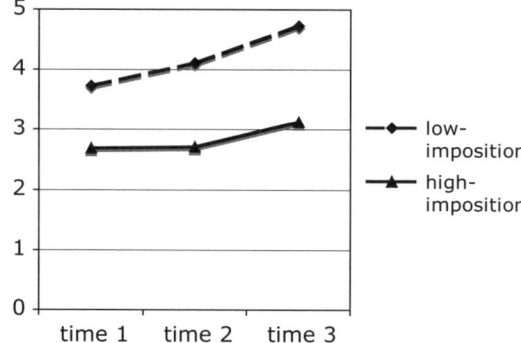

Figure 4.5 Changes in PST appropriateness scores, low- and high-imposition speech acts

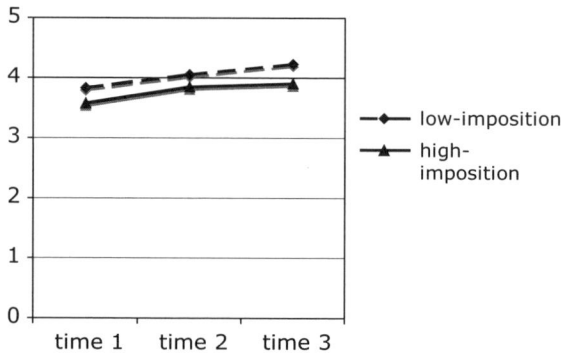

Figure 4.6 Changes in PST grammaticality scores, low- and high-imposition speech acts

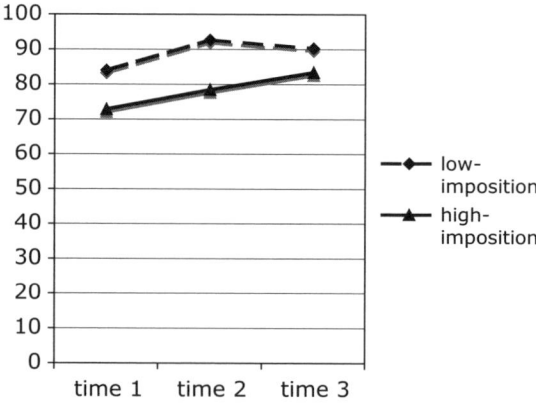

Figure 4.7 Changes in PST speech rate, low- and high-imposition speech acts

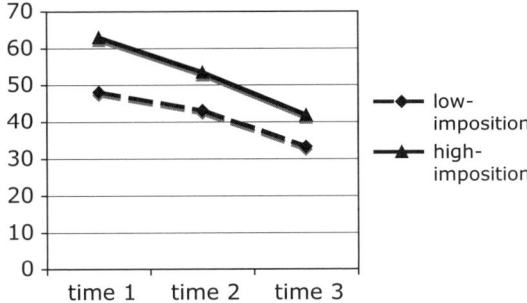

Figure 4.8 Changes in PST planning time, low- and high-imposition speech acts

time points for the low-imposition speech acts but not for the high-imposition speech acts.

Similar to the grammaticality scores, planning speed showed a profound development over time regardless of the situation type. Repeated-measures ANOVA revealed a significant effect of time on low-imposition planning time, $F = 25.93$, $p = 0.000$ ($\eta2 = 0.54$), and the gain was significant in all time contrasts: $t = -2.69$ ($p = 0.010$) for Time 1–2, and $t = -6.35$ ($p = 0.000$) for Time 2–3. The pattern was exactly the same for the high-imposition speech acts. Planning time differed significantly across time points, $F = 34.51$, $p = 0.006$ ($\eta2 = 0.61$), and the difference was detected at all time contrasts: $t = -3.15$ ($p = 0.003$) for Time 1–2 and $t = -6.14$ ($p = 0.000$) for Time 2–3. Hence, despite the cognitive and psychological demand involved in the high-imposition speech acts, the EFL learners' ability to prepare for these speech acts quickly improved over time.

The speech rate showed slightly different patterns of development. There was an overall impact of time on the low-imposition speech rate, $F = 4.33$, $p = 0.019$ ($\eta2 = 0.16$), and a significant difference was detected between Time 1 and 2 ($t = -2.93$, $p = 0.005$) but not between Time 2 and 3 ($t = -0.77$, $p = 0.45$). This pattern was the same for the high-imposition speech acts. Speech rates differed significantly across time, $F = 11.63$, $p = 0.000$ ($\eta2 = 0.34$), but the difference was found only at Time 1–2 ($t = -2.64$, $p = 0.011$), and not at Time 2–3 ($t = -2.11$, $p = 0.041$). Hence, we can conclude that the speech rate became faster in the first time period but stagnated in the second period. However, the borderline probability of error for the high-imposition speech acts suggests that there was some tendency for gain in speech rates in the second period. See Table 4.11 for a summary of the post hoc analyses.

In summary, this study revealed different developmental patterns and rates among functions and attributes in pragmatic production. Situational variables (low- vs. high-imposition) affected the gain in the appropriateness scores of production. Over time the EFL students showed a solid gain in the low-imposition speech acts, demonstrating an almost perfect score at

TABLE 4.11 Post hoc analyses of PST measures between time points

	Differences	
	Time 1–2	Time 2–3
Low-imposition speech acts		
Appropriateness	$t = -3.42^*$	$t = -10.46^*$
Grammaticality	$t = -2.34^*$	$t = -2.87^*$
Planning time	$t = -2.69^*$	$t = -6.35^*$
Speech rate	$t = -2.93^*$	n.s.
High-imposition speech acts		
Appropriateness	n.s.	$t = -4.84^*$
Grammaticality	$t = -3.74^*$	n.s.
Planning time	$t = -3.15^*$	$t = -6.14^*$
Speech rate	$t = -2.64^*$	n.s.

Notes. $^*p < 0.025$. The results are based on the paired-sample t-test.

Time 3. The absence of gain in the first time period for the high-imposition speech acts tells us that the effect of 'time' did not kick in at early stage, probably because of the pragmalinguistic sophistication required for these speech acts. Similarly, the situational variable somewhat constrained the grammaticality gains. Unlike low-imposition speech acts that showed incremental development at every time juncture, grammaticality in high-imposition speech acts showed a strong initial gain, but this gain was not sustained in the later period. The average score at Time 3 was 3.86 out of 5.00, lower than the average of low-imposition speech acts (mean = 4.26). The results indicate that, similar to the appropriateness, the accurate production of high-imposition speech acts takes a longer time to develop.

In sharp contrast, the situational variable had no effect on gains in planning speed or speech rate. Regardless of situation type, the EFL learners in this study showed significant, steady progress in planning speed. Over time, they became able to read and understand situational descriptions quickly and react to them without delay. This promptness kept improving at every measurement point. Similarly, the speech rate marked a large gain regardless of situation type, but this gain was found only initially. Later, the rate plateaued – there was no growth in the second period. It seems that, compared with planning time, speech rate required a longer time to register a significant gain among the EFL learners studied here.

Analyses of Linguistics Expressions in Speech Acts

The relatively slow progress of high-imposition speech acts found in this study was probably due to the pragmalinguistic difficulty involved in these speech acts. To illustrate this, I conducted post hoc analyses of linguistic expressions of speech acts. All expressions of requests and opinions were categorized using a coding framework. (See Appendix H for a copy of the frameworks.) The frequencies of each expression type were tallied and compared in order to capture changes across time. The data were coded by four graduate students in the programs of Applied Linguistics, TESOL and Teaching Japanese as a Second Language. Intercorder agreement was 0.95. Native speaker data ($n = 24$) formed the baseline data.

Analyses of requests

Tables 4.12 and 4.13 present the frequency distributions of the request expressions for the two low-imposition situations: asking a friend for a pen and asking a friend to repeat what he/she has said. The coding framework was adapted from the previous literature (Blum-Kulka *et al.*, 1989; see Appendix H).

As shown in Table 4.12, a notable difference between EFL learners and native speakers was found in learners' use of imperatives with 'please' (e.g. 'Please lend me your pen.'). Almost 40% of the learners used this expression type, while none of the native speakers used this form. This syntactic

TABLE 4.12 Frequencies of request head acts, low-imposition situations

	EFL learners			NS
	Time 1	Time 2	Time 3	
(I) Direct expressions				
(1) Imperatives	37.5% (36)	35.4% (34)	28.7% (27)	0
(2) Performatives	0	0	0	0
(3) Obligation statements	0	0	0	0
(4) Want statements	4.2% (4)	3.1% (3)	3.2% (3)	0
(II) Indirect expressions				
(5) Preparatory questions	30.2% (29)	27.1% (26)	40.4% (38)	29.2% (14)
(6) Permissions	17.7% (17)	15.6% (15)	22.3% (21)	27.1% (13)
(7) Suggestions	0	0	0	0
(8) Mitigated expressions	0	0	0	0
(9) Hint	4.2% (4)	3.1% (3)	3.2% (3)	2.1% (1)
(III) Conventional questions	17.7% (17)	19.8% (19)	11.7% (11)	41.7% (20)

Notes. Numbers within parentheses show the raw counts. Frequency % was calculated by dividing the raw frequency by the total number of requests analyzed. There were 48 L2 learners at Time 1 and 2, and 47 at Time 3. There were 24 native speakers (NS). Each participant produced two low-imposition requests, and so the total number of EFL learners' requests analyzed was 96 at Time 1 and 2, and 94 at Time 3. The total number of native speaker requests was 48. See Appendix H for the coding framework.

TABLE 4.13 Frequencies of request modifications, low-imposition situations

	EFL learners			NS
	Time 1	Time 2	Time 3	
(1) Hedging	0	0	1.1% (1)	0
(2) Amplifier	0	0	0	0
(3) Reason	82.3% (79)	65.6% (63)	67.0% (63)	35.4% (17)
(4) Apology	32.3% (31)	35.4% (34)	38.3% (36)	27.1% (13)
(5) Preparator	3.1% (3)	1.0% (1)	0	0
(6) Confirmation	0	0	0	0
(7) Appreciation	1.0% (1)	0	2.1% (2)	4.2% (2)
(8) Request for suggestion	0	0	0	0
(9) Conditional	1.0% (1)	0	0	0
(10) External 'please'	5.2% (5)	2.1% (2)	3.2% (3)	8.3% (4)
(11) Other benefit/right	0	0	0	0
Total	125.0% (120)	104.2% (100)	111.7% (105)	75.0% (36)

Notes. The % greater than 100 means that more than one modification appeared per speech act. See Appendix H for the definition of each category.

form decreased over time to below 30% at Time 3, approximating the target pattern. This decrease occurred incrementally over time. Their progress was also seen through their gradual increase of preparatory question use (e.g. 'Could you lend me a pen?') and permission questions (e.g. 'May I borrow your pen?'). Both of these structures appeared fairly often in the native speaker data. However, there is one area where the learners made very little progress – the use of conventional questions, namely questions or statements with implicit reference to the requested object or action (e.g. 'Do you have a pen?'). While over 40% of the native speakers used this expression, the EFL learners used it under 20% of the time. The percentage actually dropped over time, from about 18% at Time 1 to about 12% at Time 3.

Table 4.13 displays frequency distributions of external modifications for the low-imposition speech acts. One notable tendency was the learners' overuse of the 'reason' strategy – giving a reason to justify their request. At Time 1, the learners gave a reason to justify their requests over 80% of the time, while native speakers only did this about 35% of the time. The use of 'reason' is clearly nontarget-like. Small, low-stake requests such as these require little facework. As a result, the expressions used to perform these speech acts should be short, simple, to the point, without much elaboration and there is no need for lengthy explanations or mitigated expressions to alleviate the illocutionary force. Hence, the learners' excessive verbosity is an indication of their limited pragmalinguistic and sociopragmatic knowledge. EFL learners used mitigating devices much more frequently than native speakers, and their overuse was particularly notable at Time 1 where this frequency was 50% greater than that of native speakers.

However, the learners gradually decreased their usage of 'reason' over time, moving closer toward the target-like pattern. A large portion of the decrease occurred in the initial period, from Time 1 to 2, marking about 17% of drop. The following excerpts from a speech act of request for a pen illustrate this tendency. At Time 1, this learner used the preparatory question 'Could you' + verb with an attention getting device of 'excuse me', plus the 'reason' strategy. This speech act became simpler and more target-like over time. At Time 2, the attention getter 'excuse me' disappeared, while the 'reason' remained. At Time 3, the attention getter returned, but the 'reason' disappeared. This student received an appropriateness rating of 3.75 at Time 1, 4.5 at Time 2 and 5.0, the full mark, at Time 3.

Learner #6 (EAP Level 1, female)

Time 1
Excuse me Ken, I, I forgot my pen, so could you borrow me a pen¿

Time 2
Could you give me a piece of paper¿ I forgot it today.

Time 3
Excuse me Ken, can I borrow your pen¿

In summary, at the linguistic level, the learners' progress with low-imposition requests was characterized at two levels: a decrease in the use of imperative forms in the head act and a decrease in the use of external modifications. While the development of the former (i.e. syntactic forms) occurred gradually over time, the progress in the latter (i.e. use of modification strategies) was rather dramatic – a large change occurring in the first half of the period, with little change in the second period. Hence, there seems to be a differential rate of development between pragmalinguistic forms and semantic strategies. The mastery of pragmalinguistic forms is a slow-developing process, while that of strategies and tactics to perform the target illocutionary act occurs relatively quickly over a short period of time. The present study lends support to the previous findings of longitudinal ILP research which found that, over time, learners gained competence in the logistics of a pragmatic event, for instance, providing credible reasons for course nominations in academic advising sessions or softening requests with small talk and by establishing a friendly atmosphere. However, the pragmalinguistics aspect, namely precise syntax and lexis needed to encode pragmatic intentions, did not develop as quickly (see Chapter 2 for review of the literature).

These observations also apply to the developmental patterns of high-imposition requests. See Tables 4.14 and 4.15 for the syntactic forms of the request head acts and external modification for the two high-imposition speech acts: asking a teacher for an extension of an assignment and asking a teacher to reschedule a quiz.

Similar to the low-imposition requests, here the learners also overused the imperative form. It appeared about 20% of the time at Time 1 and increased to 28% at Time 2. However, it decreased to 15% at Time 3, indicating a slight sign of progress. The learners instead increased their use of preparatory questions (e.g. 'Could you' + verb), approximating the native speaker pattern. One area that revealed no progress over time was the use of mitigated preparatory expressions. These expressions were almost completely absent in the learners' system, although they appeared almost 80% of the time in the native

TABLE 4.14 Frequencies of request head acts, high-imposition situations

	EFL learners			NS
	Time 1	Time 2	Time 3	
(I) Direct expressions				
(1) Imperatives	20.8% (20)	28.1% (27)	15.0% (14)	0
(2) Performatives	3.1% (3)	0	0	0
(3) Obligation statements	0	0	0	0
(4) Want statements	28.1% (27)	19.8% (19)	33.0% (31)	2.1% (1)
(II) Indirect expressions				
(5) Preparatory questions	21.9% (21)	24.0% (23)	38.3% (36)	10.4% (5)
(6) Permissions	20.8% (20)	29.2% (28)	25.5% (24)	14.6% (7)
(7) Suggestions	0	0	0	0
(8) Mitigated preparatory	2.1% (2)	1.0% (1)	1.1% (1)	79.2% (38)
(9) Hint	1.0% (1)	0	1.1% (1)	0
(III) Conventional questions	0	0	1.1% (1)	0

Notes: Numbers within parentheses show the raw counts. Frequency % was calculated by dividing the raw frequency by the total number of requests analyzed. There were 48 L2 learners at Time 1 and 2, and 47 at Time 3. There were 24 native speakers (NS). Each participant produced two low-imposition requests, and so the total number of EFL learners' requests analyzed was 96 at Time 1 and 2, and 94 at Time 3. The total number of native speaker requests was 48. See Appendix H for the coding framework.

speaker data. Mitigated preparatory expressions include syntactic forms that make reference to the hearer's ability and involve embedded questions or bi-clausal structures. See examples in native speaker samples in response to the situation of requesting for an extension of an assignment:

Native speaker #1 (male)

Excuse me, Professor Lee, um, I wanted to t, talk to you about tomorrow's paper. Umm, it's ten pages and I've already written two but I, I've caught a bit of a cold, and I am not sure I can finish the rest of it before tomorrow, so I was wondering if I could get an extension for a couple of days, maybe.

Native speaker #16 (female)

Uh, hi professor Lee, I've been working on this paper, but I got, um, sick and I haven't been able to finish so I was hoping I could get uh, an extension, so that I could put a little more time into developing the paper. I probably should have started earlier but, um, I am hoping that it would be ok if I turn it in a little bit late.

TABLE 4.15 Frequencies of request modifications, high-imposition situations

	EFL learners			NSs
	Time 1	Time 2	Time 3	
(1) Hedging	1.0% (1)	3.1% (3)	2.1% (2)	52.1% (25)
(2) Amplifier	0	7.3% (7)	2.1% (2)	52.1% (25)
(3) Reason	92.7% (89)	94.8% (91)	113.8% (107)	97.9% (47)
(4) Apology	28.1% (27)	29.2% (28)	25.5% (24)	18.8% (9)
(5) Preparator	5.2% (5)	5.2% (5)	7.4% (7)	12.5% (6)
(6) Confirmation	1.0% (1)	1.0% (1)	5.3% (5)	6.3% (3)
(7) Appreciation	0	0	0	10.4% (5)
(8) Request for suggestion	0	0	1.1% (1)	0
(9) Conditional	0	0	1.1% (1)	0
(10) External 'please'	11.5% (11)	2.1% (2)	3.2% (3)	0
(11) Other benefit	0	0	1.1% (1)	14.6% (7)
(12) Minimizer	2.1% (2)	2.1% (2)	1.1% (1)	0
Total	141.7% (136)	144.8% (139)	163.8% (154)	264.6% (127)

Notes: The % greater than 100 means that more than one modification appeared per speech act. See Appendix H for the definition of each category.

The excerpt below illustrates EFL learners' production of the same high-imposition request – asking a teacher for an extension of an assignment. Over time, this learner abandoned the imperative form with 'please' and used a preparatory question, but the target-like structure, mitigated preparatory, did not appear in the entire study period. The appropriateness score of this student was 2.0 at Time 1, 3.0 at Time 2 and 3.5 at Time 3.

Learner #11 (Level 1, male)

Time 1
Dr. Lee, I, I had a cold, so so please, please put off the deadline more two days.

Time 2
Mr. Robinson, I was very busy with two exams and meeting doctors. So please wait two, two days more to work on it.

Time 3
I don't have enough time to finish my homework, so could you postpone the deadline?

In addition to the mitigated preparatory expressions, the learners in this study were also found lacking appropriate external modifications to soften the utterances. Table 4.15 shows frequency distributions of the modifications.

In contrast to the low-imposition speech acts where learners' speech was long-winded and crammed with unnecessary modifications, the high-imposition speech acts were characterized by their under-use of the mitigating devices. Hedging and amplifiers were almost completely absent and showed no change over time, although these lexical devices appeared over 50% of the time in the native speaker data. The total frequency of the modifications, however, increased by 20% from Time 1 to Time 3, indicating a sign of progress.

To summarize, the learners' progress in high-imposition requests was characterized at two levels: a decrease in imperative forms and an increase in external modifications. However, the development was only marginal, as shown in the absence of the bi-clausal request forms (i.e. mitigated-preparatory) and extremely limited use of hedging and amplifiers. I will discuss reasons for the learners' limited use of syntactic and lexical mitigations later in this chapter.

Analyses of opinions

As there was no existing coding framework for the opinion expressions, I developed the original taxonomy. The first step in the process was to define 'utterance', the basic unit of analysis in the speech act of opinion.

Following Garcia (2004), I defined utterance as a complete and cohesive thought unit expressed in a connected group of words. False starts, fragments and stutters were treated as part of the utterances that they preceded or followed. Responses, routine expressions (e.g. 'Thank you.') and confirmations (e.g. 'OK' or 'Right') were treated as independent utterances. Multiple dependent clauses joined with 'if' or 'so' were considered part of the main independent clause. Based on these criteria, I marked the speech act of opinion for utterance breaks. Then, I assigned each utterance a pragmatic function. A total of eight pragmatic functions were identified in the speech act: expressions of personal opinions, expressions of 'wish', requests, suggestions, requests for suggestion, grounding (reason), positive comments and invitations. When deciding on the functions, I referred to the previous literature on speech acts of disagreements, complaints and negative opinions (e.g. Beebe & Takahashi, 1989; Murphy & Neu, 1996). This hand-coding process required multiple readings of the speech acts to check initial judgments and confirm coding decisions. After assigning functions, the utterances were further divided into a mono-clausal or bi-clausal (mitigated) structure. In addition to the main categories, five external modifications adapted from the framework of requests were coded: hedging, amplifiers, preparator, apology and external 'please'. The coding framework was tested by having another rater mark utterance boundaries and assign the functions based on the categories. About 20% of the data were coded by a second rater, yielding an agreement rate of 0.90. After some modifications, the framework was finalized. Four graduate students in the programs of Applied Linguistics, TESOL and Teaching Japanese as a Second Language used the framework to code speech acts. Intercorder agreement based on the 20% of randomly sampled data was 0.95. (See Appendix H for the final version of the coding framework.)

Table 4.16 displays frequency distributions of strategies used to formulate opinions in two low-imposition situations: expressing opinions to a friend about his/her clothes and paper.

The type and proportion of the expressions used here were largely comparable between the learner and native speaker group, with a majority of these expressions falling in 'opinion' and 'suggestion' categories. In these categories, learners increased their usage of mono-clausal structures (e.g. 'Brown is not your colour.' 'Why don't you try something else?'), and became less elaborate in this informal situation. Similar to the native speakers, they also gave positive comments when framing their opinions (e.g. 'It's nice, but ...'). See below for sample learner production. This is a speech act of expressing opinion to a friend about his/her paper.

Learner #49 (Level 2, male)

Time 1
I think you should summarize your introduction more plainly.

TABLE 4.16 Frequencies of opinion strategies, low-imposition situations

	EFL learners			NS
	Time 1	Time 2	Time 3	
(1) Opinion	81.3% (78)	93.8% (90)	103.2% (97)	89.6% (43)
(a) Bi-clausal	60.4% (58)	52.1% (50)	70.2% (66)	43.8% (21)
(b) Mono-clausal	20.8% (20)	41.7% (40)	33.0% (31)	45.8% (22)
(2) Want	0	1.0% (1)	3.2% (3)	0
(a) Bi-clausal	0	0	0	0
(b) Mono-clausal	0	1.0% (1)	3.2% (3)	0
(3) Request	2.1% (2)	2.1% (2)	1.1% (1)	4.2% (2)
(a) Bi-clausal	0	0	0	0
(b) Mono-clausal		2.1% (2)	2.1% (2)	1.1% (1)
(4) Suggestion	80.2% (77)	80.2% (77)	81.9% (77)	70.8% (34)
(a) Bi-clausal	25.0% (24)	21.9% (21)	16.0% (15)	22.9% (11)
(b) Mono-clausal	55.2% (53)	58.3% (56)	66.0% (62)	47.9% (23)
(5) Request for suggestion	0	0	0	0
(a) Bi-clausal	0	0	0	0
(b) Mono-clausal	0	0	0	0
(6) Grounding	2.1% (2)	0	0	2.1% (1)
(7) Positive comments	54.2% (52)	52.1% (50)	56.4% (53)	62.5% (30)
(8) Invitation	3.1% (3)	3.1% (3)	2.1% (2)	0
(9) Hedging	6.3% (6)	17.7% (17)	7.4% (7)	121.0% (58)
(10) Amplifiers	26.0% (25)	3.1% (3)	34.0% (32)	64.6% (31)
(11) Preparator	0	0	0	0
(12) Apology	0	3.1% (3)	0	2.1% (1)
(13) External 'please'	0	0	0	0

Notes. Numbers within parentheses show the raw counts. Frequency % was calculated by dividing the raw frequency by the total number of requests analyzed. There were 48 L2 learners at Time 1 and 2, and 47 at Time 3. There were 24 native speakers. Each participant produced two PDR-low requests, and so the total number of L2 requests analyzed was 96 at Time 1 and 2, and 94 at Time 3. The total number of native speaker requests analyzed was 48. Percentage greater than 100 means the strategy appeared more than once in some cases. See Appendix H for the definitions and examples of each category.

Time 2
I think the structure is very well, well done, but you should, you should more details conclusion, you should write more detailed conclusion.

Time 3
Your paper is good. It will be better if you shorten the introduction.

This learner received the appropriateness score of 2.0 at Time 1, 3.5 at Time 2 and 5.0, a full mark, at Time 3. The learner's gradual progress was evident in the sophistication of his pragmalinguistic forms. At all time points, the speech act took the form of a suggestion, but the syntax and lexis used to formulate the suggestion changed greatly over time. At Time 1, he used a rather direct form of suggestion with the modal auxiliary of obligation, 'should'. The modal still remained at Time 2, but the expression was mitigated with the hedging phrase 'I think' and a positive comment about the structure of the paper. At Time 3, the modal 'should' disappeared, and the suggestion intent was further softened with the conditional clause 'if', combined with the positive comment, 'Your paper is good.'

In contrast to their progression with the low-imposition situations, the EFL learners made little progress with high-imposition opinions. Table 4.17 displays the frequency distributions of opinion strategies in two high-imposition situations: expressing a negative opinion to a professor about his/her class and expressing disagreement about the mid-term grade received.

EFL learners and native speakers were similar in that their strategies largely fell into two categories: opinions and requests. These two appeared about 30–60% of the time. Another area of small progress found in the EFL data was the use of positive comments and grounding (reason), which were also common strategies found in the native speaker data. Each strategy increased by 10% over time. The EFL learners seem to have learned that when giving a negative opinion about a class or complaining about a grade, it is effective to begin with a positive comment (e.g. 'I like your class, but ...') or a clear justification. Another slight developmental trend was found in the syntactic properties of the opinion expressions. Over time, learners increased their usage of bi-clausal structure and decreased their usage of mono-clausal structure. At Time 1, in about 20% of the opinion expressions, the EFL group used the mono-clausal structure, but at Time 3, the percentage decreased to about 6%. The excerpts below illustrate this point. This is the situation of expressing disagreement with a teacher about receiving a 'C' for mid-term grade.

Learner #25 (Level 2, female)

Time 1
Excuse me professor, I don't know why my mid, mid semester's grade is C. I hand, I hand in my homework on time every, every, every I, I hand, I hand, I hand in every homework on time and I got 80, 80% of exam, so it is unfair that I got, I got C.

Time 2
Excuse me professor, I don't think my grade is fair. Could you explain why I got grade C?

TABLE 4.17 Frequencies of opinion strategies, high-imposition situations

	EFL learners			NS
	Time 1	Time 2	Time 3	
(1) Opinion	54.2% (52)	32.3% (31)	34.0% (32)	54.2% (26)
(a) Bi-clausal	35.4% (34)	21.9% (21)	27.7% (26)	37.5% (18)
(b) Mono-clausal	18.8% (18)	10.4% (10)	6.4% (6)	16.7% (8)
(2) Want	40.6% (39)	60.4% (58)	68.1% (64)	14.6% (7)
(a) Bi-clausal	0	8.3% (8)	6.4% (6)	8.3% (4)
(b) Mono-clausal	40.6% (39)	52.1% (50)	61.7% (58)	6.3% (3)
(3) Request	66.7% (64)	63.5% (61)	54.3% (51)	50.0% (24)
(a) Bi-clausal	4.2% (4)	14.6% (14)	6.4% (6)	37.5% (18)
(b) Mono-clausal	62.5% (60)	49.0% (47)	47.9% (45)	12.5% (6)
(4) Suggestion	1.0% (1)	3.1% (3)	3.2% (3)	2.1% (1)
(a) Bi-clausal	0	1.0% (1)	2.1% (2)	0
(b) Mono-clausal	0	2.1% (2)	1.1% (1)	2.1% (1)
(5) Request for suggestion	0	0	2.1% (2)	18.8% (9)
(a) Bi-clausal	0	0	2.1% (2)	18.8% (9)
(b) Mono-clausal	0	0	0	0
(6) Grounding	45.8% (44)	53.1% (51)	55.3% (52)	50.0% (24)
(7) Positive comments	40.6% (39)	45.8% (44)	47.9% (45)	47.9% (23)
(8) Invitation	0	0	0	0
(9) Hedging	3.1% (3)	2.1% (2)	5.3% (5)	60.4% (29)
(10) Amplifiers	11.5% (11)	1.0% (1)	11.7% (11)	60.4% (29)
(11) Preparator	8.3% (8)	8.3% (8)	10.6% (10)	17.0% (8)
(12) Apology	0	1.0%(1)	0	0
(13) External 'please'	4.2% (4)	1.0% (1)	1.1% (1)	2.1% (1)

Notes. Numbers within parentheses show the raw counts. Frequency % was calculated by dividing the raw frequency by the total number of requests analyzed. There were 48 L2 learners at Time 1 and 2, and 47 at Time 3. There were 24 native speakers. Each participant produced two PDR-low requests, and so the total number of L2 requests analyzed was 96 at Time 1 and 2, and 94 at Time 3. The total number of native speaker requests analyzed was 48. Percentage greater than 100 means the strategy appeared more than once in some cases. See Appendix H for the definitions and examples of each category.

Time 3

Excuse me Professor, professor William. I don't think this, this grade is, I don't think this grade is fair. I always turn in the homework and I got always more than 80%. Although I, I missed three, three classes, I always do your homework.

At Time 1, this learner used the negative phrase 'unfair' but at Time 2 and 3, she prefaced it in a bi-clausal structure, 'I don't think this grade is fair.' Although the justification (grounding) was missing at Time 2, at Time 3, the student provided enough evidence to support her position. In addition, she acknowledged her shortcomings (i.e. missing classes) and gave a balanced assessment of her academic performance.

Although the learners' progress was marked by their increasing use of bi-clausal structures, the overall percentage of the opinion strategy use decreased by 20% over time. Instead, the learners increased their usage of the expression 'want' by almost 30%. This change occurred rather quickly from Time 1 to Time 2, and remained stable at Time 3. The abrupt increase of 'want' is a divergence from the target pattern, as native speakers used this strategy only 15% of the time. Instead, they used the strategy 'request for suggestion' more often, which was rare in the EFL data. The excerpt below illustrates this strategy.

Native speaker #16 (female)

Hi Professor ... I, I just saw my midterm grade. I was wondering if, if you thought there'd be any way for the rest of the semester that I could do something to, uh, inc, to to to make my grade a little bit better umm ... I'd really like to get a B or an A this semester, so if you had any suggestions that would be, that would be great.

As shown here, rather than confronting the professor directly, this participant chose to circumvent the illocutionary intent by asking for a suggestion as to how to improve her grade toward the end of the semester. At an underlying level, this could be taken as an indirect disagreement with the professor's assessment, but it also can be taken as a strategy to learn about the professor's grading criteria so that she can understand the source of discrepancy. Although none of the EFL learners used this strategy at Time 1 and 2, two students used it at Time 3, indicating a slight move toward the target norm.

Turning to the strategy category of requests, the syntactic properties of requests showed very little progress over time. The learners' use of monoclausal forms (e.g. 'Can you explain the grade?') was much greater than that of bi-clausal forms (e.g. 'I wonder if you could explain the grade.'), while this pattern was reversed in the native speakers' data. Here again, the learners' limited knowledge of mitigated request structures became evident. However, there are some exceptional cases, as illustrated in the excerpts below. When complaining about the unwarranted grade, this learner made some progress at Time 2: she started with a greeting ('Hello') and used the 'preparator' strategy, 'I have a question about my grade.' She made further progress at Time 3 by using the mitigated, bi-clausal structure with 'I think' to frame her disagreement. Her request for an explanation at the end was also in the embedded sentence structure (i.e. 'could you explain' + verb). This is a marked improvement from the earlier time when she used the direct request form with 'would/could you'. Most importantly, the content of the request changed over time. At Time 1 and 2, she asked the professor to change the grade, but at Time 3, she asked him to explain his grading criteria, which is less direct and intimidating.

Learner #39 (Level 2, female)

Time 1
Ah, I can't understand why my grade is C. Actually, I I missed three classes and I didn't participate in class much, but I always turned ah by doing homework and I always get 80% grade in the exam, so would you would you think about it again please.

Time 2
Hello, I have a question about my grade. Actually I, ah, . . . I, I don't attend, attend two classes and I skipped some homework assignment, but I got 80% on the test, so could you, could you reconsider about my grade, please⸮

Time 3
Hello. I'm afraid of my grade. I think aah actually I I absent I was absent three class. And I didn't participate so so much. But I think I did better than my grade. So so could you explain why I got grade C⸮

The excerpts below further illustrate learners' increasing awareness of appropriate semantic moves to use to mitigate the face-threat. At Time 1, this learner started the speech act with direct expression of his frustration, 'I don't think it's fair,' and he closed the speech act with the same tone. However, at Time 2, he prefaced the complaint with 'I have something to tell you.' After providing sufficient grounding, the student asked for an explanation for the grade he received. This request for an explanation appeared again at Time 3, but this time in a more open-ended question, 'Is there any reason for that⸮' Although syntactically this form belongs to the mono-clausal request, the content of the question is less direct and threatening. Also, note that there was a change in the lexis from 'I don't think it's *fair*' at Time 1 to 'I don't think it is *reasonable*' at Time 3. The phrase 'not reasonable' is more solicitous than 'not fair' and appropriate in this formal situation.

Learner #30 (Level 2, male)

Time 1
Ah excuse me ah this is not I think it's I don't think it's fair. While it may be true that I I didn't I didn't participate in your class much, but I I I have something to do well ah homework, so it is not unfair, I think.

Time 2

Ah, I have something to tell you about my grade in mid-semester, mid-term. Ah, actually I missed two class and, ah, three homework, but ah, ah my test was, ah, 80%, and I always speaking, I was always speaking up in class. How do you explain about it?

Time 3

Ah Professor William. Ah I have something to talk about talk about with you. Well ah I checked, I checked my grade. And I don't think it is reasonable. Ah actually I missed three classes but ah I may, I made it on my exam on exam every time. Is there any reason for that?

Despite these qualitative gains, a large difference between the EFL and native speaker group was found in the use of 'want' strategy. This strategy was a characteristic to the EFL group, and it appeared more than 40% of the time, while native speakers used it less than 15%. When complaining about a grade or commenting on the professor's class, most learners directly stated their wishes and interests. They mostly used the mono-clausal structure in expressing their wish (e.g. 'I want to know about recent things.'), rather than softening it with the bi-clausal structure (e.g. 'I wish we talked about recent things,' 'I'd love it if we talked about recent things.'). The use of the mono-clausal structure increased by 20% over time, further diverging from the target pattern.

Another striking difference was found again in learners' under-use of hedging and amplifiers. While they appeared over 60% of the time in the native speakers' data, the percentage of hedging was about 5% or less in the EFL data while that of amplifiers was about 10% or less. These findings further confirm that the learners were lacking these pragmalinguistic resources that could soften the impositive force or intensify their stance. By using elements of hedging and indefiniteness, for example, speakers do not have to specify their precise intentions, and they can consequently avoid the potential provocation of being precise. These indirect markers serve as status-saving strategies and thus are considered appropriate and polite when voicing an opinion to someone with greater power and higher status. As lexical items such as 'maybe', 'possibly', 'kind/sort of', 'very' and 'absolutely' are linguistically simple, the absence of these in learners' production is probably due to their lack of knowledge about the pragmatic function of these phrasal devices.

In summary, compared with their progress in making low-imposition opinions, the learners' performance in constructing high-imposition opinions was below average, and their progress was only marginal. This was largely due to their under-use of the target pragmalinguistic structures. However, the learners' speech acts contained all the necessary semantic strategies: they expressed how they felt about the grade or class, they supported their points with justifications and they voiced how they wanted to see the situation improve by making requests and suggestions to the professor. These semantic moves, which were essentially the same as those used by native speakers, were present in the learners' production from the beginning of the study. What differed from the native speakers were the linguistic toolkits used in putting together these semantic moves, namely syntactic and lexical mitigations.

Summary and Interpretations of the Findings for Pragmatic Production

This study revealed different developmental patterns and rates in pragmatic production across functions (i.e. low- and high-imposition speech acts) and attributes (i.e. appropriateness, grammaticality, planning time and speech rate). There was a constant, even-paced development in planning speed regardless of the situation type. Appropriateness showed a strong increase for the low-imposition speech acts over time, but for the high-imposition speech acts, the 'time' effect did not take effect in the beginning. Similarly, for the low-imposition speech acts, grammaticality showed a strong gain at every juncture, but for the high-imposition speech acts, the gain was detected only in the initial period and no gain in the later period. Speech rate, on the other hand, showed a significant increase initially for both situations, but this rate later stagnated. These developmental patterns are explained in the following section with qualitative data collected from interviews, class observations and journals.

There were three areas of speech acts that the learners made constant progress over time: grammaticality and appropriateness of low-imposition speech acts and fluency. As for the grammaticality, the learners became able to produce more syntactically well-constructed low-imposition speech acts, and the progress was detected at every juncture. This pattern can be explained by their increase in general proficiency. Their TOEFL scores demonstrated a steady increase in proficiency over time: the mean score of 459.35 (SD = 17.76) at Time 1, 511.90 (SD = 90) at Time 2 and 524.32 (SD = 24.02) at Time 3. Hence, it seems that, as the learners' general proficiency improved, they acquired linguistic means to articulate their speech acts more accurately. But this effect was found only for the low-imposition speech acts. High-imposition speech acts showed a significant gain in the initial but not in the later period, suggesting that mastery of these speech acts takes a longer time. Because of the greater amount of speech produced, grammatical errors in the high-imposition speech acts were probably more noticeable than that in the low-imposition speech acts.

On the other hand, there was no effect of situation type on the development of fluency of speech act production (planning time and speech rate).

This can be directly attributed to the context of learning. Being in a bilingual, immersion context, the learners probably had intense practice with target language input on a daily basis. General processing practices and exposure to input in a variety of everyday situations seemed to have transferred to pragmatic processing and assisted its gain over time. Without focused practice on the target speech acts, a naturalistic gain still occurred with planning speed and speech rate, regardless of the situation type, suggesting that the speedy processing of pragmatic functions is a product of overall time-on-task.

Similarly, a strong, steady progress found in the appropriateness of low-imposition speech acts can be explained by the frequent occurrence of those speech acts on campus. Making a small request to a friend or giving a personal assessment on a subtle matter seemed to be part of daily communication among the learners studied here. In their speaking journal entries, the speech act of request appeared about 70 times, all of which were low-imposition requests. Although it was about 5% of the total entries, this frequency is notable considering that the learners had unlimited choices of topics for this assignment. In their entries about request, they sometimes jotted down their sociolinguistic analysis of the target pragmatic forms, as shown in the example entries here:

Learner #24 (Level 2, female)

The other day I learned that using imperative sentence is a little rude when I ask someone a favor. I said 'Please help my homework.' when I wanted an international student to help my homework. When I wanted Leo to help my homework, I said 'Can you help my homework?' I'll use 'Can you' or 'Would you' when I ask someone a favor.

Learner #33 (Level2, female)

Today I talked with an international student. I told him what I was learning in EAP classes. I asked him 'What's the difference between Can I and May I?' So he answered 'may I' is more polite than 'can I.' Until then, I was using these phrases without knowing the difference between them. But I forgot to ask him, 'What situation should I use these words?' So I try to ask the question next time.

Low-imposition requests were also pervasive in the teachers' directions in class. In the EAP classes I observed, teachers produced a variety of request as part of class instruction. Common forms included: imperatives, modal expressions ('Could you' + verb), 'want' statements ('I'd like you to' + verb) and suggestions ('Maybe you can' + verb). The number of request forms ranged from 5 to 18 per class session. See example directions below from two different classes:

Teachers' directions in the EAP Level 2 writing class, section A (November, 2008)

- Think about this question a little.
- I'd like you to do X.
- Can someone explain X?
- Anyone can help out?
- Can I ask you to do X?
- Think about it.
- Take 10 min.
- Maybe you can X.
- Maybe you can use X.
- I can suggest X.

Teachers' directions in the EAP Level 2 writing class, section B (November, 2008)

- If you get cold, let me know.
- Look at your previous essays.
- If you don't understand, you need to talk to your classmates, or call me.
- Please put your textbook out.
- Open the textbook to X.
- If you have questions, you are free to call me over.
- You can just leave it.
- Move to get together with your partner.
- Remember X.
- Ask your partner for specific feedback.
- Don't just hand in your paper to them.
- Let me know what you want from them.
- Go over the paper.
- Check your name before you turn in.

In addition to classroom directions, teachers frequently gave written feedback to the students' essays, which often took the form of low-imposition opinions (see sample teacher feedback in the next section). In addition to such input from teachers, students also had plenty of opportunities to practice express opinions in class through discussion, debate and essay writing.

Hence, the linguistic and opportunistic resources available in the context seemed to have had a direct impact on the learners' fast-paced acquisition of low-imposition speech acts. They picked them up naturally along their way without explicit instruction or correction, and they gained the ability to produce them appropriately in a prompt manner.

In contrast, the appropriateness of high-imposition speech acts was found to be late-emerging. Linguistic analyses showed that the key pragmalinguistic forms used by the majority of native speakers (i.e. bi-clausal structures, hedging) were largely absent in the EFL learners' data even after eight-month exposure to the immersion context. The learners had a limited range of pragmalinguistic resources and overgeneralized one or two forms over a range of functions. They were slow in adopting a new form–function mapping and expanding their pragmalinguistic repertoire, lending support to the previous literature (see Chapter 2, literature review).

Several explanations could account for the slow acquisition of the target pragmalinguistic forms. First, eight months was not long enough for the learners to internalize the associations between these pragmalinguistic forms and their contextual requirements. Recall that at the beginning of the study, I administered a grammar test that measured learners' knowledge of target pragmalinguistic forms. Those forms were sampled from native speakers' baseline data, and included a list of bi-clausal structures (e.g. 'I wonder if' + clause; 'Is there any way that' + clause; 'I wish' + clause), modals, and hedging/amplifier expressions (e.g. 'a bit', 'a little', 'maybe', 'I think' and 'absolutely') (see Appendix H for the copy of the grammar test). The learners scored 95.5% in average on the test, indicating that they had almost complete receptive knowledge of these linguistic forms at the onset of the study. Their lack of demonstration of the target forms in speech acts, then, could be due to their lack of knowledge of the contextual requirements of these forms and their socio-pragmatic functions.

A variety of data collected on campus also point to learners' implicit knowledge of the target linguistic devices. The bi-clausal structures often appeared in their textbooks and I occasionally observed teachers explaining these structures to their students in class. Hedging devices such as 'maybe' or 'I'm not sure' often appeared as stance markers in students' journal entries as well as orally during their speaking tests in class. Mild disagreements and suggestions were exemplary in the teachers' feedback in student essays in forms such as 'It seems' + verb, 'you might want to' + verb and 'you could' + verb. See below, for example, feedback comments collected from three different writing instructors:

Level 1 Section A instructor
'You offer these specific situations and these specific remedies. You met the assignment instruction, but <u>I wonder if you might</u> have been able to develop three remedies for one situation? Anyway, this was very clear and specific.'

'<u>It seems</u> you are trying to do two different things in this paragraph. <u>It may be better</u> to focus on one thing.'

'You don't fully answer the assignment instructions, so it gets <u>a bit</u> confused. <u>It might have been clearer</u> if you first explained what you expect of teachers. <u>It seems</u> you had many good experiences to choose from, but

I wasn't <u>completely</u> sure whether you really expect all these things or not. <u>I think you could have</u> shortened and tightened the paragraph <u>if you could have</u> ordered it more carefully.'

Level 2 Section A instructor
'I think your introduction <u>can be</u> better. Write your description in a narrative style and avoid putting yourself in the picture.'

'Not bad, but you <u>can use</u> logic DNA more clearly to move from thesis to logic to detail. Your coherence is <u>a little</u> off.'

Level 2 Section B instructor
'Overall, nicely written! Structurally, your second paragraph page 1 <u>could have been</u> further developed. <u>It might even have been</u> expanded to another paragraph.'

'You <u>could have</u> developed several points <u>a bit</u> more.... . An example <u>would</u> help your reader understand the dynamics better.'

As shown here, the teachers' comments are filled with mitigated expressions – conditional forms, modals, hedging and occasional intensifiers. Despite these frequent encounters with the target linguistic forms, the learners in this study were not able to produce them in the pragmatic speaking task, probably because they did not have a firm-grounded knowledge of the pragmatic functions served by these forms in social interaction. In the retrospective interviews, when asked to name all possible request-making expressions, eight out of 12 participants included bi-clausal forms in their lists (e.g. 'I wonder if' + clause; 'Would you mind if' + clause). This is additional evidence that the absence of the target pragmalinguistic forms in the data was not caused by the absence of these forms in the learners' systems or in the input. Rather, it was caused by the learners' incomplete understanding of what these forms do 'pragmatically' and where they are ranked in the politeness hierarchy. Among the eight learners who verbalized the bi-clausal forms as a way of requesting, only three were able to rank them in the upper-end of the politeness scale. Other learners did not know where to place them or how appropriate these forms are compared with other forms in the given situation. Having no explicit knowledge of the form–context mappings, the learners' actual form choice was influenced by other factors, namely using the simplest and most familiar forms just to get through the task. There was a tendency for the learners to produce the first form that came to their minds, rather than exploring other options for comparison or making an informed decision on which form to use. The excerpts from introspective verbal interviews below illustrate this point. These learners reflected on their choice of pragmalinguistic forms when performing high-imposition speech acts (i.e. expressing a negative opinion about a teacher's class). The italic lines are their speech acts, followed by their introspective interview responses:

Learner #37 (Level 2, male)

I like your lecture of French history and I enjoy it always, but actually I'm interested in French pop culture and music, so I want you to talk about it.

I said 'I want you to' because it was the first thing that popped into my head. I considered 'would you mind' for a split second but I had a trouble completing the sentence, like which subject to use. I wasn't confident, so I prioritized communicating my message and used the form I know. In my every day conversation, often several forms come to my mind, but I never take risks. I communicate with the forms I'm most comfortable in using. Communicating intention clearly is the priority.

Learner #12 (Level 1, male)

I'm interested in French pop culture and music, so could you tell me more about them?

I was going to say 'I like your class', but if I say that first, I might forget the most important part of what I wanted to say. So rather than being unclear in my communication, I thought I should make my point up front.

Learner#25 (Level 2, female)

Professor I like you lecture and I'm interested in French history, but I'm more interested in French pop culture so next time I'd like to hear your lecture about modern France.

I said 'I like your class' at front to soften my opinion. I also used 'I'd like to', in stead of 'I want to', to make it politer. [Researcher: What could you have said to make it even politer?] I could say, 'If, if, if it is possible, I'd like to know...' I was thinking about using it, but it didn't come out. I was saying it in my heart though.

These excerpts point to several reasons why learners did not use more appropriate mitigated forms although they were conscious of them. One reason is their limited processing capacity. The learners were not able to retrieve the expressions from their long-term memories because they had to cope with the demand of online production. They reported that, because the structure was complex, if they focus too much on the form, they might forget to convey the most important thing – the actual illocution. They were afraid of sounding ungrammatical and not getting their meaning across or losing a train of thought by trying to use long, complex structures that they had not mastered completely. Hence, they prioritized clear communication of intention by sticking to the forms they were comfortable using and sacrificing the politeness.

To support this, the learners' attention on content, rather than on form, was evident in their introspective interview responses. I asked them what aspects of speech acts they were attending to most when producing high-imposition speech acts. In 25 out of the 36 verbal reports analyzed (3 high-imposition situations × 12 learners), they reported paying attention to the content and strategies (i.e. what to say). The linguistics aspect (i.e. how to say it) was their secondary concern. They were primarily occupied with giving an adequate reason to support their argument, and some learners considered this a politeness strategy. See excerpt below on the speech act of asking for a homework extension:

Learner #46 (Level 2, female)

Excuse me, I have a cold, so I can't finish my paper, so I want extra two days to finish my paper.

This is a situation with a teacher, so I tried to be as polite as possible. [Researcher: How did you try to make it polite?] I gave a reason. When asking for two extra days, I have to give a valid reason.

The following excerpt also illustrates the learners' priority on content and illocution rather than on form. What is striking in this comment, and other similar comments found in the data, is that the learners did not care how they sounded. This learner had a clear understanding that the modal 'should' sounds 'too imposing' when talking to a professor. He knew less direct ways of saying the same thing, but he did not bother to take time to locate the alternatives and formulate them. Instead, he stuck to 'should', which was immediately accessible in his linguistic repertoire.

Learner #31 (Level 2, male)

I'm interested in French pop culture and music, so you should talk about it more.

I think it's better to say what I want directly. [Researcher: Did you pay attention to the language?] I thought about making it politer, but I couldn't come up with a good sentence. I couldn't come up with anything other than 'you should.' ... The modal 'should' sounds too imposing, so maybe I should have said 'I want to learn French pop culture' instead. I don't know why it didn't come up. If this were in Japanese I could probably say it, but in English, I think about what I can say with my vocabulary. Then, the modal 'should' came up. It wasn't that I mulled over among expressions. It was an immediate decision. I thought about being polite, but what came out of the mouth was that.

While processing demands involved in online production were obvious, these learners' attitudes were not entirely due to their limited processing capacity because there was no time limit in this task: the learners were allowed to take as much time as they needed to plan their speech acts. Instead, these attitudes, in part, seem to come from their lack of sociopragmatic knowledge and sensitivity. The learners did not seem to be aware that some strong expressions like 'should' are inappropriate in this particular social interaction, and that using them could lead to negative social consequences. As they were lacking knowledge about the different interpersonal effects coming from different pragmalinguistics forms, the use of inappropriate forms probably did not appear so detrimental to them. Their limited sociopragmatic knowledge and priority on direct communication over politeness seem to be attributable to their lack of target sociocultural practice in context. I asked the learner in the excerpt above why he used 'should' even though he knew that it was not appropriate in this situation. He responded: 'I knew it's not appropriate but I couldn't act on it. I think it's because lack of experience. I don't have real life experience like this.'

In summary, these descriptions point to a range of reasons for the underdevelopment of high-imposition speech acts observed among the EFL learners in this study. Despite a frequent encounter with the target pragmalinguistic forms through input as well as their receptive understanding of the forms, the learners were not able to produce them in the pragmatic speaking task. Three major reasons were gleaned from the qualitative data: limited processing capacity, a priority on conveying meaning over using elaborate language and a lack of sensitivity for polite language use. These factors were intertwined with one another. The learners opted out of elaborate pragmatic forms and used simpler, more direct expressions because they were not able to formulate them on the spot. Because their processing capacity was limited, they stuck to the forms they were most familiar with, without attempting alternative, more polite forms. Their lack of effort in this regard was grounded in their main concern of communicating their intentions clearly. They sacrificed politeness over clarity in their speech act production.

Qualitative data revealed that these students' attitudes were reinforced through the context of learning. Although opportunities for formal language use were generally limited on campus, the only occasions on campus that allowed for such formal register for the students were interactions with their teachers. However, qualitative data revealed that these interactions did not encourage formal language use on the students' part. Similar to the PST situations, in real-life communicative situations, the students did not use polite language with their teachers nor received corrective feedback on their inappropriate language use. I have two episodes to support this interpretation. Both episodes involved conflict situations between a teacher and students that I witnessed in one of the EAP classes.

The first face-threatening incident happened to Brian, an instructor of the EAP speaking class, half way into the second semester. Brian was feeling resistance from the class because the students were not cooperative. They spoke too much Japanese in class, and they sometimes rolled their eyes when he reminded them of an assignment. They also did poorly on speaking tests because they did not follow his instructions. Since this was going on for quite some time, Brian sent an email to everyone in the class and asked what their problems were and what he could do to change the situation. A couple of days later, two female students came to his office with a letter listing a number of complaints about his class. Below is an abbreviated version of the letter that contained a list of bullet points:

Dear Brian,

- We think the amount of speaking is not enough in the class. We don't have time to practice in small groups for tests. Nevertheless, when we take a speaking test, you require high-level skills. We don't understand what you want us to do in the test.
- We don't want you to give us a kind of art project. It takes a lot of time to make. Our skills don't improve by making these things.
- What do you want us to write in the journal? We can't understand the purpose. You teach us vocabulary including slang in every class but sometime we ask international students, 'Do you use these vocabulary in daily life?' and most say 'No.' So we are not willing to learn phrases you teach us. The purpose of the journal is to talk with international students. It is good because it gives us many chances to talk with them. But you are strict about the content. Why it is not good to talk about any topics we want talk?

This is hardly a letter in format, but it represents the students' perceptions of the problems in class. They did not like the format of class that did not allow for much speaking practice, and they sensed a mismatch between class activities and assessment. They also questioned the value of some homework assignments. In particular, they felt that the format of the speaking journal did not allow for much flexibility, and the vocabulary they learned in class was not useful when talking to international students. I interviewed Brian twice about this incident. Brian acknowledged the issues brought up in the letter, saying he probably did not communicate these well with the students. He felt that he could accommodate most of the requests they made. The only thing that he felt offended was the third bullet point.

He sensed a lack of trust from the students about his ability to teach the right words.

Aside from the content, the letter was filled with direct language. The students used an expression of prohibition, 'we don't want you to' to convey their dislike of the art project. The use of direct questions, 'What do you want us to write in the journal?' and 'Why is it not good to talk about any topics we want to talk?,' sound accusatory without an appropriate preface. The sentence, 'We are not willing to learn phrases you teach us,' contains explicit negation, indicating resistance to the teacher and a lack of compliance. There was almost no use of positive or negative politeness strategies or syntactic and lexical mitigations to downplay the face-threatening tone. Hence, the students' performance in a real-life setting was no different from that of the pragmatic speaking task: they used direct, explicit expressions with minimum supporting devices to mitigate the potential face-threat.

I interviewed Kaori, one of the students who wrote the letter to complain to Brian, about her perception of the language in the letter. She told me that she did not pay attention to her language because she could not afford it. The most she could do was to get meaning across, and she did not care about the politeness aspect of the speech. Besides, she believed that native speakers of English communicate things more directly and that her manner of speech conforms to that of native speakers. These differences between Japanese and English communication methods were formed through her experiences in the bilingual university. She gave me one instance of miscommunication that she experienced earlier in the semester. When refusing an invitation to a party from an international student, she didn't explicitly say 'no'. Instead, she used circumlocution, 'maybe no', following the Japanese norm. She said that the international student did not understand what she meant. These instances of miscommunication probably lead to her one-sided understanding of English communication and to her use of direct speech style to her teacher.

While the students' tone of speech to Brian was clearly inappropriate, what was interesting in my observation was that Brian did not mind their directness at all. Rather, he welcomed a direct, explicit manner of communication because it helped him understand his students better. To my surprise, when I went to his office to interview him about this incident, I saw the letter from the students posted on his book cabinet. He told me that he 'framed' the letter because he was so happy and proud to receive it. It helped him to understand the students' frustrations and opened the window for discussion. What appealed to him was that the students took initiative: they organized themselves and cared enough to talk to him about the problems. I asked him how he felt about the students' language. He responded that he was impressed with it, and nothing was offensive or rude to him.

Brian told me that the biggest cultural adjustment he had to make in teaching Japanese students was getting their feedback. It was his first time teaching Japanese students, after teaching ESL in the United States for almost 20 years. He compared Japanese students with other cultural groups and said:

> When I was teaching in the States, I basically had two groups – Hispanics and Asians (Chinese and Koreans.) The Spanish group, because I speak Spanish, it was very easy to control because they were very talkative, they were very expressive, they didn't hold back. My Korean students were a little bit quiet and reserved, but they started developing their attitudes, and in two to three weeks they were getting more expressive. They were comfortable. So with all students, there was always feedback. I spoke, they spoke. There was always 'Shut up', 'Be quiet', not 'shut up' in the sense of like 'I'm talking, you need to stop.' 'Pay attention', that kind of thing. But here I don't understand. There is no feedback. (December, 2008)

This excerpt shows that Brian was craving for direct, explicit communication. He felt challenged to teach Japanese students because they were passive and did not react much to him or the class. He was not used to this. From the interviews, I noted that getting feedback from students was important to Brian for two reasons. One was for his professional development – the students' comments and responses would help him to assess his teaching and to improve on it. The other reason relates to his psychological need to connect with someone. Brian mentioned that, when living alone in a foreign country, the students are his closest connections, and thus he wanted to do his best for them and wished they would reciprocate in some way. See his comments:

> I think what comes to my mind is that I wanna be a good teacher. I really totally believe or want to believe that I wanna be a good teacher. For that, I need feedback. I need to know, I need reassurance that what I'm doing is good or bad. I need reassurance to know that people are learning or not. ... When I was teaching ESL in the last couple of years, I was in a trailer, the last trailer. School is overpopulated in the States right now, so there aren't enough classrooms for everyone. So instead of building, they put trailers there. So I was in the very last trailer from the center of the school, so the teachers never came to talk to me, because I was teaching ESL. There were two ESL teachers, and we were the farthest, so we never got feedback. We never got anything. My students were the only thing I had to get feedback. And here in this university, I feel like I'm treated like an adult, someone who knows what they are doing, but I don't get feedback. The feedback we give each other among teachers, we just write good things. But I really never feel that I ever got true, honest feedback. So my students are the only thing I have. So when they do give me something like that [feedback], I crave for it, because if

I made a mistake, I wanna know so that I don't do it again. If you don't say anything, I can assume it's OK, but if you tell me when I make a mistake, then I know how to fix it. So whoever the student it comes from, Hispanics, Mexicans, or Koreans, anybody, if it's said in a constructive point of view, I'd accept it. (December, 2008)

These descriptions tell us why Brian did not care about students' direct language use in the letter. He actually preferred it. He wanted students to come forward and say explicitly what was going wrong in class. Not getting such direct feedback in Japan caused a culture shock for Brian and required him to make a cultural adjustment. For him, receiving the students' letter was a strong sign of progress in this adjustment process, and thus he embraced it and took their comments seriously, rather than getting annoyed with their language use. He focused on what they said, not on how they said it. Pragmatic lesson on inappropriate language use was not given because correcting students on their language was almost counterproductive for creating a healthy learning environment. He wanted to encourage students to speak up so that they could help construct a productive learning atmosphere. Polite, elaborate language was not necessary in this process. In this respect, the teacher and students had the same priority in communication. The teacher was concerned about getting direct feedback from the students, and the students were concerned about communicating this feedback in the most effective manner. Sociocultural aspects of communication such as politeness and appropriateness in speech were not an issue for either party.

These observations are supported by another example incident which happened to Tom, an instructor of the EAP reading class, earlier in the second semester. A group of four students showed up in his office and expressed their frustrations with the class. Two members of this group were the same students who complained to Brian. They brought a letter, as they did to Brian, and expressed concerns about Tom's class. Their main problem was the class format. They wanted to have more timed reading practice and fewer vocabulary exercises. What was unique in this case is that, unlike Brian, Tom was actually aware of the rudeness in the students' language but still did not give them a corrective feedback. See the interview excerpt:

Kaori challenged me several times. She said things like, this is what I perceive as rude or too direct, when student talks to the teacher like that. She talked to me like my friend would talk to me. She said … she said …what did she say … ah … ah … 'We need to do more timed reading', oh no, no, she said, 'Why are we doing X? Why are we doing that?' Direct. And it wasn't like as if we had been building up. It was the first thing she said, so I was like, 'Oh.' But I think she was frustrated. (November, 2008)

I asked Tom whether other students spoke in a similar manner as Kaori did. He responded:

They were fine. They didn't do that. They were much, much, much more respectful. Ippei, he was really uncomfortable, and I got an impression that he had never done something like that before, so he was very deferential. He said things like, I had to ask him directly, 'So you want me to do this?' and he was like, 'Well, ah, oh, ah, yeah . . . ' Not like Kaori. She was much more direct than that. Haruyo was direct, but she had the right tone. She would say, 'I wonder if, ah, it just seems we might be doing a little bit too much of reading log' or 'I don't know why we should be doing X' or 'I don't understand why' instead of 'We should do X' or 'why are we doing this.' But her English is much better than Kaori's. Her fluency is much, much better.

As shown in the excerpts, Tom had a clear idea of the normative, appropriate language use in this confrontational situation as well as how the students' language deviated from this norm, giving an impression of a rude, inappropriate manner of speech. He felt that Kaori's starting a conversation with a direct question, 'Why are we doing X?' without any preface, was abrupt and impolite. The 'right tone' to use in this situation, according to Tom, was the use of bi-clausal, mitigated preparatory structure, as in 'I wonder if', modal expressions of indefiniteness such as 'it seems' and 'we might', and hedging devices such as 'a little bit' and 'just.' These syntactic and lexical mitigations help downgrade the face-threat, but Kaori did not use them, making her appear too direct and confrontational. Tom noted that it was clearly the wrong register, wrong tone and wrong manner. It was too direct.

Despite this explicit awareness of the proper pragmalinguistic forms for the situation and lack of them in Kaori's speech, Tom did not correct her inappropriate language use. The only intervention he made during her speech was when she was insisting on her point, and was not considering Tom's perspective. See the illustration:

There was a big thing about timed reading. Kaori would not get off on that point. She insisted in the same manner. She insisted that we should do timed reading. She said, 'Why we are not doing timed reading? We should do timed reading. I learned a lot when we were doing timed reading.' So I started out with conceding, I said, 'Yes, you're right, timed reading is a good thing. You know, we will do some of that this semester. But you have to understand that the content changed. You're not reading literature any more. That's finished. You have to deal with academic reading, so in order to handle that, you have to learn skills that make you to do that.' But she was very resistant with that idea, so finally I said,

'That's not going to change. We're going to do this, this, and this, but that's not gonna change.'

As shown here, Kaori was refusing to accept the point Tom was trying to make, which added to his frustration. But the actual negative feedback that Tom gave was on her behavior and approach (i.e. going overboard and not taking 'no' for an answer), but not on her speech. He did not correct her on language because, like Brian, he wanted students to be direct with him. Unlike Brian, Tom had more experience with teaching Japanese students in other schools. As he was familiar with the quiet, reserved attitudes of Japanese students, he was happy that they opened up and communicated the problems directly. Polite, appropriate language use in such communication was beyond the scope, considering that the students were doing it in their second language. The excerpt below illustrates this point:

You know, they are language learners, so I didn't expect them to have appropriate, perfect register, tone, and so that. They are all intermediate students. Part of the surprise, which made me feel good, is that they would come to me and tell me this. Most Japanese students would NEVER, NEVER, EVER [stress added] do something like that. They would just put them in course evaluation and say just how bad, they didn't like this, they didn't like that, but they wouldn't tell me. So I was actually happy about this.

Tom continued:

If they had come to the class and said these, and they were disruptive and caused problems, then we have a big problem, but these guys didn't do that. I'm glad they came to talk to me in my office. I'm glad they gave me the letter, and I'm glad they had the confidence.

Tom and Brian's incidents together inform us why some teachers in this particular school context do not correct students' pragmatic inappropriateness in language use. In these highly face-threatening real-life situations, students were clearly too direct. While not intentional, they used the wrong tone and manner in communicating their thoughts, which could easily lead to negative consequences such as cultural stereotyping and prejudices. However, such misunderstandings did not occur here because the students and teachers were in agreement at an underlying level: the teachers wanted direct comments from their students, and the students wanted to communicate their wishes clearly. Elaborate, long-winded ways of communicating, typical features of polite language, were not necessary for or even the obstacles in the process of direct communication. Hence, the teachers did not correct the students' language nor give them a lesson on more polite, formal register. There was simply no need for such language, even when the teachers were aware of the inappropriateness, as shown in Tom's case. Feedback and correction on speech form could even be detrimental to creating open communication between the students and teachers, particularly considering the cultural background of the Japanese students.

These observations offer some insights as to why the EFL learners in this study did not make much progress in their appropriateness scores of high-imposition speech acts. Their lack of attention to and knowledge of sociocultural aspects of language use, as well as their priority on direct communication over politeness, form part of the explanation. These attitudes were reinforced through the environment in which direct communication was encouraged between teachers and students, even at the cost of politeness. As a result, there was a lack of feedback on the pragmatic aspect of language use. Without being corrected on their inappropriate language usage, the students probably developed a wrong assessment of the target form–function–context mappings. Since there was no negative consequence from their manner of speech, they probably felt that their language was indeed acceptable. Politeness considerations were not mandatory in their social interaction, and simple, direct language, which they were capable of managing at their English level, sufficed.

These observations are further detailed in the next chapter. Chapter 5 presents case histories of eight students, with more in-depth discussions about the classroom environment, teacher–student relationships and social networks that account for the restricted pragmatic development found in this study.

Note

(1) Tables 4.6 and 4.9 and 4.14 appeared in Taguchi (2011b). I would like to thank *Modern Language Journal*, the National Federation of Modern Language Teachers' Association and Blackwell Publishing for the permission to reproduce these tables.
(2) Partial descriptions of the test development process appeared in Taguchi (2009).
(3) Twenty-five native speakers completed the task, but data from one native speaker was not recorded due to the equipment failure.

5 Individual Differences in Pragmatic Development

Chapter 4 presented group-level analyses of pragmatic development of 48 participants. Results revealed different patterns and pace of development among pragmatic functions (i.e. comprehension of conventional vs. nonconventional implicatures, and production of low- vs. high-imposition speech acts) as well as among attributes (i.e. accuracy scores, appropriateness scores, response times, planning time and speech rate). This chapter presents individual-level analyses of pragmatic development by analyzing qualitative data collected from a subset of the participants. The chapter answers the second research question: What types of learning resources and experiences are available in context and how do they shape developmental trajectories of individual learners?

Informants and Their Backgrounds

A subset of 12 students (six males and six females) from the participant group was recruited as informants in order to gain insight into the relationship among the patterns of pragmatic change, types of sociocultural experiences available in context, and individual differences in these experiences. Since the purpose of the qualitative analyses was to explore reasons behind individual variations observed in pragmatic development, I used the maximum variation sampling strategy (Dörnyei, 2007) to select the target informants. This strategy allows us to select cases from different outcome levels (i.e. high, mid and low pragmatic gain) so that we can explore variations among the respondents as well as commonality across the sampled diversity. Score differences between Time 1 and Time 2 were computed, and lists of five students who gained most and least was complied. Since this study analyzed gains on multiple pragmatic functions and attributes, separate lists were prepared for each aspect of gain. Three students who were in the top and bottom for most pragmatic aspects were selected. The remaining six showed mixed patterns of development across different pragmatic aspects. Due to space limitations, this book reports findings of eight focal informants, four males and four females, from these groups.[1]

Table 5.1 displays background information for the eight informants. Two of them were from the first level in the EAP program (i.e. beginner level), and the rest of the group was from the second level (i.e. intermediate level). All participants were the same age, except for Keita who spent two years in *yobiko*, a college preparation school after graduating from high school. Four students had a short-term home-stay experience in an English-speaking country. All students improved their TOEFL score over time, but the degree of gain varied. It should be noted here that general proficiency did not perfectly correspond with pragmatic performance. For example, although Tomoyo was most pragmatically competent in the group, her TOEFL score was the lowest at Time 2 and her TOEFL gain was the smallest in the group. Ippei, on the other hand, achieved the fourth highest TOEFL score at Time 2, but his pragmatic gain was minimal.

Data from the Language Contact Profile (LCP) are also displayed in Table 5.1. (See Appendix A for the copy of the survey.) The survey was administered in order to document the amount of target language input and use outside the class. The questions in the survey asked participants to indicate how many hours per week they spent doing certain activities, such as using each of the four basic language skills in English (i.e. speaking, reading, writing and listening), interacting with native or fluent speakers of English, and using their native language, Japanese. The product of these two numbers (i.e. the number of days per week and hours per day) provided an estimate of total time per week for each activity. The survey was administered six times over two semesters at approximately 1.5 month intervals. Table 5.1 provides the average amount of language contact.

The informants showed a great variation in their reported amount of language contact. Keita reported using English only 8.6 hours per week on average outside the class, while Mitsu reported about 40 hours of contact per week. The purpose of their English usage also varied. Yuko reported using English most when talking to friends, 10.3 hours per week in average, while Ryota and Keita used English most time when watching TV and DVDs. The rest of the students used English most when studying or doing homework. Similar to TOEFL, the amount of language contact did not correspond with pragmatic performance. Ryota reported the most contact and Keita reported the least, but both of them made very small pragmatic gain over time.

Table 5.2 shows the informants' performance on pragmatic measures at Time 1 and 2.

In pragmatic listening, Tomoyo and Yuko were high achievers in both accuracy scores and response times. At Time 2, Tomoyo achieved the score of 26 with a gain of 6 points from Time 1, the highest score in the participant group. Yuko achieved the third highest score of 21 in the group with a gain of 5 points. Yuko's average response speed was the fastest at Time 2, and her speed improved by more than 4 seconds from Time 1. Tomoyo's response time was also among the top five in the group. In contrast, Ryota, Keita and

TABLE 5.1 Informants' background information

	Gender	Age	ESL level	Previous study (years)	Overseas (week)	TOEFL score at Time 1	TOEFL score at Time 2	Average LCP hours	LCP activity with most hours
Ryota	Male	18	1	6	0	453 (39)	503 (48)	48.17 hrs/ week	Watching TV (14.6 hours/week)
Keita	Male	20	1	8	0	427 (40)	497 (48)	11.3	Watching TV (4.5 hours)
Tomoyo	Female	18	2	6	1	457 (49)	487 (55)	34.3	Talking to friends (13.8 hours)
Mitsu	Male	18	2	8	1	477 (47)	533 (50)	43.9	Studying (33.8 hours)
Asako	Female	18	2	6	0	473 (46)	503 (47)	30.5	Studying (16.2 hours)
Shoko	Female	18	2	6	1	477 (49)	513 (54)	41.7	Studying (22.8 hours)
Yuko	Female	18	2	8	2	463 (40)	543 (56)	23.3	Talking to friends (10.3 hours)
Ippei	Male	18	2	6	0	463 (41)	503 (51)	36.3	Studying (8.3 hours)

Notes. Names are pseudonymous. 'Previous study': the number of previous formal English study. 'Overseas': living experience in an English-speaking country. The numbers in the parentheses in the TOEFL columns refers to the score in the TOEFL listening section. 'ESL level': Level in the ESL program. 'Average LCP hours': average number of hours per week spent using English. 'LCP activity with most hours': Activity which participants spent most English on.

TABLE 5.2 Informants' performance on pragmatic measures at Time 1 and 2

| Name | Pragmatic listening test | | | | Pragmatic speaking test | | | | | |
| | Score | | Response times | | Score | | Planning time | | Speech rate | |
	Time 1/2	Dif	Time 1/2	Dif	Time 1/2	Dif	Time 1/2	Dif	Time 1/2	Dif
Ryota	14/9	− 5	14.4/13.4	− 1.0	27.5/25.5	− 2.0	55.1/46.4	− 8.7	59.3/55.0	− 4.3
Keita	12/7	− 5	26.3/23.3	− 3.0	26.0/26.5	+ 0.5	56.5/57.3	+ 0.8	81.7/75.2	− 6.5
Tomoyo	20/26	+ 6	10.1/10.0	− 0.1	29.0/34.5	+ 5.5	27.3/19.7	− 7.6	115.6/111.8	− 3.8
Mitsu	20/16	− 4	12.9/9.8	− 3.1	21.0/30.0	+ 9.0	34.2/46.4	+ 12.2	74.2/78.8	+ 4.6
Asako	11/22	+ 11	23.5/17.1	− 6.4	28.5/28.0	− 0.5	46.1/42.6	− 3.5	53.0/56.4	+ 3.4
Shoko	19/14	− 5	15.1/15.5	+ 0.4	28.0/33.5	+ 5.5	36.1/32.7	− 3.4	93.0/68.5	− 24.5
Yuko	16/21	+ 5	11.7/7.3	− 4.4	23.5/28.5	+ 5.0	43.2/43.8	+ 0.6	90.6/104.0	+ 13.4
Ippei	8/15	+ 7	11.6/12.9	− 1.3	28.0/23.0	− 5.0	70.8/42.6	− 28.2	83.5/84.20	+ 0.7
Ave	**15.8**		**13.6**		**27.3**		**48.3**		**85.0**	

Notes: Time 1/2: Time 1 data/Time 2 data. Dif: Time 2 value subtracted from Time 1 value. PLT response times: average number of seconds taken to answer items correctly. PST planning time: average number of seconds taken to prepare for each speech act. PST score range: 0–40. PLT score range: 0–32. PST score range: 0–40. PST speech rate: average number of words spoken per minute. Ave: average of the whole participant group (N = 48) at Time 2.

Shoko were low achievers in pragmatic comprehension. Their score dropped 3–5 points from Time 1 to Time 2 and were all below average score of 15.8. Their response speed was also slow, below an average of 13.6 seconds. Mitsu and Asako, on the other hand, showed distinct patterns of development. While Mitsu's accuracy score dropped by 4 points at Time 2, his response speed became faster by 3 seconds, much faster than the group average. Asako's pattern was opposite to Mitsu's: she was accurate in comprehension but slow in response. She made a phenomenal gain of 11 points in accuracy scores at Time 2, the largest gain in the group, reaching the second highest after Tomoyo. Her gain in response speed was also remarkable: it was the largest decrease of 6.4 seconds in response time, but it was still far above the group mean. Ippei improved both on accuracy scores and response times, and his performance was about average.

Similar to their performance in pragmatic listening, Tomoyo and Shoko were high achievers in pragmatic speaking, both in appropriateness score and fluency. They increased their appropriateness scores by more than 5 points at Time 2. Both of them were fast in planning. Tomoyo's planning time at Time 2 was less than half of the group mean. Shoko also decreased her planning time by over 3 seconds at Time 2 and placed herself as the third fastest planner in the group. The opposite trend was found in Ryota and Keita: their appropriateness scores were low and their planning speeds were slow. Ryota became faster in planning over time, but his planning time at Time 2 was still either below or near the group mean. Keita made little change, and he was particularly slow in planning – averaging 57 seconds at Time 2.

Ippei, on the other hand, showed an unbalanced development. His planning speed became faster by 28 seconds at Time 2, but his appropriateness score dropped by 5 points. Mitsu and Yuko also showed unbalanced progress but in the opposite direction: their appropriateness scores were high but their planning speeds were slow. Mitsu's improvement in appropriateness was particularly impressive: he recorded a gain of 9 points at Time 2, the largest gain in the group. Yuko made a gain of 5 points. Her score was less impressive than Mitsu's but was still beyond the group mean. Neither of them improved on planning speed. Mitsu became slower in planning by more than 12 seconds. Asako made very little improvement in appropriateness score, but her score was above the group mean. Her planning speed was below the group mean.

Tomoyo and Yuko's speech rate was well beyond the average: they spoke at the rate of over 100 words per minute. While Tomoyo's speech rate was already fast at Time 1, Yuko made a large gain at Time 2. The rest of the students had below average speech rates. Shoko's speech rate became even slower over time by about 24 words per minute.

In summary, the eight informants varied greatly in their developmental trajectories. Tomoyo and Yuko clearly excelled in most aspects of pragmatic abilities at Time 1 and Time 2. Their scores on the PLT and PST were strong, and they were also fluent in their comprehension and production. Ryota and

Keita were generally on the low end of pragmatic competence. Their scores on the PLT and PST were low, and they were slow in processing. Ippei's scores and fluency were about average for both pragmatic comprehension and production. Shoko, Mitsu and Asako, on the other hand, demonstrated unbalanced performance across different aspects of pragmatic competence. Asako's improvement on the PLT score was impressive, but her appropriateness score on the PST was near the average. In contrast, Mitsu was strong in pragmatic production but weak in comprehension. Shoko was not very strong in pragmatic comprehension, but she made a large gain in appropriateness scores in pragmatic production.

These variations in the eight participants are discussed in the following case histories of individual participants. In order to analyze individual cases, this study used a data triangulation method and collected qualitative data from five sources: student interviews, teacher interviews, class observations, student journals and field notes. (See Chapter 4 for the descriptions of each data source.)[2] These qualitative data revealed unique opportunities and experiences for pragmatic learning available on campus and their interaction with individuals' developmental trajectories. I will present the findings in the following order: Shoko, Yuko, Keita, Ryota, Asako, Mitsu, Ippei and Tomoyo.[3]

Case Histories

Shoko

Figures 5.1 through 5.8 show the group average on the pragmatic listening test (PLT) ($N = 48$) as well as the accuracy score and response times that Shoko recorded at every time point. Shoko's pragmatic listening was erratic. Her initial PLT score was only slightly above average and her score dropped at Time 2, but she made a large gain afterwards and achieved the highest score

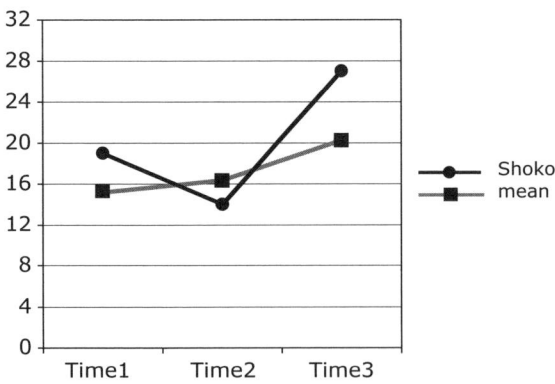

Figure 5.1 Shoko's change in PLT accuracy score

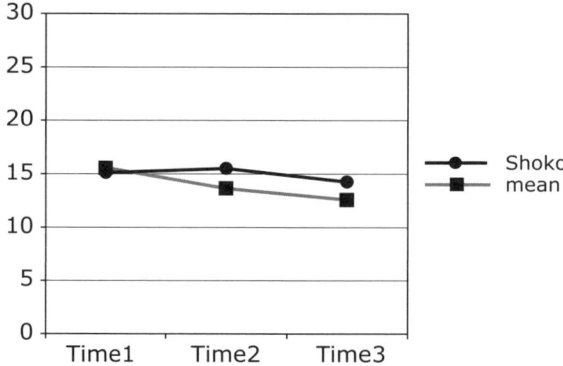

Figure 5.2 Shoko's change in PLT response times

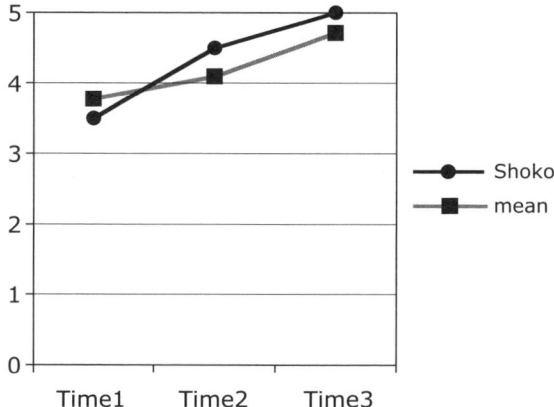

Figure 5.3 Shoko's change in PST appropriateness score, low-imposition speech acts

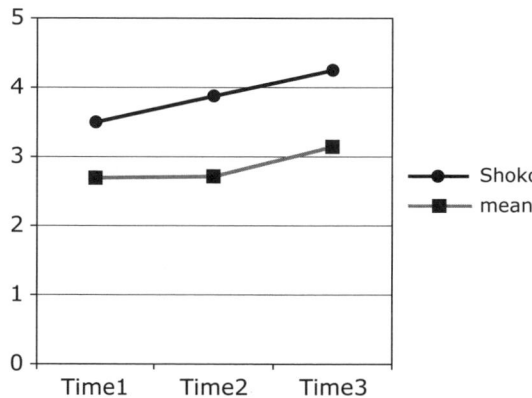

Figure 5.4 Shoko's change in PST appropriateness score, high-imposition speech acts

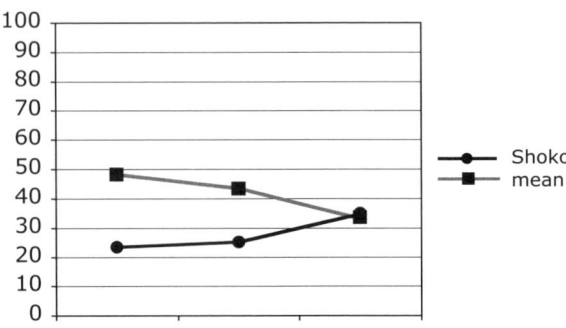

Figure 5.5 Shoko's change in PST planning time, low-imposition speech acts

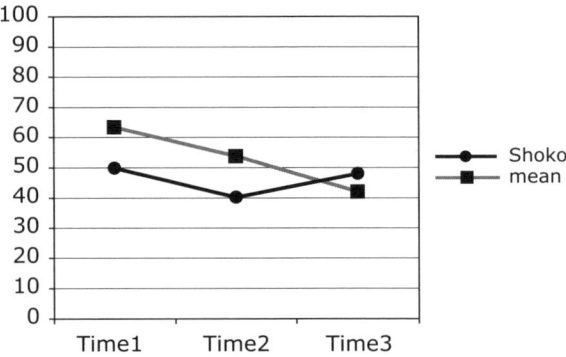

Figure 5.6 Shoko's change in PST planning time, high-imposition speech acts

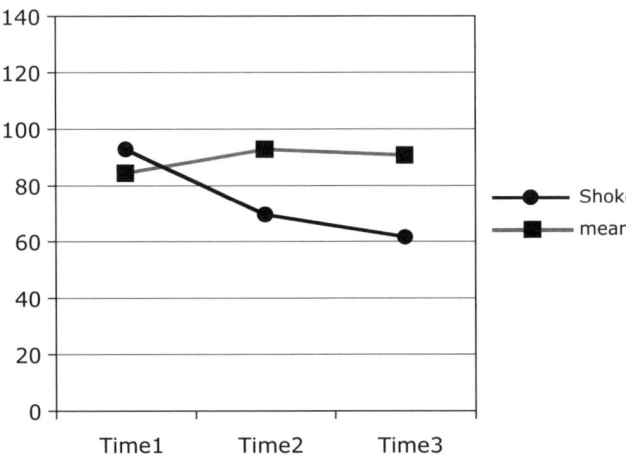

Figure 5.7 Shoko's change in PST speech rate, low-imposition speech acts

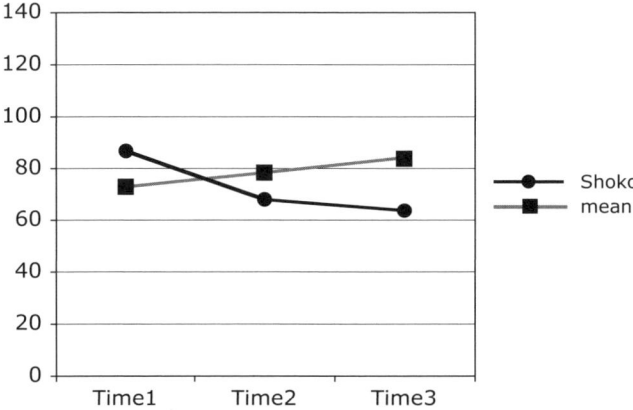

Figure 5.8 Shoko's change in PST speech rate, high-imposition speech acts

at Time 3. However, Shoko's processing speed was rather slow. Response times remained below average and improved only negligibly over time.

On the other hand, Shoko's appropriateness scores on the pragmatic speaking test (PST) was very strong. Her score on low-imposition speech acts started out slightly lower than group mean, but it improved by more than 1.5 points over two semesters and reached the maximum score of 5.0 at Time 3. Her performance on high-imposition speech acts is even more impressive. She made steady progress at every time period, and excelled the group mean by more than one point throughout the term. Her score at Time 3 was the highest in the group. However, Shoko's fluency on the PST measure was not very strong. Although Shoko started out above the average speech rate at Time 1, her speech rate dropped at Time 2 and remained below average at Time 3. Similarly, her planning time increased only gradually, while the group average decreased significantly over time. These patterns were similar for low- and high-imposition speech acts.

Shoko's developmental trajectories can be summarized as follows: she was strong in the knowledge dimension of pragmatic competence as illustrated in her high appropriateness scores on the PST, but she was weak in the processing dimension of pragmatic competence as evident in slow comprehension speed and production fluency. Her accuracy score on the PLT showed a nonlinear development. Interpretations of these developmental trajectories are described below.

Shoko is from Sapporo City, the capital of the northmost prefecture, Hokkaido, with a population of 1.8 million. She went to a regular public high school but she was in *eigo-ka* or English-track in which students have more English classes than regular-track students. She had seven hours of English classes every week co-taught by Japanese instructors and an English-speaking instructor. Her English class had a range of traditional and more communicative activities. She named 'side translation' as a common class activity: in pairs, one student reads aloud a text line by line, and the other student translates. Another typical activity was textbook presentation. In addition, her school had a debate competition as part of the curriculum, and Shoko was on the organizing committee. Her interaction with the native speaker instructor was sporadic: she talked to him only in her senior year when she asked him to proofread her essays as she prepared for the college entrance exam. However, she had an opportunity to interact with international students. Every year her class hosted a student from an English-speaking country. She became friends with the students and shared a variety of activities with them, such as having lunch together, preparing for the school festival, or organizing and participating in a sports meet. Communication was almost always in English. She home-stayed in Australia for two weeks when she was in high school.

What attracted Shoko most to the English-medium institution was the 'English-only classes'. She repeatedly said that she was disappointed with her high-school English classes because they were not conducted entirely in English. She had a strong desire to study abroad in order to improve her communication skills and later use them in a position with UNICEF or other international organizations. She said that she is satisfied with the college environment that forces her to use English to communicate. She had four English-speaking friends during the first semester from Australia and Taiwan. She got to know them through their mutual friends and club activities. She talked to them in the cafeteria, library or in the residence hall, for over a couple of hours at a time. After the first semester, her friends went back to their home country and she had less contact with English speakers. In the second semester, her English contact was reduced to once or twice a week for five to ten minutes at a time. In order to compensate for this decreased contact, she watched English-language DVDs extensively, five to seven hours per week.

Throughout the interview sessions, Shoko was polite and rather quiet. Her responses were relevant and to the point but short: she usually provided a one- to three-sentence response and elaborated on it only when probed. In class, she was always on task and followed teachers' directions well. She had her electric dictionary placed on her desk all the time and looked up new vocabulary occasionally. She reported spending three hours on homework daily, mostly on reading assignments. The three EAP teachers I interviewed unanimously commended her for her English ability. They identified Shoko as one of the most competent students in class. However, they also shared the impression that Shoko was not very active and did not participate much in class. Chris, her writing instructor, said:

> (Shoko is) a great student, a well-rounded student. I hope her confidence grows. She needs more confidence. She might be the best student in that

class. All of her skills are polished, but I'm not sure how well she knows that. If she internalizes that kind of knowledge, she would be better. (She participates) sporadically, when I ask her. She doesn't often freely participate. (November, 2008)

To support this comment, I rarely saw her speaking up or volunteering answers in class: of the 22 class periods I observed, I observed her speaking up in class six times.

Among the 12 informants, Shoko was one of the three students who identified the sociolinguistic aspect (e.g. formal vs. informal language, register variation) as a major difference between Japanese and English communication styles. She said that the Japanese language is more polite than English because of its elaborate honorifics systems. She admitted her lack of knowledge of formal vs. informal speech styles in English, but she confidently said that register variation does exist in English, and English speakers differentiate speech styles according to situation. I asked her if she usually changes her way of speaking between teachers and friends. She said 'yes' and gave me several examples: when asking a favor, she used 'Could you' instead of 'Can you' and used the hedging 'I'm afraid' as a politeness marker, which she picked up in class by observing her peers' usage. She also recalled the instance when a teacher explained the politeness nuance between 'Can I' and 'May I'.

These sociocultural sensitivity and attentiveness, as well as fragmental but explicit pragmalinguistic knowledge, were reflected in her above-average appropriateness scores. She made a large gain in the low-imposition speech acts in the first semester. Her score rose up to 4.5 at Time 2 and increased to 5.0 at Time 3. Her score on the high-imposition speech acts was at the level of 'fair' (band 3) at Time 1 and 2, but at Time 3 it rose to the level of 'good' (band 4). The excerpts of her high-imposition speech acts below illustrate her progress over three time points. A qualitative difference in her Time 3 speech act is found in the emergence of bi-clausal structure, 'I wonder if' + verb, in the request:

High-imposition request (asking a teacher for an extension of a paper)

Time 1
Excuse me professor Lee, I caught a cold, so I couldn't get up, and I have written only two pages, so could you give me extra two days to finish the paper?

Time 2
Im very sorry, but I haven't finished your report, so can I, can you give me extra days to finish it?

Time 3
Excuse me professor Lee, I, I have, have a question about due date of the essay. I caught a cold and I wrote essay only two pages so far. I know the due is tomorrow, tomorrow, but I wonder if I, I, I could turn in two days later.

Shoko was the only student who produced this mitigated preparatory request form at Time 3. Although the forms were not grammatically perfect and contained some lexical errors, the leap from 'could/can you' to the embedded sentence structure is remarkable, particularly because the rest of the 47 students did not attempt the use of this pragmalinguistic form.

There was a story behind this extraordinary progress. At the introspective verbal interview, she reported that she was conscientious about using the form 'I wonder if' because about three weeks ago, her teacher and academic advisor, Tom, gave her corrective feedback on an email message she had written to him. He explicitly told her to use 'I wonder if'. Below is the email message she sent to the teacher, requesting to schedule an appointment for an academic advising, followed by the teacher's reply (cited with permission):

Shoko's email to Tom (November, 2008)

Good afternoon. I'm Shoko. I want to see you on Tuesday, 25th to talk about my registration. Do you have time? I can meet you anytime except from 9:00am to 10:15am and after 4:30pm. Sorry to late the appointment.

EAP 3-H
Shoko Ikeda

Tom's reply to Shoko

Shoko,

Well, I do have some time, but you have to learn how to be a bit more polite in your emails. You must use a more polite form with teachers than you do with your friends. For example, with a friend you say 'I want/I need/Let's go' but with a teacher you write: I am wondering if I can set up an appointment with you next week sometime to discuss my winter term registration. Are you free at all next week? I look forward to hearing from you.

Sincerely,
Shoko

I know it sounds very formal, but you can't email me the same way you would your friends. The email you sent sounded too demanding. Be careful. I can see you on Tuesday afternoon, okay?   Tom

This email was a total surprise to Shoko. I could tell her excitement from her smile and high-pitched voice when describing this incident. She said that she was shocked simply because it had never happened to her before. She had sent similar emails to Tom and other instructors before but they never corrected her. After comparing the two emails, she realized that the expressions were completely different. This was obviously a memorable event for her because she was able to recall the incident and apply the knowledge three weeks later when she took the PST. Her follow-up action probably reinforced the learning: she revised her email message following Tom's suggestion and sent it back to him with an apology. Clearly Shoko took this as an opportunity for pragmalinguistic practice. As Tom's email closed with 'I can see you on Tuesday afternoon, okay?', Shoko's original message had a clear perlocutionary effect (i.e. setting up an appointment). The speech act of request was complete, and there was no reason for her to send a new message with the same intention, other than to practice the pragmalinguistic forms.

Interestingly, Shoko had prior knowledge of the form 'I wonder if' as a polite request-making expression. Her high-school textbook listed the expression with a footnote saying that it is a formal request form, and so she memorized it. She said that she could not use it until she saw Tom's email because she did not know when to use it. As the textbook only said 'formal expression', she was not sure in what type of formal occasions she can use it – whether it is something she can use in daily conversation or in some special, ceremonial occasions. The form sounded too formal and polite to her, and she thought that it is not something she can use to a teacher whom she had known for some time. However, the form–context mapping clicked when she saw Tom's email. She learned that she can use the form in this type of situation.

Later I sent an email to Tom and asked why he corrected Shoko. I found this unusual of Tom, considering that he did not care about students' use of direct, disrespectful language when they came to his office to complain about his class (see Chapter 5). This time he gave a corrective feedback to Shoko's inappropriate language use. Tom replied:

> Good question really. I think Steve (director of the EAP program) had voiced concern over it, and at the last faculty development seminar for the university, many professors talked about how rude students were in their emails. I would say partly it's because of the discussion we have been having on the topic, but more importantly, I just didn't like the tone of the email. I am very busy during the last three weeks of any semester and Shoko was just demanding something from me. I just felt annoyed by the tone. I know that Shoko had no ill feelings towards me, but the email was so direct, like an order. (December, 2008)

Tom's reply indicates that students' politeness was a major topic of discussion in the school community around the time he received Shoko's email. The saliency of the issue, combined with his personal reaction stemming from the busy time of the year, prompted him to give explicit feedback to Shoko.

The robustness of this learning experience was also evident in the introspective verbal interview with Shoko. During the interview, she completed five items taken from the PST in front of me (two requests and three opinions) and reflected on her performance immediately. She produced the form 'I wonder if' again in the high-imposition request we went over together. In addition, she was able to transfer the form to another high-imposition speech act – the speech act of opinion. See below for Shoko's speech act of expressing a negative opinion to a teacher in italics, followed by her accounts for the choice of the form (see Appendix D for the complete situational scenarios used in the PST):

High-imposition opinion (expressing a negative opinion to a teacher about his class)

I like your class and I'm interested in French history, but I, I am wondering if I could learn about French pop culture or some recent culture of France.

'I paid attention to my language. This is a suggestion, but I tried to make it politer. I remembered Tom's email. It was in my mind, so I used 'I'm wondering if'. Maybe in the last test session I didn't use it for this situation, but for request-making situations, I used it. Here I wanted to express that I like the class but I want to learn other things too'.

This excerpt demonstrates her solid understanding of the form 'I wonder if + clause' and its contextual requirements. Tom's email was powerful enough for her to internalize the form and apply the knowledge to a different situation that shares similar contextual features.

An additional episode here suggests that affect and emotion, as well as learnability, also contributed to the robustness of Shoko's learning. Yosuke, another informant in this study, witnessed the whole email exchange between Shoko and Tom. Yosuke was Shoko's boyfriend, and he was in the same class with Shoko. During the interview, he told me that he saw Tom's email to Shoko. By reading the email, he also learned that 'I wonder if' is a polite request form and should be used in communication with a teacher. However, this knowledge was not internalized well in Yosuke's case because he did not use the form in his speech acts. Instead, he used a direct form 'please + verb' in high-imposition requests. When I asked him why he did not use 'I wonder if', he said that he thought about the form but decided not to use it because he was not confident with formulating a clause structure after it. Consequently, he avoided the difficult structure and opted for the simple form, 'please + verb'. This story suggests that from the same experience, Shoko learned the form but Yosuke did not. It is possible that the emotional arousal and surprise associated with the experience might have facilitated

Shoko's learning. Alternatively, due to his shaky grammatical knowledge and lack of familiarity with the target structure, Yosuke was not able to use the request form, although it remained in his long-term memory.

During the interview Shoko expressed that, after coming to the college, she started paying attention to polite expressions in English in her peers' talk and emails, and she sometimes recorded them in her journal. She learned mitigating devices such as 'I'm afraid' and 'I wonder' through observation and teacher feedback, but she admitted that it was difficult to use them while coping with the processing demand of online speech. When she was focused on the organization and content, she could not pay attention to details. Situational descriptions sometimes slipped her mind, and after skipping one or two words, she could no longer continue talking with confidence. Speaking in English was demanding in itself, and speaking 'politely' was even more so.

Shoko's processing difficulty was also evident in her fluency in speech acts. At Time 3, her speech rate was slower than average, projecting a clear asymmetry relationship with her high appropriateness score. Her planning time was also notably longer than average: it even increased from Time 2 to Time 3, while the group mean decreased. Her stagnation in fluency development over time could be explained by her limited contact with English-speaking friends and teachers, as explained in the previous section. She had only three international student friends. Although she spent extensive time with them in the first semester, in the second semester her contact with English speakers became periodic and short, reduced to a few times a week for about five to 10 minutes. She spent the majority of her time studying alone and watching DVDs.

This case history revealed a range of elements required for pragmatic development. Explicit feedback and modeling on pragmalinguistic forms are important, but learner's positive stance toward them is equally vital. The forms are noticed, internalized and retained if learners act on them through practice and recycled use, and the process can be facilitated through learner's internal characteristics such as affect, emotion and linguistic readiness. Their personality and attitudes could also influence this learning. Among the 12 informants, Shoko stood out as a student who was attentive and inquisitive about formality, politeness and register variation in English. She observed how people say things and kept mental notes of lexical and syntactic mitigations and hedging forms she overheard. It is possible that this sociopragmatic sensitivity helped her to appreciate the corrective feedback she received from her teacher and fostered the learning. While the acquisition of pragmalinguistics forms could result from a single, eye-opening learning occasion combined with learners' positive stance toward learning, fluency gain could be a product of accumulative practice and time-on-task. Pragmatic fluency, like other levels of fluency, may require abundant, sustained communication practice to develop.

Yuko

Figures 5.9 through 5.16 show the group average on the PLT measure and Yuko's accuracy score and response times at every time point. Yuko's competence in pragmatic listening was clear. Although she started out at about average score at Time 1, her score increased greatly at Time 2 and again at Time 3, further widening the gap with the group mean. Her score was the highest in the group at Time 3. Her comprehension speed, measured by response times, was also much faster than average from the onset of the study, and it became faster gradually over time. Overall, she did very well on the pragmatic comprehension measure.

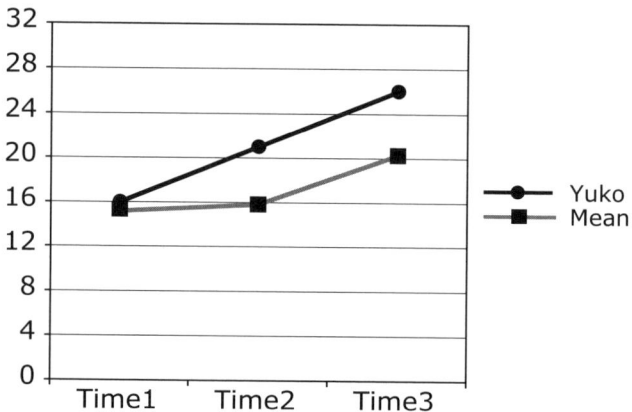

Figure 5.9 Yuko's change in PLT accuracy score

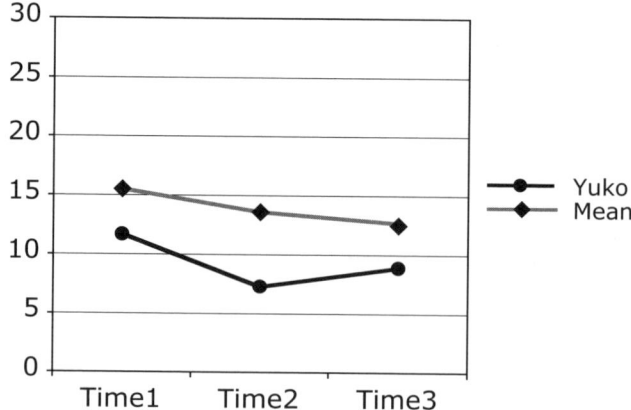

Figure 5.10 Yuko's change in PLT response times

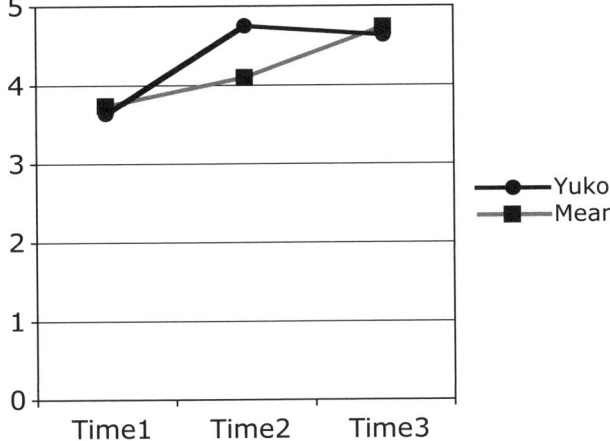

Figure 5.11 Yuko's change in PST appropriateness score, low-imposition speech acts

Yuko's pragmatic production, on the other hand, was not as impressive, but she made some gain over time. Between the two types of speech acts, she did better on low-imposition than high-imposition speech acts. Although her score was near the group average at Time 1, it increased by almost one full point at Time 2, and she maintained the score at Time 3. Her score on the high-imposition speech acts, on the other hand, was below average and showed little progress from Time 1 to Time 2, but it increased by half of a

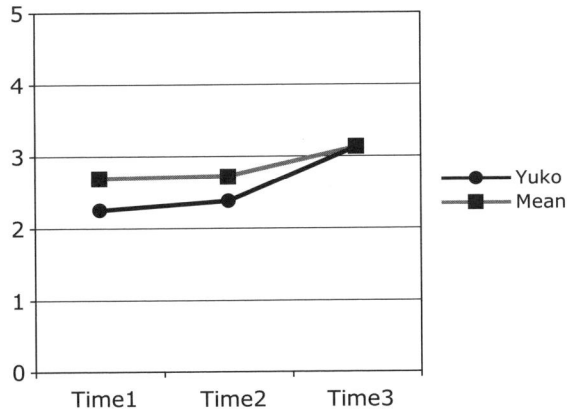

Figure 5.12 Yuko's change in PST appropriateness score, high-imposition speech acts

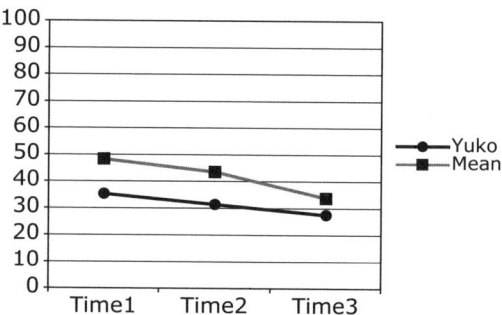

Figure 5.13 Yuko's change in PST planning time, low-imposition speech acts

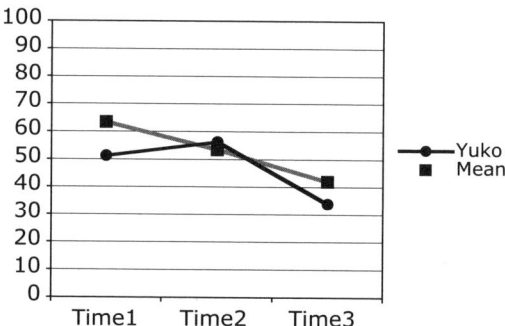

Figure 5.14 Yuko's change in PST planning time, high-imposition speech acts

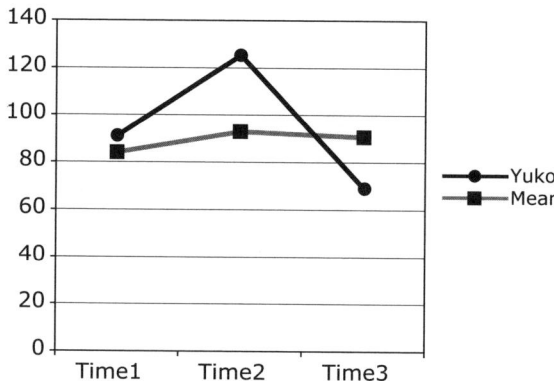

Figure 5.15 Yuko's change in PST speech rate, low-imposition speech acts

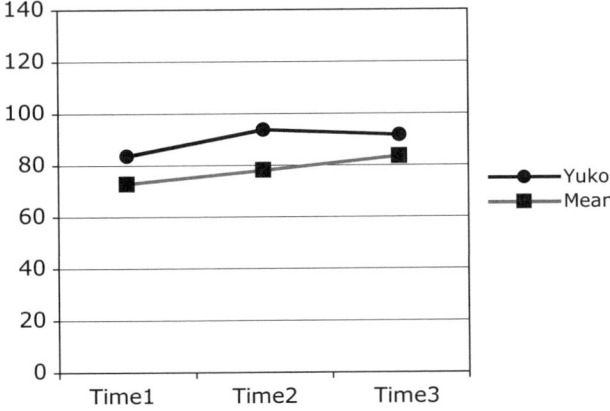

Figure 5.16 Yuko's change in PST speech rate, high-imposition speech acts

point at Time 3 to the level of the group mean. Yuko's fluency in pragmatic production, however, was above the average most of the time. Except for the strange drop in her low-imposition speech rate at Time 3, her speech rate was consistently faster than the group mean. Her planning time for both situation types was also shorter than average most of the time. Yuko's trajectories of pragmatic development are summarized as follows: she exhibited a strong pragmatic comprehension in both accuracy score and response times; an above-average appropriate production of low-imposition speech acts and fluency; and a below average appropriateness score of high-imposition speech acts. The following section provides insights into her patterns of development.

Yuko is from Sendai City in the Miyagi prefecture. Sendai is a medium-sized city with a population of one million, located about 220 miles north of Tokyo. Yoko went to a regular public high school, but like Shoko, she was in *eigo-ka*, and received more contact hours in English than other regular-track students. She had 10 hours of English instruction per week. Her English class incorporated CALL, and common classroom activities involved computer-based conversation practice, narrative animation and essay writing based on the story introduced via computer. She also received more traditional-style English instruction, such as word-by-word translation of English texts, reading comprehension exercises and grammar exercises. The classes were taught by a Japanese instructor and two native speaker instructors. English-speaking instructors team-taught the CALL classes, and their responsibilities mainly involved proof reading students' essays. Yuko told me that she had daily contact with the native speaker instructors. After school, she visited their desks in the teachers' office to chat, and she and the teachers often walked home together. They talked about many things entirely in English, such as tourist attractions in the United States and England and their experiences in

Japan. She home-stayed for two weeks in the United States during her junior year. She was also enrolled in a private English conversation class when she was in junior high school.

Yuko explained that she chose this university for its all-English classes and study-abroad opportunities. She wishes to work in a place where she can use English in the future. Although she was initially worried that she may not be able to keep up with all-English classes, her adjustment to the university was not difficult. After the first week, she became able to understand classroom directions. She said that her understanding improved when she started spending time with international students. Her social circle was in the dormitory lounge. Right next to the entrance, there is a spacious area with several couches and a large plasma screen television. The area is surrounded with floor-to-ceiling windows to give an open feeling. Yuko told me that many international students hang out there in the evening, and so it became her routine to have dinner with them at the cafeteria and move to the lounge to chat. Yuko was not shy at all in approaching them. When she saw a group of international students, she often went to join the group by saying 'Is this seat open?' She was also active in making new friends. At the beginning of the semester, she volunteered for being a 'peer supporter'. She assisted in orienting new comers to the dormitory by helping them to unpack and by showing them around. The next day, when she saw the students whom she assisted, she went up to them and asked if they remembered her name. She approached them like this several times until they finally remembered her name. In the informant group I interviewed, no other student was socially as proactive as Yuko.

Yuko's outgoing personality and social skill, along with her competent spoken English she developed in high school through daily interaction with native-speaker instructors, seemed to have helped expand her social network with foreign students quickly. She told me that she had 20 English-speaking friends and that she talked to them almost every day. Her reported amount of language contact with friends was over 10 hours per week on average, often reaching 3–4 hours per day (see Table 5.1 for the summary of LCP). While other students reported more contact hours on homework assignments, Yuko used English the most when talking to friends. She also had an intense interest in foreign languages and was a member of Spanish, Hangul and Latin clubs. Since international students and faculty typically were instructors of those languages, club activities served as another venue for Yuko to expand her English-speaking network. Talking to international students was the only source of listening and speaking practice she reported having on campus. She told me that she never practiced for TOEFL listening section, but she nonetheless made an impressive gain of 16 points over two semesters. Although her listening skills were strong, her writing skills, particularly grammatical accuracy and vocabulary density, were weak.

Yuko was an active participant in class: when asked for a list of strong, motivated students in class, all EAP instructors named Yuko. In all classes I observed, she sat in the front row, right in front of the teachers. She could not even tell me how often she usually spoke up in class because she participated so frequently. Out of the 12 classes I observed, I saw Yuko speaking up 17 times. She was always attentive in class. Yuko was usually the one who responded to teachers' questions promptly. One instructor mentioned that her spoken ability was beyond EAP level – far more advanced than the class average. However, the instructors also shared concerns about her poor performance on vocabulary quizzes and her habit of producing written work in haste.

From these observations, it is not surprising that Yuko made a large gain on the pragmatic listening test. She was exposed to authentic English for extended hours through her daily contact with international students. She had a number of resources and personal qualities – competent oral skills, previous communication experience with native speakers, an outgoing personality and social skills – that helped her gain access to these international students and establish membership in their community. Her expanded social circle brought her numerous occasions for sustained listening practice as well as opportunities to practice speaking, which probably contributed to her fluency gain on the pragmatic speaking task.

While Yuko was clearly excelled in pragmatic listening, both in accuracy and response speed, her appropriateness score, particularly that of high-imposition speech acts, was not impressive. Her score was below average at Time 1 and Time 2, and barely reached the group mean at Time 3. These statistics further confirm that students do not necessarily gain in all aspects of pragmatic competence simultaneously: some aspects develop quickly while others are much slower to develop. The course of developmental trajectories that students follow is determined by types of pragmatic opportunity available in context, learners' agency in accessing the opportunity and personal qualities that arbitrate the access. In the case of Yuko, frequent, extended interaction with international students boosted her inferential listening ability and oral fluency, but it did not help her to acquire an appropriate linguistic means for performing formal high-imposition speech acts.

Like Yuko, most students in this study had difficulty with high-imposition speech acts. As was discussed in Chapter 4, there are several potential reasons for this difficulty, including a lack of opportunity to perform such speech acts, an absence of explicit information and teaching on formal language use, a processing demand stemming from complex linguistic structures required for those speech acts, and students' preference toward simple, direct communication style at the expense of elaborate politeness strategies. Yuko's case can be explained by some of these reasons. Knowledge of linguistic forms in a formal register does not develop naturally in the immersion context studied here, unless, as observed in Shoko's case, there is an opportunity to notice and internalize the forms through explicit teaching and feedback.

However, Yuko demonstrated an emerging level of pragmatic awareness and sociocultural sensitivity. Among the 12 informants I interviewed, Yuko was one of the three students who assertively said that register variation exists in English, and English speakers change speech styles according to situation. She said that in comparison with politeness in Japanese, which is grammatically encoded through special verb endings and noun particles, politeness in English is expressed in a less visible manner. When I asked her whether English has anything equivalent to Japanese honorifics, she responded:

> Maybe there is something like that, though it doesn't show in grammar. For example, vocabulary. There are words used for formal situations vs. informal, casual words used among friends, like slang. (October, 2008)

Yuko's sociopragmatic awareness was also evident in the introspective verbal interviews conducted at the end of the semester. During the interview, she completed five speech act items taken from the PST in front of me and reflected on her performance immediately. The italics below are the low- and high-imposition requests she produced, followed by her accounts for the choice of linguistic forms (see Appendix D for the complete situational scenarios in the PST):

Low-imposition request (asking a friend for a pen)

Ken, can I borrow your pen?

I used 'can I' because it's among close friends, and the speech was casual. There are other expressions, like 'could you', 'would you', and 'may I', but the first thing that came to my mind was 'can I'. I came across similar situation before, asking an international student to open the door.

High-imposition request (asking a professor for an extension of a paper)

I have a cold, so I don't think I can finish my assignment so could you please give me extra two days?

This one was to a professor, so I gave him a reason why I needed an extension. I tried to be polite, and used 'could you please'. It's politer than 'can I'.

See other examples on a low- and high-imposition opinion speech act:

Low-imposition opinion (expressing an opinion to a friend about his clothes)

You can try another colour. How about black one?

(In response to a question whether other expressions like 'you should' or 'why don't you try' are viable) If I use 'you should', it sounds like the clothes look terrible. It's too strong, forceful. 'You can' is much softer, and 'why don't you try' is probably OK too. I used 'you can' here because I use it often, for instance, when I offered international students local food, I said 'You can try'. When I was in high school, I learned that the modal 'should' is used for obligation, and 'can' is conditional, and it's used for a mild suggestion. I saw it in a junior high school textbook too.

High-imposition opinion (expressing an opinion to a professor about his class)

I like your class, but I'm interested in French pop culture, so I'd like you talk about present French culture.

I used 'would like to' because it is to a professor. I thought 'want to' probably means the same thing, but 'would like to' is politer, so I used it instead. It was in the high school English textbook.

These verbal protocols clearly exemplify Yuko's pragmalinguistic and sociopragmatic knowledge. She was aware of the situational differences between low- and high-imposition speech acts and was conscientious about using English that matched the required degree of formality. She had a range of modal expressions in her repertoire that serve the functions of request, suggestion or expression of wish (e.g. 'can I', 'could you please', 'you should', 'you can', 'would like' and 'want to'). She was able to articulate subtle shades of meaning among them, compare and contrast options and make an informed choice of particular expression over another. For instance, she knew that 'could you please' is higher in politeness ranking than 'can I', and she used the former in the high-imposition situation. While Yuko possessed some sociopragmatic knowledge and ability to style-shift appropriately from informal to formal situations, her repertoire of syntactic and lexical mitigations required in formal situations was still incomplete. She was not able to use complex, bi-clausal structures that the majority of native speakers in this study used in high-imposition requests (e.g. 'I wonder if' + clause). She knew those forms as she learned them in high school, but they were not easily retrievable under the task condition. During the interview, I asked her if she could make a request by using the word 'wonder' and 'mind'. She immediately recalled the request-making expression 'I wonder if' and 'would you mind if' and told me that those structures were in high-school English textbooks, and that she practiced them in grammar exercises. However, they never occurred to her while doing the PST because she did not have opportunities to use those forms or observe other people using them outside of her studies.

Yuko also shared an insight with me about how she learned these request-making expressions. She memorized the entire sentences that contained the structure, such as 'Do you mind if I smoke?' and 'Do you mind if I open the window?' This hindered her from using the structure in a productive manner: she did not memorize it as a fixed core with an open slot that can be filled with a variety of words (i.e. 'do you mind if' + clause). As a result, it restricted her usage to asking for permission to smoke or open the window, not for other types of request.

Yuko's case history revealed several key issues related to pragmatic learning. First, different aspects of pragmatic competence exhibited unbalanced development, and the developmental trajectory was constrained by the types of pragmatic opportunity available in context, learner's agency in accessing the opportunity, and personal qualities that arbitrate the access. Opportunities for a long, sustained communication with international students could improve pragmatic listening because of the inferential listening practice available in such interaction. However, the informal register involved in such talk does not afford opportunities to use formal linguistic features such as lexical and syntactic downgraders, which are essential devices to perform high-imposition speech acts. Without frequent encounters with formal language forms and occasions to use them in real-life interaction, it is unlikely that learners make progress in this particular domain of pragmatic knowledge on their own. This is probably why Yuko's understanding of politeness stayed at the high-school level of knowledge and never went beyond the use of modal auxiliaries. Her linguistic repertoire did not extend to bi-clausal structures, although she learned those forms in high school. She learned the structure but did not have sufficient pragmalinguistic control over its use. What is essential in pragmatic expansion, then, is an environment in which learners are exposed to a range of registers and linguistic input associated with them. When the environment does not afford such opportunities, the only way that learners can internalize new form–function–context mappings may be through explicit teaching and feedback, as shown in Shoko's case.

Keita

This section presents a case history of Keita. Figures 5.17 through 5.24 show the group average on the PLT and PST, and Keita's performance recorded at every time point. Keita was clearly an under-achiever in pragmatic listening. His accuracy score remained below the average throughout the time, and his gain from Time 1 to Time 3 was minimal – three points. His comprehension speed remained slow as well. Although his response times dropped by seven seconds over time, they were still the second longest at Time 1 and again at Time 3.

Keita's performance on pragmatic speaking was not impressive either. While his appropriateness score for low-imposition speech acts was above

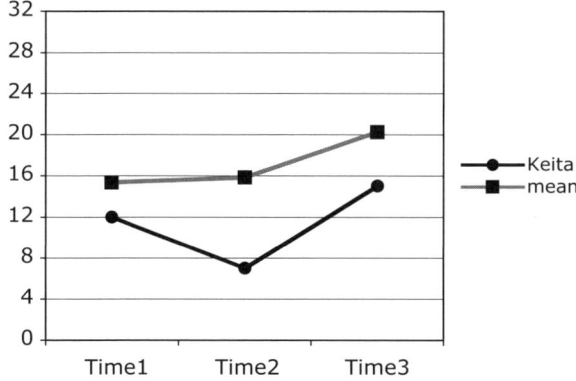

Figure 5.17 Keita's change in PLT accuracy score

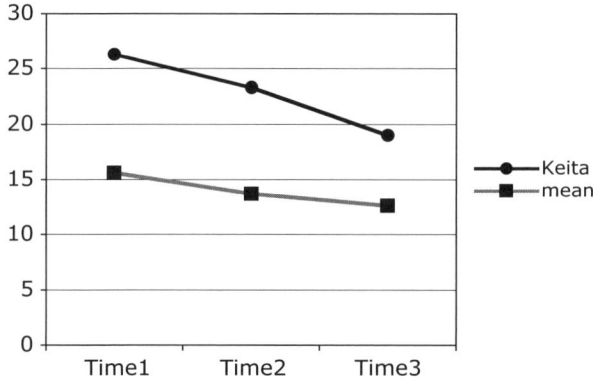

Figure 5.18 Keita's change in PLT response times

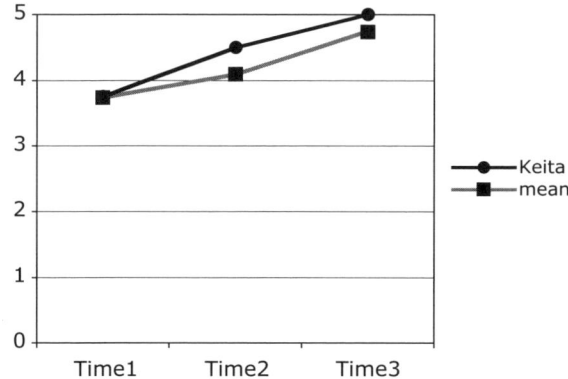

Figure 5.19 Keita's change in PST appropriateness score, low-imposition speech act

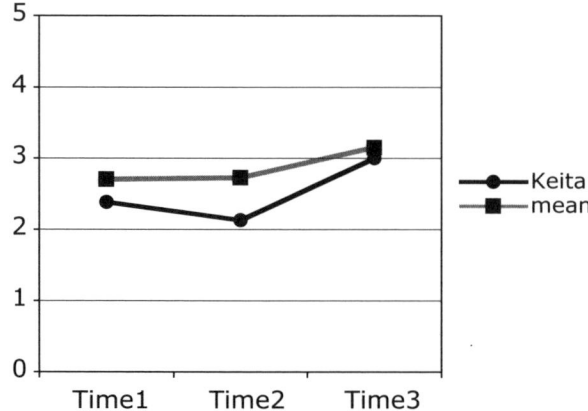

Figure 5.20 Keita's change in PST appropriateness score, high-imposition speech acts

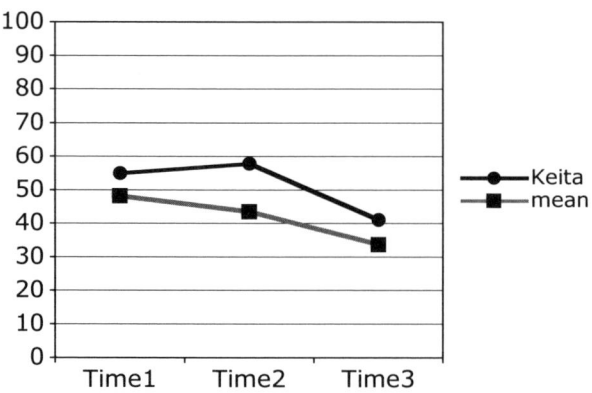

Figure 5.21 Keita's change in PST planning time, low-imposition speech acts

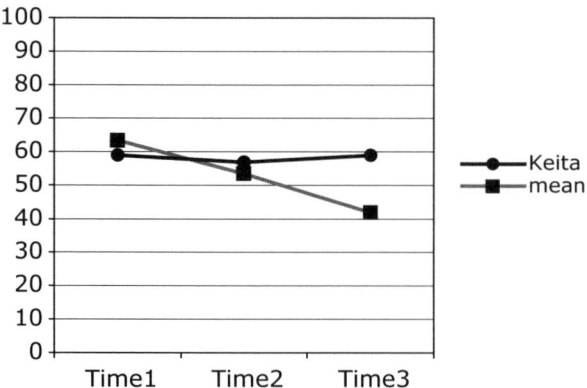

Figure 5.22 Keita's change in PST planning time, high-imposition speech acts

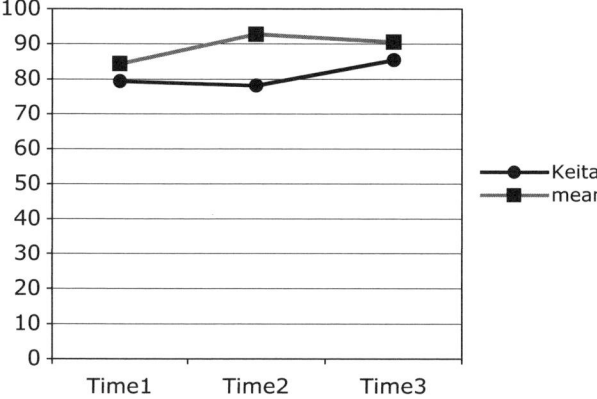

Figure 5.23 Keita's change in PST speech rate, low-imposition speech acts

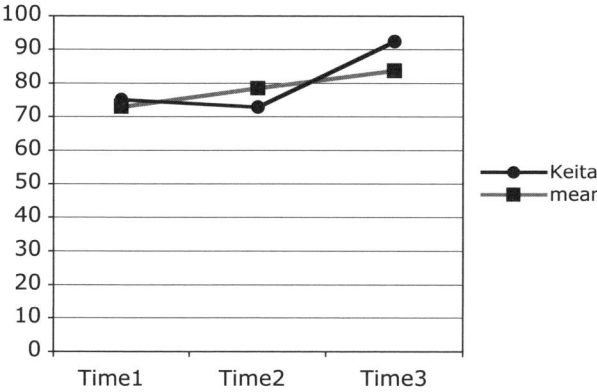

Figure 5.24 Keita's change in PST speech rate, high-imposition speech acts

average, his score for high-imposition speech acts remained below average throughout the period. He was also a slow planner: he needed more time to prepare for speech acts than average regardless of the situation type. It is notable that his planning time for high-imposition speech acts did not change at all over time, while most students recorded a large drop in planning time, as shown in the average drop of 21 seconds from Time 1 to Time 3. His speech rate was also either below or at the average at all time points, except for the average performance he showed at Time 3 for the high-imposition speech acts.

Keita's underdevelopment in all aspects of pragmatic competence came as a surprise to me. Through my observation in class, my direct interaction with him and my interviews with his teachers, Keita appeared to be the most social, outgoing and vocal student in class, one who was not shy about initiating a conversation or expressing himself in English. He was the one who volunteered answers when the rest of the class remained silent at teachers' prompting. He sometimes raised his hand and asked questions in class, which was not common among the students in his class. I saw him asking questions 10 times in out of the 14 class sessions I observed. He said that he never feels nervous about speaking up and being under the spotlight in class.

Keita's name often came up in teachers' conversations. He was always on the teachers' list of the most active students in class. Three out of four teachers I interviewed named him as their most favorite student in class. They said that he is a pleasant student to work with – diligent, hard-working and active – and that he also has charming personality because he often stays after class to initiate a personal conversation or ask questions. His questions were not limited to English: he often asked questions about current issues like the presidential election and solicited teachers' opinions of them. See the interview excerpt below for further support. The writing instructor, Jennifer, said:

> Keita tends to ask me questions about anything but grammar. He is always interested in beyond the task. He is interested in philosophical questions. He likes to read. He likes to talk about different things…. Last semester no one came to my office. This semester, Keita has come twice to hand in his journal. (October, 2008)

Keita was functional in English too. Although he started out with a relatively low TOEFL score of 423, his score went up to 490 at Time 3.

I initially thought that Keita, with his functional English skills and his extrovert personality, would make strong progress in pragmatic abilities. Although his oral and aural abilities were not as strong as those of Yuko or Tomoyo, Keita shared similar traits with these students: he was not afraid of speaking up in front of people or approaching people to use English. He himself said that he is extremely friendly and social, and these qualities are compatible with people from English-speaking countries. However, through my interviews with him, I found that these traits were largely limited to the classroom, and his social network outside the class was a totally different matter. Below I will describe Keita's academic and social involvement in the university community, and his subjectivity that shaped the patterns and degree of the involvement. I will then discuss them in relation to his modest improvement in pragmatic abilities.

Keita is from Nagasaki city in the Fukuoka prefecture located in the southern island Kyushuu. He is older than most students in the group, because after graduating from high school, he studied in *yobiko* (college preparation school) for two years after failing to receive acceptance to the universities that he wanted to enter. He went to a private high school and received eight to 10 hours of English instruction per week taught by Japanese teachers in Japanese. His classes were focused on grammar and reading, and he had no recollection of practicing communication skills in class. When asked about the most common classroom activity, Keita reported vocabulary memorization: he received a list of vocabulary in Japanese and memorized English translation of them, which he was quizzed on every week. His contact with native speakers was rare. Listening to the textbook passages on tape and dictating them was the only source of listening practice for him in high school.

Keita came to the English-medium university because he liked English; however, he also emphasized that English was not the only area of competence he wanted to polish. Although he had a desire to be able to speak English fluently, he also wished to gain a wide-ranging academic knowledge and cultural competence in Japanese and English. His future goal is to work in an international organization such as the United Nations (UN). Referring to his brother who is pursuing a medical degree, Keita said that although doctors can save a small number of people who they are directly in touch with, nonprofit humanitarian activities such as building schools in Africa could save thousands of people at one time, and this is why he would like to be involved in the UN in the future. He stressed the invaluable role that Japan can play in the UN as the only country that experienced the nuclear bomb firsthand during the World War II. He said that the peace constitution is unique to Japan and should be publicized more to the world. He would like to participate in this process, and this is the reason why he is studying English. His hometown, Nagasaki, was one of the atom-bombed sites, which might have added to his motivation. His relatives fought in the war, and he is a third-generation survivor of the atom-bombing.

This interview description is an example of Keita's maturity observed elsewhere during my interaction with him. No other students in the group gave me such a lengthy explanation of the reason for studying English, or talked about the position and responsibility of Japan in the global society in relation to their career goals. Keita's manner of interaction and topics of conversation were also different from other students I interviewed. For instance, he was the only student who called me *Taguchi-san* (Ms Taguchi) while other students called me *Taguchi-sensei* (Teacher Taguchi). In Japanese, the affix *sensei* followed by last name is a common address term for someone whose job involves teaching. It also serves as an index of asymmetrical relationship and is typically used for someone superior to or older than the speaker. Since the students knew that I teach at Carnegie Mellon University and that I am older than them, it was natural for them to call me *Taguchi-sensei*. Besides, ESL instructors introduced me or referred me as *Taguchi-sensei* or Professor Taguchi in front of the students.

The affix *san* followed by last name that Keita used, on the other hand, is often used between interlocutors in a formal relationship (e.g. colleagues, acquaintances) but does not assume power difference like the affix *sensei*. It is used in an equal power relationship, although in a senior–junior relationship in school, juniors may call their seniors with *san* or *senpai* (senior), which marks power difference. The fact that Keita always used *san* instead of *sensei* to me shows his desire to position himself at an equal level to me, like a colleague who shares the same lifetime goal of mastering English, but not as a student of mine.

Another example of Keita's maturity comes from my class visits. I sometimes visited his class between classes to distribute a schedule for the upcoming data collection session. The class was usually chaotic during break. Students were scattered elsewhere chatting, listening to iPods or sending text messages, and nobody even noticed me entering the classroom. In those occasions, Keita helped me to gather students' attention quickly. He would usually shout to the class, 'Everybody, pay attention!' No other students in any classes were as proactive as Keita.

Keita's independent and autonomous personality was also apparent in his learning style. When asked about his difficulty in adapting to the new university environment, he told me that teachers were sometimes too imposing with their beliefs about effective ways to learn English. For instance, Keita did not like the weekly assignment of recording new vocabulary in the notebook because it did not work for him before. He liked to study vocabulary from commercially available textbooks because they usually give a list of vocabulary in English with Japanese translation next to them. Although he turned in the vocabulary assignment, he confessed that his work was sloppy, just a list of words randomly put together for the sake of course credit. Another example of independent learning style was found in his selective attention in class. He distinguished between what is important and not important to his study, and paid attention to the teachers only when they discussed important materials. For instance, once he determined that his grammar knowledge is above the class level, he only pretended listening to the teachers' grammar explanation, and he was actually self-studying vocabulary with an electronic dictionary aside. He said that he did not want to listen to the things he already knew.

Keita was one of the two students among the 12 informants who constantly relied on Japanese translation in their English study, rather than learning English directly from English. He watched two to three English movies every week, following Japanese subtitles and comparing them with English expressions. While watching, he often jotted down English phrases that do not have literal translation. For example, 'No day but today' was translated to *Kyo-o ikiro* ('Live today') in Japanese. He found this translation interesting and kept note of it. In another example, he picked up a phrase 'I got it' from a movie and used it in class. He was thrilled when the teacher responded by saying 'You got it?' This experience prompted him to look for more phrases from movies and try out with teachers. Keita's reading habit also involved translation. He used to check up every single word, but having realized that it is too time consuming, he limited his dictionary usage to looking up two to five words per paragraph. However, he continued to analyze sentences for grammar. He also translated from Japanese to English when he wrote essays, and he had a habit of switching to Japanese when discussing complex issues in English. In the speaking class, I sometimes saw Keita speaking in Japanese with his partner for the entire period. He switched to English when the teacher came near his desk, but switched back to Japanese after he left.

Reflecting on his translation habit, Keita said that he is often too cautious. When he sees sentences that he cannot comprehend, he feels upset. He gets stuck there and cannot proceed to the next segment because he is too occupied with the previous section. His reading instructor, Lin, shared her observation:

> Keita is slow when putting answers on the board, probably because I embarrassed him in the fist class when he put down answers. I pointed out grammar mistakes in his answers. Nobu is opposite. He put down answers quickly, he goes back to his desk, looks at the answer, and if mistakes, he goes again to revise his answer. Keita doesn't. He writes, erases, modifies, and doesn't leave until he is done. (September, 2008)

These observations revealed Keita's struggle in his transition to the English-only environment. The word-for-word translation habit that he acquired in high school and in *yobiko* discouraged him from processing texts directly in English, consequently slowing down his reading speed. He was clearly form-oriented in his learning. He prioritized accurate, precise translation of structural units in sentences over more top-down strategies such as skipping unknown vocabulary, understanding the main idea and making inferences using contextual information. Because of this translation habit, Keita also struggled with expressing ideas in English spontaneously. He had difficulty in thinking in English and locating the right expressions to convey his thoughts, particularly when the topics involved complex, abstract issues.

His adjustment difficulty was also found in his limited social network on campus. In contrast to his active class participation and interaction with teachers, he had no friends to converse in English outside the class. He rarely talked to his English-speaking suitemate. He had some contact with international students through club activities, but it was limited to brief, informal small talk that took place once a week. He reported that he had no opportunity to speak English outside the class. Chatting with teachers in class and watching DVDs were the only sources of speaking and listening opportunities on campus. In LCP, his reported amount of time spent talking with friends in English was 15 minutes per week in average, which was the second smallest amount in the group of 48 participants.

These observations point to several reasons why Keita made so little progress in fluency aspects of pragmatic listening and speaking tested in this study. He took much more time than average in identifying implied meaning and preparing for speech acts. Although his speech rate for high-imposition speech acts was about average, it was notably slow for low-imposition speech acts. These processing weaknesses seemed to be a consequence of his consistent use of Japanese as a medium of understanding English. His habit of thinking in Japanese and translating sentences into Japanese, combined with his meticulous personality, probably slowed down his processing speed in pragmatic tasks. In addition, he had almost no contact with English speakers outside the class, which further restricted his opportunities for practice and prevented him from developing fluency as quickly as other students. Hence, similar to Shoko's case, development of pragmatic fluency could be a result of abundant time-on-task and skill-based practice. Students may need accumulative listening and speaking practices that help improve their overall processing efficiency. A general level of fluency developed through repeated use of target skills transfers to specific areas of fluency, such as pragmatic fluency.

Keita's case reiterates the importance of processing English in English, not through Japanese, for fluency development. Understanding information in two languages is more costly than understanding meaning directly from one language. The additional cost stemming from translation is likely to negatively affect processing speed particularly in a listening test. Because in listening, auditory information is transient, and there is no text to refer back to after the information is heard; as a result, listeners need to process meaning simultaneously as they hear. Translation inhibits this process of direct meaning access, resulting in comprehension failure. This could explain why Keita's accuracy score in the PLT remained low throughout the period. The introspective verbal interview also revealed numerous cases where Keita misunderstood key vocabulary items in the listening texts.

Keita expressed that the PLT was a difficult test. The speakers spoke too fast, and he could not keep up with naturally spoken English. When I asked him why he did not approach international students for opportunities to listen to authentic English, he said that he felt more relaxed and comfortable being with Japanese friends and speaking in Japanese. I also asked him why he approached the teachers so often but not international students. He responded that talking to teachers was more beneficial than talking to international students because he could ask questions about English, such as which connectors to use to combine two sentences or whether certain expressions are appropriate to use in essays. From his response, I collected that Keita's motivation toward using English was instrumental rather than integrative. He had a clear idea about what types of English practice benefits him most or least, and he was selective in choosing specific situations and interlocutors to use English in a way that they were most profitable for him.

He perceived that grammar-related information was necessary for him to advance in academic English abilities, but the daily informal conversations with international students were not useful for these purposes and thus were not necessary. He was interested in talking *about* English, not talking *in* English.

These descriptions, together with descriptions about his view of English and approach to learning, illustrate Keita's subjectivity and personal stance that shaped the type of practice that he gained in the learning environment. Clearly, he viewed English as a set of syntactic forms and lexical items that need to be rote memorized. Explicit information about them would help him accumulate linguistic resources in stock that can be used to perform academic tasks in English. He wanted to get them in a quick, easy manner via direct translation from Japanese. His focus on language knowledge rather than skill was shown in his belief that conversations with international students are not beneficial because they contain no tangible language-related information that he can gain. He did not consider them as an opportunity for skill practice and fluency development, or as an opportunity for access to a target-language community that he could bond with. This utility-based stance toward learning helped him to gain a stock of phrases he could use occasionally with teachers or isolated bits of grammatical knowledge useful for academic work, but did not lead to a social circle where he can be exposed to natural, authentic English. The result was his limited progress in the fluency aspect of pragmatic performance.

Keita's personality probably solidified his stance toward English and his learning style. As he was more independent and autonomous compared with other students, Keita was obstinate in pursuing the learning materials and methods that he preferred, and he resisted those that he determined to be useless by ignoring them completely. Because of his confidence in his own method of learning and his inflexibility in dealing with different views and approaches, he probably ended up not accepting other opportunities that could have profitably improved his speaking and listening skills.

On the other hand, Keita's appropriateness scores on the pragmatic speaking test demonstrated a mixed pattern of development. Although at Time 3 he outperformed the group mean for the low-imposition speech acts, his performance for the high-imposition situations remained below the average throughout the time. This unbalanced development between formal and informal speech acts was indeed typical among the students in this study: students generally progressed much faster for low-imposition speech acts than for high-imposition ones. However, Keita's case presents a unique insight: frequent experience with target speech acts is not enough to make progress on the speech acts. Students do not learn pragmatic appropriateness just from experiencing the speech acts like Keita's case; rather, explicit feedback and correction are necessary.

Outside of this study, perhaps due to his outspoken personality, Keita occasionally expressed his opinions about teaching style or class format directly to the teachers, face-to-face, the target high-imposition speech act. Among the 12 informants, Keita and Ippei were the only students who had ever expressed disagreement directly to their teachers, but Keita far outperformed Ippei on frequency. For instance, he went to Lin's office one day and told her that her quiz was not motivating because everyone could get a high score by just studying the textbook. He wanted her to incorporate more outside reading materials. In another occasion, he complained to her that the information she presented on the board was not well organized. These instances were similar to the situations encoded in the PST (Appendix D for the instrument). I asked Keita's teachers how he expressed his opinions and what they thought about his manner. Jennifer responded:

> He said something like 'you should', 'you should', not like 'you should take care of it'. Something like 'you should do something'. So it was a command, but when he said it, he was joking. I could tell because he was laughing.

I followed up on Jennifer's comment and asked why the modal 'should' did not bother her even though she clearly recognized it as a command rather than a polite request. She said:

> Yes, it's a command, but it's also soft, in terms of what he was taught in junior high school. I worked in junior high school and I remember how students used to be taught things like 'you had better' as a polite expressions. When I first heard that, I was shocked. No it's not. It's like you are telling me 'if you don't do it, I'll beat you up.' So I think students sometimes use the word like 'should' which sounds stronger than they are. I guess maybe I think that all the time I never take it as a strong command. He is just voicing his opinion. (October, 2008)

I asked her whether she feels the same way if the expression 'should' come from a native speaker of English. She immediately said:

> Probably not, probably not. Again, it depends on how they said it. I have a relationship with Keita, as anybody who talks a lot. We joke a lot. Because he will come up to me after the class to talk to me, not in a great deal but more than anybody else.

As shown in these excerpts, Keita's linguistic manner of requesting or expressing an opinion was inappropriate and the teacher was aware of the inappropriateness, but she did not provide him with corrective feedback. This lack of feedback probably explains why Keita did not improve on the appropriateness of high-imposition speech acts, despite his frequent use of them in his daily contact with teachers. Jennifer revealed two reasons for not giving Keita negative feedback. First, she knew that high-school English classes often provide incorrect pragmatic information, like teaching the modal expression 'had better' as a polite request. When compared with 'had better,' Keita's use of 'should' is much softer and thus was more forgivable to her. Another reason is Jennifer's perception of the illocutionary force of the speech act. Although the modal 'should' function as a strong command, paralinguistic features associated with the use of 'should' – tone of voice and facial expressions – indicated that it was not actually a command, but a mild request because Keita said it jokingly with a smile. Her familiarity with Keita's outspoken, forthcoming personality also seemed to have contributed to this perception.

When I asked Keita if he paid attention to his language when he talked to the teachers, he said that in some occasions he considered politeness, such as using 'I'd like to' instead of 'I want to' or using 'could you' instead of 'can you'. He learned these forms and their pragmatic nuances from high-school grammar books and at private English classes he had attended. This pragmatic knowledge, however, did not correspond well with his awareness of formality and register variation. When asked about differences in communication styles between English and Japanese, Keita said that the Japanese language has *keigo* (honorifics) but English does not. He thought that in Japanese, people distinguish speech styles according to formality, and honorific forms are used to mark speech styles, but he did not think that people encode formality in English. According to him, English speakers are casual and do not differentiate language use in situations as much as Japanese speakers do. He shared with me one instance that led to this generalization. He learned that the title 'sir' signifies the highest form of respect to the addressee in English. One day when a teacher was taking attendance, he responded with 'yes sir' as a joke. The teacher started laughing immediately. Keita said that Japanese people would never laugh at the most respectful form of language even if it is situationally inappropriate. The teacher's reaction made him think that linguistic formality is not so pervasive in English. Another example he gave me is the difference between 'can you' and 'do you' when asking about someone's ability to do something. He learned in high school that it is more polite to say 'do you' (e.g. 'Do you speak English?') rather than 'can you' (e.g. 'Can you speak English?') because 'can you' implies the person's inability. However, after observing people's conversations on campus, he realized that 'can you' is frequently used, which further confirmed his hypothesis that English is an informal language.

These descriptions indicate that Keita formed an incorrect sociopragmatic understanding of formality and register difference in English through his selective observation and hypothesis testing in the university community. In addition, Keita had limited repertoire of pragmalinguistic expressions.

Similar to Yuko, Keita demonstrated sociopragmatic awareness of situational differences between low- and high-imposition speech acts, and he was conscientious about using appropriate forms to convey required degree of formality. However, his linguistic repertoire did not include a complete range of polite expressions, as shown in the example below. Here he produced two requests, formal and informal, and provided an account of his pragmalinguistic choices:

Low-imposition request (asking a friend for a pen)

Excuse me Ken, I left my pen in my room, so would you borrow me a pen?

The person I was speaking to was a friend, so I didn't try to make it so polite. First I thought about using 'can I' but I felt it's better to use 'would you' and make the interlocutor the focus of the speech, not myself. 'Can I' sounds a bit arrogant.

High-imposition request (asking a professor for an extension of a paper)

I'm sorry, I'm not finished with my assignment, so could you put off the deadline?

Because I was speaking to a professor, I wanted to use a polite expression, so I used 'could you'. I heard that 'could you' is politer than 'would you'. There are other expressions like 'I want you to' + verb. It might be OK to use it to a friend but maybe not to a teacher.

I asked him if he can make the expression even politer, but he was not aware of other polite expressions. In his repertoire 'could you' was ranked as the most polite form of request.

These verbal protocols illustrate the degree of Keita's pragmalinguistic knowledge and sociopragmatic awareness. He was aware of situational differences and was able to differentiate linguistic expressions accordingly. Similar to Yuko, he had a range of modal expressions in his repertoire (e.g. 'can I', 'could you' and 'would you'), and he was able to rank order them according to their politeness value. However, his repertoire of syntactic and lexical mitigations for formal situations was still incomplete. In his system, the modal 'could you' was ranked as the politest, as he learned in high school, and he was not aware of other options such as bi-clausal structures or embedded sentences that were often used by native speakers in a high-imposition speech act. He did not use mitigation devices such as positive politeness strategies or sufficient explanation.

In summary, the slow pragmatic development found in Keita's case was not uncommon among the Japanese students studied here. Due to the scant English input and limited listening and speaking practice in high school, the students' challenge in the English-medium university involved building up sufficient listening skill to keep up with lectures given in authentic English and developing functional speaking skills that allow them to communicate everyday needs with class instructors. This was typically the case for those who came from regular high schools, not from English-focused schools like Yuko or Tomoyo. The pragmatic speaking and listening tests used in this study were challenging for those students because they drew on skills that they did not have much of a grasp on. As comprehending meaning and expressing ideas in English were difficult enough, higher-level listening and speaking tasks, namely understanding implied intentions or expressing ideas with attention to politeness, were even more taxing. These task demands stemming from modality were probably part of the reason for the slow pace of pragmatic development found in this study.

Even under this circumstance, some students still made rapid progress through a variety of means, such as incidental opportunities for pragmatic learning (Shoko), establishing membership in English circle through routine participation in their activity (Asako) and conscious use of strategies in pragmatic learning (Mitsu). But other students made little progress because of their lack of pragmatic practice. What is unique in Keita's case, however, is that it was his subjectivity and investment that precluded his access to opportunities for pragmatic growth. Keita consciously chose to approach teachers but not international students because he believed that informal conversations with international students would not increase the grammatical and lexical knowledge that he was looking for. This skewed social contact, shaped by his view of language as forms and structures, probably resulted in his slow progress in pragmatic competence, which was particularly notable in the areas of pragmatic comprehension and fluency of pragmatic production.

Keita's limited gain in the appropriateness of pragmatic production, on the other hand, seemed to have resulted from a lack of knowledge in a full range of pragmalinguistic expressions. His repertoire did not expand over time for a variety of reasons, including his lack of correction on his wrong usage of pragmatic forms and his failure to confirm the use of formal language in his surroundings. It seems that frequent experience with target speech acts alone does not help to acquire knowledge of appropriateness speech acts. The experience needs to be accompanied by negative feedback, positive evidence and reinforcement, as shown in Shoko's case.

Ryota

Ryota and Keita were in the same Level 1 class throughout the study period and received the same class instruction and assignment. Figures 5.25 through 5.32 show group average on the PLT and PST, and Ryota's performance recorded at every time point. Similar to Keita, Ryota was clearly an under-achiever on the PLT. He started near the average score at Time 1, but his score dropped by five points at Time 2 and marked the second lowest in

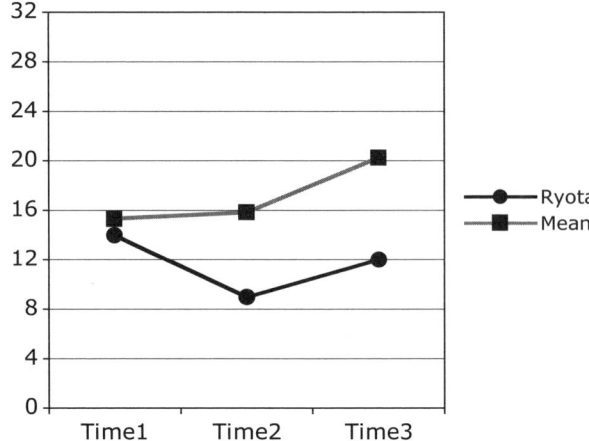

Figure 5.25 Ryota's change in PLT accuracy score

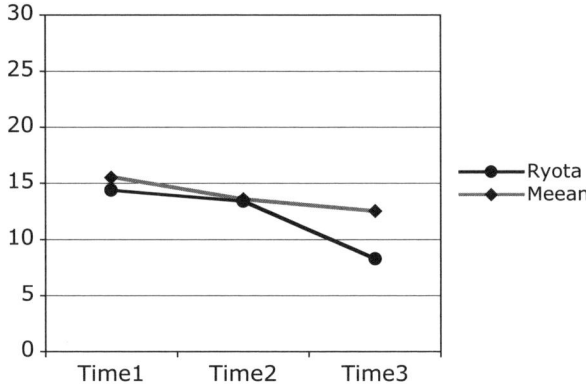

Figure 5.26 Ryota's change in PLT response times

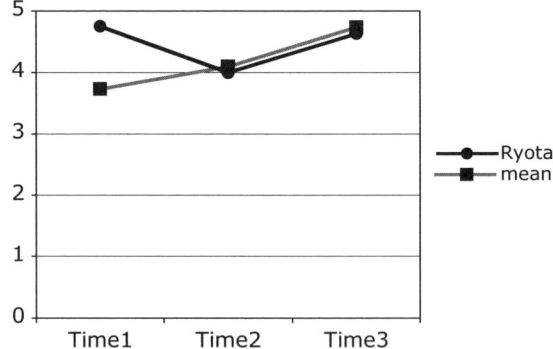

Figure 5.27 Ryota's change in PST appropriateness score, low-imposition speech acts

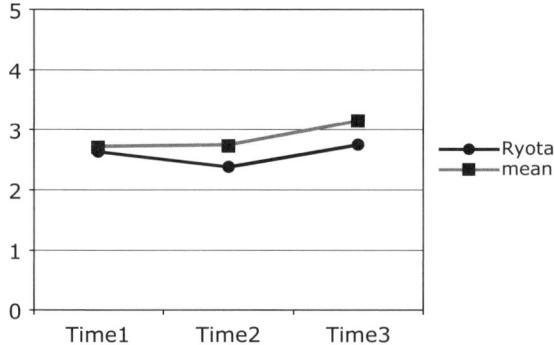

Figure 5.28 Ryota's change in PST appropriateness score, high-imposition speech acts

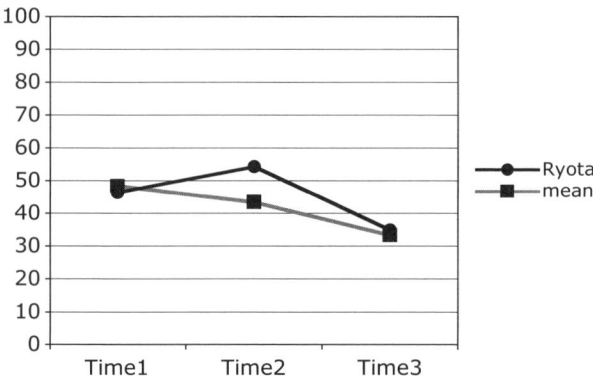

Figure 5.29 Ryota's change in planning time, low-imposition speech acts

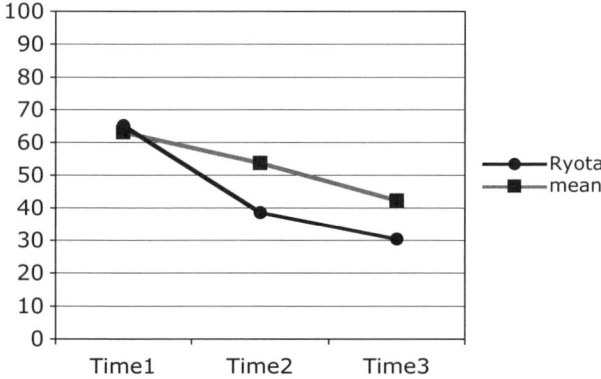

Figure 5.30 Ryota's change in planning time, high-imposition speech acts

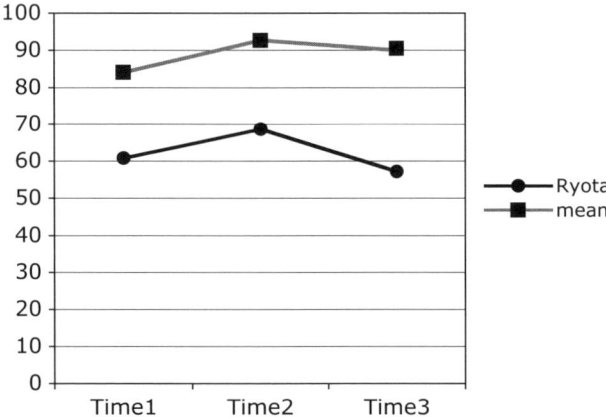

Figure 5.31 Ryota's change in PST speech rate, low-imposition speech acts

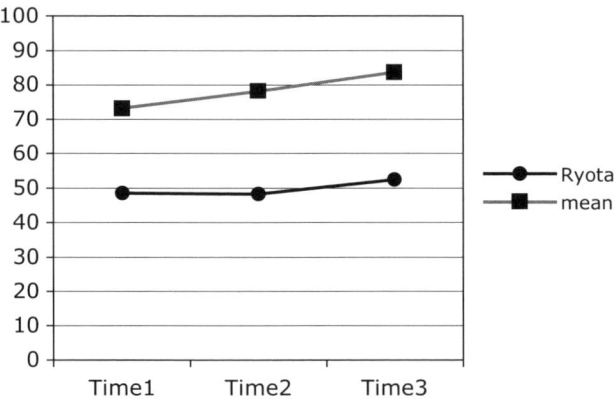

Figure 5.32 Ryota's change in PST speech rate, high-imposition speech acts

the group. At Time 3 his score rose by a few points but it was the lowest in the group. His PLT response times, on the other by a few points, were generally shorter than the group mean.

Again, similar to Keita, Ryota's performance on the PST was weak. He started out with an above-average appropriateness score for the low-imposition speech acts, but at Time 2 his score dropped by almost one point on the five-point scale, and then closely followed the pattern of the group mean. His score for the high-imposition speech acts, on the other hand, stayed below average most of the time. Ryota's change in planning time was idiosyncratic: although the group average was shorter for low-imposition than high-imposition speech acts, Ryota showed an opposite pattern. Except for Time 1, his planning time was shorter for the high-imposition than low-imposition speech acts. On the other hand, regardless the situation type, his speech rate was much slower than average and remained slow for the entire period.

As described above, although their actual paces were different, Ryota and Keita exhibited similar patterns of change. They were both under-developed in pragmatic abilities: they had low comprehension accuracy of conversational implicature, and below-average appropriateness and speech rate of speech acts. However, they differed in their pragmatic fluency: Ryota was faster than Keita in comprehending implicature and planning for the speech acts. The section below provides descriptions of Ryota's experiences on campus that could explain his patterns of development.

Ryota is from Chiba city in the Chiba prefecture, about 20 miles east of Tokyo. He went to a regular public high school and received seven to eight hours of English instruction taught mostly in Japanese. The class was concentrated on reading and grammar, with little focus on communicative activities. The most common class activity was to go over key English words with their Japanese translations and study their derivations. Ryota had no contact with native speakers in high school. He said that he chose this English-medium university for three unique characteristics: its boarding school environment, all-English classes and international students on campus. He is interested in pursuing a career in an international job, such as a bilingual translator or diplomat. He also wishes to travel overseas, visiting world heritage sites and European ruins.

In contrast to his initial interest in English learning, his university life seemed to be constrained to the Japanese-speaking community. When I asked him what he likes most about the school, he said that the small class size in the ESL program makes it easier for him to make friends, and he enjoys talking to his peers with diverse experiences and regional backgrounds. He also enjoys the school's small-community atmosphere in which he can talk openly. Although the opportunity to interact with international students was one of the reasons why he chose this university, he had not yet made any international friends. He practiced listening mostly through TOEFL exercises, and he limited his speaking practice to classroom interaction because he saw no opportunities for practice outside the class. He played baseball four times a week, but there was only one international student on the team. He said that it took courage to enter the circle of international students because they have their own community. Besides, he was satisfied with his Japanese network and felt no need for another community with international students.

Ryota was also aware of the gap between his initial commitment to master English and the current reality that he was not making much effort toward this goal. He said that his motivation went down after he entered this university, as evident in his poor study habit and lack of concentration.

His average daily study time ranged from 30 minutes to one hour, and he spent the majority of this time on homework. In LPC he reported that he used the most English when watching TV or DVDs, about 15 hours per week on average. He started missing classes because of fatigue from club activities and part time job. He said that he frequently lost concentration in class. Once or twice a day, he had to ask his classmates what was going on in class.

Ryota's lack of motivation was often a topic of conversations among teachers. Several times teachers complained about Ryota for skipping homework, failing quizzes and not paying attention in class. His reading instructor, Lin, mentioned that one time she scolded him in class for his numerous missing assignments. His listening instructor told me that he never turned in assignment. Two teachers had an individual meeting with him because they were concerned about his grades. Ryota was also on the teachers' list of least active, least motivated students in class. See Lin's comment:

> Ryota failed two quizzes so far. . . . Ryota seems not really into the class. He is always spaced out. He is not there because he sometimes falls sleep. He sometimes looks outside. When we are on page 11, he is looking at page 13. Class participation is minimum. . . . He might not be able to pass the class. (September, 2008).

In the same class, I observed him arriving to class for 20 minutes late. Lin said to him, 'You are always late for my class. No more!' Ryota nodded silently and sat down to join the group activity. Of the 14 classes I observed, I saw Ryota asking questions to the teacher once, only when she came to his desk. He never volunteered to answer in class.

Among the 12 students I interviewed, Ryota was the only one who received a large amount of disapproval from multiple teachers. Given his low motivation toward the course work and limited contact with English speakers on campus, it is not surprising that his pragmatic performance was weak. Similar to Keita, his listening practice was limited to watching DVDs with Japanese subtitles, and he had almost no speaking practice in or outside the class. Like Keita, he had a habit of translation. He usually started out with an English–English dictionary but after reading one to two pages, he gave up and switched to English–Japanese dictionary. When writing an essay, he would jot down ideas in Japanese first and then translates them to English. Because basic listening and speaking abilities are the prerequisite to pragmatic listening and speaking, insufficient practice on these target skills seemed to be the direct cause of his minor pragmatic progress. When I asked him why he never approached international students, he responded:

> Before I came here, I believed that English skill will bring about numerous possibilities and open up future directions. But after I came here, my poor English abilities became apparent, and that lowered my motivation

for studying. There are many students who are more fluent than me. I was placed in the lowest level in the EAP program. That's why my motivation went down. Before I came here I thought that there are abundant opportunities to talk to international students, and my English will improve quickly, but the reality was different. (November, 2008)

Although he was aware of the gap, Ryota did not try to change his situation. He said that he felt intimidated when he saw a large group of international students gathering together, and he could not enter the social circle. He had no point of contact with them. When he saw his friends speaking fluently within the group of international students, he began to feel even worse and started to develop an inferiority complex. He also expressed that his introvert personality had a significant influence on his feeling of intimidation. During my interaction with him, I found him shy and less verbal than other students. In a 30-minute interview, there were six instances in which he paused for a long time, more than eight seconds, before answering my question. As a post hoc analysis, I examined his oral fluency in Japanese. I analyzed a three-minute extract from his interview for speech rate and pause length, and compared them with those of three other students whom I selected randomly from the 12 informants. Ryota was clearly disfluent in Japanese. His speech rate was about 25% slower than other students, and his pause length was twice longer. Hence, it seemed that his communication difficulty in English was not an English-specific problem. Instead, it was closely related with his introvert personality and hesitant speech style in Japanese.

Ryota's restricted social network with English speakers seemed to have affected his sociolinguistic knowledge as well. On the topic of politeness, he expressed that he knew very little about polite English usage because he rarely have a conversation in English. His high-school teachers told him that in English formality exists only in exceptional occasions such as talking to the president, and people do not change speech style in their everyday conversation. He believed this and concluded that register variation in English is not as distinct as in Japanese. Like Keita, he ranked 'could you' + verb as the most polite form of request, followed by 'would you' + verb. The only other form he knew was 'please' + verb. Complex, bi-clausal structures (e.g. 'I wonder if' + verb) or other syntactic and lexical mitigations were not in his repertoire.

In summary, because of imperfect understanding of linguistic politeness in English, combined with scant contact with English speakers and low motivation toward English study in general, Ryota made little progress in pragmatic development over time. Keita and Ryota's cases together inform us that sustained practice in basic communication skills is a likely condition for pragmatic growth. Neither student voluntarily accessed opportunities for such practice, but the factors that constrained their access were different.

While Keita exercised his subjectivity and elected not to interact with international students because he thought that they would not help strengthen his knowledge of grammar and lexis, in Ryota's case, it seems that it was his introvert personality and limited oral skills that discouraged his participation in the English-speaking community.

The next case history, Asako, presents similar restraints on students' access to opportunity for pragmatic practice stemming from their personality. Like Ryota, Asako was introverted, shy and slow in expressing and articulating her thoughts. Because she came to the university with little previous contact with native speakers, her oral skills were weak. However, in sharp contrast with Ryota, she successfully established her membership within the English community and gained regular access to target language input, which led to her dramatic gain in pragmatic comprehension. What was instrumental in her change was the class assignment that forced her to seek opportunity for practice. The following section describes the strategies that she exercised to complete the assignment, which eventually led to her routine participation in the community.

Asako

Figures 5.33 and 5.34 show the group average on the PLT, and the accuracy score and response times that Asako recorded at every time point. Her pragmatic listening was exceptionally strong. She made a remarkable increase in her score from Time 1 to Time 2, a gain of 11 points, which was more than six times larger than the average gain of 1.8 points. It was the second highest in the group, and she sustained the score at Time 3. Her comprehension speed, on the other hand, was not so impressive. Although her response

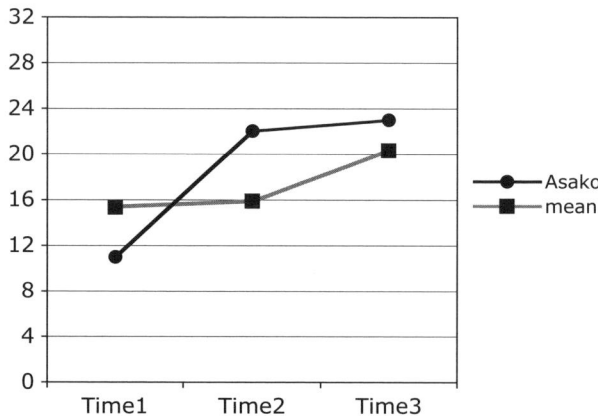

Figure 5.33 Asako's change in PLT accuracy score

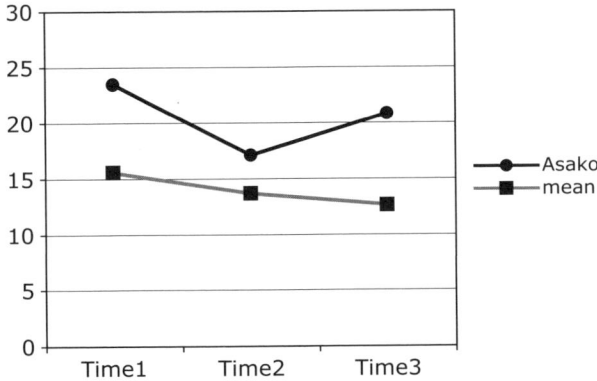

Figure 5.34 Asako's change in PLT response times

times dropped by about six seconds from Time 1 to Time 2, her response speed was always slower than the group mean.

Figures 5.35 through 5.40 display Asako's change in score and fluency on the PST measure. Compared with her extraordinary improvement in comprehension of implicature, her performance on the production of speech acts was no more than average. Although she started out with a high appropriateness score on low-imposition speech acts, her score dropped at Time 2 and then followed the group curve to Time 3. Her scores for high-imposition speech acts were slightly better than average. Her planning time dropped over time, but again, the pattern of change was similar to that of the group. Asako's speech rate, however, was notably slower than average for both

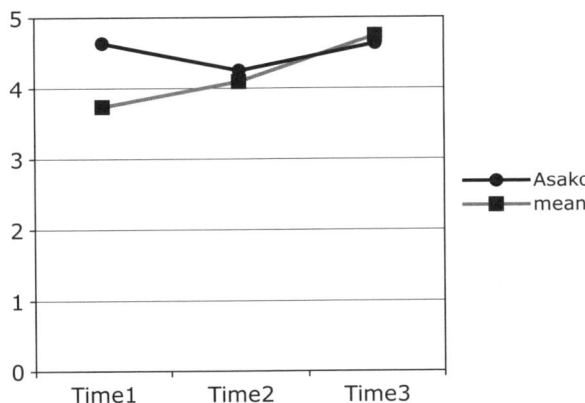

Figure 5.35 Asako's change in PST appropriateness score, low-imposition speech acts

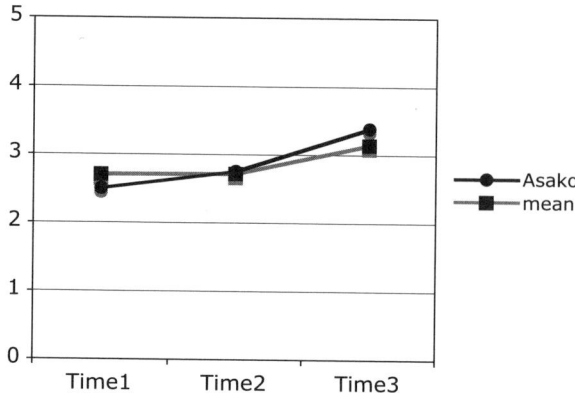

Figure 5.36 Asako's change in PST appropriateness score, high-imposition speech acts

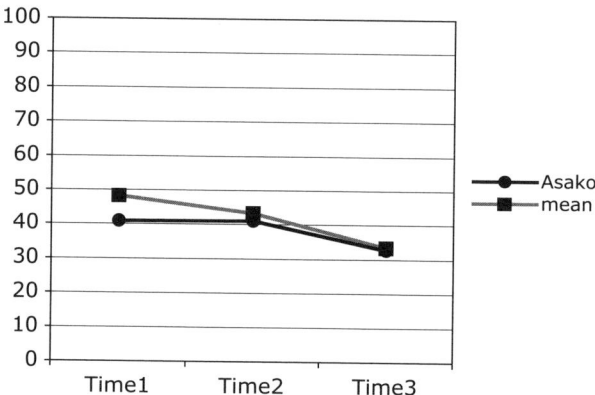

Figure 5.37 Asako's change in PST planning time, low-imposition speech acts

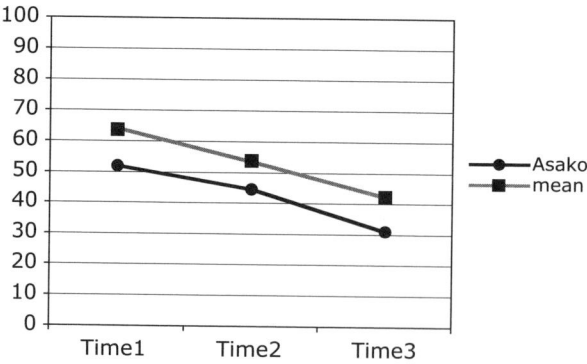

Figure 5.38 Asako's change in PST planning time, high-imposition speech acts

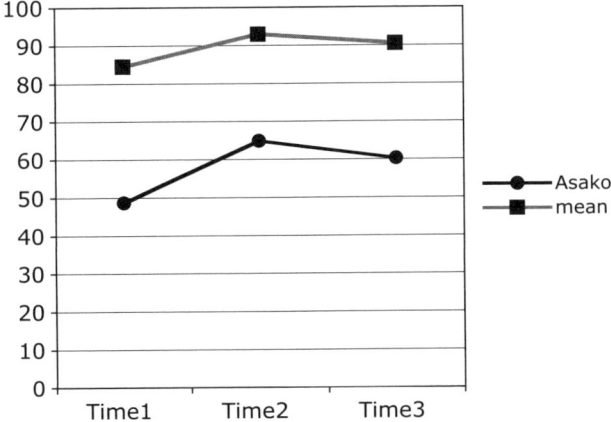

Figure 5.39 Asako's change in PST speech rate, low-imposition speech acts

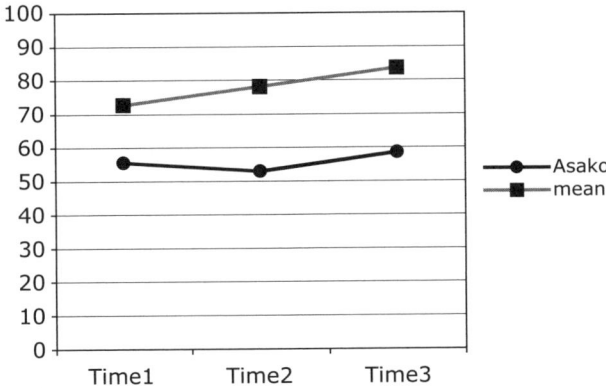

Figure 5.40 Asako's change in PST speech rate, high-imposition speech acts

situation speech acts, and the gap remained wide throughout the period. This pattern was similar to her response times in the PLT. Hence, it seems that she demonstrated an exceptionally high PLT score and average-level PST appropriateness score, but her speed at which these tasks were performed was slow. The next section presents qualitative analyses that explain her developmental trajectories.

Asako is from Kushiro City in Hokkaido, a city with a population of 200,000. She went to a regular public high school. Her previous English experience was fairly typical and traditional. She received English instruction five to seven hours per week. Her English class was focused on reading and writing and was taught by a Japanese instructor in Japanese. She said that 'shadowing' was the most common classroom activity: students listened to a CD and repeated what they heard simultaneously. She had no contact with a native speaker instructor in high school. She mostly studied grammar to prepare for the college entrance exam.

She told me that she chose this English-medium university because one year of study abroad is part of the school curriculum. She is interested in foreign countries and cultures, and she wishes to work in a place where she can use English after graduation. During the first 40-minute interview, the term *ryugaku* (study abroad) appeared 15 times in a context such as *ryugakusei* ('international students') or *ryugaku-suru* ('go study abroad'), signifying her intense interest in study abroad and foreign students. She expressed that a close distance between Japanese students and international students on campus is an asset of this university, which made her feel most appreciative about coming to this school.

Asako was a serious student with a good study habit. She typically spent three to four hours daily doing homework and even longer when she had essay assignments. In all classes I observed, she usually positioned herself in the middle of the classroom. She was attentive and followed directions well. Her diligence was also evident in the large proficiency gain she made over two semesters. Her TOEFL score improved by 80 points from 470 to 550, the largest gain in the entire group of 48 participants. Tom, the instructor of her reading class, and Chris, the instructor of her writing class, named Asako as one of the top students in class and consistently praised her polished literacy skills. However, they also pointed out Asako's shy and quiet personality, and said that she never participates in class. See the interview excerpts:

> Asako is very strong in class. At the beginning I thought she would fail, but she made a huge improvement over time. She is very quite in class. She probably spoke up four times during the semester. She makes a strong contrast with Haruyo who started out strong but didn't improve.... (Tom, September, 2008)

> Asako is a good student, ah ... she is not so assertive, and I think that hurts her a bit. If she were more assertive and participating, and she tried to take control of her education, she would be better. She is a good student but lacking assertiveness. Her writing is good. Her grades are good. (Mike, November, 2008)

Over the 22 class periods I observed, I saw Asako volunteering answers only once. When reading a newspaper article, she asked for the meaning of the word 'intent'. This was a memorable incident for the class instructor. After the class, the instructor was elated and said:

> Today first time ever, ever, ever Asako raised hand. Asako, who never said anything, never raised hand before, asked a question!

While Asako's strong English abilities clearly stood out in reading and writing classes, in a speaking class where students were expected to participate orally, her passivity was an obstacle, and she was labeled as a less competent student. Brian, the instructor of her speaking class, ranked her as one of the weakest students in class, and his evaluation remained the same throughout the term. Brian said:

Asako … (long pause). She is a great writer, I'd, I still think she is very shy. Lacks confidence, sweet, yeah (laugh). I like her, but if I had a class with a full of students like her, I would go crazy because they are so quiet in class. They don't raise hand or speak up. (December, 2008)

In Brian's class, students had three speaking tests during the semester. Students formed a pair or group and talked for two to three minutes on an assigned topic. Their speech was evaluated based on five criteria: accuracy, fluency, pronunciation, vocabulary usage and communication strategies. Asako's score was always the lowest in class. See Brian's comment:

Asako is the only one who failed this speaking test. She got 51%. Getting something out of her was just painful. Too much time thinking. I asked, 'What did you do last weekend?' and she said, 'I ah … I ah … , I ah …' It took a long, long, long time to get her answer. She couldn't come up with any answers that I was looking for. She said, 'I would, I would, I would, I would do this…' She did something similar in the previous tests. (November, 2008)

Asako's difficulty in self-expression was also evident in her native language, Japanese. During the interview, I often found her hesitant and at a loss for words. In a 40-minute interview, there were 11 instances in which she paused for more than eight seconds and did not provide a straightforward response to my question. As a post hoc analysis, I examined her oral fluency in Japanese. I compared her speech rate and pause length to those of three other students who I selected randomly. Results showed that Asako was clearly disfluent. Her speech rate was 40–50% slower than that of other students, and her pause length was two to five times longer. Hence, it seemed that her communication difficulty was not specific to English, but instead came from her reserved personality and limited social skills in general. Asako expressed:

I'm not social. Talking to people is not my strong suit. I don't talk much in Japanese, and even less in English. I'm not good at expanding on conversation, in Japanese or in English, so I'm envious when I see my peers who can talk for an extended period. I'm not a good story-teller. I can't build on topics, and my stories often come to an end quickly. (October, 2008)

Given her introvert personality and weak speaking abilities, I was surprised that she performed so well on the pragmatic listening task. In fact, from my observation of her in class, her name never occurred to me as someone who could increase their score by 11 points in a short period of three months. However, my initial impression changed quickly as I learned her experience in the university environment. Through interviews, I learned that she tactfully established her community within a small group of international students and gained continual access to the opportunity to listen to authentic, naturally spoken English. This sustained listening practice seemed to have contributed to her outstanding performance on the PLT measure. Subsequently, I will describe Asako's interaction with the English-speaking community.

During the first interview in September, I asked her in what ways she had changed most after coming to the university. She said that she became more proactive, taking the initiative by acting rather than reacting to events passively. One instance that denotes this change is her attempt to overcome her communication difficulties with international students. In contrast to her initial optimism, she quickly learned that attending classes does not alone improve her English skills dramatically. This realization was reinforced by her observation of and interaction with her competent peers. She recognized a large gap in speaking ability between her peers who had studied abroad before and herself who had never left Japan. When her peers were conversing with international students fluently, Asako was not able to jump in the conversation and take the floor. She named listening and speaking weakest among the four English skills, and the weakness often became apparent when she could not express herself well in front of the international students or when she could not understand them and had to clarify what they said. These experiences added to her growing inferiority complex.

Her inferiority complex, however, was gradually cured with an increasing contact with international students she established over time. She told me that she is competitive by nature. Her competitiveness motivated her to exercise various means to access opportunities to practice English, with a strong commitment to making English-speaking friends in order to improve her English. She had to be strategic in creating opportunities because she had less contact with international students through extracurricular activities, and her roommate was Japanese.

One strategy she used to gain access to English was to go to the library regularly and sit at a desk where international students were studying. This became Asako's routine earlier in the first semester. She spent a total of five hours everyday in the library, from 8:00 pm to 1:00 am, and did her homework while sitting next to the international students and eavesdropping on their conversations. There were three international students – an American, a German and a Hong Konger – who always came to the library and sat at the same table. They talked in their common language, English, about mundane things – their plans for the day, daily experiences, Japanese classes, families and friends and their hometowns. Asako said that she was not a participant in the conversation but was an active listener. This was the only source of extracurricular listening activity she was engaged in outside the class.

I asked her why she never goes to the lounge in the dormitory where most international students hang out. The lounge was the place where Yuko and Tomoyo, other high-scorers on the pragmatic listening test, spent most of their time. Asako said that the laid-back, nonacademic atmosphere in the lounge did not appeal to her. There were many international students in the lounge, both familiar and unfamiliar ones, and they were always watching TV or playing computer games. She preferred the library because she could talk to a small group of international students who she felt comfortable with, and she could also do her homework there.

The event that triggered this library routine was the speaking journal assignment she received from her speaking class. She recorded her experiences in speaking English, three to five entries per week (see Chapter 1 for descriptions of the assignment). This assignment was stressful for Asako, who did not have a social network with English speakers. Because she did not have anyone to talk with regularly, she was often desperate to find someone in the cafeteria or lounge to do the assignment. Talking to strangers in this way often required a lot of courage. But her struggle ended when she came to know the group of three international students. One day during the first semester, she mentioned the speaking journal homework to an American student in the same club. The student offered to help with the assignment and invited her to come to the library at night. From that day, Asako started her day-to-day routine of going to the library at 8:00 pm and sitting next to the group of three international students, listening to their conversation, while doing her own homework.

This unintentional, incidental listening practice that she gained daily by sitting next to English speakers probably contributed to her dramatic gain in the pragmatic listening score. Her PLT score increased by 11 points by the end of the first semester, and she maintained the ability throughout the academic year. Among all the informants interviewed, Asako, Tomoyo and Yuko were the only students whose PLT scores were consistently high, and they occupied the first three places in the entire group of 48 students. All three of these students had extensive daily contact with international students. While other students reported a sporadic contact of 10–30 minutes per week, mostly while passing through the hallway or cafeteria, they were engaged in a continuous, prolonged conversation all in English. Because the only common experience among these three high-scoring students was the opportunity to engage in a prolonged conversation with English speakers, it is likely that the experience with a long, sustained communication, rather than small chunks of daily exchange, helps students to develop the ability to comprehend indirect, nonliteral meaning.

This interpretation is reasonable when we consider the construct of pragmatic comprehension that involves inferential ability to understand meaning behind a given utterance. Pragmatic comprehension involves the ability to understand what words and sentences mean, as well as to understand what speakers want to do by using them. This type of inferential communication is less likely to occur in a greeting or small talk that typically involves a brief conversation exchange on a trivial matter. Because those talks are constrained by time, they are usually short and simple, and people stick to factual communication and avoid embellishment. Only in a long stretch of discourse among people who share everyday experiences indirect communication is likely to occur. In an extended discourse, indirect communication is less risky and becomes an economical mode of communication. Shared context and knowledge that people construct over numerous turns make it possible to understand meaning that is conveyed implicitly. An involved conversation of multiple parties often include a variety of conversational implicature, as well as other forms of indirect communication such as jokes, sarcasms, figurative language and metaphors. Hence, it is probable that the long, extended conversations that Asako, Yuko and Tomoyo were exposed to on a daily basis assisted their gain in the PLT score. Considering that Asako's TOEFL listening score was much lower than Yuko and Tomoyo's score and that other students who had higher TOEFL scores made smaller gains than Asako, this particular form of listening (i.e. extensive listening), not listening proficiency alone, seemed to be the contributing factor in the development of pragmatic comprehension.

Despite the clear commonality among Asako, Yuko and Tomoyo's experience and their achievement on the PLT, Asako's means to access the experience was different because of her introvert personality and limited communication skills. Both Yuko and Tomoyo reported that they had 10–20 close international friends and spent time with them for three to four hours everyday in the student lounge. They came with strong English skills developed through daily interaction with native speaker teachers in high school, which allowed them to participate in the English-speaking community on campus. In contrast, Asako, having no native-speaker instructors in high school, came with limited spoken skills that discouraged her from attaining membership in the mainstream social circle. Unlike Yuko and Tomoyo, who spent a large chunk of time in the dormitory lounge and interacted with a number of students, Asako's social circle was in the library, in an intimate space with three international students. Although her initial access to this social circle occurred by chance, Asako was persistent in maintaining this access by participating in the circle everyday. She told me that she was a listener and observer rather than a speaker. She did not contribute to conversation so much, but she tuned in to their talk for an extended period and was absorbed in spontaneous, authentic English spoken at a natural speed. In this sense, Asako was strategic and instrumental in her own learning. She knew what types of learning resources and opportunities were available in the learning environment and exercised her subjectivity in accessing those opportunities. Once she gained the access, she made an effort to sustain it on a regular basis. She was aware of the limitations to her English ability, as shown in her inferiority complex expressed at an earlier stage of study, but she also knew that contact with English speakers was indispensable to improve this ability. Her competitive personality, along with the speaking journal assignment that pushed her to approach English speakers, created a chance to pursue her goal in this direction.

In this sense, Asako's case was different from Ryota's case discussed in the previous section. Both of them had similar backgrounds: they received traditional English instruction in high school in which communication skill was de-emphasized, and they had little contact with native speakers in class. They were both shy and almost never participated in class, and had limited social network with international students. They developed inferiority complex about their communication skills by comparing themselves with fluent peers. Under these constraints, Ryota was not able to secure an opportunity for sustained interaction with English speakers, but Asako successfully established daily participation in a small English-speaking community through the journal assignment required in class. Hence, for Asako, the speaking journal was part of the learning resources that created an opportunity to expand on her English-speaking circle outside the class. Had Ryota been given a similar assignment, it could have served as a venue for him to explore social network to practice English. Asako's story tells us that a combination of multiple factors – learners' personality, commitment in learning goals, subjectivity to access opportunity and a circumstance that necessitates such access – could support language development.

Although the specific form of practice that Asako gained over time (i.e. extensive listening) helped her to make a remarkable gain in pragmatic comprehension, this opportunity did not bring about the same level of success in pragmatic production. Her appropriateness score was barely average, and her fluency was below the group mean most of the time. These scores form a sharp contrast with Yuko and Tomoyo, who demonstrated a strong gain in all aspects of pragmatic fluency. This contrast is probably due to the fact that Asako's English practice was exclusively limited to listening, and speaking was not part of her routine practice. Although she was capable in reading and writing, as her teachers reported, she seldom spoke up in class or initiated a conversation in English. In the LCP survey, she reported spending on average only half-an-hour per week on speaking. It seems that, due to a lack of actual oral practice, her pragmatic fluency barely developed and remained below-average throughout the period.

Asako's appropriateness score, on the other hand, was slightly above average. It is noteworthy that she made particularly strong improvement on the high-imposition speech acts, whereas the majority of students struggled with this area throughout the period. The following excerpts of high-imposition opinion situations illustrate Asako's change over time. In this scenario, a professor invites feedback from a student about his class, but the student feels that the class is not quite what he/she had in mind. The participants assumed the role of the student and expressed mild criticisms about the professor's class. (See Appendix D for the situational scenario.) The linguistic form that Asako used to express her opinion changed from the direct form 'I want to' + verb at Time 1 to the indirect, polite form 'I'd like to' + verb at Time 2, and she maintained the form at Time 3. Her speech act in the retrospective interview was even better. Not only that she used the form 'I'd like to' + verb to convey her wish, but she also provided a reason for the wish.

> High-imposition opinion (expressing an opinion to a teacher about his class)
>
> Time1
> *French class is great, but I'm interested in French, ah, modern culture music, so I want to listen to the stories of modern France culture.*
>
> Time 2
> *Um professor, I like your class, but I think um I'd like to um learn more presentation skill. So . . .*
>
> Time 3
> *Uh I like your class, but I'd like to know, uh, French pop culture and music.*
>
> Retrospective interview
>
> *I like your class very much, but I'm interested in more French pop culture and music, so I'd like to study pop culture and music.*

During the introspective interview, Asako told me that she was conscious about using the form 'I'd like to' instead of 'I want to'. Although these two forms are functionally equivalent, she learned that the former is politer than the latter and thus more appropriate in a situation like this in which one needs to soften the tone of speech. Her journal entries also revealed her sociopragmatic sensitivity and conscientiousness about polite language use. See below for sample entries. In the first entry, she demonstrated her fine distinction between the two request-making forms: 'please' + verb and 'Can you' + verb. The second excerpt about her interaction with an EAP instructor illustrates her understanding of the forms 'Can I' and 'May I' in relation to their politeness cost. It also demonstrates that she was not able to implement the knowledge on the spot due to lack of practice.

I learned that using imperative sentence is a little rude when I ask someone a favor. I used to say 'Please help my homework.' when I wanted an international student to help my homework. So this time when I wanted Leo to help my homework, I said 'Can you help my homework?' (June, 2008)

I needed one chair, and I went to Noriko *sensei*'s office to borrow a chair. I said 'Can I borrow chair?' She said 'How many chairs do you need?' I said 'One'. And then I borrowed one chair. After this conversation, I thought I should say, 'May I borrow your chair?' I learned the difference between 'Can I' and 'May I' but I cannot use these two words properly. I need practice. I want to use what I learned in class. (October, 2008)

This type of reflection on pragmatic aspects of language use was not common, found only in four instances in the total journal entries examined, the fact that two of them came from Asako's journal indicates that she had a high level of sociocultural awareness and sensitivity and she consciously tried to implement her knowledge of polite language use in her real-life communication. It is possible that her small, yet incremental, improvement found in the high-imposition speech acts was a reflection of her consciousness toward pragmalinguistic appropriateness. Perhaps what she needed in order to improve more on her appropriateness score was actual communication practice in which she could put her knowledge into action. Plentiful, sustained speaking practice, combined with an opportunity for extensive listening, could have aided her in achieving a more balanced development in pragmatic production and comprehension.

Mitsu

This section presents the case history of Mitsu. Figures 5.41 through 5.48 display his changes on PLT and PST in comparison with group means. Mitsu's pragmatic development is characterized as rather weak pragmatic comprehension but strong pragmatic production. He started out with above-average PLT accuracy, but this score dropped at Time 2 to the level of the group mean. He made very little gain from Time 2 to Time 3, and his score was below average. Mitsu's response speed, on the other hand, was faster than the group mean at Time 1 and Time 2; however, it became slower at Time 3 and fell below the group average.

Mitsu's pragmatic appropriateness, on the other hand, was very strong. Although he started out with a below-average appropriateness score at Time 1, he made a large gain at Time 2 with an increase of more than one point, surpassing the group mean. He continued to improve afterward and reached the perfect score at Time 3. His progress on the high-imposition speech acts

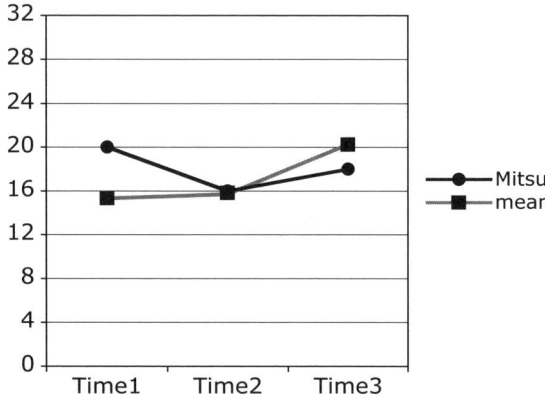

Figure 5.41 Mitsu's change in PLT accuracy score

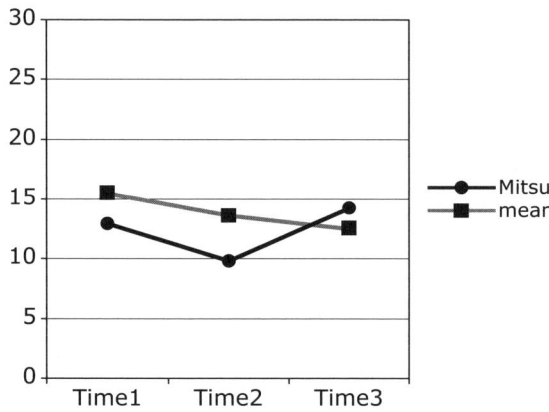

Figure 5.42 Mitsu's change in PLT response times

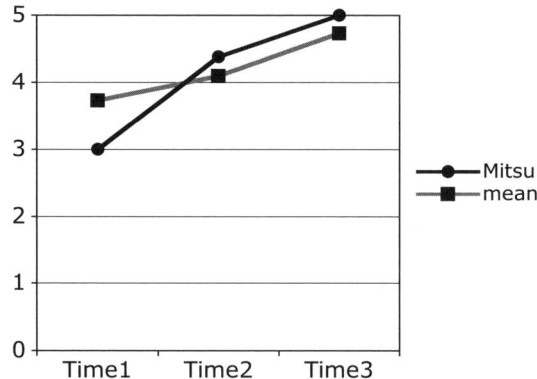

Figure 5.43 Mitsu's change in PST appropriateness score, low-imposition speech acts

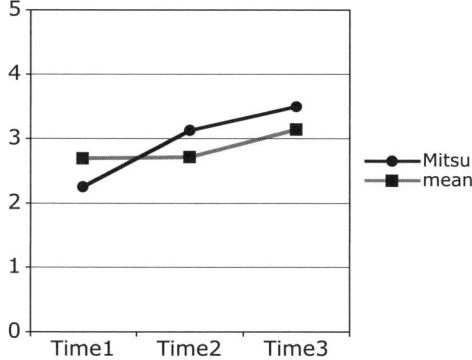

Figure 5.44 Mitsu's change in PST appropriateness score, high-imposition speech acts

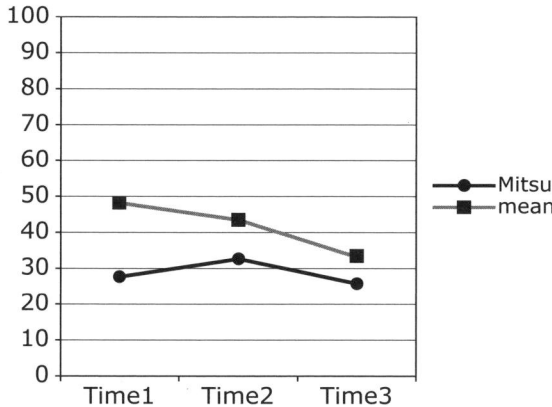

Figure 5.45 Mitsu's change in PST planning time, low-imposition speech acts

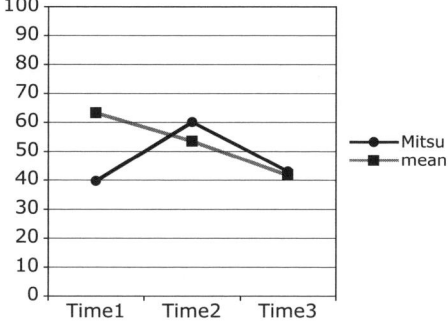

Figure 5.46 Mitsu's change in PST planning time, high-imposition speech acts

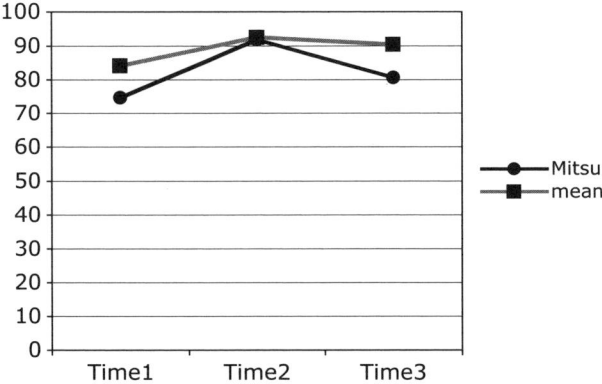

Figure 5.47 Mitsu's change in PST speech rate, low-imposition speech acts

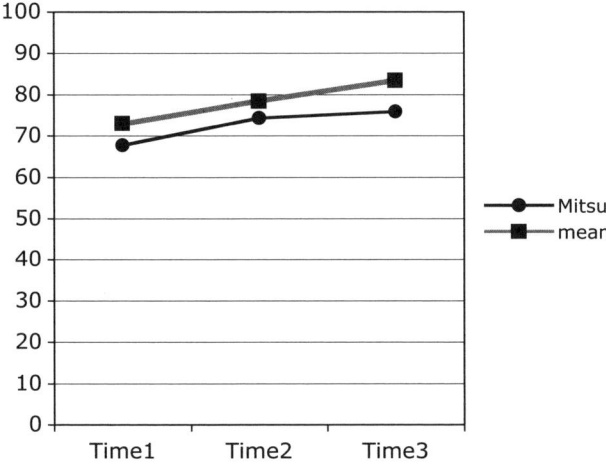

Figure 5.48 Mitsu's change in PST speech rate, high-imposition speech acts

was even more impressive. Again, he started out below average at Time 1, but after that, he made a steady, incremental gain at every time point, and his score was above the mean constantly. Mitsu's planning time, however, showed a mixed pattern of development: for the low-imposition speech acts, it was shorter than average at all time points, but this pattern was opposite for the high-imposition speech acts. He started out with shorter planning time than average at Time 1, but it increased by 20 seconds at Time 2. It decreased again at Time 3 but remained longer than the average time. Mitsu's speech rate, on the other hand, was below average for the whole time regardless of the situation type, and the degree of improvement was very small. The following section presents interpretations of these seemingly erratic patterns of development in relation to his experiences and his approach to pragmatic learning.

Mitsu is from a local prefecture. He went to a public school located in Honjo City in the southwest coast of Akita. He received five hours of English instruction per week focused on reading and taught in Japanese by a Japanese instructor. He named translation exercises and vocabulary quizzes as two common class activities. He had a native speaker instructor occasionally in class, but only in his first year. The only contact he had with the native speaker instructor was having him edit his writing when he participated in the essay competition. He home-stayed in Minnesota for one week during his first year.

His initial motivation to study English was instrumental. He came to this university because he wanted to acquire enough English skills to do international business and travel overseas without communication difficulty. He likes this university environment because he can make friends easily across levels and programs, and everyone is motivated and hardworking. He told me that he did not speak up much in high school because he did not want to stand out in class, but here, he can freely participate because everyone else in class participates. He also enjoys workshop-style classroom and group projects, which were rare in high school. The collegial, positive atmosphere in class motivated him to be active and vocal. In the 17 classes I observed, I saw him asking questions and volunteering to answer 20 times. Teachers also unanimously listed Mitsu as one of the most outspoken and active students in class. See this quote from Brain, his speaking class instructor:

> Mitsu is matured and intelligent. He gained confidence over time. He shows certain level of honesty. If he doesn't understand something, he says he doesn't understand what everybody said. (December, 2008)

From my observation of him in class and with teachers, I found that Mitsu is a serious and likable student. I saw teachers often teasing him in front of the class, and he had the personality and interaction skill to deal with teachers' ridicule upfront. In those occasions, he actually talked back to the teachers with a sense of humor. His manner was different from other students who typically did not know how to deal with teasing other than to remain silent with a wry smile. I have one classroom episode that illustrates this point. In a speaking class, Brian presented a list of target phrases on the board. He teased Mitsu by using one of the phrases, 'a wishful thinking'. He said in front of the class, 'Mitsu said that someday he wishes he would be handsome. I'd say it is wishful thinking'. The whole class laughed at Brian's joke, but Mitsu immediately responded, 'Uhm . . . uhm . . . whatever'. Despite the hesitation and pauses, he was able to come up with the right response on the spot and use it in a naturalistic interaction. Reflecting on this episode and other interactions with Mitsu in class, Brian shared the comment:

> I feel with him (Mitsu), and Ippei, Tomoyo, Kaori, I do try to push them. I do try to get reaction from them. For example, I call them crazy boy or crazy girl. I say these things to kind of get them to talk back. The other day I was teasing Mitsu singing a song about him in class, and he is like, 'OK, you can shut up now' or something along the line, so I was like, 'Dude, good!' I was happy that he reacted that way. Ippei, on the other hand, would say, 'I don't think so'. When I push his button, that's his response. I try to get him react, but that's as far as he could respond. (December, 2008)

These observations show that Mitsu was comfortable in his interaction with teachers and classmates. He was natural even when he was singled out in class. He was aware of cultural script of joking and teasing, and he was able to demonstrate a conventional reaction to them in a spontaneous manner.

Another side of Mitsu I found through interviews and observations is his strong commitment in English learning, which was evident in his study habit. He reported studying for two to three hours everyday, sometimes up to five hours, mostly doing home assignments, but he was also constantly seeking additional study materials. Among the 12 participants I interviewed, he was the only one who reported using a variety of self-study materials on a regular basis. For instance, he told me that he made his own vocabulary notebook by compiling unfamiliar words he encountered elsewhere on campus. He was on his third notebook when I interviewed him early in the second semester. In addition, to improve his listening ability, he started watching CNN programs through iTunes and listening to English conversation programs on the radio almost everyday for about 15 minutes. He also subscribed to English newspapers and read them on weekends. Mitsu told me that this extra effort and motivation toward studying came from his 'provisional student status'. As part of the admission process, the university gives a pending admission to a small group of promising students who did not quite reach the admission criteria but have the potential to do so. These students receive an official student status only after they prove their academic capabilities at the end of the first year. Since Mitsu fell in this provisional category, he had to work hard to prove himself. He said that initially he struggled to keep up with assignments and fast-paced classes because he was not very strong, but in the second semester, he settled in the routine and started to absorb information coming in English. He gradually became more comfortable with naturally spoken English as he spent more time with international students.

Although he took his academic work seriously, his motivation toward social contact and networking was also apparent in the extensive extra-curricular activities he was involved in. He belonged to three clubs – tennis, music and French – and spent one or two hours everyday in club activities. He volunteered in the support group for international students and helped them with language and other needs on monthly basis. He was also strategic in creating opportunities to interact with international students. For instance, he and his friend made a flyer called 'Let's Talk Together' and invited international students to converse informally in both Japanese and English. Two British students and one Singaporean student contacted them after seeing the flyer, and they started meeting once a week to chat.

Despite his strong desire to speak English, Mitsu's actual amount of communication time was not very extensive. The 'Let's Talk Together' gathering that he initiated lasted for only a couple of weeks. He communicated with his American suitemate frequently, once or twice a day, but their conversations were all very short, about 10 minutes. Besides his suitemate, he had a few international friends whom he interacted with regularly. They mostly helped him with his speaking journal assignment. As Mitsu was keen on practicing new vocabulary and phrases with them, each contact inevitably became brief. More than 50% of his journal entries were short descriptions of vocabulary practice. See sample excerpts below:

> At the cafeteria, I met an international student who I've not seen recently. And I said 'long time no see' [target phrase]. She answered, *'so-dane!'* in Japanese. It was easy to use and I liked it. (June, 2008)

> In the conversation between Scott and I, he said, 'I spoke Japanese all day, so I'm tired', and I said 'Is it tough for you?' [target phrase]. 'Yes', he said. (October, 2008)

Mitsu mentioned that he preferred practicing vocabulary with international students rather than having a free conversation because it gave him something tangible and concrete. With vocabulary, it was easy to write up what he learned from the communication, which was part of the requirement for the assignment. When I asked him in what ways the journal assignment was helpful in improving his English, he responded that it helped to expand his vocabulary knowledge. He was not sure if it helped him with his speaking skill.

These observations point to possible explanations for Mitsu's rather slow development of pragmatic comprehension and speech rate of pragmatic production. His motivation and desire to expand social network, willingness to communicate and proactive attitudes facilitated his access to the English-speaking community, but the types of practice he gained from this contact was a series of sporadic, brief interactions, rather than a sustained and engaged

communication. While he was proactive and instrumental in creating opportunities to practice English through off-campus volunteer activities, the 'Let's
Talk Together' gathering that he organized and the use of radio programs,
these activities did not lead to a routinized, sustained communication practice
lasting for an extended stretch of time. The speaking journal assignment,
which served as one of the few venues of recurrent speaking practice in
Mitsu's life, became a mere vocabulary practice that involved a brief exchange
of small talk. It is possible that these short but frequent encounters with
English speakers helped him with his ability to respond spontaneously, which
might have been reflected in his above-average response times and planning
times in the pragmatic measures. However, these small chunks of communication did not seem to contribute to the development of inferential ability and
oral fluency, which are likely to require sustained time-on-task to develop, as
is suggested in the cases of Yuko and Asako.

In sharp contrast to his pragmatic comprehension scores and oral fluency,
Mitsu's appropriateness score of pragmatic production was very strong. It
was constantly above average and showed a large, steady increase over time,
a gain that was detected in both low- and high-imposition speech acts. This
pattern is unique because most students in this study struggled with high-
imposition speech acts and recorded only a negligible gain over time. The
excerpts below from his PST illustrate his upward trend in the appropriateness score. This is a high-imposition opinion situation in which a student
expresses disagreement with a teacher about the mid-term grade:

> High-imposition opinion (expressing an opinion to a teacher about an
> unwarranted grade)
>
> Time 1
> *Ah excuse me ah this is not I think, it's I don't think it's fair. While it may be
> true that I, I didn't I didn't participate in your class much, but I, I, I have
> something to do well ah homework, so it is unfair, I think.*
>
> Time 2
> *Ah, I have something to tell you about my grade in mid-semester, mid-term. Ah,
> actually I missed two class and, ah, three homework, but ah, ah my test was,
> ah, 80%, and I always speaking, I was always speaking up in class. How do
> you explain about it?*
>
> Time 3
> *Ah Professor William. Ah I have something to talk about, talk about with you.
> Well ah I checked, I checked my grade, and I don't think it is reasonable. Ah
> actually I missed three classes but ah I may, I made it on my exam, on exam
> every time. Is there any reason for that?*

While Mitsu's disfluency of speech, as marked with repetitions,
hesitations, and false starts, is noticeable throughout the time points, his

appropriateness score made a strong, gradual increase over time: he received a rating of 2.0 at Time 1, 3.0 at Time 2, and 4.0 at Time 3. At Time 1 he started off with the topic (i.e. disagreement on the grade) right away and framed his opinion with an explicit negative comment ('it's not fair'). He emphasized the confrontational tone at the end by repeating the phrase again. At Time 2 his tone became much softer. He learned to preface the speech act of disagreement with 'I have something to tell you about my grade' and provided a more detailed explanation of his class performance in order to justify his point. Rather than voicing disagreement explicitly, as he did at Time 1, he left the judgment to the teacher at the end by asking for his explanation. His speech act improved further at Time 3. He addressed the teacher with the title 'professor' for the first time. He used the term 'not reasonable' instead of 'unfair' to question the credibility of the grade. He ended the speech act with a question 'Is there any reason for that?' to invite the teacher's perspective on the issue at hand. This strategy helped to take off the tension in this face-threatening situation and turn it into a constructive discussion about his class performance, rather than a conflict situation.

From these analyses, it is clear that Mitsu made a strong gain in high-imposition speech acts. Qualitative data suggested that Mitsu's competence in this area came from his sociopragmatic sensitivity combined with his conscientious approach to pragmatic learning. As shown in the descriptions of his learning style, Mitsu was clearly an autonomous and independent learner who cultivated a variety of learning strategies and self-study materials. This attitude was evident in his pragmatic learning as well: Mitsu was constantly attentive to social aspects of language and employed self-directed strategies to absorb pragmatic implications of everyday language use. Below I will present detailed accounts of Mitsu's pragmatic learning strategies.

Like Shoko, Mitsu was one of the three students who cited the sociolinguistic aspect (e.g. formal vs. informal language, register variation) as a major difference between Japanese and English communication styles. He said that the degree of politeness encoded in language is different between English and Japanese. For instance, in Japanese, the use of honorifics marks age difference between interlocutors, but this is not the case in English. When asking for a favor in Japanese, he would say '*yatte kureru?*' ('do' + donative auxiliary verb *kureru* in informal form) to a friend, but '*yatte moraemasenka?*' ('do' + donative auxiliary verb *moraeru* in formal negative form) to someone of higher status than him. He said that such informal vs. formal speech variation also exists in English. For instance, 'can you' + verb is the equivalent of Japanese '*yatte kureru?*', while 'could you/would you' + verb is the equivalent of '*yatte moaremasenka?*' He gave another example, 'yeah' vs. 'yes': the former is a response form in a casual talk, while the latter is used in a formal situation. He learned these forms from his self-study conversation textbooks.

Mitsu's sociolinguistic sensitivity and awareness stood out in his introspective verbal interviews. He was aware of the delicate differences among pragmalinguistic expressions, and he was able to articulate these differences verbally and use the pragmatic knowledge to guide his choice of forms in the given situation. In this regard, he was different from Ippei who used the form that first popped up in his head without reflecting on its pragmatic value (see the next case history). The excerpt below from Mitsu's verbal protocols illustrates this point. Here he expressed an opinion to a teacher and provided an account of his pragmalinguistic choices:

High-imposition opinion (expressing an opinion to a teacher about an unwarranted grade)

Excuse me Professor William, I'd like to talk about my grade. I check my grade yesterday and I was surprised that my grade was C. Actually I, I did not appear in the class and skipped three or four times, but I, I, I was always turning in my homework every time, and I got 80% on the test, so I'm afraid it is not fair. So can you, could you explain about it¿

I paid attention to the situation. Here I had to admit my fault because I missed three classes, and I did not speak up. But the grade C is not right. I missed three classes but I turned in homework, and I did all right with the test. I wanted to convey that the grade is not right, but I was also careful with the tone. I was conscious about using 'could you'. Initially 'can you' came out from my mouth, but this is a polite request, so I changed to 'could you'. Other than that, I wanted to say that I always turned in homework.

As shown in his reflection, Mitsu's choice between the modals 'can you' and 'could you' was a deliberate one. It is notable that 'can you' first came out of his mouth but he quickly self-corrected it and switched to 'could you'. Since other students did not bother to cancel the form once they said it even when they knew the more appropriate form, Mitsu's conscious self-correction is a strong indicator of his attentiveness to sociocultural aspects of language use. See the excerpts below for further support. Here he produced low- and high-imposition requests.

Low-imposition request (asking a friend for a pen):

Hey Ken, I forgot my pen. Can I use yours¿

High-imposition request (asking a teacher for an extension of an assignment):

Excuse me, I have something to tell you. Actually I have a cold and I did, I did my homework, but I'm afraid I need more, two extra days, so is it possible to put off my deadline¿

This is to a professor, so I was careful not to use casual language. I tried to add more words so that it sounds softer. I explicitly said the reason, 'I caught a cold'. I probably won't give a long excuse like this if I were talking to a friend. I compared the expressions 'I think' and 'I'm afraid' to frame 'I need two extra days'. I decided to use 'I'm afraid' because it conveys a regret, and it's politer than 'I think'. I learned it after I entered the university through an English conversation book published from NHK (Japanese Broadcasting Corporation). I didn't know that 'I'm afraid' had a meaning of regret before I saw it in the book. I used the expression 'is it possible' because 'can I' didn't sound right here. I thought that 'is it possible' is more formal and polite, but now I feel that I could have used 'would it be possible' instead to make it even politer.

This verbal protocol presents additional evidence of his sociopragmatic awareness, conscious assessment of pragmalinguistic forms and ability to implement pragmatic knowledge in real-time production. He did not use the same form in the request to a friend vs. to a professor, which reflects his sociopragmatic awareness of situational differences. He was also aware that the high-imposition situation warrants lengthy explanation, but an excuse is not needed in a small request to a friend, illustrating his understanding of appropriate semantic moves in this situation. He used a syntactic mitigation 'I'm afraid' which he learned from his self-study material, and he was able to articulate the subtle differences between 'I'm afraid' and 'I think' based on their politeness cost. In addition, he reevaluated the request-making form 'is it possible to' that he used. He said that it could be further mitigated by using the modal 'would' as in 'would it be possible to', which was more appropriate in the formal situation here. These multiple layers of knowledge and thoughtful examination of target form – function – context mappings were largely absent in other students' protocols. Yuko and Asako, for example, exhibited some level of pragmalinguistic knowledge, but the actual style shift between formal and informal situations was marked only with the modal type in the target head act (e.g. 'I want to' vs. 'I'd like to' and 'can you' vs. 'could you'). They did not attend other aspects such as internal/external mitigation and semantic moves that contribute to speech acts' overall tone. Hence, Mitsu's knowledge of pragmalinguistic devices at multiple levels clearly stood out among the participants in this study. Although he did not employ bi-clausal structures as native speakers did, he was able to use other lexical and syntactic devices that alleviate the potential face-threat of high-imposition speech acts.

Mitsu's sociopragmatic awareness started to develop when he participated in the North-East Asian Students Conference organized on campus during summer. A group of Korean students came from Seoul and had a debate with Japanese students on a variety of topics. During the event, he met a senior Japanese student, a business major, who had been to Korea several times. The student lamented that very few Japanese university students can speak proper, appropriate English in professional business meetings. This incident triggered Mitsu to apprehend the concept of situationally appropriate language use. Since then, he became conscious about register variation in English and started to pay attention to the sociocultural function behind linguistic expressions. For example, one day he saw the expression 'I'm afraid' in a conversation book with a footnote indicating that the expression is more formal than 'I think'. He wrote this information down in his notebook so that he could actually use it to mitigate a negative opinion in a formal situation. At another time, he found the expression 'Is there any reason for that?' in a movie and memorized it as a useful expression to soften the tone of disagreement. In addition, whenever he checked the dictionary for an unfamiliar word, he developed a habit of looking for usage notes. If the dictionary said that the word has a formal usage, he recorded it in his notebook and then tried to use it in a formal situation such as talking with a teacher or giving a presentation in class.

These descriptions tell us that Mitsu was clearly a strategic learner. His effort to learn about appropriate speech behavior in situation was evident. He was consciously directing his attention to pragmatic functions of everyday language use and making mental notes as he encountered them. This self-directed learning habit helped him to notice and mentally rehearse target pragmalinguistic features and semantic formulas, and he was committed to actually try them out when opportunities arose.

Mitsu's case history revealed the importance of subjectivity and investment for pragmatic learning. While Shoko's case suggests that learners stand to benefit from explicit correction and teaching on pragmatics, rather than simply being exposed to target pragmatic forms, Mitsu's case implies that if learners have strategies for learning pragmatics, they can turn everyday materials into opportunities for pragmatic learning. They can look for pragmatic information behind the ordinary usage of the forms or analyze different forms for their force and impact on the interlocutor. These bits of information that learners accumulate elsewhere over time could lead to a body of pragmatic knowledge that becomes available for retrieval in occasion, as shown in Mitsu's progress with speech act production.

One intriguing question here is how Mitsu came to invest so much in pragmatic learning. His interest was initially piqued when a senior student told him about English usage in specific business situations. However, a close analysis of qualitative data indicated that Mitsu's strong commitment to improve his English in general served as a driving force for pragmatic learning as well. Supporting evidence comes from his introspective verbal interview. In the speech act of request of asking a teacher to reschedule a quiz, Mitsu used the request head act 'When can I make up for it?' Since many students used 'please' + verb to put forward the request, I asked him why he used this indirect question form instead. He responded:

The form 'please' + verb becomes an imperative sentence without 'please'. When we add 'please' it becomes softer. But for me it's sounds like just a list of words, so ... I don't know how to say this, but I've been studying English for a while, so I want to raise my English level and attempt to approximate native speakers. I know 'please' + verb already, so I wanted to use new expression. (December, 2008)

Mitsu's motivation in pushing himself forward was also evident in his teachers' comments. Brian shared with me several episodes that illustrate Mitsu's assertiveness and strong desire to learn. He said that while other students would talk about simple topics like TV programs or movies, Mitsu would push himself and talk about deeper issues such as politics. See Brian's comment below:

In class he (Mitsu) pushes himself. He tries to speak with eloquence. He tries to speak with complex ideas, complex vocabulary. From April, in the speaking journal he is the one who uses more complex, difficult vocabulary, like once he used the word 'discombobulated'. I was so impressed. This kid can use the word. He learned the word, he likes it, he's using it properly, and he has even used it in the journal. So when he is on and he wants to talk, he talks to sound intelligently. He has made an effort to learn academic vocabulary. It's funny because from reading his journal I sensed that he didn't want to be here. This school wasn't his first choice, but he is here and he is trying to make most of it. That's what I feel. (December, 2008)

To support this observation, Brian shared one of his experiences with Mitsu:

Last week we had a mini lesson on sarcasm. For example, when someone has really ugly shoes and I say, 'Oh, I really love your shoes'. – What does it mean? So we had a little discussion on how to say sarcasm. I tried to teach them that when you say sarcasm you say opposite thing, and you kind of slow your speech, kind of emphasize the sound. And so later we are talking about future, and Haruko said, 'I'm going to be alone on Christmas' and I said, 'Wow that sounds really like fun'. And Mitsu was the first person who said 'That's sarcasm'. As soon as he said it, everybody caught on. They understood it meant opposite to what I said, and they started laughing. Then Mitsu asked, 'What is the response? When someone says sarcasm, what do I say back?' I said, maybe typical response is 'thank you', again being sarcastic, saying opposite.

This lesson about sarcasm revealed Mitsu's positive attitude and determination to constantly improve himself in English. He not only learned the meaning and functioning of sarcasm but also applied this knowledge to his observation of teacher–student dialog and demonstrated the knowledge in class promptly. Moreover, he asked the teacher for a common response pattern in sarcasm to further expand his knowledge base of sarcasm. From these observations, I interpreted that Mitsu's orientation and curiosity toward learning in general transferred to pragmatic learning and improved his pragmatic knowledge. He was attentive to sociocultural rules associated with everyday usage of language, trying to absorb such information as he encountered it in his study, and consciously tried to implement the knowledge in real-life interaction. This positive stance on pragmatics and other levels of learning led to a set of learning strategies that he developed and exercised over time. One positive outcome of this self-directed learning process was Mitsu's strong growth in the area of appropriate production of speech acts. Mitsu's case reiterates the importance of subjectivity and investment in pragmatic development, which contrasts sharply with Ippei's case described in the following section.

Ippei

This section presents the case history of Ippei. Figures 5.49 through 5.56 display his changes on PLT and PST in comparison with group means. Similar to Keita and Ryota, his pragmatic competence was clearly underdeveloped. His initial PLT score was about half the group mean. Although this score reached the group mean at Time 2, it dropped again at Time 3 and marked the lowest score in the group of 48 students, at the same level as Ryota. In addition, his PLT response speed decreased over time. Ippei's performance on PST was not impressive either. Although his appropriateness score on low-imposition speech acts recorded a large gain, it remained below average for the whole time. His high-imposition speech acts made no improvement at all: the score remained the same from Time 1 to Time 2,

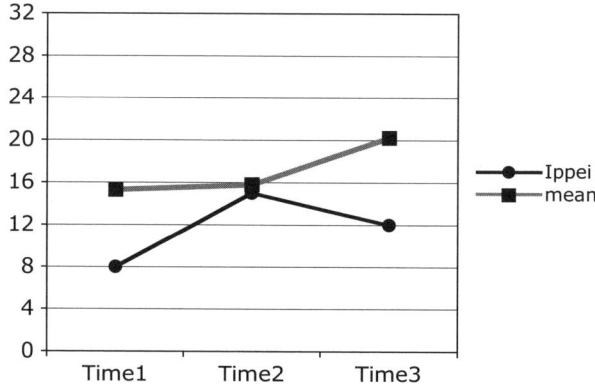

Figure 5.49 Ippei's change in PLT accuracy score

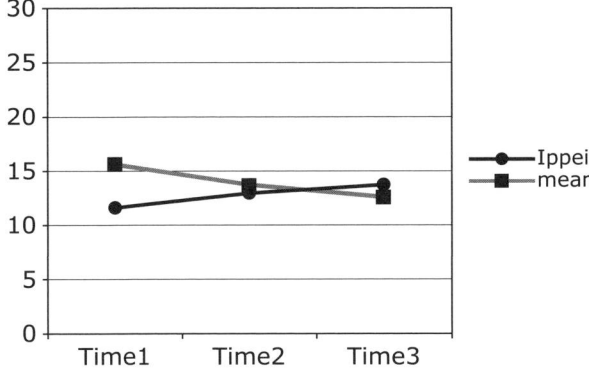

Figure 5.50 Ippei's change in PLT response times

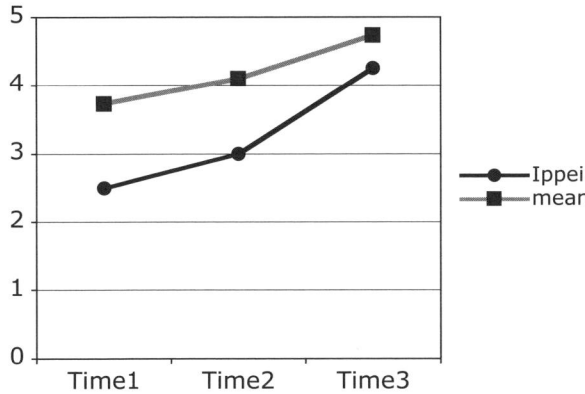

Figure 5.51 Ippei's change in PST appropriateness score, low-imposition speech acts

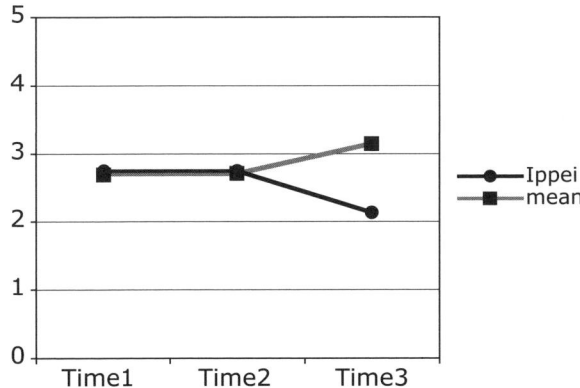

Figure 5.52 Ippei's change in PST appropriateness score, high-imposition speech acts

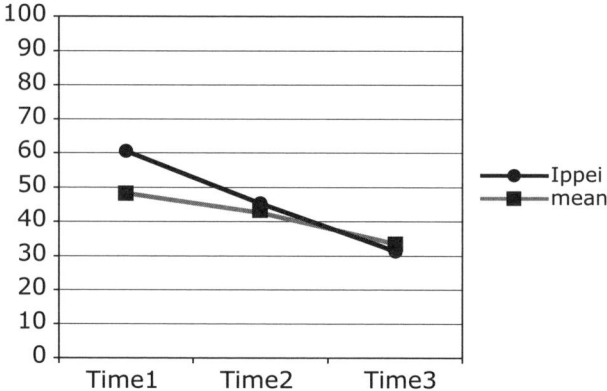

Figure 5.53 Ippei's change in PST planning time, low-imposition speech acts

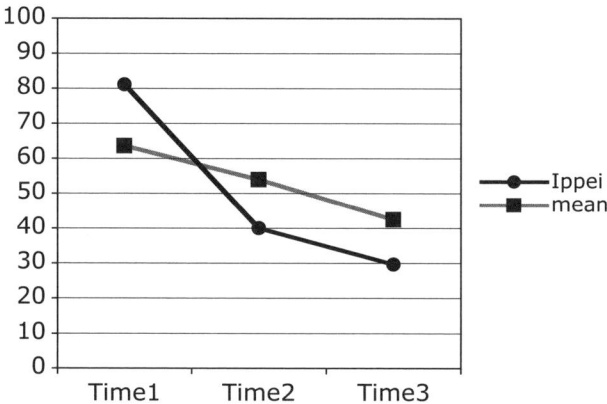

Figure 5.54 Ippei's change in planning time, high-imposition speech acts

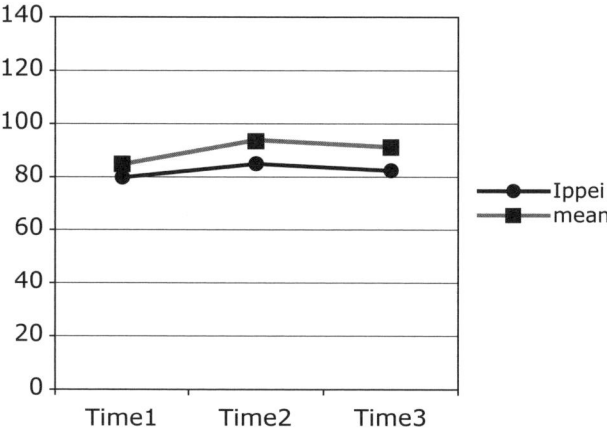

Figure 5.55 Ippei's change in PST speech rate, low-imposition speech acts

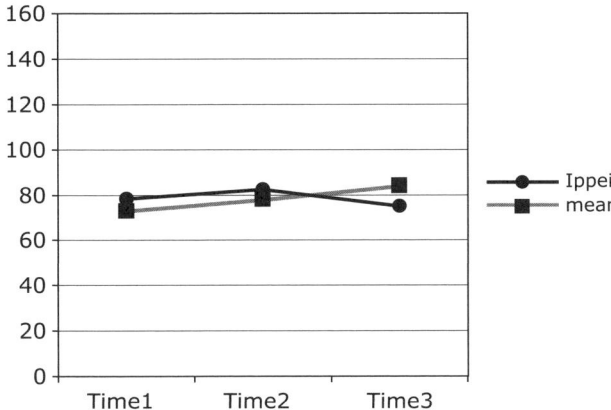

Figure 5.56 Ippei's change in PST speech rate, high-imposition speech acts

and dropped by almost one point at Time 3. His speech rate was below the group mean for the low-imposition speech acts, and about average for the high-imposition speech acts. Planning time was the only area in which he demonstrated above average performance. Although he started out as a slow planner, his planning speed became faster to the average level at Time 2 and Time 3 for low-imposition speech acts. For high-imposition speech acts, his planning speed was faster than the group average by about 10 seconds.

A close examination of his social experience on campus suggested that his slow pragmatic development was largely caused by lack of interaction with English speakers outside the class, just like Ryota and Keita. I assessed his personality, motivation and willingness to communicate to be somewhere between Ryota and Keita. He was not as diffident or introverted as Ryota, and instructors did not indicate any problems with his attitude in class. Although he was not as verbal or forthcoming as Keita, his class participation was moderate, and he did not hesitate to approach teachers to ask questions. However, what was markedly different in Ippei's case was not only his lack of knowledge of pragmalinguistic expressions but also his almost complete lack of sociolinguistic sensitivity. At times, he directly complained to the teachers about classes. In those occasions, his manner of speech was clearly inappropriate, but he was not aware of the potential negative consequence of this inappropriate manner. This insensitivity toward politeness probably led to his restricted pragmatic development, particularly in the area of appropriateness score in speech acts. These descriptions are provided below in his case history.

Ippei is from Akashi City in Kobe Prefecture, about 310 miles west of Tokyo. He came from a typical public high school and received seven hours of English instruction per week taught by Japanese instructors in Japanese. He identified translation as the most common classroom activity. His contact with English speakers was sporadic. During his first year he had a native speaker instructor in class once every two weeks, but he talked to the instructor only one time outside the class when he was preparing for the college entrance interview. From the fifth grade to his senior year in high school, he attended a private English conversation class taught by a Japanese instructor once a week. Although his school was a conversation school, class activities involved a variety of tasks, including conversation practice, listening exercises and preparation for the English certificate exam.

Ippei said that he chose this university because he wanted to study English seriously. His interest in English started in elementary school when he first attended private conversation school. His motivation is largely instrumental; he feels that English competence will be a plus when he enters the job market. When I asked him what he likes most about the university, he said that he likes students' diligence and seriousness. The term 'TOEFL' appeared eight times during the first interview, which I interpreted as a sign of his high instrumental motivation. Improving scores on TOEFL was a driving force in his study of English. When I asked him about his adjustment difficulty in the new university, he said that he initially felt inferior because his TOEFL score was lower than that of other students. This contrasts with Ryota and Asako who developed inferiority complex because of their weak speaking ability. He said that he is competitive and does not want to be looked down upon by his peers in class. He reported spending about two to three hours everyday on homework, and he expressed frustration that he could not secure enough time for TOEFL study. He said that he devoted almost no time to listening practice, except for listening to TOEFL CDs. Sometimes he watched movies with Japanese subtitles. He practiced speaking for about 30 minutes per week only in order to complete the speaking journal assignment. Other than that, he does not speak English outside the class.

Because of this strong instrumental motivation toward academic English, it is possible that Ippei was not very interested in expanding his network in the international student community. In the first semester, he had a couple of international friends he talked with occasionally, a few times a week for about 30 minutes, but they have since gone back to their countries, and had nobody to talk to at the time of this study. He did not even talk to his American suitemate. The speaking journal was a burden for him. According to him, international students who came in the second semester were *hachamecha* (wild and crazy) and not very approachable, and so he did not enjoy the assignment that required a communication with English speakers. His typical approach to the assignment was to find someone in the lobby or cafeteria and have a five- to ten-minute conversation, which mainly involves him asking for vocabulary meaning. He does not engage in conversation with them. The following journal excerpt illustrates this observation. Compared with Asako or Tomoyo's entries, his entries were usually short, running for six to eight lines, and they were focused on forms. Out of the 68 entries, 48 (about 70%) were on vocabulary and grammar practice:

> I asked an international student how to use the phrases 'I would' and 'I could' because I couldn't use them in my interview. Then he said to me, 'If I had one million yen, I would travel all over the world'. I was almost able to understand them. I want to practice and use them. (June, 2008)

Ippei's limited social contact was not restricted to the English-speaking community. In two out of the three interviews, he expressed his frustration with living in the dormitory because in a small school like this, human relations are constrained and rumors spread easily. He said that he could not wait to live off campus and get out of this small community. Ippei's detachment from Japanese community was also evident in that he spent most of his time alone. Although he belonged to three clubs (music, Japanese calligraphy and Italian club), except for classes and club activities, he stayed in the room and surfed the internet. He reported staying on the internet until 4:00 or 5:00 am, mostly watching YouTube videos in Japanese, and then sleeping for about three hours before going to class. Because of this habit, he started to miss classes. Of the 12 informants I interviewed, Ippei and Ryota were the only ones who overtly expressed that their motivation gradually diminished in the second semester. Ippei was the most negative about his classes. He complained that class activities were repetitive from the first semester, and that the reading class was particularly boring because it focused too much on vocabulary rather than actual reading exercises. He liked his writing class because the instructor was new, but other than that, his overall motivation decreased in the second semester.

Teachers' impressions about Ippei were neither positive nor negative. I interviewed three teachers, and Ippei's name never came up on their lists of strong or weak students at any point of time. Of the 22 classes I observed, I saw him volunteering answers 10 times. His participation in the group work was moderate. He did not take a leadership role nor was he particularly vocal, but he participated adequately when required. I was impressed with his group presentation in the speaking class that I observed around the end of the academic year. Ippei's group organized a debate in class. The class was divided into two groups to discuss whether or not one should give up their career for their family. Ippei was active throughout, giving directions, facilitating discussion and summarizing opinions. All three teachers I interviewed mentioned that Ippei was making slow but good progress. See their comments:

> He is very soft spoken, mild personality, and in terms of his language, he ... he is very sincere about asking questions. Sometimes he has to stop,

and ah . . he gets kind of mixed up and he wants to say in Japanese, and he'd say, 'wait, wait, wait', and he goes back to English and says it in English. It's not perfect, but he is actually quite clear, and his personality actually helps him not to take off any edge off from the mistakes he makes, like tense or pronoun mistakes. He is a little bit shy, but ... he's got very friendly character, so I think that's helpful. When he makes any mistakes, it's easy kind of not to notice the mistake. (Tom, September, 2008)

Ippei has made some improvement. He came to have lunch with us. I was surprised that he was assertive that way. There are a plenty of places he could sit, so I was impressed. In class he still occasionally falls into Japanese, but I think he tries. I think he could have done more. He has good attitudes. In class he tries, but I see some immaturity. I don't think he pushes himself enough as a speaker. He does minimum required. (Brian, December, 2008)

As shown in these comments, Ippei is a shy but likable student. His fluency is weak, and he struggles in expressing himself in English, but he continues to try.

These observations both inside and outside of the class point to some reasons why Ippei was slow-developing in pragmatic abilities. One obvious reason for this slow development is his lack of daily interaction with English speakers. Since pragmatic listening and speaking are built on basic listening and speaking abilities, his lack of practice for communication is a likely explanation for his pragmatic underdevelopment. Similar to Keita and Ryota, Ippei did not establish a social network within the international student community; as a result, his listening and speaking practices outside of the class were limited to TOEFL listening exercises, DVD watching and brief, sporadic exchanges with English speakers for the purpose of the speaking journal assignment. Two factors seemed to have constrained Ippei's access to target language input: personality and instrumental motivation. Because of his introvert personality and indifference toward social interaction in general, he closed himself in his room and engaged in net-surfing, which he called his 'hobby'. He was also most interested in improving his TOEFL score so that he could advance in the EAP levels. In this instrumental goal, contact with English speakers was not a priority at all.

While Ippei's case shares many similarities with Ryota and Keita's cases, and it reiterates the importance of sustained interaction for pragmatic growth, this case reveals an additional factor to consider for pragmatic development – sociocultural sensitivity. Recall that Ippei was particularly weak in appropriate production of speech acts. His score for low-imposition speech acts was below average for the whole time. His score for high-imposition speech acts was about average at Time 1 and Time 2, but it dropped by a large margin at Time 3 when the group mean increased. See the excerpts of Ippei's high-imposition speech acts:

High-imposition opinion (expressing an opinion to a teacher about an unwarranted grade)

Time 1
Why is my grade is C? I took a good grade.

Time 2
I think my grade is incorrect because I do in class well and ah, please think about it again.

Time 3
I think this grade is unfair because I turned all of homework and I got high score in quiz. So you should think about it again.

His speech act at Time 1 received a score of 2.0, 'poor'. The question at the beginning has an accusatory tone without adequate framing. It is very short and lacking a sufficient explanation of his argument. The score remained at 2.0 at Time 3. Although he provided some explanation this time, the speech act ended as a command because of the use of the modal of obligation 'should'.

In real-life situation, Ippei performed the same speech act to the class instructors several times. In at least two occasions, this performance involved a serious confrontation. He directly complained to the teachers about their quizzes, assignments and selection of class activities. Here, I will describe one of the occasions I witnessed. Brian, his speaking instructor, told me about an incident that took place in the first semester. Ippei came up to him after class and complained about the quiz:

He (Ippei) was angry. He had failed the listening test again. He said, 'I hate your listening test. This is the speaking class, but you give us listening test. Speaking class, speaking test!' He was the only one who actually came up and said that. (September, 2008)

This incident also appeared in Ippei's speaking journal. At the end of the first semester, Brian asked students to write a short paragraph in response to a question: If you were a teacher, how would you teach a class? Ippei wrote:

I would teach like you because your class is funny, but I think you have some points at which you must improve. First, I don't like your speaking test. I don't like a listening test. Why did you do listening? I think it was good to do speaking interview, so you should only do a speaking interview as a test. Second, you should not say 'I want to kill you' because the words made us frightened. We don't like such words. I think your class was exciting, so I want you to care about these two points. (July, 2008)

While this is a well-organized opinion with explicit transition markers and clear introduction and conclusion statements, the actual language that Ippei used to make his point was clearly rude. He started out with an explicit expression of dislike, 'I don't like', and a direct question, 'why do you do X?' He also used the strong obligation modal of 'must' and 'should' elsewhere to express his wish and request to the teacher. Ippei was probably not intentional in his use of strong, impolite language because he prefaced his opinion with a positive politeness strategy, 'your class is funny', and emphasized it again at the end.

I had a follow-up interview with Ippei specifically about this journal entry in order to gain his perception about pragmatic appropriateness. He said that he did not think the message was particularly rude. He wrote his honest opinion because Brian is friendly and approachable, and he invited everyone to give direct feedback. He said that he would not be able to say the same thing to a different instructor who was more authoritative. I asked him if he had paid attention to his language or content before he turned it in. Ippei said he did not because he was in a hurry. I asked him to look over the text to see if he would change anything in the text. He said that the sentence 'I will teach like you' sounded a bit confusing because of 'teach' and 'like' next to each other. He also pointed out that the collocation in the sentence 'Why did you do listening?' is a bit off, so he would probably revise it. His comments were concentrated on grammar and lexis, and there was no mention of the pragmatic aspect of language use.

These descriptions highlight Ippei's incorrect assessments of contextual features and lack of knowledge of proper pragmalinguistic forms in this situation. He did not employ syntactic and lexical mitigations that could soften the tone of speech. For example, he could have used different modals than 'must' or 'should' or hedging devices such as 'a little' or 'a bit' to reduce potential face-threat. He could have used an indirect question, 'I don't understand why you used listening test', instead of a direct question, 'Why did you do listening?' Alternatively, he could have used a bi-clausal, embedded sentence structure with 'I wonder' or 'I think' to make his opinion less direct. These pragmalinguistic forms were either completely absent in his system or he had no intention of using them because he was not able to point out his pragmalinguistic misuse in the follow-up interview. An important observation here, however, is that Ippei did not seem to care much about the politeness aspect of the message. He thought that his manner of speech was perfectly fine for Brian who was friendly and open. Communicating intentions explicitly and clearly took priority, and the facets of sociocultural appropriateness and politeness were not even in his consciousness during his interaction.

Brian's personality and his casual interaction style with students in class seemed to have influenced Ippei's assessment of the contextual factors involved in this real-life speech act. Through my interviews with Brian, it became clear that he did not mind students' frankness. In fact, he was constantly encouraging students to be direct and forthcoming, and he never corrected students' pragmalinguistic inappropriateness. In this regard, the teacher and students were on the same page: if students prioritized direct communication of meaning over manner of communication, the teacher did too. The following email and interview excerpts illustrate this point. I asked Brian what he thought about Ippei's manner of speech, and he responded:

No (I didn't get offended by Ippei), because I want to get feedback from the students. He made his point clearly, and he backed it up. There was an inconsistency between what I was teaching and what I was testing. The materials and assessment didn't match. I felt that in his own way he was trying to help me and improve my teaching. He didn't go behind my back and tell everybody that he hated my class or that I was a bad teacher. He came directly to me and made his point. I was proud of him. (email communication, September, 2008)

What Ippei did to me was actually to help me out. He was right, and while I had my reasons to do what I was doing, here was an 18-year-old student, with limited English speaking abilities, within a bicultural setting, and a teacher-student dichotomy, telling me about a mistake I was making. It took an incredible amount of courage (generated from a deep frustration) for him to express his anger and tell me what I was doing wrong. He opened my eyes. He taught me a lesson. Why would I be angry with him? (email communication, September, 2008)

To me when they (students) give me feedback, they like me, and they want me improve, and I feel that. It's my own personal . . . I don't think this is the teacher thing. This is 'Brian thing'. I want students feel, yes, I'm the authority figure, I'm the teacher, but somebody that they can trust, they can feel comfortable with, they can play with language, and they can talk back, they can . . . Have some kind of joking, kind of like peer, because now I kind of feel like me and them, me on top of them. What I want is something like this, yes, I'm the authority figure but they can, they can joke, they can tease, and they can do that kind of stuff, and it's a one year process. I think they are very, very, very, very afraid. (interview, October, 2008).

These excerpts clearly illustrate Brian's stance toward teaching and his perception of an ideal student–teacher relationship. He wanted to create a cooperative learning environment where teachers and students jointly contribute to the goal of learning—construction of target language knowledge and skills. In this process, feedback from students is essential, and students have to feel comfortable in speaking up to teachers and telling what is helpful and not helpful for their language development. Ippei did just that. As Brian acknowledged, what Ippei said upfront actually made sense. Students were not tested on what they learned in class. Although Brian had his own reasoning for using the listening test, he obviously did not communicate this rationale or how it could benefit their speaking clearly. Ippei's message made him aware of this lack of communication. Hence, from Brian's perspective, Ippei's courage to write the message was something to be commended, and not something to be reproached for its inappropriate use of language.

It was also evident in Ippei's perception of formality and register variation in English that he prioritized transaction of meaning over politeness. He admitted that he did not know whether register variation exists in English or whether English speakers change their speech style in situation as Japanese people do with honorifics and polite language. In high school, he gained some pragmalinguistic knowledge, such as using 'had better' + verb when making a suggestion is impolite or 'would you' is politer than 'will you' when making a request. But in real-life communication with teachers, he did not care about politeness. Because he did not want his teachers to misunderstand his intention, he focused on making his point clearly and directly. He cared about the actual content of the message—what to say—and was not thinking about how to say it. The excerpts below from the introspective verbal interview session further illustrate his stance:

High-imposition request (asking a professor for an extension of a paper)

Actually I caught a cold, so I didn't finish my homework, so please give me two extra days.

I thought that I need to give a reason first. Otherwise, the teacher wouldn't give me two days of extension. I used 'please' but I have no particular reason. I knew that this is a situation with a professor. I used 'please' because it was the first thing that popped up in my head. Maybe 'would you' might have been better, but it didn't come up.

High-imposition opinion (expressing opinion to a professor about an unwarranted grade)

I think my grade is unfair because I got 80% on the test, so why my grade was C?

I paid attention to how to say it in a way that the professor would understand it. The main point was why the grade was C. I got 80% on a test, so it's not C. It's B. That's what I wanted to say. I didn't care about how to say it. I just wanted to complain. I wanted to convey what I wanted to say.

These excerpts reveal Ippei's focus on content, not on form. He used whatever expressions were salient and most accessible at the given point of time to convey his intention, and he did not evaluate the expressions for politeness value. These attitudes seemed to be reflected in his planning time. Among the various aspects of pragmatic competence examined in this study, planning speed was the only area in which Ippei excelled in the group. Ippei's speedy planning could be a reflection of his approach to each speech act item. He used the expression that first came to his mind, rather than evaluating multiple expressions for pragmatic appropriateness and choosing one that best fits the given context. In this sense, Ippei's pragmatic act was rather impulsive, both in real-life and test settings.

In summary, Ippei's case points to several reasons why some students are slow-developing in the acquisition of pragmatic competence. Pragmatic listening, as tested in this study, is built on general listening skill, and so exposure to authentic target language input and time-on-task are vital for its growth. In the learning environment studied here, such opportunities are likely to be present in a long, engaged conversation with international students outside the class. Hence, lack of access to an English-speaking community seemed to be the major cause of Ippei's below-average pragmatic comprehension. Like Asako, Ippei had the weekly speaking journal assignment that could have potentially helped him to expand his social network, but he considered this assignment to be a nuisance rather than an opportunity to practice English. Ippei's competitiveness in academic attainment and his strong instrumental motivation toward TOEFL, together with his preference for solitude, probably shaped his social experience in the university community.

Ippei's case suggests that sociopragmatic sensitivity is one of the key elements for the development of pragmatic speaking. Understanding language in relation to their contextual requirements (e.g. interlocutor relationship, setting and topic), as well as considering others' perceptions of one's linguistic behavior, seems to be a prerequisite to pragmalinguistic development. If students do not care about the social dimension of language use and its consequence on interpersonal relationships, they see no value of implementing pragmalinguistic knowledge even if they own it. Pragmalinguistics involves a conscious decision about which modal to use or whether to employ mitigating devices. This decision depends on one's knowledge of those pragmalinguistic forms and one's ability to accurately assess the contextual features that require them. However, equally vital in this decision is one's awareness about the importance of those forms in social interaction and motivation to use them. As shown in Ippei's case, for second language speakers, basic communication of message is primary, and politeness or appropriateness issues associated with communication is secondary or even unaddressed. To be able to attend both dimensions, speakers first need to orient themselves to them: lack of sensitivity or interest in the sociocultural dimension of language provides little basis for pragmatic development.

Another important finding related to this observation is the role of environment for the development of sociocultural sensitivity. As shown in Ippei's real-life speech acts, the teachers were so keen on getting students' feedback that they did not care much about the manner in which this feedback was delivered. They responded to the content of the message but not to the language, either neglecting to correct Ippei's misuse of pragmalinguistic forms or feeling no need to correct it. Similar findings were presented in Keita's case history and also at the end of Chapter 4 in the discussion of contextual constraints on pragmatic development. Ippei's case reiterates the complex interaction among students' qualities (e.g. goal, motivation, ability and history), contextual factors that promote or discourage certain type of practice and input and development of pragmatic abilities.

The final case history presented in the next section further illustrates this complexity among individuals, context and pragmatic development. Tomoyo, who was in the same class with Shoko, Asako, Mitsu and Ippei, started out with a fairly developed pragmatic competence, but one aspect of her pragmatic ability gradually diminished over time, corresponding to the type of interaction and experiences she accumulated in this particular context. I will discuss this unique case of pragmatic backsliding in detail below.

Tomoyo

Figures 5.57 through 5.64 present Tomoyo's change in pragmatic measures in relation to group means. Tomoyo clearly excelled in pragmatic listening. Her score was always well above average, and she made a large gain of seven points over two semesters. Her comprehension speed was fast as well. Her response times were below the average at all time periods, and her time decreased by about three seconds at Time 3. She was also fluent in pragmatic speaking. Her planning time was short and her speech rate was fast, and this pattern was the same for low- and high-imposition speech acts. Her appropriateness score, however, showed idiosyncratic changes: her score on the low-imposition speech acts remained high. Her score on the high-imposition speech acts was also strong at Time 1 and Time 2, but her score dropped drastically in the second semester by more than one full point on the five-point scale.

These changes in the appropriateness scores are reflected in the type of linguistic expressions Tomoyo used to formulate high-imposition speech acts. While Shoko was the only student who produced the mitigated-preparatory form (bi-clausal structure) at Time 3, Tomoyo was one of the

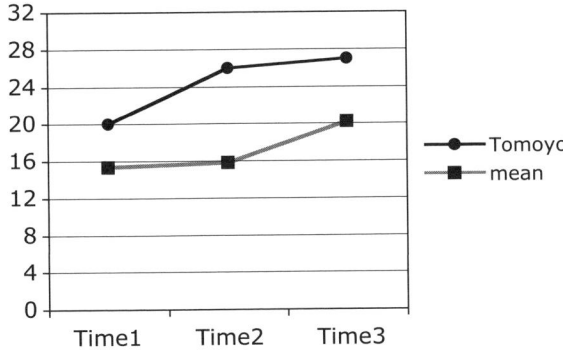

Figure 5.57 Tomoyo's change in PLT accuracy score

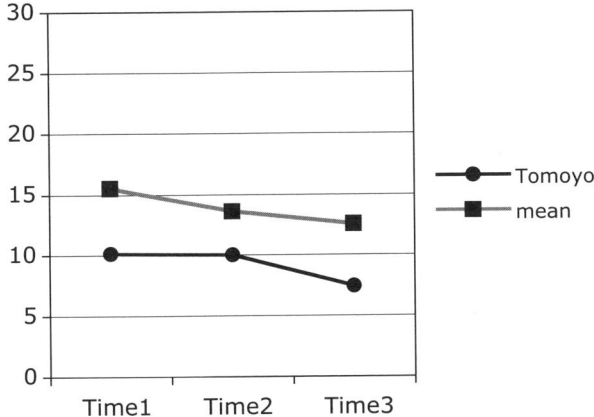

Figure 5.58 Tomoyo's change in PLT response times

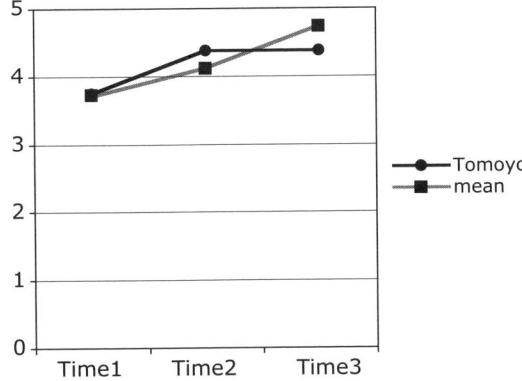

Figure 5.59 Tomoyo's change in PST appropriateness score, low-imposition speech acts

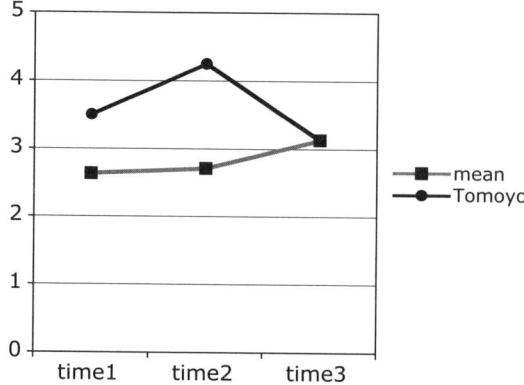

Figure 5.60 Tomoyo's change in PST appropriateness score, high-imposition speech acts

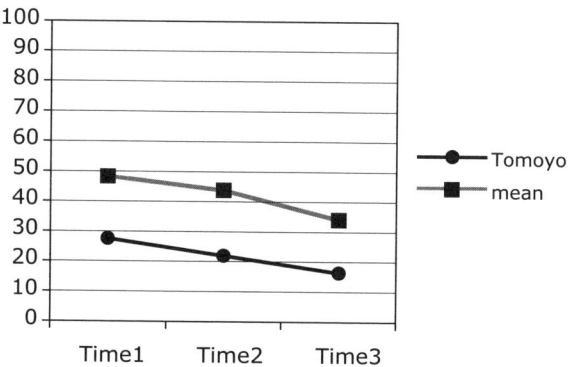

Figure 5.61 Tomoyo's change in PST planning time, low-imposition speech acts

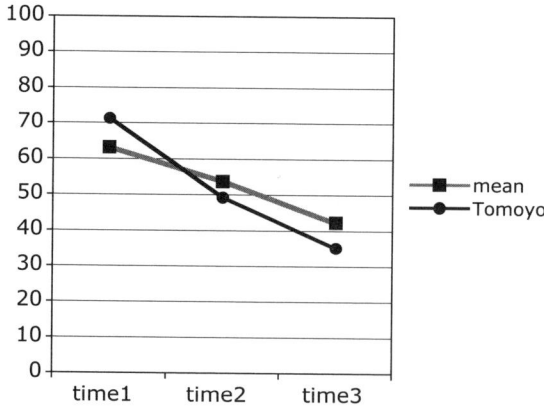

Figure 5.62 Tomoyo's change in PST planning time, high-imposition speech acts

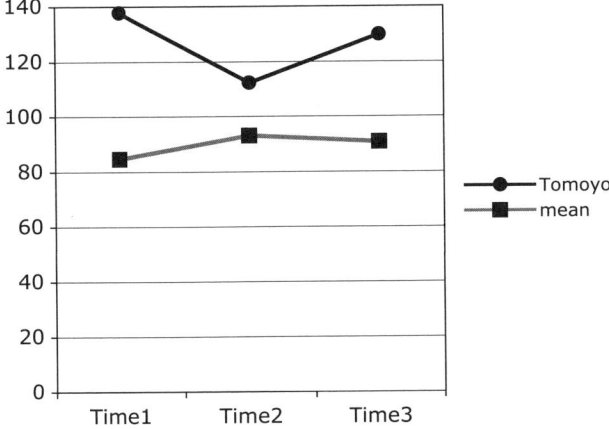

Figure 5.63 Tomoyo's change in PST speech rate, low-imposition speech acts

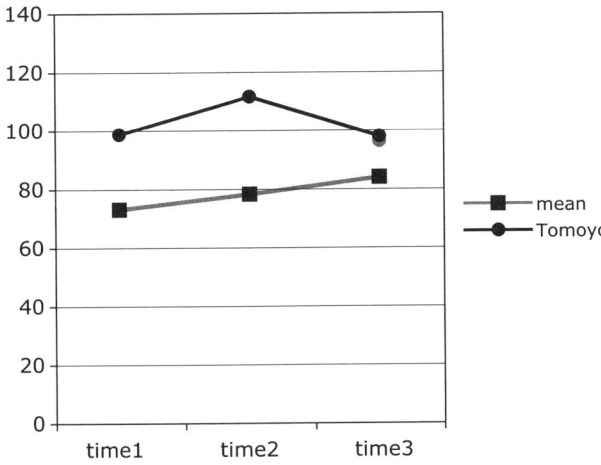

Figure 5.64 Tomoyo's change in PST speech rate, high-imposition speech acts

two students who used it at Time 1. This pragmalinguistic form was already in her repertoire as a high-imposition request, and her processing skill was sufficient for implementing the use. However, puzzlingly, the target form disappeared eight months later, as illustrated in these excerpts:

High-imposition speech act (asking a teacher for a permission to take a test other time)

Time 1
I'm so sorry, but Mr. Smith, but I'm going to have my cousin's wedding I need to prepare, I was wondering if you change the schedule test.

Time 2
Excuse me professor, I have a doctor appointment on the same time as you are gonna have a test and I really need to see a doctor. I know that the test is important, but I'm not feeling well these days, so I was wondering if you arrange the test for different time.

Time 3
Next week we are gonna have a test but I can't attend the class on that today because my cousin is gonna have a wedding. And I need to go out. So I wanna thinking for making up the test another day.

At Time 3 she stopped using the mitigated expression, 'I was wondering if', and instead encoded casual tone throughout with the contractions 'gonna' and 'wanna'. Her speech in the introspective verbal interview was even worse. She used the form 'I want you' + verb, which was an order rather than a request. Qualitative analyses revealed a matrix of factors stemming from context, learner subjectivity and persona that caused this pragmatic backsliding.

Like Mitsu, Tomoyo was a local student. She went to a public high school in Akita City. Like Shoko and Yuko, she was in *eigo-ka*, English-track, and received 10 hours of English instruction per week taught by Japanese teachers and an English-speaking instructor. From her descriptions, I found her English class different from other typical high-school English classes that are grammar- and vocabulary-oriented: it was highly interactive, content-based and four-skill-based. About two years ago her high school was nominated as one of the experimental schools under the nationwide 'Super High School' project and received a large grant from the government to implement unique English instruction and her class is a representative example of the unique English education implemented through the grant. Tomoyo's high-school teacher, Chris, who was also a part-time instructor at the target institution, gave me a description of typical classroom activities:

> The theme of the class was 'communicating with empathy'. Students read a number of opinions on a range of societal issues, such as environmental problems or death penalty. They read something and hear opinions from the text. They would have to take a pro or con position and explain it to their conversation partner. Then they turn to a person with opposite opinion and then they have to give their opposite opinion so that they understand both sides. We did that twice a week. Tomoyo's class ended up being most expressive, openly expressive, by the end of the time I taught them. They freely gave answers. They shouted for answers. Tomoyo was one of the three or four top students in class who were never shy about sharing her opinions. (September, 2008)

Tomoyo maintained close contact with Chris throughout her high-school years. With a few other friends, she visited his desk in the teacher's room almost everyday and talked about trivial things. She also belonged to the English Club that he supervised, and she spent one to two hours daily with him and other club members. Chris, who had Tomoyo in class over three years, said:

> Tomoyo has a lot of leadership quality and she is the type that always volunteers, always active. That built part of her confidence to approach me, talk to me, and continue, which is not for everyone. . . . She was one of my closest students, because she took a chance to offer herself as a person. When she came, she talked about personal thing, about school, something funny. It was all English practice. But it was a successful English practice because it was a natural, real communication. As a result, teacher–student relationship became stronger, and the trust became stronger, and obviously the end goal of English became stronger too. (September, 2008)

These intense, authentic communication practices in high school contributed to Tomoyo's advanced speaking skills. She was fluent, articulate and spontaneous, and there was almost no awkwardness in her interaction with native-speaker instructors. She was natural. She knew how to joke, resist and be assertive in English. Chris said that Tomoyo could occupy the entire class time. The class can become almost a conversation between the two of them if he was not careful to involve other students'. Her journal entries were also qualitatively different from other students'. They were not dry, monotonous descriptions, but showed emotion and personal perspective. See the example excerpts from her journal:

> Mr Miller always mistakes Haruyo and me. He sometimes looks at me and says Haruyo. I always correct his mistake, but recently he doesn't even listen to me. On Wednesday, he did the same thing as usual and I was frustrated, so I stomped the ground. I knew it was childish but I was that angry. After the class, I met Peter at cafeteria and I told him, 'I stomped the ground with frustration'. He laughed . . . (June, 2008)

> On Wednesday, Chris told us about global marriage. Since his wife is Japanese, he knows the system of marriage. In Japan, when people become family, we need to register to the government. But Chris is not Japanese, so his wife's register paper has only her name. I told him it's strange, old, bad Japanese culture and he should complain about it to the government. Then he said, 'I think it's old, traditional Japanese culture, so it will get better in the future'. But I strongly disagree with that idea. In Japan Chris doesn't exist. It's not fair. (September, 2008)

Tomoyo was also quick in learning a new phrase and using it in a different context. Her journal often contains a description of an international student giving her a lesson on usage of English and her recycling it in a different sentence. Brian, the teacher who assigned the speaking journal homework, often commended Tomoyo on her ability to absorb new vocabulary. See the excerpt below followed by Brian's comment to one of her entries:

Tomoyo's journal entry:

The other day my mom called me on very early morning and talked to me a lot. She was so mad because I did something wrong and I put her into trouble. I was in Happo town and stayed there with several international students. One of them listened to my mom screaming behind the phone. Then, after that, she asked me if my mom lectured me. I didn't know what 'lectured' mean but after a while, I got it. Then I asked her how to use the word. I asked if 'my mom lecturing me yesterday' is correct, but she said it must be 'my mom lectured me yesterday'. After all this conversation, I thought I should have known 'lecture' as verb because it's useful. I'll try to use it more often.

Brian's comment:

Tomoyo: Reading your journal was like a breath of fresh air. This level of thinking is much more appropriate for someone with your experience, knowledge, and fortitude. This was one of the best things I have read from you and one that makes me proud. I'm happy you tried to push yourself. I'm glad you saw an opportunity for growth and you took it. You will go far if you can continue this approach. So you make a mistake here and there ... this is how one learns. FABULOUS! ☺

These journal entries clearly not only illustrate Tomoyo's expressiveness in English, but also show the extent of her social network with international students. She named about 10 close friends she interacted with regularly. She hung out with them in the dormitory lounge and usually spent 30 minutes to five hours talking in English, sometimes staying overnight to continue the conversation. She also volunteered to assist English classes in local elementary schools and made day-long or overnight trips with international students. While other informants reported spending most of their time studying and doing homework, Tomoyo's English activities centered around the interaction with international students. She told me that her average study time was 30 minutes per day. Her 'English circle' clearly existed in a different space than the circles of students who reported DVDs or journal assignment as primary sources of listening and speaking practice. For Tomoyo, practice came naturally in authentic communication opportunities and was a part of her life. She was also the only student who often went to the teachers' office to talk about personal topics. She was particularly close to two instructors and regularly visited their office once or twice a week. Tomoyo expressed that she is social and talkative, both in Japanese and English, and she wants to master English so that she can expand her social network more. It is likely that, as found in Asako and Yuko's cases, these intense, routine communication opportunities with international students contributed to her strong gain in pragmatic listening.

While Tomoyo's network with international students was extensive, her contact with Japanese students was rather limited. When I asked about her adjustment difficulty in the new university environment, the first thing she talked about was her Japanese peers. She said that the Japanese students were immature and that they gave her 'goose bumps'. They talked loud at night in hallways in the residence hall, and they did not calm down even after she complained about the noise. They did not do homework and just chat in the library. It seems that her tie with international students was strengthened through a temperamental dislike that she developed for her same-age Japanese peers.

While Tomoyo's integrative motivation to study English was apparent, her instrumental motivation was questionable. Unlike the rest of the informants who mentioned study abroad and an international career as incentives for studying English, Tomoyo did not provide a clear reason for her English study. She entered this university because it was in her hometown, and she liked English. Unlike other students, she did not show much interest in study abroad, saying that all the paper work involved in the application process is a nuisance. She acknowledged her weaknesses in grammar, vocabulary and reading, as reflected in her TOEFL score. Among the 48 participants, her score was the third lowest at Time 3 with the increase of 30 points from Time 1, the smallest gain size among the 12 informants. It is worth noting here that all three EAP instructors I interviewed nominated her both as one of the most active participants in class and as someone who needed most work in academic achievement. Chris, Tomoyo's writing instructor, commented:

> Tomoyo knows a kind of details that need to go to the essay to make it a good essay, and her vocabulary and grammar are fair, above average, but she does poorly on quizzes and she doesn't do homework sincerely. So I don't know how good she is as a student. For someone who uses English, she is one of the best students in the whole EAP program but in terms of being a student, she is probably one of the worst. (September, 2008)

This excerpt shows that Tomoyo is outspoken and participates well in class, but she is not very serious about her academic work.

During the interviews, I found Tomoyo expressive, articulate and confident. She often gave me an extended answer and explained things in great detail without any kind of prompting. This openness and honesty became most visible in her interaction with teachers. She told me that teachers often asked for her feedback about their class on topics such as the amount of homework or pace of instruction. This had happened almost every month in high school and about five times since she came to the college. She said that teachers seemed to appreciate her frankness, trusting her even more for the directness and maturity she demonstrated in handling class situations. When I asked Chris whether he could recall an episode of seeking her feedback, he said:

> Yeah, I do actually, fairly early on in her class. I think students always take time to adapt to the class, so I asked her why students are disinterested ... why they don't speak up, and why do they sleep? In my own mind I was thinking they are Japanese and teenagers, so these two combinations ... (laugh) ... And ... I don't know if she had a real answer or anything in depth, but she assured me that keep doing what I'm doing and enjoying it. Eventually the dynamic changed and the class became *genki* (active). And I think it's useful to have a student who is willing to tell you the truth. (September, 2008)

The degree of trust that Tomoyo gained from teachers was clearly at a different level than the rest of the students. An incident that supports this observation happened after the middle of the semester. Brian, the EAP speaking class instructor, arranged an informal hearing in response to the tension he was feeling with the students. He was 'pulling teeth' with the students because they were speaking too much Japanese in class. He wanted to form a small representative group to discuss, and he asked Tomoyo to take a leadership role. Brian said that Tomoyo was initially surprised and hesitant, but she eventually agreed to take up the role. I asked him why he chose Tomoyo, and he responded:

> She is the one I trust, because she would never sugarcoat something from me. Because even when students are totally angry with me but totally Japanese and not tell me, she would. ... I feel like she is most acclimated to Americanism. I mean Haruyo is pretty good too but Haruyo is also ... I'd say, maybe, afraid that she might be offensive or she might say something. ... They are both smart, but I'd trust Tomoyo more to tell me straight up this is what's wrong. And if I had to explain something in English, I'd trust her to be able to say that to the group, like a perfect translator. (October, 2008)

This excerpt demonstrates that it was the combination of Tomoyo's English ability and forthright personality that helped her to gain teachers' trust and further deepen her relationship with them. 'Most acclimated to Americanism' was the phrase that Brian used to describe Tomoyo. According to Brian, the 'Americanism' here referred to an environment in which students and teachers construct learning as a reciprocal activity: teachers provide materials and students provide reflections about their learning. This type of inclusive community and open communication between teachers and students is not common in a traditional Japanese class. In fact, Brian mentioned that the biggest cultural adjustment that he had to make in Japan after teaching in the United States was to get students' feedback. Because students did not give any feedback, he had to push students and encourage them to get reassurance that they were learning, as described before in his interaction with Ippei. In that sense, Tomoyo was probably an atypical Japanese student. She was open, expressive and direct, and did not hesitate to cast opinions. She had the exact quality that the teachers were looking for. I visited Brian's class a couple of days after the incident. There I saw Tomoyo standing in front of the class, summarizing in Japanese to her peers the meeting outcome and Brian's message.

This incident with Brian also came up during my interview with Tomoyo. She told me that Brian emailed everyone in class and asked for their input about his class. Soon after, she received his email saying that he wants to talk to her personally about the issue. Tomoyo said that she was half expecting the email. I asked her how she handled the situation, and she said that she handled it well. She struggled to explain the complaints from the class with her limited vocabulary, but she was happy to see Brian listening to her explanation in a thoughtful manner. When Brian showed his private side and expressed his stress over this incident, Tomoyo realized that she was successful in making her points understood.

Another instructor, Chris, also occasionally mentioned that he would trust Tomoyo and Haruyo, another student in class, to be direct with him. I asked him why he would trust them, and he replied:

> It's because how freely they communicate, how openly. They spontaneously communicate without any kind of prompting. When I might say something, they are very happy to reply. They are not afraid of mistakes necessarily, they are willing to take a risk, and that's kind of communication, I think, is the kind of communication that could be valuable between students and teachers because I feel like it shows that they are not afraid to confront something, even if it's not necessarily their comfort zone, so when I ask them to share any feeling that the class might have, I told them directly that I can trust them that they won't be afraid of saying things directly to me. (November, 2009)

I interpreted Tomoyo's openness in a teacher–student relationship as an indication of her sociopragmatic development. She learned that it is perfectly fine in the United States or other cultures for students to complain or say things directly to teachers if these comments include constructive feedback. This socialization into the target sociocultural norms occurred and was reinforced through repeated experiences of being asked for feedback by teachers in high school and college. However, this sociopragmatic knowledge and rapport with teachers did not help Tomoyo with her pragmalinguistic knowledge. Recall that over time she made progress in all aspects of pragmatic competence except for appropriateness of high-imposition speech acts. Her score dropped dramatically from Time 2 to Time 3, and she stopped using the syntactic mitigation, the bi-clausal structure in high-imposition requests (i.e. 'I was wondering if' + clause). This decline probably occurred because of the relationship between her and teachers in real life. Over time, her relationship with teachers became casual, and as a result, her manner of speaking became direct and informal. Formal situations, as they were defined in the PST did not exist in her real life. Due to the lack of sustained practice, the target pragmalinguistic forms gradually disappeared from her systems.

During the introspective verbal interview, I showed Tomoyo transcripts of her high-imposition requests from previous recordings, and pointed out to her that she was using the mitigated, bi-clausal expression ('I was wondering if' + clause) at Time 1 and 2, but not at Time 3. She was surprised and gave me her account of the change:

> It never came across my mind this time. I'm surprised that I was using this kind of form before. I think it's because I studied this for the college entrance exam. This structure was in the textbook, and I memorized it, practiced it. There was a footnote saying that this is a formal expression. ... Maybe because I don't use it here. I talk casual with international students, so I forgot it? Before I came here, someone told me that some teachers are picky with language, like telling students to use 'Dr.' or 'please'. Saying 'Can you explain?' is not good, and I have to say 'Would you explain?' They warned me, but in reality, the teachers I had are all casual. I don't think it's bad, but ... say ... I came here prepared, but now it's like, there is a hole in the bag and everything is falling off.... I don't have anybody to use it. I don't have the situation to use it. (December, 2008)

Tomoyo told me that she was more conscientious about her language at the beginning of the academic year when she did not have much contact with international students. While planning for the speech acts, she was thinking about the intention that she was supposed to convey as well as linguistic expressions to express the intention and evaluated them for formality. However, in the most recent test session, she never thought about the forms but just content of her speech.

A lack of opportunities to use formal language on campus also seemed to have influenced Tomoyo's metapragmatic awareness. On the issue of politeness and formality, she said that situational variation in speech is not very important in English. She formed this assessment from her own experiences in the bilingual college environment. In this environment, students use peer talk regardless of age differences because little hierarchical relationship exists between seniors and juniors on campus. She said that this rationale also applies to the teacher–student relationship. She often mentioned how friendly and approachable Brian and Chris were. They encouraged her to speak up, and they did not mind her using slang and other informal language. Because she felt relaxed and unguarded when she talked to them, polite language or formal register often slipped her mind. Besides, the relationship she had established with them over time – and the degree of trust and support – was not an ordinary teacher–student relationship in which formal register could apply. Tomoyo shared one episode that illustrates this point. One day she skipped Brian's class when he gave guidelines for an upcoming presentation assignment. Since she missed the directions, she dropped by his office in the afternoon to ask about the assignment. Without elaborate explanations or polite request expressions, she just said to Brian, 'I have no idea what I need to do on Monday.' She told me that she did not pay attention to her manner of speech because talking to Brian did not feel like a formal interaction for her.

This case history revealed that the type of experiences in context plays a decisive role in learners' pragmatic change, and it is powerful enough to override what learners already had in their systems. In the case of Tomoyo, she initially had a complete understanding of the target pragmalinguistic forms through her preparation for college entrance exam, and she had automatized the use of them through memorization and drill practice. In addition, unlike other informants, she came with sufficient processing skills that helped her to implement the forms in spontaneous production. However, after being exposed to the casual, informal register among peers on campus, she became less conscious about those formal expressions. Extensive, personal-level contact with her teachers, which resulted from her persona and stance toward learning, also altered her perception of formality and speech, therefore leading to her casual tone in the high-imposition speech acts at Time 3. These new experiences during academic socialization, on the other hand, did not affect her fluency aspect of pragmatic production or comprehension of implied meaning. Those skills continued to develop robustly, indicating that mere exposure to input and practice is sufficient to improve these areas of pragmatic abilities.

Chapter 6, the last chapter in this book, synthesizes the findings from the analyses of both the qualitative and quantitative data described in this chapter and Chapter 4. I will discuss what it means to be pragmatically competent in this particular English-medium university in Japan by summarizing general patterns of developmental trajectories found in the data. Then, I will discuss complexities of pragmatic change based on contextual and individual-level analyses and interpret why pragmatic development forms a formidable challenge for some learners but not for others. I will conclude the book with limitations of the study and implication for future directions of longitudinal studies in interlanguage pragmatics.

Notes

(1) Owing to the space limit, analysis of grammaticality of pragmatic production is excluded from the individual-level analysis. Group-level analysis of grammaticality appears in Chapter 5.
(2) Student interviews were conducted in Japanese. Interview responses appearing in this chapter were translated into English by the author.
(3) A portion of Shoko and Tomoyo's case histories appeared in Taguchi (2011b).

6   Summary and Conclusion

This book has described development of pragmatic competence among Japanese learners of English in an English-medium university in Japan (see Chapter 1 for descriptions of the school). This study had two purposes: (1) to reveal patterns and the rate of pragmatic development across different pragmatic functions; and (2) to reveal resources and experiences in the learning context and link them to individual developmental trajectories. Forty-eight first-year students in the university completed two pragmatic measures: a pragmatic listening test which assessed their ability to comprehend conversational implicatures and a pragmatic speaking test which assessed their ability to produce appropriate speech acts. These measures were administered three times over one academic year to capture relevant changes in pragmatic competence. In addition to describing changes, this study sought to explain them. To do so, a subset of the participants were interviewed to learn the nature of their social contacts, domains of contact and types of social activities in order to examine the relationship between pragmatic gains and types of sociocultural experiences which are available for individuals. Results revealed a variety of tendencies and paces of development across pragmatic functions, and these variations were in part explained by contextual and individual difference factors. The following sections provide a summary and implications of this study's findings in two main areas: implications for the construct of pragmatic competence and implications for the second language acquisition process.

Implications of the Study Findings for the Construct of Pragmatic Competence and Development

This study proposes an original theoretical framework based on the synthesis of previous models of communicative competence and L2 proficiency (Bachman & Palmer, 1996, 2010; Bialystok, 1990b; Canale & Swain, 1980; Hymes, 1972) that situate *knowledge* and *processing* as two major subcomponents of pragmatic performance (see Chapter 3 for the theoretical framework). The framework reflects the view that language-related performance is largely based on language knowledge, but that other cognitive and noncognitive factors also have an important effect on performance. It is the combination of language knowledge and processing capacities that provides learners with the ability to engage in pragmatic tasks. As Skehan states, 'performance will not be some pale reflection of competence, but will be subject to all manners of processing factors which impinge on the nature of the performance required' (Skehan, 1995: 100). Linguistic knowledge and processing dimensions are both considered elements of the second language development process and provide complementary explanations for different problems (Bialystok, 1990a; Segalowitz, 2003, 2007).

Following these theoretical foundations, this study tracked development of *knowledge* and *processing* components of pragmatic abilities separately. Pragmatic *knowledge* was measured as knowledge required for comprehension and production of speech intentions, which encompasses a wide range of properties, including: linguistic knowledge, knowledge of Grice's (1975) maxims of conversation and assumptions about relevance, functional knowledge (form–meaning associations), knowledge of discourse (i.e. coherence and cohesions), sociocultural knowledge (e.g. notion of politeness and norms of interaction) and knowledge of linguistic and social conventions. Inferences about pragmatic knowledge were drawn from analysis of pragmatic comprehension accuracy and pragmatic production appropriateness. The *processing* component was measured in terms of the ability to process pragmatic knowledge fluently in real time. This skill involves higher-order execution abilities that aim to efficiently integrate knowledge bases and maximize the effectiveness of pragmatic performance. Inferences about processing capacity were drawn from analysis of fluency aspects of pragmatic comprehension and production, namely response times, planning time and speech rate.

Great variation was found in the patterns and rate of development between *knowledge* and *processing*, as well as among the various sub-constructs measured in each dimension (see Chapter 4 for the findings). Between the two types of conventional implicature items – indirect refusals and routines – comprehension of the former showed a steady, linear progress at every time junction, but that of the latter showed no gain in the first period followed by a large gain in the second period. Relative ease of indirect refusal is explained by common conventions between the participants' L1 and L2. As it is customary in both Japanese and English to give an excuse when refusing someone's invitation or offer, the Japanese participants were able to transfer their L1-based knowledge of refusal conventions to L2 comprehension. Comprehension of routines, on the other hand, required participants to draw on conventions of linguistic forms. Because the L2-specific forms needed to be newly learned and not inferred from L1 transfer, comprehension was likely not as easy as that of indirect refusals.

In the case of nonconventional implicatures, lack of any familiar conventions made comprehension of this item type even more difficult. Development of comprehension accuracy of nonconventional implicatures was slow with significant gains detected only later. Scores in the TOEFL listening section correlated significantly with those of conventional implicatures but not with nonconventional implicatures. Hence, it seems that comprehension of conventional implicatures develops naturally along with the increase in general listening skill, while comprehension of nonconventional implicatures takes a longer time to develop, and the developmental path does not coincide with the development of general listening proficiency.

The hierarchy of developmental order found in accuracy scores somewhat coincided with that of response times. Similar to accuracy, comprehension of nonconventional implicatures showed a significant decrease in response times only later, and not initially. Again, the effect of 'time' did not kick in immediately for this item type due to the lack of conventionality available to facilitate comprehension. In contrast, comprehension of indirect refusals was found to have a significant drop in response times directly related to conventionality, but it later reached stagnation – no change in response times occurred in the second period. Hence, development of accuracy and response times was observed in differing timescales: a longer time span was needed to detect a measurable gain for response times than for accuracy. Routine items, on the other hand, showed no change in response times, even though their accuracy scores improved significantly. This somewhat unexpected finding is explained by the multiple choice question format of the listening task. In this task, the target routine expression was embedded in a conversation, and after participants listened to this conversation they were required to choose the option that matched the target. This task required a process of evaluating individual response options and comparing them with what they heard in the conversation. It is possible that comprehension speed barely improved because of this bottom-up process induced from the task rather than a top-down process of associating routine expressions directly with their correct option.

In summary, variations in patterns and rate of development found in pragmatic comprehension are summarized in the following three main points: (1) distinct patterns of development were found between *knowledge* measured by accuracy scores and *processing* measured by response times; (2) conventionality of response patterns in indirect refusals (i.e. expected ways of refusing someone's requests or invitations) facilitated comprehension and its effect was observed in immediate and incremental increase in scores; and (3) nonconventional implicatures and routines that involve linguistic conventions were found to be slow in development, showing a trend of progress only at later time periods.

As shown in this summary, conventionality encoded in implicatures clearly mediated these developmental trajectories. While conventional pattern of refusals facilitated comprehension, ability to understand less conventional implicatures did not develop as quickly due to the extensive inferential bridge needed to understand meaning. Because there was no symbolic cue to guide comprehension, learners needed to go through word-by-word, bottom-up processing that involved analysis of syntactic and lexical information, as well as contextual cues. Due to the multiple levels of processing required, nonconventional implicatures showed a slower developmental pace than conventional implicatures.

The present findings conform to the generalization established in previous literature: L2 learners' comprehension follows a progression from the stage where meaning is conveyed through strong cues (i.e. signals of conventionality) to the stage where a message does not involve any obvious signals and thus require a series of inferential clues to arrive at meaning (see Chapter 2). What is new in this study is the finding that linguistic conventionality has a differential effect in contrast to the convention of discourse patterns used in indirect refusals. In this study convention of linguistic forms encoded in routines was not as strong or salient enough to boost the pace of development. In fact, the results were quite similar with those of nonconventional implicatures: there was no sign of development in the initial period, and this development occurred in the later period. Conventionality, then, exhibits a different order of accessibility. L2 learners can utilize the conventions of discourse patterns immediately to assist comprehension, probably by relying on L1 transfer, but convention of forms takes some time to utilize because they need to be newly learned.

These findings are in line with previous longitudinal studies that examined the comprehension of a range of implicatures among EFL and ESL learners (Bouton, 1992, 1994; Taguchi, 2007a, 2008b). Taguchi (2008b), for instance, found that, regardless of learning context (ESL or EFL), indirect refusals were easier and faster for learners to comprehend, and they showed a larger size of gain than indirect opinions which do not involve any conventional, predictable response patterns.

Now I will turn to a summary of the pragmatic production results. Similar to pragmatic comprehension, great variation in developmental tendencies were found among the four variables measured: appropriateness scores, grammaticality scores, planning time and speech rate. What was common across these variables was the relative ease of low-imposition situation speech acts: appropriateness and grammaticality scores were higher than those of high-imposition speech acts, and these speech acts were produced more promptly at a faster speech rate. Significant gains were found at all time junctions for low-imposition speech acts in the case of all four variables except for speech rate, but this was not true for high-imposition speech acts because in these speech acts, appropriateness developed slowly, with gains detected only at a later period, and not in the initial period. In terms of grammaticality scores, high-imposition speech acts exhibited a significant increase in the initial period but no development in the second period. The situational variable, however, did not affect the patterns of change in fluency. For both low- and high-imposition speech acts, planning time showed an incremental drop at every time point. Speech rate showed a large gain in the initial period but reached stagnation in later periods, and this pattern was the same for both situation types.

These variations found in the data indicate that the situational factor clearly constrained the patterns of development of the *knowledge* dimension of pragmatic competence. Adapting Brown and Levinson's (1983) politeness theory, this study used social and interpersonal factors to operationalize low- and high-imposition speech acts, based on the premise that power difference between interlocutors and the size of the imposition influence the degree of politeness that one needs to demonstrate in speech acts. More specifically, in a situation where a speech act involves a high-degree of imposition and is addressed to a person who has more power (e.g. asking a teacher for an extension on a paper), a greater degree of politeness is required to allow the interlocutor to save face. In contrast, when the speech act involves a low-degree of imposition and is produced for a person in an equal relationship (e.g. asking a friend for a pen), a lesser degree of politeness is required. Thus, the social factors of power and imposition are thought to make high-imposition speech acts more demanding to perform than low-imposition speech acts. Greater attention to politeness, as well as longer, more elaborate pragmalinguistic expressions and a variety of face-saving strategies that are required to convey politeness, probably led to the small amount of gains and slow development in appropriateness scores of high-imposition speech acts.

These findings lend support to previous findings that revealed the effect of situation type on pragmatic production. Taguchi's (2007c) cross-sectional study examined the effect of general proficiency and situation type on production of speech acts in L2 English. This study found an advantage of low-imposition speech acts on appropriateness scores and fluency. The present study confirmed these differential effects of speech act situations through a longitudinal design: situational variables affect the rate and patterns of development.

The linguistic demand involved in high-imposition speech acts becomes evident in the post hoc analyses of the pragmalinguistic forms used to produce these speech acts. Frequency analyses of expression types revealed various syntactic and lexical mitigations that appeared frequently in native speaker data but were almost completely absent in L2 learners' data (see Chapter 4). These forms include: embedded questions or bi-clausal structures (e.g. 'I wonder if' + clause and 'I think' + clause), hedging expressions (e.g. 'a bit/little' and 'sort/kind of') and amplifiers (e.g. 'really' and 'very'). Because there was some progress in the participants' use of semantic moves, it seems that more profound changes took place in strategies and tactics used to perform the speech acts than in use of the target-like pragmalinguistic forms. The present findings lend support to the previous findings that learners were slow in acquiring the target pragmalinguistic forms compared with their acquisition of sociopragmatic rules (e.g. Bardovi-Harlig & Hartford, 1993;

Schauer, 2004; Taguchi, 2006; Takahashi, 1996; Warga & Schölmberger, 2007). Learners tend to start out with a limited range of pragmalinguistic resources, often symbolized in the overgeneralization of one or two forms over a range of functions and slowly expand their pragmalinguistic repertoire by adopting a new form–function mapping into their systems (see Chapter 2 for literature review).

In summary, variations in patterns and rate of development found in pragmatic production are summarized in the following three main points: (1) distinct patterns of development were found between *knowledge* as measured by appropriateness and grammaticality scores, and *processing* as measured by planning time and speech rate; (2) the situational and linguistic demands involved in high-imposition speech acts slowed the progress in appropriateness scores, but situation type had no effect on planning time and speech rate; and (3) emergence of target-like norms was negligible in the area of pragmalinguistic forms, but a small trend of development was found in the area of semantic strategies used to put together these speech acts. These developmental trajectories were clearly mediated by the degree of imposition and potential for face-threat encoded in speech act situations. Due to their low-stake, informal nature, low-imposition speech acts were easier and faster to perform, and showed a steady, incremental development over time, but high-imposition speech acts did not develop as quickly, because of the greater degree of politeness required to counter the potential threat to face.

A major source of difficulty in high-imposition speech acts was the complex nature of linguistic expressions and a larger number of supporting moves required in production. The fact that the participants were not able to use target-like syntactic and lexical mitigations tells us that they were in the stage of 'unpacking' in Kasper and Rose's (2002) five-stage sequence of pragmatic development (see Chapter 2). Building on R. Ellis' (1992) model of developmental sequence for request-making expressions, Kasper and Rose proposed a developmental scale consisting of five phases: a 'pre-basic' stage characterized by a context-dependent use of linguistic forms, a 'formulaic' stage characterized by reliance on unanalyzed chunks, an 'unpacking' stage where formulae are incorporated into productive language use, an 'expansion' stage characterized by a growth of pragmalinguistic repertoire with increased use of complex syntax and mitigation, and a 'fine-tuning' stage where target form–function–context mappings are realized. The EFL learners showed some small changes in pragmalinguistic forms, for instance, a shift from imperatives using 'please' to conventional preparatory questions (e.g. 'Could you' + verb) when making a request, and a shift from using a mono-clausal to bi-clausal structure (e.g. 'I think' + verb) when expressing an opinion. These shifts are characteristic of the 'unpacking' phase. However, negligible use of more complex syntax or external modifications indicates that they still fell short of the 'fine-tuning' stage.

What was interesting in pragmatic production was that the low- vs. high-imposition contrast constrained the developmental patterns of the *knowledge* dimension (i.e. appropriateness scores), but it did not constrain the *processing* dimension of pragmatic performance. Planning time and speech rate showed similar patterns of change regardless of situation type. The findings suggest a close correspondence between pragmatic fluency and generally fluency: oral fluency gained through repeated practice and exposure to input could transfer to fluency in sociocultural tasks. These findings further confirm the differing developmental paths between knowledge and processing components of pragmatic competence.

As summarized above, in both pragmatic comprehension and production, development was found to be a nonlinear process with a differing rate of change found for different aspects of pragmatic construct. Comprehension and production of pragmatic functions present different patterns of change, and the variations are constrained by factors inherent to the target constructs – degree of conventionality involved in implicatures and degree of formality encoded in speech act situations. Variations in patterns and rates of development gleaned from this study confirm that pragmatic competence is a multifaceted construct. Comprehension of implicatures or production of speech acts alone does not represent the whole construct consistently. Differential characteristics involved in modality, task and attributes affect underlying pragmatic traits differently, resulting in variation in pace and timing of development. An important implication generated from the present findings is that analyses of the two attributes, knowledge and processing capacity, provide complementary information and jointly contribute to our understanding of pragmatic competence and its development.

Implication of the Study Findings for the Second Language Acquisition Process

Common questions in SLA research include: how do people develop competence in a second or additional language?; what internal and external factors affect their development?; and what variations are observed in the process and outcome of their development? This study precisely addressed these questions as they are found in the domain of interlanguage pragmatics.

The study sketched evolving pathways toward pragmatic abilities of a cohort of learners transitioning through institutional time, by analyzing group-level patterns of development measured at key turning points, as well as by providing in-depth, individual-level analyses of case studies of eight focal informants. These multilevel, multidimensional investigations were meant to generate meaningful interpretations of developmental trajectories shaped by individual and contextual factors. To this end, the present study is an orthodox SLA research that combines descriptions and explanations of developmental change in a longitudinal design.

The present study was also profoundly informed by the recent epistemology of SLA theories that underscores a dynamic, complex systems perspective in the investigation of language development. Dynamic Systems Theory (DST) (de Bot *et al.*, 2007; de Bot, 2008), chaos/complexity theory (Larsen-Freeman & Cameron, 2008), and emergentism (MacWhinney, 2006; N. Ellis & Larsen-Freeman, 2006) are major forerunners of this emerging theoretical paradigm that avers the centrality of context and individuals, and interactions between them as explanation for language growth. They view language development as a dynamic, nonlinear process in which cognitive, social and contextual factors interact and coregulate the course of development. Because individuals and contexts constantly change, L2 development is characterized as an irregular and unevenly paced process. As such, this process is susceptible to backslidings, jumps and stagnations, and involves a great deal of intra- and intervariability in the development and in its outcomes. There are no simple cause–effect relationships in the sense of one or two decontextualized variables causing change in another. Variables collectively explain change, not in isolation (see Chapter 2 for detailed examination of the theoretical paradigm).

The variation of developmental scaling across pragmatic attributes summarized in the previous section certainly conforms to the dynamicity, nonlinearity and variability of developmental process. Pragmatic development was found to be unevenly paced, with differing rates of change and differing time distributions of stability for different aspects of the construct. While these idiosyncratic patterns were largely explained by construct-inherent factors such as conventionality of implicatures and degree of imposition in speech acts, qualitative data revealed context-generated factors that could explain these nonlinear changes. For instance, a profound, steady progress found in the appropriateness of low-imposition speech acts was explained by the frequent occurrence of those speech acts on campus. Making a small request to a friend or giving a personal assessment on a small matter often appeared in the students' journal entries. Low-imposition requests were always present in teachers' classroom directions in a wide range of structures. Teachers also frequently gave written feedback to students' essays, which often took the form of low-imposition opinions. Hence, it seems that opportunistic resources available in the learning context, along with linguistic simplicity of the low-imposition speech acts, boosted students' acquisition of these speech acts. They picked them up naturally along their way, without explicit teaching or modeling (see Chapter 4 for descriptions).

Appropriateness of high-imposition speech acts, on the other hand, was found to be late-emerging. The target pragmalinguistics forms (e.g. bi-clausal structure, hedging) were almost absent in the EFL learners' data, even after eight-months of exposure in the immersion context. However, qualitative data indicated that they had plenty of exposure to the target pragmalinguistic forms through class materials. Bi-clausal structures were present in textbooks and were taught explicitly in class. Hedging devices such as 'maybe' or 'I'm not sure' often appeared in learners' journals and in their speech. Mild disagreements and suggestions appeared frequently in teachers' feedback to students' essays. Moreover, introspective verbal interviews revealed the learners' implicit knowledge of the target pragmalinguistic forms: when I asked the focal informants to name all the request-making forms that they were aware of, half of them included bi-clausal forms in the list. In addition, more than 95% of the learners achieved perfect score on the pre-test that assessed their receptive knowledge of target pragmalinguistic structures. Hence, the absence of the target forms in the present data was not solely due to absence of these forms in the learners' systems. Rather, they were not able to retrieve them from their systems for use because of their limited processing capacity while coping with the demand of online production. Several learners mentioned that, because of complexity of these structures, too much focus on form would interfere with communication. They were focused on clearly communicating intention by sticking to forms they were confident in using, even though they had to sacrifice politeness as a result (see Chapter 4 summary and interpretation section for details).

These learners' attitudes, in part, seemed to have stemmed from their lack of sociopragmatic knowledge and sensitivity toward linguistic politeness. They were not aware of the potential negative consequences of inappropriate language use in interpersonal relationships. These attitudes were attributed to limited practice with high-imposition speech acts on campus, but an even more prevailing explanation is their teachers' attitudes toward learners' pragmatic misdemeanors. Real-life confrontational occurrences between teachers and students described in Chapter 4 clearly illustrate the teachers' main interest in getting direct, explicit comments from students over correcting their language or the manner used to express their comments. Giving corrective feedback on language or having students use elaborate, polite expressions to convey intentions was considered discouraging to the flow of open dialog, and this was a major reason that teachers did not react to their students' pragmalinguistic and sociopragmatic inappropriateness in real-life interaction.

These findings are in line with the dynamic, complexity systems view of SLA. Unbalanced development in appropriateness scores between low- and high-imposition speech acts was a product of the intricate interaction among the subsystems – the elements, agents and processes – in this specific learning context. There were a range of agents and elements in the university environment: teachers, students, their resources and backgrounds, the English-medium curriculum and classroom arrangements, instructional materials and learning goals. These subcomponents were not independent from one another, and interactions between elements were not fixed but also changed over time themselves. The teachers, students, curriculum and the bilingual environment coadapted to each other, giving rise to the skewed pattern of development toward the sociolinguistic norms of interaction.

As described in Chapter 4, the teachers adapted to the students' passivity and inexpressiveness by welcoming their forwardness in sharing their concerns about the class and their requests for changes, despite the students' direct, impolite language use that resulted from their forwardness. The teachers' historicity – their prior experience with the multicultural student population in the United States and their adjustment process in teaching homogeneous Japanese group – was another element that probably influenced their attitudes. The students, on the other hand, adapted to the system of the Western style classroom where independent, self-directed learning was valued. The students' increasing ownership of their learning experience led to their self-initiated evaluation of classroom activities in terms of its benefit for them. Their initiative in broaching the problems directly to their teachers was a sign of their adaptation to the Western university system and was an integral part of their academic socialization. When expressing problems to their teachers, students adapted these expressions to their limited processing capacity and English skill. Because fluent use of elaborate forms was beyond their proficiency level, they prioritized simple, straightforward communication over a polite, face-saving communication style. Lack of negative consequences to inappropriate language use, in the form of teachers' corrections, off-putting reactions or disagreement, seemed to have further reinforced the students' incorrect assessment of form–function–context mappings: highly mitigated linguistic forms are not necessary, and simple, direct forms are sufficient. Hence, the students' manner of communication and the teachers' tolerance of this style were in a reciprocal relationship, adapting to each other's needs and resources in the context. These descriptions present a picture of reciprocal causality (Thompson & Varela, 2001): an emergence of specific behavioral patterns from the interaction of agents was constrained by the historic trajectory of the agents in the system and by their current state in the changing environment.

These analyses reiterate the importance of integration of context and agents as explanations for language change. As Larsen-Freeman and Cameron (2008) state, context is not a stable background variable outside of individuals that affects their linguistic choices. Instead, the individual and context are coupled, and every change to the individual in a system is influenced by context. Larsen-Freeman and Cameron observe:

> The context-dependence of complex applied linguistic systems is threefold: language is developed in context, as use in context shapes language resources; language is applied in context, as context selects the language action to be performed; language is adapted for context, as the experience of past language use is fitted to the here and now. (Larsen-Freeman & Cameron, 2008: 69)

The present study aligns with this theoretical position, which delegates central power to context in the process of second language acquisition. As such, this study has abandoned traditional cause–effect, linear predictions and treats pragmatic development as nested systems that are interconnected at multiple levels, responsive to context and always adapting to context as well as changing it. A quantitative approach combined with qualitative, ecologically rich forms of inquiry captured the patterns and amounts of change over time and possible explanations for these changes. Explanations stemmed from two separate but complementary resources: internal, or within the learner (e.g. language abilities, processing capacity, personal perspective and attitudes, sociolinguistic awareness and sensitivity), and external, or outside the learner (e.g. environment, input, interacting agents, time, materials, reinforcement). Interaction and complex adaptations of these resources formed a basis to explain stabilities and increases of pragmatic abilities that were observed in this study.

Second language acquisition as a complex, dynamic, nonlinear, and adaptive process becomes even more apparent in the analyses of case studies presented in Chapter 5. The eight case histories analyzed here exemplify individual learners' contributions to the ongoing developmental process. Learner characteristics such as motivation, affect, learning styles, learning strategies and personality were found to interact with each other and with the environment, and jointly accounted for the unique trajectories of pragmatic change. The case studies revealed a process-oriented, situated nature of learner characteristics mediated through context and time, which corroborates with Dörnyei's view:

> They (individual learner characteristics) are not stable but show salient temporal and situational variation, and they are not monolithic but are complex constellations made up of different parts that interact with each other and the environment synchronically and diachronically. Simple cause-effect relationships are unable to do justice to these multi-level interactions and temporal changes. (Dörnyei, 2009: 194)

The view of learner characteristics as dynamically changing and evolving through time and context precisely situate the analysis of individual characteristics within the paradigm of the dynamic, complexity systems theory perspective. The case histories in this study illustrate an intricate constellation of individual factors that interact with each other and with their environment at multiple levels, which, in turn, generates variation in the routes and rates of pragmatic change.

Graphs of individual trajectories and group means displayed in Chapter 5 show that an assumption of progressive conformity to majority norms does not hold. We saw that different participants were following different routes toward full mastery of pragmatic abilities, although they had similar prior experiences and living arrangements. Take the trajectories of Yuko, Shoko and Tomoyo as examples. They were placed in the same EAP level and had the same amount of instructional hours, course requirements and textbooks, and lived in the same dormitory throughout the year. Their academic experiences prior to college were also similar. They went to a regular public high school but belonged to the English-track and received intensive, skill-focused English instruction taught by native speaker and Japanese instructors. Their high schools regularly hosted international students, which provided them opportunities to share activities and school events with English-speaking peers. All of these participants had traveled overseas for about a week.

Despite these similarities, they followed remarkably different trajectories of pragmatic development. Tomoyo and Yuko clearly excelled in pragmatic comprehension and fluency aspect of pragmatic production. Their comprehension accuracy and response speed were far beyond the group average throughout the study, while those of Shoko were only average. Tomoyo's and Yuko's planning speed and speech rate were also above average and showed strong progress over time, but those of Shoko barely improved or even decreased. The picture is quite different when it comes to the analysis of appropriateness scores. All of them showed a very similar developmental pattern for low-imposition speech acts, but the pattern of high-imposition speech acts were strikingly different. Both Shoko and Tomoyo started out with similar appropriateness scores, but it was Shoko who continued to develop at Time 3, almost to the perfect level. Tomoyo, on the other hand, experienced a huge drop in score in the second semester. Yuko's score remained below average throughout the study with only a marginal increase at Time 3. The data tell us that group averages conceals a great deal of intra- and intervariability. There is immense variation within and among individuals both in terms of when and how they move through key milestones of pragmatic development. Individuals react differently to different environmental conditions, making simple generalizations impossible.

Potential reasons behind these individual variations were closely related to the nature of individuals' target language contact and experiences, as described in Chapter 5. In the unique immersion context where classes are taught in English and international students are on campus, EFL learners had presumably equal access to target language input, but in practice they differed in the type and intensity of contact, leading to differing paths toward pragmatic mastery. In the case of Yuko, her outgoing personality and social skills, combined with her competent spoken English ability and her fluency, helped to expand her network with international students. She reported having 20 English-speaking friends with whom she interacted on daily basis. She participated in a range of extracurricular activities and volunteer work in order to connect with international students and to further expand her network. She was also active in class participation. While these opportunities for sustained communication with English speakers seems to have contributed to her strong gain in pragmatic comprehension and fluency in pragmatic production, the informal register involved in such interactions did not help her to progress in the appropriateness score of high-imposition speech acts. Linguistic forms required for such speech acts (e.g. lexical and syntactic mitigations) never appeared in her production, and her pragmalinguistic repertoire did not expand beyond high-school level.

Yuko's case indicates that input exposure alone is not sufficient to acquire new pragmalinguistic forms. Explicit teaching and feedback are necessary for new form–function–context mappings to get internalized for use, as suggested in Shoko's case. Shoko's strong development in the appropriateness of high-imposition speech acts was a product of her teacher's direct correction and modeling. Through her teacher's corrections of her language use in an email she sent to request an appointment, the target pragmalinguistic form (i.e. bi-clausal form 'I wonder if' + clause in request-making) was internalized in Shoko's system (see Chapter 5). This email exchange functioned as a triggering event for noticing of the new form–function–context mapping. Shoko's personality, attitudes and motivational orientations were found to be equally important in building toward this crucial moment of noticing and for taking advantage of it to expand her pragmalinguistic repertoire. Shoko's curiosity toward sociocultural aspects of language, and her tendency to observe people's ways of communicating politely, seemed to have facilitated her noticing. The fact that she revised her email message following the teacher's correction, and sent it back to him with an apology, further illustrates her interest and motivation toward mastering sociocultural rules of speaking.

These various descriptions reflect dynamic relationships among individual traits, experience, and context as mutually reinforcing factors in shaping the course of language development. Shoko's case presents evidence to support the current view that cognition, emotion, and motivation are conceptually distinct but interrelated mental systems (Dai & Sternberg, 2004; Dörnyei, 2009; Lewis, 2005). Various cognitive functions interact with motivational and emotional processes, forming complex relationships within a system. As Dörnyei (2009) claims, our thinking is guided by emotion toward perceptions, interpretations and memories that are relevant to the specific emotion, and emotional response leads to motivated actions.

Shoko's case also reiterates the role of attention, noticing and explicit teaching in pragmatic learning. Noticing and attention have been a topic of SLA research for over two decades. As Schmidt (1990, 1993) originally claimed, noticing is the prerequisite for input to become intake and lead to acquisition. Attention to linguistic forms, functional meanings and relevant contextual features are necessary conditions for pragmatic input to become intake. These conditions were present in Shoko's situation. Her teacher's explicit feedback and modeling helped her to notice crucial pragmalinguisitc and sociopragmatic connections – the connection between form, function and social factors that constraint form. The present findings correspond to previous literature that have documented the facilitative effect that native speaker modeling, corrective feedback and observation have on naturalistic pragmatic development (e.g. Belz & Kinginger, 2003; DuFon, 2000; Hassall, 2006).

What was quite different from the acquisition of target pragmalinguistic forms was Shoko's slow progress in the processing aspect of pragmatic competence. Her underdevelopment in fluency was considered to have resulted from her limited network in the English-speaking community and insufficient amount of communication practice. Hence, it seems that development of pragmatic fluency, like other levels of fluency, requires accumulated practice and time-on-task, which Shoko did not have in her context.

In sharp contrast, Tomoyo had an extensive network with English speakers, which provided her abundant opportunities for practice and boosted her oral fluency. Like Yuko, the resources Tomoyo brought to the university setting – functional English skills, outgoing personality and an expressive communication style – helped her to connect not only with international students but also with teachers. Tomoyo was the one whom the teachers turned to for advice when they had problems with their class. The degree of trust that Tomoyo gained from teachers elevated her to a unique level of teacher–student relationship and strengthened her bond with her teachers. The intense language practice that she accumulated over time with teachers and international students boosted her gain in pragmatic comprehension and fluency of pragmatic production. However, ironically, it counteracted with her development of appropriateness of formal, high-imposition speech acts. Target pragmalinguistic forms (e.g. bi-clausal form 'I wonder if' + clause, when asking a favor of a teacher) were initially present in her system as she produced them at Time 1 and Time 2, but they disappeared over time, resulting in a large score drop at Time 3. This happened because, after being exposed to informal register among peers, she became less conscious about formal language. With increasing personal contact and the bonds she established with her teachers, her perception of formality changed, and her language with teachers became informal and casual (see Chapter 5 for descriptions). These findings are consistent with the findings from Matsumura's (2007) study, which illustrated the attrition of pragmatic competence after returning from a sojourn abroad. Learners' choices of appropriate pragmalinguistic expressions gradually diverged from target-like choices because their perception of sociocultural norms changed upon returning to home country.

This episode of pragmatic backsliding presents an interesting portrayal of a learner's history of participation in a community and socialization in relation to pragmatic change. Tomoyo's case corroborates with the view of language development in the dynamic, complexity theory perspective that learners assemble their language resources interacting with a changing environment (Larsen-Freeman & Cameron, 2008). Language development is a nonlinear and interactive process, and is ratified by real-life experiences. Tomoyo's onset performance, that is, the use of bi-clausal form in requesting, instilled from memorization and drill practice in high school, shifted over time because of the new practice and experiences she accumulated in the university environment. Tomoyo's pragmalinguistic choice was being constantly transformed by the uses embedded in the complex system.

From a complexity theory perspective, it is essential to understand how variation works at the individual level – why individuals do and do not conform to expected patterns. Intraindividual variability is an essential source of information about the underlying developmental process. Shoko's abrupt development and Tomoyo's pragmatic backsliding revealed such insights about the developmental process from the individuals-in-context perspective. The rest of the six case histories also equally contribute to our understanding of the developmental process. Ryota and Asako, for instance, demonstrated interesting differences in their stance and orientations toward opportunities for practice, resulting in variation in pragmatic development. These two students were similar in their background, prior experience and level of English. Unlike Tomoyo, Yuko and Shoko, they received traditional, grammar-focused English instruction in high school where communication skills were de-emphasized, and had almost no contact with native speaker instructors in high school. They were introverted, quiet, seldom spoke up in class and had limited social networks with international students. Both formed an inferiority complex about their poor oral skills as a result of comparing themselves with fluent peers. While Ryota's social network and practice remained limited throughout the period, and his motivation decreased because of this, Asako successfully established her membership in an English-speaking community and gained routine access to target input. She became acquainted with a group of three international students who regularly came to the library to study and soon after, it became her evening routine to sit at the same desk with them and do homework while eavesdropping their conversation for a few hours. The result of this continual, sustained listening practice was a dramatic gain in the pragmatic listening task at the end of the first semester. Ryota, on the other hand, made almost no gain in pragmatic listening, and his score remained far below average throughout the period of the study.

The event that triggered this routine for Asako was the speaking journal assignment which required her to talk to someone in English and record the experience. Because she did not have many English-speaking friends, she needed to take advantage of the relationship she established with the three international students in order to complete this weekly assignment. She made an effort to sustain this relationship by participating in their activities every day, although her participation was peripheral: mainly as a listener and observer rather than a speaker. Had Ryota had the same assignment, it could have served as a similar drive to explore a social network to practice English. Hence, Asako's access to the opportunities for practice was both circumstantial and strategic. It was circumstantial and context driven because she was under the pressure of completing the assignment and met, by chance, the three international students who were willing to serve as her conversants. At the same time, it was strategic and learner driven in that, while not completely an insider, she created her own space in their community and maintained it by filling it on a routine basis.

Asako's case history, once again, lends support to the dynamic, complexity systems perspective of language development. The agents and elements, and various internal and external resources within them, interacted and coadapted to each other, and shaped her developmental trajectory in pragmatic comprehension. Context contains a set of opportunities and resources, and it interacts with individuals who act on these opportunities and resources. Individuals' self-determination in learning, circumstances that pushes them to move toward the goal, and a context that affords optimal resources to support this goal-oriented behavior may promote learning. These interpretations correspond with Dörnyei's (2005, 2009) 'L2 motivational self system' that illustrates the interaction between individual learner characteristics and context. According to Dörnyei, motivated learning is organized according to three components: ideal L2 self, ought-to L2 self and L2 learning experience. The ideal L2 self refers to what one wishes to become as an L2 speaker. It is a motivating force because of the desire to close the gap between the actual and ideal selves. The ought-to L2 self describes the attributes that one believes one ought to possess to meet expectations and avoid possible negative outcomes. L2 learning experience refers to situated motives related to the immediate learning environment and experience (e.g. influence of the teacher and curriculum, experience of success, peer group). These three components function as 'attractor basins' that guide learners through the learning process, and influence the direction and persistence of their behavior (Dörnyei, 2009: 218). Asako had all these three levels in harmony. The gap between her and her fluent peers, and the inferiority complex that she initially experienced, led to the conceptualization of the ideal L2 self and the ought-to self. Motivation stemmed from these two types of self-images was reinforced through motivation from the third level – successful engagement with the actual language learning process, which consequently led to her accomplishment in pragmatic comprehension. In Ryota's case, the two self-images might have existed, but he did not have access to the environment – actual experiences – to endorse them. Asako's limited progress in pragmatic production, on the other hand, could stem from a lack of alignment of these three components: she did not have the actual engagement in speaking in formal or informal register.

These three systems of motivation also apply to Mitsu's case. Similar to Asako and Ryota, he came to the university with limited resources.

He received grammar-oriented instruction in high school with little practice with communication skills, and did not have much contact with native speaker instructors in high school. Despite this background, similar to Asako, Mitsu was strategic in creating opportunities for himself and resources for practice. He was an autonomous, independent learner who cultivated a variety of learning strategies and self-study materials to improve in his English. These strategies include: keeping records of new vocabulary in notebooks, watching CNN programs, listening to English conversation programs on radio and reading newspapers in English. Through interviews, I discovered that pragmatic learning was part of his self-directed learning process. He was constantly attentive to sociocultural aspects of language and employed learning strategies to absorb pragmatic information about everyday language use. He directed his attention to the social functions of language and made mental notes as he encountered them. For example, he developed a habit of looking for usage notes whenever he used his dictionary for vocabulary check. He kept notes of formal vs. informal use and functions of expressions so that he could use them when a situation requires them. He also paid attention to hedging and mitigating expressions in movies and radio conversations and kept track of them in a notebook for future use.

Qualitative data revealed that Mitsu's orientation toward pragmatic learning and a set of self-efficacy strategies he developed over time came from his higher-level motivation to push his overall English ability forward. At one point, he explicitly said that he wanted to be like a native speaker by expanding his linguistic repertoire and using new forms. The ideal self, in Mitsu's case, was to go beyond the 'current self' and to sound like a native speaker. It worked synchronously with the ought-to self and L2 learning experience, as he proactively tried to implement his pragmatic knowledge whenever opportunities arose in context. The result of these motivations and motivated actions led to his strong, steady increase in the appropriateness scores of speech acts in both low- and high-imposition situations.

The subjectivity, stance and investment that Mitsu and Asako exercised over time and their corresponding pragmatic gains are in sharp contrast with Keita and Ippei's cases. These two students were clearly under-developed in all aspects of pragmatic competence. Keita's accuracy scores and response times on pragmatic comprehension remained below average throughout the study period. His planning speed and speech rate also remained below group mean. Although his appropriateness score of low-imposition speech acts made some progress over time, that of high-imposition speech acts was below average at all time points. Ippei's patterns were similar. The only area in which he outperformed Keita was planning speed, where he showed above average performance.

The pragmatic underdevelopment found in Keita and Ippei's cases is explained in part by their lack of social experience and networking in English. Neither of them was able to establish a social network within an

English-speaking community. As a result, their listening and speaking practice outside of the class were limited to movie watching, TOEFL listening exercises and occasional brief exchanges with international students in passing. What was common for these two students was their strong instrumental motivation, which in turn constrained their access to target language practice. Ippei was most interested in improving his TOEFL score so that he could advance in the EAP program. The topic of TOEFL came up eight times in his first interview, symbolizing his strong commitment and priority in TOEFL. Keita, on the other hand, was keen on increasing knowledge of grammar and vocabulary. He often stayed after class and approached teachers to ask questions about English or to talk about current issues. He explicitly said that he did not approach international students because there was no merit: there was no tangible language-related information that he could gain from daily, casual conversation with them. This utility-based motivation toward learning English, shaped by each learner's subjectivity and stance, helped them gain in general English proficiency as shown in their large increase in TOEFL scores over time. However, it did not lead to social networking or exposure to English that could provide authentic listening and speaking practice. This resulted in underdevelopment for both of them in most aspects of pragmatic comprehension and production.

Regarding their below-average appropriateness score of high-imposition speech acts, qualitative data revealed additional insights. Keita and Ippei were the only students who had real-life experiences with high-imposition speech acts outside of the study. For example, Keita sometimes complained to teachers directly about the format of a quiz or course materials. Ippei's situations were more confrontational. In one occasion, he went up to a teacher after class and complained about the format of the quiz that he failed several times. He wrote about it in his journal, expressing how unfair the quiz was. In another occasion, he went to a teacher's office to complain about the amount of homework and class style. In those real-life instances, the language they used was clearly direct and impolite and lacking pragmatic considerations. For instance, Keita used the modal 'should' as in 'you should' + verb, which the teacher took as a command rather than a request. Ippei, on the other hand, used an explicit expression of dislike, 'I don't like the listening test', and direct questioning, 'Why do you do listening?' He also used the strong modal of obligation 'should' and 'must' in making a request to the teacher. These descriptions highlight their inappropriate sociopragmatic assessments of contextual features and formality, as well as their lack of knowledge of proper pragmalinguistic forms for performing high-imposition speech acts. Chapter 5 describes in detail potential factors for their pragmatic inappropriateness: limited sensitivity to politeness in English, inaccurate sociopragmatic understanding of formality and register variation, incomplete range of pragmalinguistic expressions, priority on content (what to say) rather than on form (how to say it) and lack of explicit feedback from teachers regarding their manner of speech. These multiple factors stemming from internal and external sources were found intertwined with each other, leading to low appropriateness scores of high-imposition speech acts.

In summary, this study achieved a situated account of the evolving trajectories of pragmatic development at both group and individual levels, provided by the general patterns and rate of pragmatic development gleaned from group-level analysis, combined with in-depth, individual-level analyses of learners' characteristics, subjectivity and investment that shaped the type of their target language experience in the unique immersion environment. This study found that pragmatic competence contains multiple subcompetencies that exhibit different developmental rates and stabilities within the timescale of one academic year, suggesting intimate relationships among pragmatic construct, time and change. Qualitative analyses revealed several elements crucial to attainment of balanced development among subconstructs and attributes. One such element is solid listening and speaking abilities on which pragmatic knowledge can be mobilized. Because pragmatic comprehension and production are built on general listening and speaking skills, mastery of these basic-level skills are prerequisite to accurate, efficient demonstration of pragmatic knowledge. To this end, frequent, sustained communication practice with English speakers is a desirable condition for pragmatic development. This generalization was drawn from the cases of Tomoyo and Yuko, high-achievers of pragmatic measures, as well as from the cases of Keita, Ippei and Ryota, low-achievers in this study. Asako's case adds to the profile in showing that exposure to sustained, prolonged discourse, rather than chunks of short speech, is likely to boost pragmatic listening.

Another important element for pragmatic growth is individuals' orientations toward sociocultural, pragmatic implications of everyday language use. Going back to the original concept of communicative competence, ability to use language entails knowledge about forms and their functional possibilities and knowledge about contextual requirements that determine form–function mappings. Learners need to be aware that learning a language extends beyond the mastery of grammatical forms and in fact entails acquisition of social usage of various forms. Learners further need to be oriented to the idea that the target language, just like their native language, is used not only to inform or express thoughts, but also to connect people in action, to establish common sentiments and to nurture personal relationships. These social parameters of language use need to be brought to learners' attention in order to inform their pragmatic choice.

This type of pragmatic awareness was present in Shoko's and Mitsu's development, apparent by their alertness to sociocultural aspects of language use. In Shoko's case, her pragmatic sensitivity was a condition, and her teacher's incidental correction on her pragmatic misuse was a trigger for her pragmatic development. In Mitsu's case, his alertness worked in tandem with self-directing learning strategies. He skilfully turned everyday materials into pragmatic materials by looking for pragmatic information behind ordinary usage of forms and by comparing various forms in terms of their assumed force and their impact on the interlocutor. These two cases together inform us about the fundamental role of orientation, attention, noticing and explicit information in pragmatic development. While Shoko's case suggests that learning pragmatic rules can occur via single-moment external force (i.e. explicit negative feedback), Mitsu's case illustrates that learning can take place independently over time through an accumulative, incremental process.

Taken together, these case studies collectively reinforce the dynamic, complex view toward second language development. Language learning is a socially constructed process and language use is socially situated and negotiated, and emerges through a coadaptation of a complex social interplay among agents, elements, and environment that change with time. Individual variation in language achievement is not necessarily attributable only to the events or conditions characterizing learners' experiences. It is in fact tightly connected to the aspirations that learners bring in to their learning experiences, and to learners' resources, both internal and external, that act on these aspirations to orient them toward learning. Developmental trajectory is thus a mirror image of individuals' characteristics, resources and environment, and a constant interaction, adaptation and change among these elements.

Limitations of the Study and Directions for Future Research

In this section I will present limitations of the present study and discuss directions for future research. This study controlled potential extraneous variables related to participants (e.g. age, gender, overseas living experience) in order to gain a clearer picture of the relationship among the target variables of interest. However, because the participants were limited to adult Japanese EFL learners, findings cannot be generalized to other age groups, other L1 and L2 groups, or learners in an ESL context. Because pragmatics is concerned with language use in social contexts, pragmatic performance is sensitive to the sociocultural backgrounds and experiences of those who interact in a given setting. Learners of different age groups, cultures and language backgrounds might follow different pragmatic conventions and sociolinguistic rules, consequently exhibiting different patterns of pragmatic development. Likewise, differing patterns could arise from differing learning environments. This study examined pragmatic development in an immersion institution located in a foreign language context. Because learners in a second language context are potentially more frequently exposed to everyday authentic practice for comprehending implicit meaning or producing pragmatic functions, when overall L2 proficiency is controlled, second language learners might progress faster in some aspects of pragmatic competence than foreign language learners. Without data from second language learners, however, this study was not able to make such a comparison.

Another limitation of this study is the small number of measures used to project pragmatic development. As found in this study, pragmatic development is a nonlinear, unevenly paced process with differing rates of change for different aspects of construct. Comprehension and production of pragmatic functions present very different patterns of pragmatic progress, and so do knowledge and processing dimensions of the construct. Hence, future treatment of pragmatic competence should involve multiple levels by incorporating additional subconstructs and attributes in a developmental study within single learner group. For instance, corresponding with the burgeoning interest in pragmatic competence in situated interactions, analytical frameworks could extend the conventional features of pragmalinguistic elements, by analyzing features of interactional competence, such as the ability to manage sequential organization and turn-taking, use of communication strategies, promptness of uptake and knowledge of rhetorical scripts. These features can be traced over time through recurring speech events within a single participant group so that their ability to participate successfully in interactions could serve as an indicator of pragmatic development.

Another implication for future longitudinal investigation relates to the optimal length of study period and frequency of data collection. This study revealed meaningful gain size across different pragmatic functions and attributes, indicating that the timescale of two semesters with the total of three data collections were appropriate for illuminating development to some extent. However, comprehension of nonconventional implicatures and production of high-imposition speech acts showed signs of gains only in the second half of the study period, indicating that a longer time span could further benefit investigation of these subconstructs. In particular, target pragmalinguistic forms almost never appeared in high-imposition speech acts even at the end of the study period, which suggests that closer examination of this specific aspect of construct is valuable. The present findings inform future theorizing about the metric of time in designing a longitudinal study. The average time span for pragmatic gain established in this study, together with the general proficiency development inferred from the participants' TOEFL scores, will help us make sensible predictions about the optimal size of gain across timescales and constructs. When situated in an educational setting, such an investigation will enable us to recognize and provide insights about the effect of institutional practices on the development of pragmatic, sociocultural aspects of language use.

Finally, the major implication of the present study relates to the ongoing need to acknowledge the complexity and individual variation involved in inquiry into pragmatic development. The intricate relationship among pragmatic gain, individual differences and context gleaned in this study confirms that pragmatic development is mediated by context as well as learners' subjective participation within the context. The idiosyncratic patterns of change found in these eight case histories and the qualitative data regarding individuals' experiences underscore the importance of an ecological approach to language data and analysis. At the same time, these observations reiterate the usefulness of the dynamic, complexity systems perspective as a lens through which pragmatic development is best examined. These insights provide strong support for continuing effort in the future to reveal learners' pragmatic change combined with in-depth analyses of sociocultural contexts and learner agency which affect this change. Such investigation will help reveal the nature of intra- and intervariability within the process and achievement of development, as well as the interconnectedness among variables that jointly shape the trajectories of the second language acquisition process.

Appendix A: Language Contact Profile (LCP)

Notes. This survey is adapted from Freed *et al.* (2004). The survey was administered in Japanese.

- Please respond to the following questions. Your responses will be kept confidential and will be used only for the purpose the current research.

1. Gender ( ) Male ( ) Female
2. Age ( ) years old
3. Grade level: freshman sophomore junior senior
4. How many years did you study English before you came to this school? _____ years
5. Have you lived in an English-speaking country more than two months? If so, please indicate the length and purpose of your stay.
   Yes, I have lived in an English-speaking country _____ months for_____.
6. Which situation best describes your living arrangements this semester?
   a. ____I live in a dormitory.
      1) ___ I have a private room.
      2) I have a roommate who is a native or fluent English speaker.
      3) I live with others who are NOT native or fluent English speakers.
   b. ____I live alone in a room or an apartment.
   c. ____Other. Please specify. _____

7.   Please reflect on your activities <u>in the past few weeks,</u> and respond to the questions below by circling the numbers.

1. How much time did you spend communicating in English with your instructors outside of class?	Typically, how many days per week? 0 1 2 3 4 5 6 7 On those days, typically how many hours per day? 0 0-1 1-2 2-3 4-5 more than 5
2. How much time did you spend communicating in English with your classmates, friends and roommate outside of class?	Typically, how many days per week? 0 1 2 3 4 5 6 7 On those days, typically how many hours per day? 0 0-1 1-2 2-3 4-5 more than 5
3. How much time did you spend in communicating with service personnels in English?	Typically, how many days per week? 0 1 2 3 4 5 6 7 On those days, typically how many hours per day? 0 0-1 1-2 2-3 4-5 more than 5
4. How much time did you use English outside the classroom for class-related things?	Typically, how many days per week? 0 1 2 3 4 5 6 7 On those days, typically how many hours per day? 0 0-1 1-2 2-3 4-5 more than 5
5. How much time did you use English outside the classroom for non-class-related things?	Typically, how many days per week? 0 1 2 3 4 5 6 7 On those days, typically how many hours per day? 0 0-1 1-2 2-3 4-5 more than 5
6. How much time did you spend reading English newspapers, magazines or books outside of class?	Typically, how many days per week? 0 1 2 3 4 5 6 7 On those days, typically how many hours per day? 0 0-1 1-2 2-3 4-5 more than 5
7. How much time did you spend doing emails or Internet in English outside of class?	Typically, how many days per week? 0 1 2 3 4 5 6 7 On those days, typically how many hours per day? 0 0-1 1-2 2-3 4-5 more than 5
8. How much time did you spend watching movies, TV or videos in English outside of class?	Typically, how many days per week? 0 1 2 3 4 5 6 7 On those days, typically how many hours per day? 0 0-1 1-2 2-3 4-5 more than 5

9. How much time did you spend writing essays or homework assignments in English outside of class?	Typically, how many days per week? 0 1 2 3 4 5 6 7 On those days, typically how many hours per day? 0 0-1 1-2 2-3 4-5 more than 5
10. How much time did you use Japanese outside of class?	Typically, how many days per week? 0 1 2 3 4 5 6 7 On those days, typically how many hours per day? 0 0-1 1-2 2-3 4-5 more than 5

- By looking back your past few weeks, please answer the questions below.

1. When, where, to whom and for what purposes do you mostly use English?
2. Please describe the most salient communication experience in English that occurred recently. (E.g. 'I had a trouble keeping up with the class, so I went to talk to the teacher. She gave me extra listening exercises, which helped me understand the class better.' 'I noticed that people call each other by their first name.')

Appendix B: Descriptive Statistics of LCP Results

Notes. The LCP was administered six times over the period of the study. The numbers indicate the average amount of hours spent for each activity per week in English.

Time 1 (April)

Amount of time spent in English for:	Mean	SD	Min.	Max.
Communicating with teachers	0.58	1.15	0	7.50
Communicating with friends	2.72	3.79	0	15.00
Communicating with service personnels	0.01	0.07	0	0.50
Doing class-related things	7.00	8.07	0	35.00
Doing nonclass-related things	2.35	3.52	0	17.50
Reading newspapers, magazines and books	3.49	3.41	0	12.50
Watching TV or DVDs	2.98	4.46	0	21.00
Browsing Internet or using emails	1.05	1.88	0	7.50
Writing essays	6.83	5.71	0.50	22.50

Time 2 (June)

Amount of time spent in English for:	Mean	SD	Min.	Max.
Communicating with teachers	0.60	0.78	0	3.50
Communicating with friends	4.98	7.44	0	35.00
Communicating with service personnels	0.02	0.14	0	1.00
Doing class-related things	14.59	13.39	0	35.00
Doing nonclass-related things	4.47	7.26	0	31.50
Reading newspapers, magazines and books	5.82	7.55	0	31.50
Watching TV or DVDs	3.02	3.91	0	20.00
Browsing Internet or using emails	1.07	2.73	0	17.50
Writing essays	12.09	11.04	0	35.00

Time 3 (July)

Amount of time spent in English for:	Mean	SD	Min.	Max.
Communicating with teachers	0.69	0.76	0	3.00
Communicating with friends	2.67	4.18	0	17.50
Communicating with service personnels	0.42	1.73	0	10.50
Doing class-related things	10.88	11.05	0	35.00
Doing nonclass-related things	2.95	5.23	0	31.50
Reading newspapers, magazines and books	3.36	3.57	0	12.50
Watching TV or DVDs	3.92	6.42	0	35.00
Browsing Internet or using emails	0.64	1.59	0	10.00
Writing essays	9.99	9.28	1.00	35.00

Time 4 (September)

Amount of time spent in English for:	Mean	SD	Min.	Max.
Communicating with teachers	0.80	1.07	0	6.00
Communicating with friends	2.50	3.98	0	17.50
Communicating with service personnels	0.18	0.44	0	2.00
Doing class-related things	12.85	9.72	0	35.00
Doing nonclass-related things	3.02	5.08	0	31.50
Reading newspapers, magazines and books	2.44	2.85	0	15.00
Watching TV or DVDs	2.45	2.21	0	7.50
Browsing Internet or using emails	1.11	2.02	0	12.50
Writing essays	9.14	7.87	0	35.00

Time 5 (November)

Amount of time spent in English for:	Mean	SD	Min.	Max.
Communicating with teachers	1.47	3.47	0	22.50
Communicating with friends	2.04	3.42	0	17.50
Communicating with service personnels	0.12	0.38	0	1.50
Doing class-related things	11.43	9.16	0	31.50
Doing nonclass-related things	3.09	4.13	0	17.50
Reading newspapers, magazines and books	2.76	3.26	0	17.50
Watching TV or DVDs	4.20	3.89	0	15.00
Browsing Internet or using emails	2.83	6.27	0	35.00
Writing essays	9.39	7.45	0	31.50

Time 6 (December)

Amount of time spent in English for:	Mean	SD	Min.	Max.
Communicating with teachers	0.73	0.73	0	4.50
Communicating with friends	1.91	2.60	0	12.50
Communicating with service personnels	0.04	0.18	0	1.00
Doing class-related things	0.43	0.16	0	1.00
Doing nonclass-related things	14.47	11.44	0	35.00
Reading newspapers, magazines and books	2.82	2.77	0	10.50
Watching TV or DVDs	4.50	4.95	0	25.00
Browsing Internet or using emails	1.36	2.42	0	12.50
Writing essays	10.19	7.35	0	35.00

Appendix C: Pragmatic Listening Test (PLT) Items

Notes. Two parallel versions of the test were prepared to minimize the practice effect coming from repeated administration. Different filler items were used, male and female speakers' roles were reversed, and slight modifications were made to proper nouns, prices and object names. The items were administered in a random order each time.

I. Conventional Implicature Items

(1) Indirect Refusals

1
A: Hey, Mike.
B: Hey Nancy. Did you just get back? How was everybody in the family?
A: Everybody was fine. We had a nice birthday party. They said hi to you. Hey look my sister made a loaf of bread today. You gotta have a piece. It's so good.
B: I'm full.

1. Mike doesn't want the bread now.
2. Mike is going to have a piece of bread.
3. Nancy is full now.
4. Nancy made bread for the birthday party.

2
A: Hey Steve, you're still on the Internet. What are you doing?
B: I'm checking out some colleges to see which one I should apply to.

A: How about this school called St. Joes college in Indiana. They sent us a lot of information. It sounds like a neat school.

B: They don't have many majors.

1. Steve wants to apply for St. Joes college.
2. Steve knows about many majors.
3. Steve lived in Indiana before.
4. Steve is not interested in St. Joes college.

3

A: Are you still thinking about a college, Mike?

B: Yeah Nancy. I'm reading information about Duke University. I fell in love with that school when I went there last summer.

A: You can always apply.

B: I don't know if I'm gonna bother, because the chance of my getting in there is small.

1. Mike is bothered by Duke University.
2. Mike has never visited Duke University.
3. Mike will not apply for Duke University.
4. Mike will apply for Duke University.

4

A: Hey, Mike, do you have plans for tonight?

B: Hey Nancy. Ah, I don't know.

A: I talked Catherine into going out tonight to see if she wants to take in a movie or something, after she comes home from work. Do you wanna go out with us?

B: I don't feel that great.

1. Mike is watching a movie now.
2. Mike wants to stay home tonight.
3. Mike wants to go out with Nancy tonight.
4. Mike thinks Catherine is great.

5

A: Hey Nancy, what are you doing? Do you wanna do something tonight?

B: I don't know. I was just gonna watch TV.

A: I wanna go out tonight. Maybe we can go to the Japanese restaurant. The new one just opened.

B: I don't have any money this week to pay the bills.

1. Nancy doesn't want to go out tonight.
2. Nancy is going out tonight.
3. Nancy got a bill from the restaurant.
4. Nancy is watching TV with Mike.

6
A: Are you finished eating Steve¿
B: No, not yet, Mom. I'm not full. I haven't eaten all day today.
A: You didn't have lunch at school¿
B: No, I was too busy. Mom, can I have more of that
       chicken stuff¿
A: There isn't gonna be anything left for your father.

1. Steve can have more chicken.
2. Steve's father cooked the chicken tonight.
3. Steve had small lunch at school today.
4. Steve should not have any more chicken.

7
A: Hi Steve, what are you looking at¿
B: Hi Mom. It's a volleyball schedule.
A: Oh, that, at the church¿
B: Yeah, it's on Sundays and Wednesdays. Can I join the team¿
       All I need is your signature so I can play volleyball on the
       team.
A: You have your piano practice every Wednesday.

1. Steve's mother is a piano teacher.
2. Steve's mother goes to church on Sundays.
3. Steve can't play volleyball on the team.
4. Steve can play volleyball on the team.

8
A: Hey Steve, where are you¿
B: What mom, I'm here.
A: I need you and Beth to carry chairs from the back yard, those four
       little white ones. They will stack, so you can stick two together, and
       carry them around here.
B: I'm on the phone right now.

1. Steve is sitting in a white chair.
2. Steve doesn't want to carry chairs now.
3. Steve is going to carry chairs now.
4. Steve bought a new phone.

(2) Routines

1

A: Hey Mom, this is the birthday gift I want you to open.
B: Oh, is this from you Steve? This is a pretty package. When did you have a chance to wrap this?
A: Last night. At home.
B: Look at this. A pair of gloves. That's so sweet of you.

1. Mother thanked Steve for the gloves.
2. Mother didn't like the gloves much.
3. Mother likes sweets.
4. Mother wrapped the gift at home.

2

A: Steve, this is the gift I want you to open. It's from me.
B: Thanks, Mom. How do you open this box? Did you ever open this?
A: Oh yeah.
B: How did you ever open this?
A: Let's see it, well, it's supposed to open on the side. There we go.

1. Steve opened the gift box.
2. Mother put the box to the side.
3. Steve gave his mother a gift.
4. Mother opened the box for Steve.

3

A: Hello. I need to pay for my summer session class.
B: OK, you have the parking ticket on file too. Did you want to pay the total?
A: Sure.
B: Four hundred dollars is your total. Do you want a receipt?
A: Yeah.
B: It'll take just a moment for that to process. Here you go.

1. The man processed the receipt.
2. The man paid $300 for parking.
3. The salesclerk gave a receipt to the man.
4. The man didn't get the receipt.

4
A: Hello.
B: Yes, how can I help you?
A: Ah, could you help me to find professor Jane Smith? I know she is in this building.
B: Jane Smith. Uhm, I don't see it on the list. Let me look into one other area and see if they got it. I'll be right back.

1. The woman's professor is Jane Smith.
2. The woman just left.
3. The woman found Jane Smith on the list.
4. The woman was right about the professor's name.

5
A: Hey, Nancy, what's up.
B: Hey Mike, I'm listing all of the things that are happening next week. I'm gonna be so busy.
A: Yeah?
B: I have two final exams, one presentation, and two papers due, one for literature class and one for Japanese class. Everything is happening next week.
A: I'm sorry.

1. Mike thinks Nancy has a hard schedule next week.
2. Mike is apologizing to Nancy.
3. Nancy is very busy this week.
4. Mike is taking a Japanese class.

6
A: Can I help who's next?
B: Hi, can I have two copies of this? Can you make it really dark?
A: Sure. Ah... It's still gonna have the line in it, not matter what.
B: All right, just give me two copies.
A: OK, it comes to two dollars. Out of five?

1. The copy service cost five dollars.
2. The man asked for four copies.
3. The man thought the copy was too dark.
4. The copy service cost two dollars.

7

A: Hi. How can I help you?
B: Hi, I'd like a cup of coffee please.
A: Do you wanna small or large?
B: Large, with room for milk. And a chocolate chip cookie too.
A: OK. Out of five? Two dollars is your change. You have a good day.

1. The man is having a good day.
2. The man asked for a small cup of coffee.
3. The man paid three dollars.
4. The man paid two dollars.

8

A: Hi how can I help you?
B: Ah, could I get a small regular coffee, with milk? And a slice of apple pie.
A: For here or to go?
B: To go please.
A: Here's a large cup, we don't have small because we ran out of the small ones.
B: OK, thank you.

1. The man ordered cake.
2. The man is taking the coffee out.
3. The man is having coffee in the shop.
4. The man ordered a large cup.

II. Nonconventional Implicature Items

1

A: Hey, Nancy. You're home. Where were you?
B: Hey. I just had dinner with people from work. We went to a restaurant called Lucca.
A: Where is Lucca?
B: It's like next town over or something like that. They serve Italian food.

A: Oh, OK. Did you enjoy the dinner⸮
B: It was late.

1. Nancy didn't enjoy the dinner very much.
2. Nancy thought the dinner was good.
3. Nancy was late for the dinner.
4. Nancy didn't go to work this morning.

2
A: So what's the plan for tonight, Mike.
B: I don't know, Nancy. I just was. ... I went shopping with Tom and his roommate this afternoon. They said they would come over here sometime.
A: Oh, are they⸮
B: So you know, if we wanna just hang out and drink, whatever.

1. Mike doesn't have formal plans for tonight.
2. Mike is going out tonight.
3. Mike thinks that they should go shopping tonight.
4. Mike wants something to drink.

3
A: So, Mary, you and your husband just moved from Florida to New York⸮
B: Yes, last year.
A: Do you like living in New York⸮
B: We looked around for two years. My husband and I went all over the United States, and we didn't find any place we liked better.

1. Mary likes living in New York.
2. Mary likes living in Florida.
3. Mary likes traveling all over the United States.
4. Mary has never lived in Florida.

4
A: So you have lived in Boston all this time, Kevin⸮
B: Thirty years. Except we did take five years off. My wife and I went to Florida. We needed a vacation, so we went there, and we moved instead.
A: Really.
B: And the first year we were there, we visited Boston six times.

1. Kevin missed Boston when he first moved.
2. Kevin likes living in Florida.
3. Kevin is visiting Boston now.
4. Kevin has lived in Boston for five years.

5
A: Hi Kevin, I saw your daughter today at school. She is beautiful.
B: Thanks, Mary. So do you have any children¿
A: My husband has two children.
B: Did you raise them in New York¿ I was gonna say, is it possible¿
A: It's possible. And they were partially raised in New York.

1. Mary has no children of her own.
2. Mary has two children of her own.
3. Mary raised children in New York.
4. Mary's husband was raised in New York.

6
A: Thank you for this birthday present, Mike. It's a really pretty sweater.
B: You're welcome, Nancy. If it's too big, your mother can take it.
A: Or I can wear some shirts underneath it. Let me try it on.
B: Is it too big¿
A: I still got room for another ten pounds.

1. The sweater is too big for Nancy.
2. The sweater fits Nancy well.
3. Nancy has put on ten pounds recently.
4. Nancy is as big as her mother.

7
A: Hey Mike, you're home. Aren't you supposed to be at work¿
B: Hey Nancy. I quit that job yesterday. I just didn't wanna work in the factory any longer.
A: What¿ Really¿ Do your parents know about this¿
B: When they come back from their trip, they'll be pretty shocked.

1. Mike's parents think he's still working.
2. Mike's parents know that he quit his job.

3. Mike's parents just came back from their trip.
4. Mike's parents work in a factory.

8
A: What are you doing, Mike? You're working hard.
B: Hey Nancy. I'm studying for the exam, SAT. I took it once, but I do need a better score for the college application next year.
A: What did you say your score was before?
B: Ten seventy.
A: Well, you'd only taken it once so.

1. Nancy is encouraging Mike.
2. Nancy thinks Mike's SAT score is very good.
3. Mike applied for a college once.
4. Nancy is talking about her SAT score.

9
A: Why are you working so hard, Nancy?
B: Hey Mike. My medical exam is coming up next week. You know I took it before, but I have to get a better score to get into a medical school.
A: What was your score before?
B: Ten fifty.
A: I'd be happy with seven hundred.

1. Mike thinks Nancy's exam score is good.
2. Mike thinks Nancy's score is poor.
3. Nancy is a medical school student.
4. Nancy's medical school exam is next month.

10
A: Hi Mom.
B: Hi Steve. You're still on the Internet. What're you doing?
A: I'm reading about colleges. I wanna go to a big university in the city, maybe New York.
B: I'll tell you what, if you're going to college to have a good time, one year is all I'm paying for.

1. Mother thinks Steve won't be serious in city.
2. Mother thinks Steve will study hard in city.

3. Steve is paying for college first year.
4. Mother likes New York.

11
A: Hi Nancy.
B: Hey Mike. How was work?
A: Fine, I'm tired though. What are you looking at?
B: I'm checking out some furniture ads. These are on sale. Hey, look at this, three hundred ninety-nine, leather sofa, brown. Looks really nice. What do you think?
A: I already looked at that.

1. Mike is not interested in the sofa.
2. Mike wants to buy the sofa.
3. The sofa is three hundred dollars.
4. Mike didn't go to work today.

12
A: Hey Steve, did you just put this t-shirt out here?
B: Not me, mom. Dad did.
A: Oh, OK, Is he still here?
B: No, he's gone to work. Aren't you washing those now?
A: Yeah I am, but see now I can't tell if this t-shirt is dirty or clean.
B: It's white.

1. Steve thinks the t-shirt is clean.
2. Steve thinks the t-shirt is dirty.
3. Steve is wearing a white t-shirt.
4. Steve's mother is wearing a white t-shirt.

13
A: Kevin, I really like that painting you have upstairs.
B: I bought it in Mexico City, ten or fifteen years ago. When I was in college. I paid two thousand dollars for that.
A: Did you say two thousand dollars?
B: Yeah, I don't know what I was thinking that time.

1. Kevin thinks he paid too much for the painting.
2. Kevin thinks the painting was reasonable.
3. Kevin has a headache.
4. Kevin lived in Mexico ten years ago.

14

A: Hi Steve. What's wrong⸮

B: Hi Mom. Dad and I got into another fight.

A: What happened⸮

B: He got upset because I said I don't wanna get a job right after college. I've been studying Japanese for years, so I wanna study abroad in Japan.

A: It sounds like he has a problem.

1. Mother likes Steve's idea about study abroad.
2. Mother thinks Steve should get a job after college.
3. Steve has a problem with study abroad.
4. Steve is studying German.

15

A: Hi Kevin.

B: Mary you're late today.

A: Yeah, I got on a train, and then realized I left my bag at home. Did I miss something⸮

B: No, ah, we were just talking about getting a new coffee maker for the office.

A: Don't you want a new one with timer⸮

B: I'm happy with ours.

1. Nancy doesn't care for a new coffee maker.
2. Nancy is interested in a new coffee maker.
3. Nancy is happy today.
4. Nancy left her bag in the bus.

16

A: Kevin, are you feeling better⸮ Did you go to the hospital⸮

B: Yeah they did a blood test, and said I picked up virus. He said I could do more tests to know more.

A: So did you have more tests⸮

B: By the time I get the results back, I'd probably be over with it anyway.

1. Kevin had just a blood test.
2. Kevin had many tests in the hospital.
3. Kevin is not sick any more.
4. Kevin didn't go to the hospital.

III.   Filler Items

1

A: Hey Mike, are you back from work? Your mom just called.

B: Oh, she did?

A: Yeah, like ten, fifteen minutes ago.

B: What did she say?

A: She just wanted to know when you got there, so we told her, seven, seven thirty.

She was happy with that and hung up.

B: OK. Thanks, Nancy.

1. Nancy talked to Mike's mother.
2. Nancy and Mike just came back from work.
3. Nancy was happy to talk to Mike's mother.
4. Nancy's mother called Mike.

2

A: Hey, Mom, I haven't had breakfast yet. Do we have any food?

B: Well, we have lots of cereal, Steve. Just no milk.

A: No milk?

B: Yeah, I just threw away the gallon. That was the last one.

A: OK, then, I'm gonna go to the store and pick up some milk.

B: OK.

1. Steve already had breakfast.
2. Steve just finished a gallon of milk.
3. Steve doesn't want cereal for breakfast.
4. Steve is going to the store to buy milk.

3

A: What's wrong, Nancy? Are you sick?

B: I need some food. I'm so hungry.

A: What did you have tonight?

B: I just had a piece of toast with butter. That's all.

A: Was that your dinner?

B: Yeah, I haven't eaten since I ate that Chinese food at school for lunch.

1. Nancy doesn't like Chinese food.
2. Nancy had a piece of toast and milk for lunch.
3. Nancy wants to eat something.
4. Nancy is full right now.

4
A: Wow, the dinner is delicious, Kevin. Did you make this?
B: Thanks, Mary. I had red beans and rice for dinner last week and it was so great, and I thought, I could make this for a dinner party.
A: Yeah, this is wonderful.
B: I just added some onions and peppers.

1. Mary had red beans and rice last week.
2. Kevin cooked the dinner.
3. Kevin didn't cook dinner tonight.
4. Kevin used some red peppers for the dish.

5
A: Do you like cooking, Mary?
B: Yeah, I love it. My cooking comes out different, differently every time I make something though.
A: Really? So ...
B: The only thing consistent is my fried chicken, pretty much tastes the same, and spaghetti meat sauce I make, tastes pretty much the same.

1. Mary likes cooking very much.
2. Mary doesn't like cooking so much.
3. Mary usually cooks fried rice with chicken.
4. Mary likes cooking different kinds of food.

6
A: Hi Mom.
B: Hey, Steve. You're home. Where were you?
A: I was at a bookstore.
B: Oh yeah?
A: I didn't buy any books though. I couldn't decide what I wanted, and then, things just got too hurried, and I just didn't think it was the right time to buy a book.
B: Oh, OK.

1. Steve bought some books.
2. Steve was in a hurry when he bought a book.
3. Steve went to the bookstore with his mom.
4. Steve didn't buy any books.

7

A: What are you looking at, Kevin?

B: Some ads on office things. I need a color printer.

A: Yeah?

B: Yeah, how much is your color printer, Nancy?

A: You can get a color version of the printer I have for, gosh, I don't know, five hundred dollars or something?

B: Oh, OK.

1. Kevin's printer was five hundred dollars.
2. Kevin works at office every day.
3. Kevin wants to buy a color printer.
4. Kevin already has a color printer.

8

A: Mom, I'm thinking about which college I should apply to. I don't know which is better, a big school or a small school.

B: They both have advantages and disadvantages, Steve. You have to see which ones fit your personality best.

A: Yeah.

B: Your uncle went to a small art school, and he loved it.

1. Steve likes small colleges.
2. Steve's uncle liked a small art school.
3. Steve's mother doesn't like big universities.
4. Mother likes big schools better than small ones.

Appendix D: Pragmatic Speaking Test (PST) Situational Scenarios

Notes. In order to avoid practice effect, two parallel versions of the test were prepared by making slight changes in the situational descriptions. The items were administered in a random order each time.

I. Requests

Low-Imposition Situations

You are in your English class. You have a free writing task in class today, but you forgot to bring a pen. You need a pen to write the essay. You want to borrow a pen from your friend, Ken, in the class. He is sitting next to you. What do you say to Ken?

It is Sunday evening at seven o'clock. You are with your friend, John, and are working on a project for English class in the library. You and John are talking about your group presentation for tomorrow's class. John said something about English class to you, but you didn't understand. What do you say to John?

High-Imposition Situations

You are taking Professor Smith's intercultural communication class this semester. You have a small test in her class next Monday, but you just realized that you have to go out of town that day because of your cousin's wedding. You want to take the test at some other time. What do you say to Professor Smith?

Tomorrow is the due date of a paper for Professor's Land's history class. The paper is a 10-page assignment. You caught a cold, and you've written only two pages so far. You don't think you can finish the paper. You want to ask for two extra days to finish. What do you say to Professor Land?

II. Opinions

Low-Imposition Situations

It's Sunday afternoon. You are shopping for clothes with your friend, Jeff. You and Jeff are very good friends and go to the same college. Jeff picked up a brown jacket and tried it on. You don't think he looks good in brown. He says, 'What do you think?' What do you say to Jeff?

You are working on a paper for Japanese Culture class with your class-mate, Cindy. You and Cindy are very close friends. Cindy asked you to check the first draft of her paper on the Japanese education system. The paper is well-written, but you think the introduction is too long. What do you say to Cindy?

High-Imposition Situations

You're taking Professor Williams' business class. He gave you a mid-semester grade of C, but you don't think it's fair. You missed three classes and didn't speak up in class much, but you always turned in homework on time and got 80% on the test. You go to Professor William's office to explain. What do you say?

You're in Professor Young's French Culture class. You like the professor, but she talks about French history most of the time and doesn't address recent things. You're more interested in French pop culture and music. One day after class she says, 'What do you think about the class?' What do you say to Professor Young?

III. Filler Situations

You are waiting for a bus to campus. You have been waiting a long time, and you are worried that you might be late for your afternoon class. You want to know what time it is. You see a man with a watch standing next to you. What do you say to the man?

It is Sunday afternoon at four o'clock. You are on your way downtown to meet your friends and see a movie. You are taking a subway downtown. The subway is very crowded. A woman accidentally steps on your foot. She says, 'Oh, I'm so sorry.' What do you say to the woman?

It's Saturday night. You have a birthday party at your friend's house. Your friend, Jack, who lives in the same dorm, is also invited. Jack doesn't have a car, so you drive him in your car. When you arrive at the house, Jack says, 'Thank you for the ride.' What do you say to Jack?

It's Saturday afternoon at four o'clock. You are in a clothing store and are shopping by yourself. You are looking for a pair of gloves. A salesperson comes to you to assist you with your shopping. You don't want the salesperson's help. The salesperson says, 'How can I help you?' What do you say to her?

Appendix E: Evaluation of Speech Acts: Grammar Rating Scale

5 **Excellent**	There are almost no grammatical and lexical errors. Almost perfect. Example: *Could I borrow a pen? What did you say?*
4 **Good**	There are one or two minor grammatical and lexical errors, which are hardly noticeable. Example: *Do you have a pens? What do you say?*
3 **Fair**	There are <u>a few major</u> grammatical and lexical errors, but <u>they do not interfere with understanding.</u> Example: *What did you speak?*
2 **Poor**	There are many major grammatical and lexical errors that cause misunderstanding. Example: *You say that?*
1 **Very Poor**	The expressions are incomprehensible because they are fragmental or contain excessive grammatical mistakes. Example: *Pen, one. No.*
0 **No performance**	No attempt to respond.

Appendix F: Evaluation of Speech Acts: Appropriateness Rating Scale

5
Excellent
	Almost perfectly appropriate and effective in the level of directness, politeness and formality. In a face-threatening situation (talking to a professor), the expressions contain conditional structures and sufficient supporting expressions to mitigated potential face threat (e.g. enough explanation, positive comments & hedging that soften the expressions)
	
	Examples:
	* Requests
	1. 'Friend' situations
	    – *Do you have a pen? / Can I borrow a pen?/ Could you say that again? / (Please) say that again. / What did you say?/ Pardon?*
	
	2. 'Professor' situations
	    – *Hi ah. . .I have a problem with the test. I know this is a last minute thing, but is there any way that I could change it to another time. I'm supposed to go to my cousin's wedding on the same day.*
	
	    – *Hi professor, I'm really sorry about this, but I was wondering if I could ask for an extension for the paper. I've been sick, and I don't think I'll be able to finish in time. So if I could, could I turn it in, in maybe two days rather than tomorrow? Thanks.*
	
	* Opinions
	1. 'Friend' situations
	    – *Nice, but it's not your colour, try another one. / How about different colour?/ You looks better in xxx. / xxx is better to you.*
	    – *The paper is good, but the introduction is a bit long. You might wanna cut it down.*

	2. 'Professor' situations – *I think your discussions about French history are really interesting, but I think the language might be more interesting if we actually talked a little more about the culture nowadays, instead of talking about the historical aspect.* – *Hi, I was just wondering about my mid-semester grade, I had a C but I turned in every homework and I got a pretty good grade on the exam, and I know I didn't, uh, I missed a few classes, so I was wondering if there was any other reason I got a C.*
4 **Good**	**Not perfect but adequately appropriate in the level of directness, politeness and formality. Expressions are a little off from target-like, but pretty good.** Examples: * Requests 1. 'Friend' situations – *Could you borrow me a pen? / Please borrow me a pen.* (not quite target-like) – *I don't know what you mean, so please tell me more detail.* (not quite target-like) 2. 'Professor' situations – *You know, Friday we have test right? My cousin has wedding on Friday. If possible, I want to take the test some other day. Is it all right?* – *Professor Lee, I caught a cold so I couldn't get up, and I have written only two pages, so could you give me extra two days to finish the paper?* * Opinions 1. 'Friend' situations – *Brown jacket doesn't go with you. / You don't look so nice.* – *I think the paper is well-written, but introduction is too long. Make it shorter.* 2. 'Professor' situations – *I really like your class, but I'd rather hear some stuff about more contemporary culture and stuff, like music and such.*

3
Fair
	Somewhat appropriate in the level of directness, politeness and formality. Expressions are more direct or indirect than the situation requires with minimum framing expressions to mitigate the directness/indirectness.
	
	Examples:
	
	* Requests
	'Professor' situations
	   – *I should go to the wedding ceremony, so I want to take the test another day*
	   – *I'm sorry actually I caught a cold so I can't finish my paper. Please give me two extra days to finish the paper.*
	
	* Opinions
	1. 'Friend' situations
	   – *Your paper is too long. You had better cut it shorter.* (without positive comment)
	   – *You don't look good. Change your clothes.*
	
	2. 'Professor' situations
	   – *Hi professor, I don't think my grade is fair since I did pretty well on the test and got in all the homework on time. Could you please explain that for me?*
	   – *I think your French class is very interesting, but I want to know pop French culture, so could you tell us French pop culture next class?*

2
Poor
	Clearly inappropriate in the level of directness, politeness and formality. Expressions sound almost rude or too demanding.
	
	Examples:
	
	* Requests (talking to a professor)
	   – *I have a wedding to attend. Please change the test day.*
	   – *I caught a cold, and I'm not done with the assignment. I want you to give me extension.*
	
	* Opinions (talking to a professor)
	   – *I don't think grade C is fair. Can you change it?*
	   – *Professor, why did I get a C? I should have a B.*
	   – *You should focus on current things in class, because old stuff is boring.*
	   – *Please teach me recent French culture.*

1 **Very Poor**	**Not sure if the target speech act is performed.** Examples: – *Please borrow my pen.* (asking for a pen) – *Please another day.* (asking to reschedule a test or asking for an extension) – *I have to go to my Cousin's wedding on Monday, so I can't attend your class. Sorry.* (asking to reschedule a test) – *It looks good.* You should buy it. (negative opinion about clothes) – *Ah I'm sorry, could you speak more lately?* (word choice mistake) – *I did my best in your class, so please.* (incomplete)
0	**No response.**

Appendix G: Grammar Test for Target Pragmalinguistic Features

Part 1:

次の英語の日本語訳を箱の中から選んで数字で答えて下さい。同じ言葉を何度使っても結構です。

(Choose the Japanese translation for each English word.)

a. a little ___
b. would ___
c. I think ___
d. might ___
e. probably ___
f. could ___
g. maybe ___
h. I'm not sure ___
i. may ___
j. should ___
k. a bit ___
l. I feel ___
m. absolutely ___
n. I know ___
o. can ___
p. completely
q. will ___
r. just ___
s. really ___
t. must ___

---

1 本当に 　　2 多分 　　3 少し／ちょっと 　　4 may の過去形 　　5 ーできる

6 ーすべきだ 　　7 完全に／全く 　8 （私は）知っている 　9 （私は）ーと思う 10 ーできた

11 willの過去形 　　12 ーしても良い 13 ーしなければならない 16 ちょうど

17 ーするだろう（未来形）18 確かではない 19 （私は）ーと感じる 　20 再度

Part 2:

英語の単語を並べ替えて、日本語訳に合う文を作って下さい。英語の単語を全部使う必要はありません。

(Re-order the words to construct a sentence that matches with the Japanese translation. You do not have to use all the words.)

例：私は英語を話す (speak / I / English) ＝ I speak English.

1 世界中を旅行できたらいいのになあ。＝————————————
(travel / must / could / tomorrow / wish / I / all over the world / think /)

2 鍵をなくしたら家に入るのが難しくなるだろう。= ————————
(that / I/ if / to / get in / it / lose / it would / be / difficult / the house / keys / feel /)

3 私の両親は中国に行ったことがある。= My —————————————
(have / to / parents / been / China / has / whether)

4 彼がフランスに住むのは可能ですか。= —————————————
(it / for him / to / be possible / France / would / live in / that / they / whom)

5 英語を勉強するのは好きですか。 = —————————————
(do / did / English / studying / you / like / don't)

6 明日雨は降るだろうか。 = —————————————
(that / I / if / tomorrow / rains / it / when / wonder / feel)

7 私がテストをスキップできる方法がありますか。 = —————————————
(whether / there / any way / is / I / skip / could / the test / that)

8 彼女がアメリカに行く可能性がありますか。 = —————————————
(she / there / goes to / is / any chance / that / America / went / might / when)

Appendix H: Coding Frameworks for Speech Act Expressions

Notes. The coding framework for request is based on Blum-Kulka et al. (1989). The framework for the speech act of opinion is original.

I. Speech Act of Request

Head act (An utterance/expression that conveys the target request intention)

(1) Direct Expressions

1. Imperatives (IMP): The illocutionary force is directly conveyed by imperative sentences.
   e.g. Lend me a pen. / Please lend me a pen.

2. Performatives (PF): The illocutionary force is explicitly stated by performative verbs.
   e.g. I'd like to ask you to lend me a pen.

3. Obligation Statements (OB): The illocutionary force is derivable in obligatory sentences.
   e.g. You should lend me a pen.

4. Want Statements (WA): The illocutionary force is derivable in want/wish/need sentences.
   e.g. I want you to lend me a pen. / I'd like you to lend me a pen.

(2) Indirect Expressions

5. Preparatory Questions (PQ): Reference to preparatory conditions such as the hearer's ability, willingness or possibility to perform the action.
   e.g. Could you/would you/can you lend me a pen?

6. Suggestions (SUG): The illocutionary intent is phrased as a suggestion.
   e.g. How about lending me a pen?

7. Permissions (PERM): The speaker asks for the hearer's permission.
   e.g. May I/Could I/Can I borrow a pen?

8. Mitigated Expressions (MIT): Reference to preparatory conditions (i.e., the hearer's ability, will and possibility) or reference to the speaker's want and wish in embedded questions or sentences (i.e., bi-clausal structures).

     e.g. Do you think you can lend me a pen? / I wonder if you could lend me a pen.

9. Hint (H): Questions or statements with implicit reference to the action.

     e.g. My pen just quit. / (asking for extension) Two more days, please.

(3) Conventional Questions (CON): Formulaic questions that convey the request intent.

     e.g. Do you have a pen? / Pardon? / What did you say?

Modifications

1. Hedging (HG): Single words that minimize self-expression.

     i.e. *a little, a bit, maybe, perhaps, just, possibly, probably, kind/sort of*

2. Amplifier (A): Single words that strengthen or heighten self-expression.

     i.e. *really, so, very, absolutely, totally*

3. Grounder (G): The speaker gives reasons, explanations or justifications.

     e.g. *I misunderstood the due date.*

4. Apology (AP): The speaker expresses his/her regret for making an imposition.

     e.g. *I'm sorry. / In my blame, but.*

5. Preparator (P): The speaker prepares the hearer for the request.

     e.g. *I'd like to ask you something. / I have a question about my grade. Could you do me a favor? / I came to talk about something.*

6. Confirmation (C): The speaker confirms if the request is acceptable.

     e.g. *Is it OK? I want to take the test some other time. Can I?*

7. Appreciation (APP): Expressions of thanking.

     e.g. *Thank you. / I appreciate it.*

8. Request for Suggestion (REQSUG): The speaker asks for suggestion.

     e.g. *What do you think I should do?*

9. Imposition Minimizer (MIN): The speaker reduces the imposition placed on the hearer.

     e.g. *If it's OK with you / If you have time / If possible*

10. External 'please' (PL): The phrase 'please' attached to intensify the request.
    e.g. *Could you extend the deadline, please*

11. Hearer Benefit (B): Expression about the hearer's benefit from complying the request.
    e.g. *I need an extension so that I can turn in a quality paper.*

12. Promise (PRO): promise to the hearer.
    e.g. I'm sure I will finish it in two days.

13. Attention getter (AT): expressions of greetings, etc.
    e.g. *Hello Professor Smith / Excuse me Dr. Santos*

II.   Speech Act of Opinion

Notes. 'Mitigated' refers to an utterance in bi-clausal structure, while 'unmitigated' refers to an utterance in mono-clausal structure.

Main strategies

1. Expressions of personal opinions, feelings and observations (OP)
    biclausal: e.g. *I'm not sure if it's really a good color. / I don't think it's your color.*
    monoclausal: e.g. *Brown is not your color. / Introduction is too long.*

2. Expressions of want, wish and interest (WA)
    biclausal: e.g. *I wish / I hope we talked about recent things.*
    monoclausal: e.g. *I'm interested in recent things. / I'd like to discuss ecent things.*

3. Request (REQ): The speaker requests the hearer for action or information that benefits the speaker.
    biclausal: e.g. *I was wondering if you could speak more about current issues.*
    monoclausal: e.g. *Could you explain that? / Why did I get C?*

4. Suggestion (SUG): The speaker suggests the hearer to do something for the hearer's benefit.
    Specific action to be taken is explicitly said or implied from the utterance.
    biclausal: e.g. *I tend to think you should cut down the introduction a little.*
    monoclausal: e.g. *You should cut it back. / Why don't you try something else?*

5. Request for suggestion (REQSUG): The speaker asks the hearer for suggestion.

    biclausal: e.g. *I was wondering if there'd be any way for the rest of the semester that I could do to make my grade a little better.*
    monoclausal: e.g. *What should I do?*

6. Grounding (G): The speaker gives reasons or explanations to justify his/her position.

    e.g. *I got C, but I always turned in homework on time, and I got 80% on the test.*

7. Positive comments (PC): Positive evaluation of the hearer.

    e.g. *I like your jacket. / Your paper is very good. / I really like your class.*

8. Invitation (INV): The speaker asks the hearer to participate in a joint activity.

    e.g. *Let's try different jacket. / Shall we pick another clothes?*

Modifications

Same with the request coding.

References

Achiba, M. (2002) *Learning to Request in a Second Language: Child Interlanguage Pragmatics.* Clevedon: Multilingual Matters.

ACTFL (1999) *Standards for Foreign Language Learning in the 21st Century.* Lawrence, KS: Allen Press Inc.

Akamatsu, N. (2006) The effects of training on automatization of word recognition in English as a foreign language. *Applied Psycholinguistics* 29, 175–193.

Alcon Sóler, E. and Martinez-Flór, A. (2008) *Investigating Pragmatics in Foreign Language Learning, Teaching and Testing.* Bristol: Multilingual Matters.

Anderson, J.R. (1990) *Cognitive Psychology and Its Implications* (3rd edn). New York: W.H. Freeman and Company.

Anderson, J.R. and Lebiere, C. (1998) *The Automatic Components of Thought.* Mahwah, NJ: Lawrence Erlbaum.

Anderson, J.R., Bothell, D., Byrne, M.D., Douglass, S., Lebiere, C. and Qin, Y. (2004) An integrated theory of the mind. *Psychological Review* 111, 1036–1060.

Austin, J.L. (1962) *How to Do Things with Words.* Cambridge: Harvard University Press.

Bachman, L.F. and Palmer, A.S. (1996) *Language Testing in Practice: Designing and Developing Useful Language Tests.* Oxford: Oxford University Press.

Bachman, L.F. and Palmer, A.S. (2010) *Language Assessment in Practice.* Oxford: Oxford University Press.

Bak, P. (1997) *How Nature Works: The Science of Self-Organized Criticality.* New York: Oxford University Press.

Bardovi-Harlig, K. (1999) Exploring the interlanguage of interlanguage pragmatics: A research agenda for acquisitional pragmatics. *Language Learning* 49, 677–713.

Bardovi-Harlig, K. (2000) Pragmatics and second language acquisition. In R.B. Kaplan (ed.) *Oxford Handbook of Applied Linguistics* (pp. 182–192). Oxford: Oxford University Press.

Bardovi-Harlig, K. (2010) Exploring the pragmatics of interlanguage pragmatics: Definition by design. In A. Trosborg (ed.) *Handbook of Pragmatics: Pragmatics Across Languages and Cultures* (Vol. 7, pp. 219–259). Berlin: Mouton de Gruyter.

Bardovi-Harlig, K. and Dörnyei, Z. (1998) Do language learners recognise pragmatic violations? Pragmatic versus grammatical awareness in instructed L2 learning. *TESOL Quarterly* 32, 233–259.

Bardovi-Harlig, K. and Hartford, B. (1993) Learning the rules of academic talk: A longitudinal study of pragmatic change. *Studies in Second Language Acquisition* 15, 279–304.

Bardovi-Harlig, K. and Hartford, B. (2005) *Interlanguage Pragmatics: Exploring Institutional Talk.* Mahwah, NJ: Lawrence Erlbaum.

Bardovi-Harlig, K. and Mahan-Taylor, R. (2003) *Teaching Pragmatics.* Washington, DC: US Department of State.

Barron, A. (2003) *Acquisition in Interlanguage Pragmatics: Learning How to Do Things with Words in a Study Abroad Context.* Amsterdam: Benjamins.

Barron, A. (2006) Learning to say 'you' in German: The acquisition of sociolinguistic competence in a study abroad context. In M. DuFon and E. Churchill (eds) *Language Learners in Study Abroad Contexts* (pp. 59–82). Clevedon: Multilingual Matters.

Beebe, L. and Takahashi, T. (1989) Do you have a bag?: Social status and patterned variation in second language acquisition. In S. Gass, C. Madden, D. Preston and L. Selinker (eds) *Variation in Second Language Acquisition: Discourse and Pragmatics* (pp. 55–74). Clevedon: Multilingual Matters.

Beebe, L.M., Takahashi, T. and Uliss-Weltz, R. (1990) Pragmatic transfer in ESL refusals. In R. Scarcella, D. Andersen and S. Krashen (eds) *Developing Communicative Competence in a Second Language* (pp. 55–74). New York: Newbury House.

Belz, J. and Kinginger, C. (2003) Discourse options and the development of pragmatic competence by classroom learners of German: The case of address forms. *Language Learning* 53, 591–647.

Bezuidenhout, A. and Sroda, M.S. (1998) Children's use of contextual cues to resolve referential ambiguity: An application of relevance theory. *Pragmatics and Cognition* 6, 265–299.

Bialystok, E. (1990a) The competence of processing: Classifying theories of second language acquisition. *TESOL Quarterly* 24, 635–648.

Bialystok, E. (1990b) *Communication Strategies*. Oxford: Blackwell.

Bialystok, E. (1993) Symbolic representation and attentional control in pragmatic competence. In G. Kasper and S. Blum-Kulka (eds) *Interlanguage Pragmatics* (pp. 43–59). New York: Oxford University Press.

Biber, D., Conrad, S., Reppen, R., Byrd, P. and Helt, M. (2002) Speaking and writing in the university: A multi-dimensional comparison. *TESOL Quarterly* 36, 9–48.

Block, D. and Cameron, D. (2002) *Globalization and Language Teaching*. London: Routledge.

Blum-Kulka, S., House, J. and Kasper, G. (1989) *Cross-Cultural Pragmatics: Requests and Apologies*. Norwood, NJ: Ablex.

Bouton, L. (1992) The interpretation of implicature in English by NNS: Does it come automatically without being explicitly taught? In L. Bouton (ed.) *Pragmatics and Language Learning Monograph Series* (Vol. 3, pp. 64–77). Urbana-Champaign, IL: Division of English as an International Language, University of Illinois, Urbana-Champaign.

Bouton, L. (1994) Can NNS skill in interpreting implicature in American English be improved through explicit instruction?: A pilot study. In L. Bouton and Y. Kachuru (eds) *Pragmatics and Language Learning Monograph Series* (Vol. 5, pp. 88–108). Urbana-Champaign, IL: Division of English as an International Language, University of Illinois, Urbana-Champaign.

Boxer, D. (2002) Discourse issues in cross-cultural pragmatics. *Annual Review of Applied Linguistics* 22, 150–167.

Brown, P. and Levinson, S. (1983) *Politeness: Some Universals in Language Usage*. Cambridge: Cambridge University Press.

Canale, M. and Swain, M. (1980) Theoretical aspects of communicative approaches to second language teaching and testing. *Applied Linguistics* 1, 1–47.

Code, S. and Anderson, A. (2001) Requests by young Japanese: A longitudinal study. *The Language Teacher* 25, 7–11.

Council of Europe (2001) *Common European Framework of Reference for Languages: Learning, Teaching, Assessment*. Cambridge: Cambridge University Press.

Cutting, J. (2008) *Pragmatics and Discourse* (2nd edn). London: Routledge.

Dai, D.Y. and Sternberg, R.J. (2004) Beyond cognitivism: Toward an integrated understanding of intellectual functioning and development. In D.Y. Dai and R.J. Sternberg (eds) *Motivation, Emotion, and Cognition: Integrative Perspectives on Intellectual Functioning and Development* (pp. 3–18). Mahwah, NJ: Lawrence Erlbaum.

Davis, J. (2007) Resistance to L2 pragmatics in the Australian ESL context. *Language Learning* 57, 611–649.

De Bot, E., Lowie, W. and Verspoor, M. (2007) A dynamic systems theory approach to second language acquisition. *Bilingualism: Language and Cognition* 10, 7–21.

De Bot, K. (2008) Introduction: Second language development as a dynamic process. *Modern Language Journal* 92, 166–178.

DeKeyser, R. (1997) Beyond explicit rule learning: Automatizing second language morphosyntax. *Second Language Studies* 19, 195–221.

DeKeyser, R. (2007) *Practice in a Second Language: Perspectives from Applied Linguistics and Cognitive Psychology.* Cambridge: Cambridge University Press.

Dewaele, J.-M. and Furnham, A. (1999) Extraversion: The unloved variable in applied linguistic research. *Language Learning* 49, 509–544.

Dörnyei, Z. (2000) Motivation in action: Towards a process-oriented conceptualization of student motivation. *British Journal of Educational Psychology* 70, 519–538.

Dörnyei, Z. (2005) *The Psychology of the Language Learner: Individual Differences in Second Language Acquisition.* Mahwah, NJ: Lawrence Erlbaum.

Dörnyei, Z. (2007) *Research Methods in Applied Linguistics.* Oxford: Oxford University Press.

Dörnyei, Z. (2009) *The Psychology of Second Language Acquisition.* Oxford: Oxford University Press.

Drew, P. and Heritage, J. (1992) Analyzing talk at work: An introduction. In P. Drew and J. Heritage (eds) *Talk at Work: Interaction in Institutional Settings* (pp. 3–65). New York: Cambridge University Press.

Du Bois, J.W., Chafe, W.L., Meyer, C. and Thompson, S.A. (2000) *Santa Barbara Corpus of Spoken American English, Part 1.* Philadelphia: Linguistic Data Consortium.

DuFon, M. (2000) The acquisition of negative responses to experience questions in Indonesian as a second language by sojourners in naturalistic interactions. In B. Swierzbin, F. Morris, M. Anderson, C. Klee and E. Tarone (eds) *Social and Cognitive Factors in Second Language Acquisition* (pp. 77–97). Somerville, MA: Cascadilla Press.

Duranti, A. and Goodwin, C. (1992) *Rethinking Context.* Cambridge: Cambridge University Press.

Ellis, N. (2003) Constructions, chunking, and connectionism: The emergence of second language structure. In C. Doughty and M. Long (eds) *Handbook in SLA* (pp. 63–103). Malden, MA: Blackwell.

Ellis, N. and Larsen-Freeman, D. (2006) Language emergence: Implications for applied linguistics – Introduction to the special issue. *Applied Linguistics* 27, 558–589.

Ellis, R. (1992) Learning to communicate in the classroom: A study of two learners' requests. *Studies in Second Language Acquisition* 14, 1–23.

ETS (2003) TOEFL Testing Program. Online at www.toefl.org, accessed 10 November 2003.

Faerch, D. and Kasper, G. (1984) *Strategies in Interlanguage Communication.* Harlow: Longman.

Freed, B. (2000) Is fluency, like beauty, in the eyes (and ears) of the beholder? In H. Riggenbach (ed.) *Perspectives on Fluency* (pp. 243–265). Ann Arbor, MI: University of Michigan Press.

Freed, B., Dewey, D. and Segalowitz, N. (2004) The language contact profile. *Studies in Second Language Acquisition* 26, 349–356.

Fukkink, R., Hulstijn, J. and Sims, A. (2005) Does training in second-language word recognition skills affect reading comprehension? An experimental study. *The Modern Language Journal* 89, 54–75.

Garcia, P. (2004) Meaning in academic contexts: A corpus-based study of pragmatic utterances. Unpublished doctoral dissertation, Northern Arizona University.

Gass, S. and Houck, N. (1999) *Interlanguage Refusals*. Berlin: Mouton de Gruyter.

Gass, S. and Neu, J. (1996) *Speech Acts Across Cultures*. Berlin: Mouton de Gruyter.

Gatbonton, E. and Segalowitz, N. (2005) Rethinking communicative language teaching: A focus on access to fluency. *The Canadian Modern Language Review* 61, 325–353.

Gershon, S. and Mare, C. (2008) *New English Upgrade*. Oxford: Macmillan Ltd.

Gladwell, M. (2000) *The Tipping Point: How Little Things can Make a Big Difference*. Boston: Little Brown.

Goffman, E. (1976) Replies and responses. *Language in Society* 5, 254–313.

Grice, P. (1975) Logic and conversation. In P. Cole and J. Morgan (eds) *Syntax and Semantics* (Vol. 3). New York: Academic Press.

Gudykunst, W. and Kim, Y.Y. (2004) *Communicating with Strangers: An Approach to Intercultural Communication* (3rd edn). Thousand Oaks, CA: Sage Publication.

Gumperz, J., Jupp, T. and Roberts, C. (1979) *Crosstalk: A Study of Cross-Cultural Communication [film]*. London: National Centre for Industrial Language Training/BBC.

Hassall, T. (2006) Learning to take leave in social conversations: A diary study. In M. DuFon and E. Churchill (eds) *Language Learners in Study Abroad Contexts* (pp. 31–58). Clevedon: Multilingual Matters.

Hellerman, J. (2008) *Social Actions for Classroom Language Learning*. Bristol: Multilingual Matters.

Holtgraves, T. (2008) Automatic intention recognition in conversation processing. *Journal of Memory and Language* 58, 627–645.

House, J. (1996) Developing pragmatic fluency in English as a foreign language. *Studies in Second Language Acquisition* 18, 225–252.

Hudson, T., Detmer, E. and Brown, J.D. (1995) *Developing Prototypic Measures of Cross-Cultural Pragmatics* (Technical Report No. 7). Honolulu, HI: University of Hawai'i at Manoa, Second Language Teaching and Curriculum Center.

Hymes, H.D. (1972) On communicative competence. In J.B. Pride and J. Holmes (eds) *Sociolinguisitics: Selected Readings* (pp. 269–293). Middlesex, Harmondsworth: Penguin.

Ishida, M. (2009) Development of interactional competence: Changes in the use of ne in L2 Japanese during study abroad. In H. Nguyen and G. Kasper (eds) *Talk-in-Interaction: Multilingual Perspectives* (pp. 351–386). Honolulu, HI: University of Hawai'i, National Foreign Language Resource Center.

Ishihara, N. and Cohen, A.D. (2010) *Teaching and Learning Pragmatics: Where Language and Culture Meet*. Harlow: Pearson/Longman.

Ishihara, N. and Tarone, E. (2009) Emulating and resisting pragmatic norms: Learner subjectivity and pragmatic choice in L2 Japanese. In N. Taguchi (ed.) *Pragmatic Competence* (pp. 101–129). Berlin: Mouton de Gruyter.

Iwasaki, N. (2010) Style shifts among Japanese learners before and after study abroad in Japan: Becoming active social agents in Japanese. *Applied Linguistics* 31, 45–71.

JACET (Japan Association of College English Teachers) (2003) *JACET List of 8,000 Basic Words*. Tokyo: JACET.

Jianda, L. (2007) Developing a pragmatics test for Chinese EFL learners. *Language Testing* 24, 391–415.

Kasper, G. (1992a) *Pragmatics of Japanese as Native and Target Language*. Honolulu, HI: University of Hawai'i at Manoa, Second Language Teaching & Curriculum Center.

Kasper, G. (1992b) Pragmatic transfer. *Second Language Research: Pragmatics of Chinese as Native and Target Language* (Vol. 8, pp. 203–231). Honolulu, HI: University of Hawai'i at Manoa, Second Language Teaching & Curriculum Center.

Kasper, G. (1995) *Pragmatics of Chinese as Native and Target Language*. Honolulu, HI: University of Hawai'i at Manoa, Second Language Teaching & Curriculum Center.

Kasper, G. (2001) Four perspectives on L2 pragmatic development. *Applied Linguistics 22*, 502–530.

Kasper, G. (2006) Introduction. *Multilingua* 25, 243–248.

Kasper, G. and Blum-Kulka, S. (1993) *Interlanguage Pragmatics*. New York: Oxford University Press.

Kasper, G. and Dahl, M. (1991) Research methods in interlanguage pragmatics. *Studies in Second Language Acquisition* 13, 215–247.

Kasper, G. and Rose, K. (1999) Pragmatics and SLA. *Annual Review of Applied Linguistics* 19, 81–104.

Kasper, G. and Rose, K. (2002) *Pragmatic Development in a Second Language*. Oxford: Blackwell.

Kasper, G. and Schmidt, R. (1996) Developmental issues in interlanguage pragmatics. *Studies in Second Language Acquisition* 18, 149–169.

Kecskes, I. (2003) *Situationally-Bound Utterances in L1 and L2*. Berlin: Mouton de Gruyter.

Kinginger, C. (2008) Language learning in study abroad: Case studies of Americans in France. *Modern Language Journal Monograph Series* 92.

Kinginger, C. and Farrell, K. (2004) Assessing development of metapragmatic awareness in study abroad. *Frontiers: The Interdisciplinary Journal of Study Abroad* 10, 19–42.

Kinginger, C. and Blattner, G. (2008) Development of sociolinguistic awareness in study abroad. In L. Ortega and H. Byrns (eds) *Longitudinal Studies and Advanced L2 Capacities* (pp. 223–246). New York: Routledge.

Koike, D. (1989) Pragmatic competence and adult L2 acquisition: Speech acts in interlanguage. *Modern Language Journal* 73, 279–289.

Kubota, R. (2002) Impact of globalization in language teaching in Japan. In D. Block and D. Cameron (eds) *Globalization and Language Teaching*. London: Routledge.

Kubota, R. and McKay, S. (2009) Globalization and language learning in rural Japan: The role of English in the local linguistic ecology. *TESOL Quarterly* 43, 593–619.

Larsen-Freeman, D. and Cameron, L. (2008) *Complex Systems and Applied Linguistics*. Oxford: Oxford University Press.

Lave, J. and Wenger, E. (1991) *Situated Learning: Legitimate Peripheral Participation*. New York: Cambridge University Press.

Leech, G. (1983) *Principles of Pragmatics*. Harlow: Longman.

Lennon, P. (1990) Investigating fluency in EFL: A quantitative approach. *Language Learning* 40, 387–417.

Leve, J. and Wenger, E. (1991) *Situated Learning: Legitimate Peripheral Participation*. Cambridge: Cambridge University Press.

Levinson, S.C. (1983) *Pragmatics*. Cambridge: Cambridge University Press.

Lewis, M. (2005) Bridging emotion theory and neurobiology through dynamic systems modelling. *Behaviorism and Brain Science* 28, 169–245.

LoCastro, V. (2003) *An Introduction to Pragmatics: Social Action for Language Teachers*. Ann Arbor, MI: The University of Michigan Press.

MacWhinney, B. (2006) Emergentism – Use often with care. *Applied Linguistics* 27, 729–740.

Martínez-Flór, A., Ester Usó Juan, A. and Guerra, F. (2003) *Pragmatic Competence and Foreign Language Teaching*. Castelló de la Plana, Spain: Publications de la Universitat Jaume I.

Márquez-Reiter, R. and Placencia, M. (2004) *Current Trends in the Pragmatics of Spanish*. Amsterdam: Benjamins.

Matsumura, S. (2001) Learning the rules for offering advice: A quantitative approach to second language socialization. *Language Learning* 51, 635–679.

Matsumura, S. (2007) Exploring the aftereffects of study abroad on interlanguage pragmatic development. *Intercultural Pragmatics* 4, 167–192.

McGroarty, M. and Taguchi, N. (2005) Evaluating communicativeness of EFL textbooks for Japanese secondary schools. In J. Frodesen and C. Holten (eds) *The Power of Context in Language Teaching and Learning* (pp. 211–224). Boston, MA: Thomson/Heinle & Heinle.

Mey, J.L. (2003) *Pragmatics: An Introduction* (2nd edn). Oxford: Blackwell.

Mikulecky, B. and Jeffries, L. (2004) *More Reading Power*. New York: Pearson.

Ministry of Education, Culture, Sports, Science, and Technology (2002) *Developing a strategic plan to cultivate Japanese with English abilities*, accessed 2 January 2005. http://www.mext.go.jp/english/news/2002/7/020901.htm/

Ministry of Education, Culture, Sports, Science, and Technology (2003) *Regarding the establishment of an action plan to cultivate Japanese with English abilities*, accessed 20 June 2004. http://www.mext.go.jp/english/topics/03072801.htm/

Morgan, J. (1978) Two types of convention in indirect speech acts. In P. Cole (ed.) *Syntax and Semantics: Pragmatics* (Vol. 9, pp. 261–280). New York: Academic Press.

Mori, J. (2006) The workings of the Japanese token hee in informing sequences: An analysis of sequential context, turn shape, and prosody. *Journal of Pragmatics* 38, 1175–1205.

Mori, J. (2009) The social turn in second language acquisition and Japanese pragmatics research: Reflection on ideologies, methodologies and instructional implications. In N. Taguchi (ed.) *Pragmatic Competence* (pp. 335–358). New York: Mouton de Gruyter.

Murphy, B. and Neu, J. (1996) My grade's too low: The speech act set of complaining. In S.M. Gass and J. Neu (eds) *Speech Acts Across Cultures: Challenges to Communication in Second Language* (pp. 191–216). Berlin: Mouton de Gruyter.

Nelson, G.L., Carson, J., Batal, M.A. and Bakary, W.E. (2002) Cross-cultural pragmatics: Strategy use in Egyptian Arabic and American English refusals. *Applied Linguistics* 23, 163–189.

Norris, J.M. (2006) Assessing foreign language learning and learners: From measurement constructs to educational uses. In H. Byrnes, H. Weger-Guntharp and K. Sprang (eds) *GURT 2005: Educating for Advanced Foreign Language Capacities: Constructs, Curriculum, Instruction, Assessment* (pp. 167–187). Washington, DC: Georgetown University Press.

O'Brian, I., Segalowitz, N., Freed, B. and Collentine, J. (2006) Phonological memory predicts second language oral fluency gains in adults. *Studies in Second Language Acquisition* 29, 557–582.

Ochs, E. (1996) Linguistic resources for socializing humanity. Rethinking linguistic. In J. Gumperz and S. Levinson (eds) *Rethinking Linguistic Relativity* (pp. 407–437). New York: Cambridge University Press.

Ohta, A. (2001) *Second Language Acquisition Processes in the Classroom: Learning Japanese*. Mahwah, NJ: Lawrence Erlbaum.

Ortega, L. and Byrnes, H. (2008) *The Longitudinal Study of Advanced L2 Capacities*. Hillsdale, NJ: Lawrence Erlbaum.

Ortega, L. and Gina I-S. (2005) Longitudinal research in SLA: Recent trends and future directions. *Annual Review of Applied Linguistics* 25, 26–45.

Pawley, A. and Syder, H. (1983) Two puzzles for linguistic theory: Native-like selection and native-like fluency. In J. Richards and R. Schmidt (eds) *Language and Communication* (pp. 163–199). London: Longman.

Pennycook, A. (1994) *The Cultural Politics of English as an International Language*. London: Longman.

Phillipson, R. (1992) *Linguistic Imperialism*. Oxford: Oxford University Press.

Riggenbach, H. (2000) *Perspectives on Fluency*. Ann Arbor, MI: University of Michigan.

Rose, K. and Kasper, G. (2001) *Pragmatics in Language Teaching*. Cambridge: Cambridge University Press.

Röver, C. (2005) *Testing EFL Pragmatics*. Frankfurt: Peter Lang.

Runtime Revolution Ltd. (1997) Edinburgh: Runtime Revolution Ltd.

Salsbury, T. and Bardovi-Harlig, K. (2001) I know your mean, but I don't think so: Disagreements in L2 English. In L. Bouton (ed.) *Pragmatics and Language Learning Monograph Series* (Vol. 10, pp. 131–151). Urbana-Champaign, IL: Division of English as an International Language, University of Illinois, Urbana-Champaign.

Sawyer, M. (1992) The development of pragmatics in Japanese as a second language: The sentence-final particle ne. In G. Kasper (ed.) *Pragmatics of Japanese as a Native and Foreign Language* (pp. 83–125). Honolulu, HI: University of Hawai'i at Manoa, Second Language Teaching and Curriculum Center.

Schauer, G. (2004) May you speaker louder maybe? Interlanguage pragmatic development in requests. *EUROSLA Yearbook* 4, 253–272.

Schauer, G. (2006) Pragmatic awareness in ESL and EFL contexts: Contrast and development. *Language Learning* 56, 269–318.

Schauer, G. (2009) *Interlanguage Pragmatic Development: The Study Abroad Context*. London: Continuum.

Schieffelin, B. and Ochs, E. (1986) Language socialization. *Annual Review of Anthropology* 15, 163–191.

Schmidt, R. (1983) Interaction, acculturation, and the acquisition of communicative competence. In N. Wolfson and E. Judd (eds) *Sociolinguistics and Language Acquisition* (pp. 137–174). Rowley, MA: Newbury House.

Schmidt, R. (1990) The role of consciousness in second language learning. *Applied Linguistics* 11, 129–158.

Schmidt, R. (1993) Consciousness, learning and interlanguage pragmatics. In G. Kasper and S. Blum-Kulka (eds) *Interlanguage Pragmatics* (pp. 43–57). New York, NY: Oxford University Press.

Schmidt, R. (1995) Consciousness and foreign language learning: A tutorial on the role of attention and awareness in learning. In R. Schmidt (ed.) *Attention and Awareness in Foreign Language Learning* (pp. 1–63). Honolulu: University of Hawaii, Second Language Teaching & Curriculum Center.

Schmitt, N. (2004) *Formulaic Sequences*. Amsterdam: John Benjamins.

Searle, J.R. (1976) The classification of illocutionary acts. *Language in Society* 8, 137–151.

Segalowitz, N. (2001) On the evolving connections between psychology and linguistics. *Annual Review of Applied Linguistics* 21, 3–22.

Segalowitz, N. (2003) Automaticity and second languages. In C. Doughty and M. Long (eds) *The Handbook of Second Language Acquisition* (pp. 382–408). Malden, MA: Blackwell.

Segalowitz, N. (2007) Access fluidity, attention control, and the acquisition of fluency in a second language. *TESOL Quarterly* 41, 181–185.

Segalowitz, N. and Freed, B. (2004) Context, contact, and cognition in oral fluency acquisition. *Studies in Second Language Acquisition* 26, 175–201.

Segalowitz, N. and Hulstijn, J. (2005) Automaticity in bilingualism and second language learning. In J.F. Kroll and A.M.B. de Groot (eds) *Handbook of Bilingualism: Psycholinguistic Perspectives* (pp. 371–388). Oxford: Oxford University Press.

Shatz, C.U. (1977) The development of social cognition. In E.M. Hetherington (ed.) *Review of Child Development Research* (Vol. 5, pp. 257–324). Chicago: University of Chicago Press.

Siegal, M. (1996) The role of learner subjectivity in second language sociolinguistic competency: Western women learning Japanese. *Applied Linguistics* 17, 356–382.

Skehan, P. (1996) Analyzability, accessibility, and ability for use. In G. Cook and B. Seidlhofer (eds) *Principle and Practice in Applied Linguistics* (pp. 91–106). Oxford: Oxford University Press.

Skehan, P. (2001) Tasks and language performance assessment. In M. Bygate, P. Skehan and M. Swain (eds) *Researching Pedagogic Tasks: Second Language Learning, Teaching, and Testing* (pp. 167–185). New York: Longman.

Spencer-Oatey, H. (2005) *Culturally Speaking: Managing Rapport Across Cultures*. London: Continuum.

Sperber, D. and Wilson, D. (1995) *Relevance: Communication and Cognition* (2nd edn). Cambridge: Cambridge University Press.

Swain, M. and Johnson, R.K. (1997) *Immersion Education: International Perspectives*. Cambridge: Cambridge University Press.

Taguchi, N. (2005) Comprehension of implied meaning in English as a second language. *Modern Language Journal* 89, 543–562.

Taguchi, N. (2006) Analysis of appropriateness in a speech act of request in L2 English. *Pragmatics* 16, 513–535.

Taguchi, N. (2007a) Development of speed and accuracy in pragmatic comprehension in English as a foreign language. *TESOL Quarterly* 42, 313–338.

Taguchi, N. (2007b) Chunk learning and the development of spoken discourse in Japanese as a second language. *Language Teaching Research* 11, 433–457.

Taguchi, N. (2007c) Task difficulty in oral speech act production. *Applied Linguistics* 28, 113–135.

Taguchi, N. (2008a) Building language blocks in L2 Japanese: Chunk learning and the development of complexity and fluency in spoken production. *Foreign Language Annals* 41, 130–154.

Taguchi, N. (2008b) The role of learning environment in the development of pragmatic comprehension: A comparison of gains between EFL and ESL learners. *Studies in Second Language Acquisition* 30, 423–452.

Taguchi, N. (2008c) Cognition, language contact, and development of pragmatic comprehension in a study-abroad context. *Language Learning* 58, 33–71.

Taguchi, N. (2008d) Pragmatic comprehension in Japanese as a foreign language. *Modern Language Journal* 92, 558–576.

Taguchi, N. (2009a) *Pragmatic Competence*. Berlin: Mouton de Gruyter.

Taguchi, N. (2009b) Corpus-informed assessment of L2 comprehension of conversational implicatures. *TESOL Quarterly* 43, 738–749.

Taguchi, N. (2010) Longitudinal studies in interlanguage pragmatics. In A. Trosborg (ed.) *Handbook of Pragmatics: Pragmatics Across Languages and Cultures* (Vol. 7, pp. 333–361). Berlin: Mouton de Gruyter.

Taguchi, N. (2011a) Rater variation in the assessment of speech acts. *Pragmatics*, 21, 453–471.

Taguchi, N. (2011b) Pragmatic development as a dynamic, complex process: General patterns and case histories. *Modern Language Journal*, 59.

Taguchi, N. and Iwasaki, Y. (2008) Training effects on oral fluency development in L2 Japanese. *Journal of Japanese Linguistics and Literature* 42, 413–438.

Takahashi, S. (1996) Pragmatic transferability. *Studies in Second Language Acquisition* 18, 189–223.

Tanabe, Y. (2004) What the 2003 MEXT action plan proposes to teachers of English. *The Language Teacher* 28, 3–8.

Thelen, E. and Smith, L. (1994) *A Dynamic Systems Approach to the Development of Cognition and Action*. Cambridge, MA: The MIT Press.

Thomas, J. (1983) Cross-cultural pragmatic failure. *Applied Linguistics* 4, 91–109.

Thomas, J. (1995) *Meaning in Interaction: An Introduction to Pragmatics*. London: Longman.

Thompson, E. and Varela, F. (2001) Radical embodiment: Natural dynamics and consciousness. *Trends in Cognitive Science* 5, 418–425.

Trosborg, A. (1995) *Interlanguage Pragmatics: Requests, Complaints, and Apologies*. New York: Mouton de Gruyter.

Ushioda, E. (2009) A person-in-context relational view of emergent motivation and identity. In Z. Dörnyei and E. Ushioda (eds) *Motivation, Language, Identity and the L2 Self* (pp. 215–228). Bristol: Multilingual Matters.

van Dijk, T. (1977) Context and cognition: Knowledge frames and speech act comprehension. *Journal of Pragmatics* 1, 211–232.

Verschueren, J. (1999) *Understanding Pragmatics*. London: Arnold.

Walters, S. (2007) A conversation-analytic hermeneutic rating protocol to assess L2 oral pragmatic competence. *Language Testing* 24, 155–183.

Warga, M. and Schölmberger, U. (2007) The acquisition of French apologetic behavior in a study abroad context. *Intercultural Pragmatics* 4, 221–251.

Widdowson, H.G. (1989) Knowledge of language and ability for use. *Applied Linguistics* 10, 128–137.

Wray, A. (2000) Formulaic sequences in second language teaching: Principle and practice. *Applied Linguistics* 21, 463–489.

Yamashita, S. (1996) *Six Measures of JSL Pragmatics* (Technical report #14). Honolulu, HI: University of Hawai'i at Manoa, Second Language Teaching & Curriculum Center.

Young, R. (2002) Discourse approaches to oral language assessment. *Annual Review of Applied Linguistics* 19, 105–132.

Young, R. and He, A.W. (1998) *Talking and Testing: Discourse Approaches to the Assessment of Oral Proficiency*. Amsterdam: Benjamins.

Index